THE STORY OF ISRAEL

A BIBLICAL THEOLOGY

C. MARVIN PATE, J. SCOTT DUVALL,

J. DANIEL HAYS, E. RANDOLPH RICHARDS,

W. DENNIS TUCKER JR. AND PREBEN VANG

InterVarsity Press
Downers Grove, Illinois

Apollos
Leicester, England

InterVarsity Press, USA
P.O. Box 1400, Downers Grove, IL 60515-1426, USA
World Wide Web: www.ivpress.com
E-mail: mail@ivpress.com

APOLLOS (an imprint of Inter-Varsity Press, England)
38 De Montfort Street, Leicester LE1 7GP, England
Website: www.ivpbooks.com
E-mail: ivp@uccf.org.uk

InterVarsity Press®, U.S.A., is the book-publishing division of InterVarsity Christian Fellowship/USA®, a student movement active on campus at hundreds of universities, colleges and schools of nursing in the United States of America, and a member movement of the International Fellowship of Evangelical Students. For information about local and regional activities, write Public Relations Dept., InterVarsity Christian Fellowship/USA, 6400 Schroeder Rd., P.O. Box 7895, Madison, WI 53707-7895, or visit the IVCF website at <www.intervarsity.org>.

Scripture quotations, unless otherwise noted, are from the New Revised Standard Version of the Bible, copyright 1989 by the Division of Christian Education of the National Council of the Churches of Christ in the USA. Used by permission. All rights reserved.

Material from The Dead Sea Scrolls Translated: The Qumran Texts in English, trans. Florentino Garcia Martinez (Leiden: Brill Academic Publishers, 1996), is reprinted with permission.

Design: Cindy Kiple
Images: Christ Redeemer with Saints: Cameraphoto/Art Resource, NY; Virgin and Child, Cain and Abel: Erich Lessing/Art Resource, NY

USA ISBN 0-8308-2748-X
UK ISBN 1-84474-055-2

Printed in the United States of America ∞

Library of Congress Cataloging-in-Publication Data

The story of Israel: a biblical theology / C. Marvin Pate . . . [et al.].
    p. cm.
Includes bibliographical references and index.
ISBN 0-8308-2748-X (pbk.: alk. paper)
1. Bible—Theology. I. Pate, C. Marvin, 1952-
BS543.S74 2004
230'.041—dc22

2004011519

British Library Cataloguing in Publication Data

A catalogue record for this book is available from the British Library.

P	19	18	17	16	15	14	13	12	11	10	9	8	7	6	5	4	3	2	1
Y	19	18	17	16	15	14	13	12	11	10	09	08	07	06	05	04			

For Chesley and Elizabeth Pruet

of El Dorado, Arkansas,

whose vision and generosity made

the Pruet School of Christian Studies

at Ouachita Baptist University

a reality.

CONTENTS

PREFACE

In a discussion a few years ago, several faculty members in the Pruet School of Christian Studies at Ouachita Baptist University concluded that the field of biblical studies really needs a good one-volume book on biblical theology, a book that focuses on integrating the biblical story into a coherent whole. After further discussions we likewise concluded that a major motif that flows throughout the Scriptures—both at the micro- and the macro-levels—and that ties the two testaments together theologically is the paradigmatic story of Israel, namely, the story of sin, followed by exile, climaxing in restoration. Thus the seeds for this work were planted and began to germinate.

Our goal for this cooperative work was to produce an overarching biblical theology that stresses large connecting motifs, a theology that attempts to step back from the trees for a moment and look at the forest as a whole. There are many outstanding New Testament theologies and Old Testament theologies but very few that try to place the entire Bible into a unified conceptual framework. This volume is an attempt to help fill that gap.

Our prayer for this work is that it will become an important tool of study for students, professors and ministers as well as for informed laity as they come to understand their own faith in light of the fulfillment of Israel's story in Jesus the Messiah. As such, the story of Israel in the Bible is transformed into the story of the gospel for the whole world. Given that reality, the story of Israel could never again be restricted to one people group.

There are numerous individuals whose commitment to this project has placed us in their debt. First, we wish to express our thanks to Dan Reid and the publishing team at InterVarsity Press. Dan shared our vision for this book from the beginning, and his expertise helped to bring it to fruition. Second, some of our student assistants at OBU provided invaluable aid with the myriad of details accompanying a work like this, including confirming references, indexing and typing. To those students—Aaron LeMay, John Thompson, Clint Followell and Jason Hentschel—we offer our sincere appreciation. Third, our students at OBU and in the Pruet School of Christian Studies in particular have encouraged us all along the way with their questions, affirmations and love for the Lord. To you we say—you inspire us.

Next, as the dedication indicates, we are most appreciative of the support that Chesley and Elizabeth Pruet have provided for OBU and for the Pruet School of Christian Studies. Our heartfelt thanks therefore go to that couple. In that connection, we would also like to thank the leadership of Ouachita Baptist University for affording us the opportunity to serve in an environment that encourages us to research and write. Finally, in the case of this publication, as with all other areas of our lives, we wish to thank our wives for their love, encouragement and patience with our busy schedules.

Soli Deo Gloria.

J. Scott Duvall
J. Daniel Hays
C. Marvin Pate
E. Randolph Richards
W. Dennis Tucker Jr.
Preben Vang

1

INTRODUCTION

The Story of Israel and Biblical Theology

Is there a big picture or an overarching theme that unfolds the message of the Bible? A significant number of scholars say there is. Some of the leading candidates for such a perspective quickly come to mind. The motif of the *kingdom of God,* for example, is a frequent nominee in discussions of the unity of the Bible. It is suggested that the Old Testament portrays God's kingdom or reign as manifested through Israel, while in the New Testament the church inherits that place of honor, and in the life, death and resurrection of Jesus Christ the transition between the two was completed. Related to the theme of the kingdom of God is the theme of *covenant,* an expression of God's intimate relationship with the patriarchs, Moses and David, culminating in the new covenant, which was anticipated by the prophets of Israel and was finalized in the person of Jesus through his shed blood on the cross. Another contender for the unifying principle of the Bible is *promise and fulfillment.* The former is the basis of the Old Testament's predictions of the coming Messiah, while the latter is realized through the New Testament's presentation of Jesus as the Christ. Other topics that can be traced throughout the two Testaments include the *people of God, gospel, eschatology* and *new creation.*

The preceding comments, however, reveal a fundamental problem that emerges when one tries to identify the central story that encompasses Scripture: Which one of these motifs can rightly claim to be *the* theme that unites the various biblical authors? Moreover, even if an overarching theme can be identified, does that imply that each of its inspired authors says the same thing about that subject? Obviously not, or why have more than one biblical writer?

Here we are also grappling with the centuries-old debate of how systematic theology and biblical theology are to be related, if at all. Mature reflection on these two disciplines has yielded the following definitions: *systematic (or dogmatic) theology* attempts to summarize the Bible through an organized system of thought carried out within a particular cultural context. As such, it covers not only the Bible but also the formulations of faith (creeds) crafted in Jewish and Christian traditions, and that with a view toward the application of those principles to one's experience of a context. Typically, the organizing system through which the Bible is interpreted by this discipline includes such categories as God, man, sin, salvation, Spirit, church, and end-times. *Biblical theology,* however, first seeks to reconstruct the individual theologies of the writings of the Bible. The accent in such a discipline is on the particular contribution to theology of the book or books in question. That task accomplished, the next step of biblical theology is to integrate the various themes across the whole Bible. For example: What does the Pentateuch teach about the categories of God, man, sin, and so forth? Then, what does Joshua through 2 Kings say about these themes? The same questions are asked of Wisdom literature and the Prophets and, in the New Testament, of the Gospels, Paul, the General Epistles, and the Johannine materials.

In the ensuing comments, we will probe more deeply into the relationship between systematic and biblical theologies by briefly tracking the history of that debate. Then we will offer a potential way out of the maze of proposed theories, arguing that the story of Israel, conceived in a particular way, is a prevailing pattern in Scripture. Finally, we will conclude with a précis of the chapters that follow. In short, the authors of this volume have joined together to work out a coherent approach: viewing the "theology" of the Bible as involving the story of Israel.

Biblical Theology: A Definition

Perhaps the best-known definition of biblical theology was formulated by J. P. Gabler (1753–1826) in his 1787 inaugural address at the University of Altdorf entitled "About the Correct Distinction of Biblical and Dogmatic Theology and the Right Distinction of Their Goals." Gabler, often called "the father of biblical theology," wrote, "'True biblical theology' is the historical study of the Old Testament and the New Testament, their authors and the contexts in which they were written. This is then to be followed by 'pure biblical theology.'"[1]

Three consequences emerged from this seminal definition. First, Gabler's statement became the basis for separating biblical theology from dogmatic theology, though he himself did not condone the polarization of the two. C. H. H. Scobie writes of this distinction, particularly as it surfaces in Gabler's phrase "pure biblical theology," that such a notion "consists of a comparative study of the biblical material with a view to distinguishing what is merely time-conditioned and what is eternal Christian truth; it is the

---

[1] J. P. Gabler, "About the Current Distinction of Biblical and Dogmatic Theology and the Right Definition of Their Goals" (inaugural address, University of Altdorf, March 30, 1787). Published in *Opuscula Academica* 1 (1831): 179-94.

latter that becomes the subject-matter of dogmatic theology. On this view, biblical theology is not merely descriptive but is also part of the hermeneutical process."[2] Unfortunately, many since Gabler have overemphasized the descriptive task of biblical theology to the exclusion of its prescriptive value. To state it another way, rather than building systematic/dogmatic theology on the foundation of biblical theology, much of academia since Gabler has set the two in opposition, often relegating systematics to a secondary status.

A second dynamic that emerges from Gabler's definition is the implicit recognition that the continual plight of biblical theology would be that of integrating both the unity and diversity of Scripture. Thus the "*historical* study of the biblical authors and their respective contexts" (diversity) would somehow have to be related to "pure biblical theology" (unity). How to resolve such a contrast constituted a formidable challenge to doing biblical theology, a struggle that persists to this day.

Third, also implicit in Gabler's definition is the inherent problem of how to relate the two Testaments, which is "the result of the historical study of the Old Testament and New Testament." That quandary continues to be the nemesis of biblical theology. Our own contention in this work is that the story of Israel will move us closer to bridging the preceding three gaps in biblical theology: biblical versus systematic, diversity versus unity, and Old Testament versus New Testament. We turn now to the debate surrounding biblical theology.

Can We Have a Biblical Theology?

Biblical scholars have provided two answers to this question since Gabler.[3] Those who have said no do so because they believe the diversity of Scripture prohibits a single biblical theology. Those who have said yes do so because of their perceptions of the unity of Scripture. These two replies may be seen as roughly corresponding to the historical periods in which biblical theology flourished: 1787 to 1878—no; and post-World War I to the 1960s—yes. It is helpful to review those two periods.

   1. The first period, 1787 to 1878: No to biblical theology. The catalyst for Gabler's separation of biblical theology from dogmatic theology was rationalism. Three assumptions accompanied such an approach to the Bible, as Gerhard Hasel has pointed out:

   (1) Inspiration is to be left out of consideration because "the Spirit of God most emphat-

---

[2]C. H. H. Scobie, "History of Biblical Theology," in *New Dictionary of Biblical Theology: Exploring the Unity and Diversity of Scripture* (Leicester, England/Downers Grove, Ill.: InterVarsity Press, 2000), 11-20, 13.
[3]Gerhard Hasel provides a helpful bibliography on the surveys of biblical theology in *Old Testament Theology: Basic Issues in the Current Debate,* rev. ed. (Grand Rapids, Mich.: Eerdmans, 1997).

ically did not destroy in every holy man his own ability to understand and the measure of natural insight into things." What counts is not "divine authority" but "only what they [biblical writers] thought." (2) Biblical theology has the task of gathering carefully the concepts and ideas of the individual Bible writers because the Bible does not contain the ideas of just a single man. Therefore, the opinions of Bible writers need to be "carefully assembled from Holy Writ, suitably arranged, properly related to general concepts, and carefully compared with one another." . . . This task can be accomplished by means of a consistent application of the historical-critical method with the aid of literary criticism, historical criticism and philosophical criticism. (3) Biblical theology as a historical discipline is by definition obliged to "distinguish between the several periods of the old and new religion." The main task is to investigate which ideas are of importance for Christian doctrine, namely, which ones "apply today" and which ones have no "validity for our time."[4]

These programmatic enlightenment assumptions set the tone for the study of biblical theology for almost one hundred years. That is to say, with Gabler the diversity of Scripture, and with it the emphasis on *theologies* in the Bible, became the dominant method of the academy.

Perhaps the most celebrated attempt to interpret the Bible in this manner was F. C. Baur's (1792-1860) application of the Hegelian dialectic to the New Testament. He argued that the thesis of Jewish Christianity (Petrine materials, Matthew, Revelation), opposed by the antithesis of Gentile Christianity (Galatians, 1—2 Corinthians, Romans, Luke), resulted in the synthesis of early Catholicism (Mark, John, Acts) of the second century. These contradictory theologies, according to Baur, argued strongly against the presence of a single biblical theology in the New Testament, not to mention the whole Bible. The Hegelian dialectic dominated New Testament studies for years, and to this day it continues to exert strong influence on German scholarship, despite the refutation of its literary assumptions by J. B. Lightfoot a century ago.[5]

Two developments, however, signaled the demise of the study of biblical theology as it was then known. First, there was the forceful response of conservatives. E. W. Hengstenberg, whose *Christology of the Old Testament* protested the application of historical-critical methodology to the Bible, defended instead the unity of the Old Testament and New Testament. But the most significant part of the conservative reaction against a diversified approach to biblical theology came from the "salvation-history school," most notably from J. Ch. Konrad von Hofmann (1810–1877). Hasel observes

---

[4]J. P. Gabler, "About the Current Distinction of Biblical and Dogmatic Theology and the Right Definition of their Goals," as quoted in Hasel, *Old Testament Theology,* 21-22.
[5]For a summary of Lightfoot's critique of F. C. Baur, see C. Marvin Pate, "Tübingen Revisited," in *The Reverse of the Curse: Paul, Wisdom, and the Law* (Tübingen, Germany: J.C.B. Mohr/Paul Siebeck, 2000), 438-40.

that the "salvation-history *(Heilsgeschichte)* school" of the nineteenth century was based on three considerations: (1) the history of the people of God as expressed in the Word; (2) the idea of the inspiration of the Bible; and (3) the result of the history between God and man in Jesus Christ.[6] Hasel expands on these crucial themes:

> Von Hofmann found in the Bible a record of linear saving history in which the active Lord of history is the triune God whose purpose and goal it is to redeem mankind. Since Jesus Christ is the primordial goal of the world to which salvation history aims and from which it receives its meaning, the OT contains salvation-historical proclamation. This an OT theology has to expound. Each books of the Bible is assigned its logical place in the scheme of salvation history. The Bible is not to be regarded primarily as a collection of proof-texts or a repository of doctrine but a witness to God's activity in history which will not be fully competed until the eschatological consummation. The influence of the "salvation-history school" on the development of both OT and NT theology has been considerable and is felt to the present day, though with great variation and in new forms.[7]

Heilsgeschichte, therefore, bespeaks the unity of the Bible.

But it was the rise of the history-of-religions *(Religionsgeschichte)* approach that dealt the deathblow to nineteenth-century biblical theology. As is often noted, 1878 marks the beginning of this approach with the publication of the *Prolegomena to the History of Israel* by Julius Wellhausen (1844–1918). Wellhausen popularized and integrated two recent scholarly developments: the JEDP theory of the Pentateuch[8] and Darwin's evolutionary theory. These two tenets, with their resulting espousal of contradictory theologies, still hold sway among Old Testament scholars. Eleven years later William Wrede called for the application of the history-of-religions approach to the New Testament in his essay "Concerning the Task and Method of So-Called New Testament Theology." It was Wrede's goal to separate theology from religion. The classic example of Wrede's work is *The Messianic Secret,* in which he contended that Jesus was a holy man (the original religious aspect) but not the Messiah (early Christianity's concept). He argued that the commands to various people in Mark's Gospel to be silent about Jesus' messiahship were creations of Mark to cover up the embarrassment that Jesus did not historically claim to be the Messiah.

The end result of the history-of-religions approach was to shatter any remaining

---

[6]Hasel, *Old Testament Theology,* 25-29, where the preceding bibliographies can also be found.
[7]Ibid., 28.
[8]Wellhausen's *Prolegomena to the History of Israel* championed the theory that Moses did not write the first five books of the OT, but rather that the Pentateuch is composed of four written sources dating up to a thousand years after the time of Moses (if he ever existed!): J = Yahwist (ca. 950 B.C.), E = Elohist (ca. 850 B.C.), D = Deuteronomy (750 B.C.), and P = Priestly writing (ca. 550 B.C.). For Wellhausen, contradictions accompanied these documents: e.g., J (pro-kingship, especially David) versus E (anti-kingship); P (liturgical) versus D (ethical).

confidence in the unity within or between the two Testaments and to protest against the assumption of the harmony of systematic and biblical theologies.

2. The second period, post-World War I to the 1960s: Yes to biblical theology. In the decades following World War I, several factors brought about a revival of biblical theology. R. C. Dentan delineates these dynamics: (1) a general loss of faith in evolutionary naturalism; (2) a reaction against the conviction that historical truth can be attained by pure scientific "objectivity" or that such objectivity is indeed attainable; and (3) the return to the idea of revelation in dialectical (neo-orthodox) theology.[9]

This dramatic turnaround in the fate of biblical theology stemmed from the realization that liberalism's naïve reduction of historical study to the mere investigation of facts was woefully inadequate, signaling the need for a new approach.[10] Those who answered this challenge spawned a new movement of biblical theology, one that—for all its diversity—nevertheless championed the essential unity of the Bible. Space permits only the mention of key advocates of this perspective, along with their respective proposals of a unifying principle of the Bible. Some of the most influential in Old Testament theology were Walter Eichrodt's proposal of a covenantal center,[11] Wilhelm Vischer's proposal of a christological center,[12] and Gerhard von Rad's kerygmatic testimonies.[13] In New Testament theology there was the redeemed Redeemer myth of Rudolf Bultmann, which was wedded to existential philosophy,[14] Joachim Jeremias's essential equation of the Jesus of history with the Christ of faith[15] and the already/not yet eschatology of Oscar Cullmann.[16]

This second wave of interest in biblical theology, whose advocates defended the basic unity of the Scripture, has often been labeled the "Golden Years" of biblical theology. Brevard S. Childs lists six components that contributed to the popularity of the movement: (1) opposition to philosophical systems; (2) contrast between Hebrew and Greek thought; (3) emphasis on the unity of the Testaments; (4) uniqueness of the Bible as against its environment; (5) reaction against the older "liberal" theology; and (6) revelation of God in history.[17]

---

[9]Robert C. Dentan, *Preface to Old Testament Theology,* 2nd ed. (New York: Seabury, 1968), 61.

[10]See especially C. T. Craig, "Biblical Theology and the Rise of Historicism," *Journal of Biblical Literature* 62 (1942): 281-94; and C. R. North, "OT Theology and the History of Hebrew Religion," *Scottish Journal of Theology* 2 (1949): 113-26.

[11]Walther Eichrodt, *Theology of the Old Testament,* 2 vols. (Philadelphia: Fortress, 1961, 1967).

[12]Wilhelm Vischer, *The Witness of the Old Testament to Christ* (London: Lutterworth, 1949).

[13]Gerhard von Rad, *Old Testament Theology,* 2 vols. (London: Harper & Row, 1962, 1965).

[14]Rudolf Bultmann, *The History of the Synoptic Tradition* (New York: Harper and Row, 1963).

[15]Joachim Jeremias, *New Testament Theology: The Proclamation of Jesus* (New York: Scribner, 1971).

[16]Oscar Cullmann, *Christ and Time: The Primitive Christian Conception of Time and History* (Philadelphia: Westminster Press, 1950).

[17]Brevard S. Childs, *Biblical Theology in Crisis* (Philadelphia: Fortress, 1970), 85; see Childs's description of biblical theology from the 1940s on, pp. 13-87.

The appeal of biblical theology, however, waned in the 1960s for at least two reasons. First, its methodology was called into question, most notably by James Barr. Barr severely criticized the supposed objectivity of the movement (Childs's point # 1) as well as its facile opposition of Hebrew and Greek thought (# 2).[18] Moreover, the growing complexity of biblical studies resulting from new discoveries and prolific output of information reasserted the diversity of the Bible and thus again raised suspicions regarding the uniqueness of Scripture (# 4), the revelation of God in history (# 5), and the unity of the Testaments (# 3). These polemical barbs basically aligned biblical scholarship of the 1960s with an older biblical approach (# 6). Second, twentieth-century biblical theology was abandoned because of changing priorities among scholars, especially in the pursuit of the sociology of religion.

Three rather recent approaches demonstrate that reports about the death of biblical theology are exaggerated, however. First, Brevard S. Childs's "Canonical Approach," which first appeared in his *Biblical Theology in Crisis* (1970), was subsequently worked out in his canonical introductions to both the Old Testament (1979) and the New Testament (1984) and later in his *Biblical Theology of the Old and New Testaments* (1992). Such a reading places its emphasis on the final form of the Scripture, not on the historical-critical process that produced the text. It is the canonical form of the text, the one that the church has come to accept, that provides the basis of biblical theology; and the unity therein approximates traditional orthodox theology. Second, the opposite view of Childs's thesis is the "whole-biblical theology" (*eine gesamtbiblische Theologie*) approach proposed in Germany by such scholars as Hartmut Gese and Peter Stuhlmacher. This method is also called the "history of traditions" approach. C. H. H. Scobie explains why:

> [The history of traditions method] is based on the assumption that in the time of Jesus the OT canon was not yet closed, and that biblical theology is concerned with a continuous history of tradition. Divine revelation is not to be located only in the earliest forms of the tradition but in the entire process, which was long and complex as traditions were continually selected, edited and reinterpreted. This approach has been demonstrated in studies of such themes as "wisdom," "law" and "righteousness."[19]

Third, though he has not employed it as such (nor perhaps would he condone it), N. T. Wright's proposal in *The New Testament and the People of God* for understanding the story of Israel may well prove to be another important catalyst in the revival of biblical theology, accounting for both the unity and diversity of Scripture. Our next section broaches that subject.

---

[18]James Barr, *The Semantics of Biblical Language* (Oxford: Oxford University Press, 1961).
[19]Scobie, "History of Biblical Theology," 181-91.

The Story of Israel: A Description

In his monumental study of the Old Testament, Jewish, and New Testament sources regarding the role and fate of the prophets in Israel's history, Odil H. Steck argues at length that Second Temple Judaism (Jewish materials written between the fall of Jerusalem in 587 B.C. and its later fall to the Romans in A.D. 70) was dominated by the Deuteronomistic view of Israel's history.[20] Steck makes a compelling case that especially by the time of Antiochus IV and the Maccabean revolt (167 B.C.), the Deuteronomistic tradition, though capable of a certain fluidity of expression, had become a relatively fixed conceptual framework with five constituent elements.

1. Israel's perpetual disobedience to God. The Deuteronomistic view of the story of Israel[21] asserts, first of all, that the nation has been "stiff-necked," rebellious and disobedient during its entire existence (see Ex 33:3, 5; Num 14:22; Deut 29:4; 31:27; Is 63:10; Jer 9:26; CD3). Using a different metaphor but pinpointing the same reality, Deuteronomy 32:5 characterizes Israel as a perverse generation, a verdict stretching across its history: "They have dealt corruptly with him [God], they are no longer his children because of their blemish; they are a perverse and crooked generation." Deuteronomy 32:20 concurs: "They are a perverse generation, children in whom is no faithfulness" (cf. Lk 7:31; 11:29 and par.; Phil 2:15). Later Jewish writings viewed their generations as continuing Israel's disobedience. Thus Baruch 1:18-19 (c. 150 B.C.) laments, "We have disobeyed him [God], and have not heeded the voice of the Lord our God, to walk in the statutes of the Lord that he set before us. From the time when the Lord brought our ancestors out of the land of Egypt until today, we have been disobedient to the Lord our God, and we have been negligent in not heeding his voice" (cf. 2 Kings 17:23; Neh 9:32; Ezek 2:3-4; 20:3-8; Dan 9:5; 1 Esd 8:73-74; 2 Esd 9:7). These passages, in their usage of the first person plural pronoun, indicate the collabo-

---

[20]Odil H. Steck, *Israel und das gewaltsame Geschick der Propheten: Untersuchungen zur Überlieferung des deuteronomistischen Geschichtsbildes im Alten Testament, Spätjudentum und Urchristentum*, Wissenschaftliche Monographien zum Alten und Neun Testament 23 (Neukirchen-Vluyn, Germany: Neukirchener, 1967). The ensuing comments on the description of the story of Israel come from C. Marvin Pate, *Communities of the Last Days: The Dead Sea Scrolls, the New Testament and the Story of Israel* (Downers Grove, Ill.: InterVarsity Press, 2000), 24-29. For the general application of the story of Israel to the Old Testament, the intertestamental period (Jewish literature written from 400 B.C. to A.D. 100), and the New Testament, Steck's work has proved to be programmatic. Other authors applying this theme to the New Testament will be identified in the course of this work.

[21]Ever since the work of Martin Noth, *Überlieferungsgeschichtliche Studien* 1, scholars have viewed Deuteronomy 1 through 2 Kings 25 as a continuous narrative, a "Deuternonimistic history" displaying, via stories and speeches, the theme that obedience to the Torah brings blessings on Israel, whereas disobedience invokes divine curses. In this manner the historian can explain the exile of the Jews as a part of God's plan rather than as a consequence of his inability to protect the nation. Furthermore, if Israel repents, God will restore its previous fortunes (Deut 30:1-10; cf. 1 Kings 8:46-51 with Deut 30:1; 2 Kings 25:27). Moreover, such a theme of sin–exile–restoration also informs Israel's preexilic history (the periods of the conquest, the judges and the monarchy), adumbrating the exile itself.

ration of contemporary Jews with the hard-heartedness of ancient Israel.[22]

2. Israel and the prophets. Already in Deuteronomy there is the hint that God will raise up prophets to call Israel to repentance. Thus we read in Deuteronomy 18:15, "The LORD your God will raise up for you a prophet like me [Moses] from among your own people; you shall heed such a prophet." God announces, "I will put my words in the mouth of the prophet, who shall speak to them everything that I command" (Deut 18:18). Here the prophet like Moses is being referred to as the prototype of God's future messengers to Israel.

3. Israel's rejection of the prophets. Israel, however, rejected God's prophets, refusing to repent of her disobedience. Speaking of the coming prophet like Moses, Deuteronomy 18:19 ominously signals such a storied rejection: "Anyone who does not heed the words that the prophet shall speak in my name, I myself will hold him accountable." Repeatedly thereafter, Israel's malignment of the prophets is highlighted in Jewish literature:

> We have not listened to your servants the prophets, who spoke in your name to our kings, our princes, and our ancestors, and to all the people of the land. (Dan 9:6)
>
> Nevertheless they were disobedient and rebelled against you and cast your law behind their backs and killed your prophets, who had warned them in order to turn them back to you, and they committed great blasphemies. (Neh 9:26)
>
> We did not listen to the voice of the Lord our God in all the words of the prophets whom he sent to us, but all of us followed the intent of our own wicked hearts by serving other gods and doing what is evil in the sight of the Lord our God. (Bar 1:21-22; see *Jub* 1:13; *1 En* 89:51; CD 3:4; 4QpHos 2:3b-6; 1QS 1:3; 8:15-16; 1QpHab 2:5-10; cf. Lk 13:34-35)

4. Israel and the Deuteronomic curses. Deuteronomy is replete with warnings of divine judgment if Israel should lapse into idolatry (Deut 27:1-26; 28:15-68; 29:19-28). Deuteronomy 29:25-28 succinctly summarizes the curses that would accompany the nation's disobedience to the law of Moses:

> It is because they forsook the covenant of the LORD, the God of their ancestors, which he made with them when he brought them out of the land of Egypt. They turned and served other gods, worshipping them, whom they had not known and whom he had not allotted to them: so the anger of the LORD was kindled against that land, bringing upon it all the curses written in this book. The Lord uprooted them from their land in anger, fury, and great wrath, and cast them into another land, as is now the case.

---

[22]On this point, see Carey A. Moore, "Toward the Dating of the Book of Baruch," *Catholic Biblical Quarterly* 36 (1974): 312-20, esp. 315. Unless otherwise specified, all quotations of intertestamental literature are taken from James H. Charlesworth, *The Old Testament Pseudepigrapha*, vol. 1 (Garden City, N.Y.: Doubleday, 1983), and *The Old Testament Pseudepigrapha*, vol. 2 (London: Darton, Longman & Todd, 1985).

With the fall of the northern kingdom in 722 B.C. and the defeat of the southern domain along with the destruction of the temple in 587 B.C., those threats came true as Jews were displaced from their land.

Gerhard von Rad observes that texts like Daniel 9, Nehemiah 9, Ezra 9 and Baruch 1:15—3:8 reflect the conviction that the catastrophe of 587 B.C. was an undiminished reality, for although that date had passed, the authors believed that Israel was still under divine judgment (cf., e.g., CD 1:3—2:4; 1 Thess 2:15-16; Acts 28:26-27).[23] Von Rad's perspective has proven compelling to a growing number of scholars.[24] Michael A. Knibb encapsulates this view of a protracted exile when he writes of Jewish literature in the Second Temple period: "Despite many differences in presentation, the writings . . . seem to share the view that Israel remains in a state of exile long after the sixth century, and that the exile would only be brought to an end when God intervened in this world order to establish his rule."[25]

Two reasons seem to have combined to give the impression to most Second Temple Jews that the Deuteronomic curses and exile continued to abide on Israel. First, the glorious Old Testament expectations of national restoration had not yet materialized. As Jacob Neusner points out, all Judaic systems emphasized the present experience of exile as a recapitulation of 587 B.C. This was so because, with the non-occurrence of a full and glorious restoration in the sixth century as their reading of Torah led them to expect, most Jews continued to push their hopes into the future and view themselves as living in an extended exilic situation.[26] Second, related to the first reason, the invasion and control of Israel by foreign rulers, especially the Greek king Antiochus IV (171 B.C.), and the Roman generals Pompey (63 B.C.) and Titus (A.D. 70), reinforced in the minds of many that divine judgment still resided on the nation.[27]

5. The restoration of Israel and the Deuteronomic blessings. Despite Israel's sin, however, Deuteronomy 30:1-8 held out the assurance of divine forgiveness

---

[23]Gerhard von Rad calls these passages "doxologies of judgment." See his *"Gerichtdoxologie"* in *Gesammelte Studien zum Alten Testament Band II,* ed. Rudolf Smend, TBS. AT 48 (Munich: Kaiser, 1973), 246-47.

[24]Steck, *Israel und das gewaltsame Geshick der Propheten*; N. T. Wright, *The New Testament and the People of God* (Minneapolis: Fortress, 1992); James M. Scott, "Paul's Use of Deuteronomic Tradition(s)," *Journal of Biblical Literature* 112 (1993): 645-65; Frank Thielman, *Paul and the Law: A Contextual Approach* (Downers Grove, Ill.: InterVarsity Press, 1994).

[25]M. A. Knibb, "The Exile in the Literature of the Intertestamental Period," *Heythrop Journal* 17 (1976): 253-72, esp. 271-72.

[26]Jacob Neusner, *Self-Fulfilling Prophecy: Exile and Return in the History of Judaism* (Boston: Beacon, 1987).

[27]See N. T. Wright's development of this theme in his *New Testament and the People of God,* 152-66, and the application of such a concept to Jesus in his *Jesus and the Victory of God* (Minneapolis: Fortress, 1996).

and restoration if the nation would repent:[28]

> When all these things have happened to you, the blessings and the curses that I have set before you, if you call them to mind among all the nations where the LORD your God has driven you, and return to the LORD your God, and you and your children obey him with all your heart and with all your soul, just as I am commanding you today, then the LORD your God will restore your fortunes and have compassion on you, gathering you again from all the peoples among whom the LORD your God has scattered you. Even if you are exiled to the ends of the world, from there the LORD your God will gather you, and from there he will bring you back. The LORD your God will bring you into the land that your ancestors possessed and you will possess it; he will make you more prosperous and numerous than your ancestors.
>
> Moreover, the LORD your God will circumcise your heart and the heart of your descendants, so that you will love the LORD your God with all your heart and with all your soul, in order that you may live. The LORD your God will put all these curses on your enemies and on the adversaries who took advantage of you. Then you shall again obey the LORD, observing all his commandments that I am commanding you today. (cf. Ezra 9:8-9, 15; Jer 31:31-34; Ezek 36:25-26; Dan 9:16-19; Bar 2:34-35)

In light of this promise, George Nickelsburg's analysis of Second Temple Jewish literature leads him to conclude that

> the destruction of Jerusalem and the Exile meant the disruption of life and the breaking up of institutions whose original form was never fully restored. Much of post-biblical Jewish theology and literature was influenced and sometimes governed by a hope for such a restoration: a return of the dispersed; the appearance of a Davidic heir to throw off the shackles of foreign domination and restore Israel's sovereignty; the gathering of one people around a new glorified Temple.[29]

As a rule, Jewish writings of the Second Temple period espousing the hope of Israel's restoration—that is, the replacement of the Deuteronomic curses with the covenantal blessings—express two convictions.[30] First, they are *nomistic* (*nomos* = law) in orientation. Israel's restoration will come about only when it sincerely obeys the Torah. This tenet is held in both Palestinian Judaism (e.g., Sir, Bar, *Pss Sol*, DSS; 4 Ezra; *2 Apoc. Bar.*) and in Diaspora Judaism (Wis, *Ep Arist*, 4 Macc, *T. 12 Patr, 3 Sib*

---

[28]Steck (*Israel und das gewaltsame Geshick der Propheten*) divides the restoration into two elements: Israel has the opportunity to repent, and restoration will follow upon taking that opportunity. James M. Scott ("Paul's Use of Deuteronomic Tradition[s]") follows Steck in this regard. We think, however, that one may just as well combine the two, for Israel's restoration necessarily involves an invitation to repent.

[29]George W. E. Nickelsburg, *Jewish Literature Between the Bible and the Mishnah* (Philadelphia: Fortress, 1981), 18. Nickelsburg's work (like Steck's) emphasizes the influence of Deuteronomistic traditions(s) on the literature of early Judaism.

[30]Regarding these two points, see C. Marvin Pate, *The Reverse of the Curse,* part one.

Or). This dynamic, however, calls for two qualifications:

1. Various Jewish groups at the time defined the Torah somewhat differently. Thus Sirach, Baruch and *Psalms of Solomon* equate the Torah exclusively with the law of Moses, believing that it could be obeyed in this present age. Fourth Ezra and *2 Baruch* reinterpret the Law apocalyptically, relegating Israel's full compliance with it to the age to come. While *1 Enoch* and the Dead Sea Scrolls redefine the Torah in terms of their respective sectarian readings, Diaspora Judaism emphasizes the moral summary of the Law in the hope that Gentiles will thereby be attracted to the God of Israel.

2. Since the seminal work of E. P. Sanders, scholars commonly recognize that despite their preoccupation with the Torah, most Jews in the Second Temple era were not consciously legalistic in their perspective. Rather, their relationship to the law of Moses is best described as "covenantal nomism"—one enters the covenant by divine grace but remains in that covenant by obeying the Torah.[31] Already in the Old Testament we hear of God's antecedent grace in saving Israel (Deut 7:7-8; 8:14-18; 9:4-5), and it was such unconditional love that would serve as the catalyst for the nation's restoration (Deut 28:15—30:10; 31:16-29; 32:1-38; Jer 31:31-34; Ezek 11:19; 36:22–37:14; Dan 9:16-19).[32]

A second conviction enmeshed in Jewish literature of the Second Temple era espousing the hope of the restoration of Israel is *particularism,* the divine election and destiny of Israel to one day rule the nations. Yet such particularism could be manifested differently. There are those Jewish writings which envision an eschatological pilgrimage of the Gentiles to Zion to share in Israel's restoration (*Pss. Sol.* 17:30-35; *2 Apoc. Bar.* 68:5; Tob 13:11; *1 En* 90:30-36; cf., e.g., Is 2:2-4; 25:6-10; 56:6-8; Mic 4:1-4; Zech 8:20-23). At the far end of the spectrum, other materials (notably the Dead Sea Scrolls) excluded from Israel's future redemption not only Gentiles but also unrepentant Jews.

Conclusion to the story of Israel. The five components of the story of Israel's history discussed above can be formulated in terms of the pattern of sin–exile–restoration, a refrain running throughout early Judaism. Thus, Annie Jaubert can refer to this pervasive Old Testament/Jewish theme as "the rhythm of the covenant."[33] Such a rhythm is heard in the penitential prayer tradition of the ancient synagogues based on passages like Daniel 9:4-19 and Nehemiah 9:5-37[34] and contributing to the formation

---

[31]E. P. Sanders called attention to covenantal nomism in his watershed book *Paul and Palestinian Judaism: A Comparison of Patterns of Religion* (Philadelphia: Fortress, 1977).

[32]Frank Thielman highlights this aspect of Deuteronomy in his work *Paul and the Law: A Contextual Approach* (Downers Grove, Ill.: InterVarsity Press, 1994), 64-65.

[33]Annie Jaubert, *La notion d'alliance dans le judaïsme aux abords de l'ère chrétienne,* Patristica Sorbonesia 6 (Paris: Éditiona du Seuil, 1963), 44.

[34]For the influence of Nehemiah 9:5-37 on the prayers of the postexilic synagogue, see Leon J. Liebreich, "The Impact of Nehemiah 9:5-37 on the Liturgy of the Synagogue," *Hebrew Union College Annual* 32 (1961): 227-37.

of what Joseph Klausner has labeled the "messianic chain," consisting of sin–punishment–repentance–redemption, which was deeply embedded in Israel's self-identity.[35]

As Steck points out, however, it is not necessary for an Old Testament or later Jewish text to contain all five elements as Baruch 1:15—3:8 does in order for it to be framed by the Deuteronomistic perspective. Indeed, some texts may emphasize certain elements more than others and may therefore omit one or more components; other passages may expand an element by including a related tradition. But all of this nevertheless takes place within the basic Deuteronomistic framework. As a result of this consideration, Steck is able to show the pervasiveness of such a tradition not only in Palestinian Judaism during the period from 200 B.C. to A.D. 200 but also in the New Testament.[36]

The Story of Israel as a Biblical Theology

It seems to us that the story of Israel does indeed qualify to be characterized as a biblical theology in its own right. This is so because it is a pervasive theme throughout the Old Testament, Second Temple (less appropriately labeled "intertestamental") literature, and the New Testament, allowing for both unity and diversity in the Bible.

In the previous section we called attention to the description of the Deuteronomistic history, or the story of Israel. Here our purpose is to highlight the prevalence of such a pattern in the Old Testament, Second Temple Judaism and New Testament, noting how it potentially encompasses both similarities and differences in the Bible. The following elaboration will also serve as a survey of the chapters that follow.

Chapter two: Pentateuch. Throughout the Pentateuch there is a deep-seated relationship between divine will and human responsibility. When human responsibility fails and the relationship is breached, there are certain expected consequences. The history presented in the Pentateuch explores the connection between sin and exile, and whether there is a hope for restoration. Genesis 1—11 serves as a prologue to the entire corpus by suggesting that the paradigm of sin–exile–restoration embodies the history of humanity—even from the beginning. With the birth of a new nation (Gen 12), specific stipulations in the tenuous relationship between divine will and human responsibility are provided (Ex 19; Lev 26). While these stipulations define sin and indicate punishment, they also sound a note of hope in their comments on restoration. The book of Deuteronomy concludes the collection by suggesting that obedience to the words of Yahweh is central to becoming the people of God. The Deuteronomic blessings and curses highlight the critical nature of their obedience. In obedience there

---

[35]Joseph Klausner, *The Messianic Idea in Israel from Its Beginning to the Completion of the Mishnah* (London: Allen & Unwin, 1956).
[36]Steck, *Israel und das gewaltsame Geshick der Propheten.*

is life; in disobedience, only death and exile. The corpus closes with a people prepared to create a nation. They know the demands of obedience—and the threat of exile.

Chapter three: Deuteronomistic history. This chapter will cover the books of Joshua, Judges, 1-2 Samuel, and 1-2 Kings. The central issue of this unit is that of Israel's required faithfulness to Yahweh and the covenant (as expressed in Deuteronomy). As they enter the Promised Land, will they remain faithful to their relationship with Yahweh? The answer is negative. Thus, this unit explains how the people of God went from Promised Land/blessing to exile/curse. Within the larger unit there are also several smaller cycles of blessing–disobedience–judgment–restoration that parallel the larger story. Furthermore, as Israel's disobedience and apostasy move to the foreground of the story, the grace and patience of God nonetheless continue to hover in the background (undeserved deliverance in Judges, the Davidic covenant, references to the Abrahamic covenant, individual deliverance in the Elijah/Elisha narratives, etc.), thus faintly anticipating the message of restoration beyond the exile.

Chapter four: The Psalms and the Wisdom literature. The Wisdom literature offers a more nuanced view of the story of Israel. While much of the literature in the Old Testament contributes to the actual story of Israel, the Wisdom literature engages the story at a different level. The book of Proverbs provides a detailed exploration of reality and the order therein, thus producing a strong case for double retribution. Consistent with Deuteronomic theology, double retribution offered a sound hermeneutic for interpreting the experiences of sin, punishment, and perhaps even exile. The books of Job and Ecclesiastes appear to decry such a worldview, arguing instead for a different reading of reality. The story continues outside the canon, however. In Sirach the author further explores the notion of wisdom, often drawing on Deuteronomic theology, and couples this approach to wisdom with the critical concept of Torah. Thus Wisdom literature has moved full circle—returning once again to the story.

Chapter five: Prophets. The message of the preexilic prophets is embedded in the context of the covenant as expressed in Deuteronomy (although Ezekiel leans on Leviticus). Their basic message to Israel/Judah can be reduced to three major points: (1) You have broken the covenant; repent and turn back to Yahweh. (2) No repentance? Then judgment (the curses of Deuteronomy—destruction by the Assyrians and Babylonians and exile) is imminent. (3) However, beyond the judgment there is hope for a glorious future restoration and a new way of relating to Yahweh.

The prophets' picture of restoration includes the concept of the "new" covenant, a shift from national to individual relationship, the inclusion of the Gentiles, and the promise of a more personalized presence of God through the pouring out of his Spirit, all of which connect directly with the New Testament. The postexilic prophets clarify that the postexilic situation is *not* the glorious restoration. Disobedience continues, and hope still looks to the future for the fulfillment of the promised restoration.

Chapter six: Second Temple Judaism. A striking question that is addressed over a
wide range of Second Temple Jewish literature is: If Israel has been restored to her
land, how is it that she is still in exile, that is, suppressed by foreign nations? While
the essential answer to that question is that Jews need to take the Mosaic law more seriously in order to be free, four different expressions of that fundamental construct surface in this literature:

   a. Theocratic works like Sirach; Baruch; 1, 2, 3 Maccabees; and *Psalms of Solomon*
      assert that the entire Mosaic code must be followed for Israel's final restoration
      to occur.
   b. Apologetic works such as Wisdom of Solomon, 4 Maccabees, *Third Sibylline Or-
      acle, Aristeas* and *Testaments of the Twelve Patriarchs* emphasize the moral sum-
      mary of the Law as the key to Israel's restoration as well as to the salvation of
      Gentiles.
   c. Apocalyptic writings like 4 Ezra and *2 Baruch* delay the restoration of Israel until
      the age to come but still stress the importance of a nationalistic reading of the
      Law much like the theocratic works mentioned above.
   d. Sectarian materials like the Dead Sea Scrolls and *1 Enoch* redefine the Mosaic law
      in terms of their respective *halakah* (way of life); for them, this is the key to Is-
      rael's restoration, a restoration no longer defined in merely ethnic terms.

Because space does not permit a full-scale analysis of all of the above works, we will
focus on one representative from each of the aforementioned categories. Chapter six,
then, will show that there is indeed a thematic bridge between the Old Testament and
the New Testament: Israel's sin–exile–restoration. This is our rationale for including
noncanonical literature such as the above in a biblical theology.

Chapter seven: Synoptic Gospels. From the climactic point of the experience of
God's visible reentrance into the life of Israel through Jesus Christ, Matthew, Mark and
Luke cast their descriptions of the coming of God's kingdom in language, and with emphases, that parallel Old Testament stories of God and Israel. They are the description
of the fulfillment of God's promises, and they function, therefore, as the explanation
for how Israel should have understood God's history with his people and the nations
all along. Beyond being theological biographies of Jesus, these three Gospels give content to the old prophetic message of God's new covenant relationship. Because of this,
their recounting of "kingdom events" in Jesus' ministry stand as corrective reinterpretations of God and Israel.

Chapter eight: John. John also uses the story of Israel to share the story of Jesus,
drawing many of the same points of comparison made in the Synoptics. Nevertheless,
John also adds several unique contributions. He usurps later Jewish Wisdom tradition,
reformulating the stories to show that Jesus was the "Wisdom" described in Proverbs
8, Sirach 24 and *1 Enoch* 42. Wisdom did not dwell among the Jewish people in the

form of Torah; rather, Wisdom "became flesh and tabernacled among us" (Jn 1:14). John's story is that God has returned to his people as promised in the restoration. *First Enoch* promised that the dispersed sheep would be regathered by the Lord. John then announces that Jesus has come to regather the lost sheep.

In the Old Testament, God dwelt among his people in the tabernacle. His presence was evidenced by signs and wonders. So now also, John proclaims, God has come to dwell among his people, as evidenced by the "signs" John describes. Nevertheless, John draws cosmic implications for the story of Israel. For John, it is the story of the world.

Chapter nine: Acts. Luke's Acts of the Apostles aims to show how the teaching and ministry of Jesus continued in the early church through the Spirit. Luke concludes the argument he made in his Gospel that God's purpose for Israel was in the process of fulfillment through the outpouring of God's Spirit upon all who through faith would participate in the kingdom. What Jesus had shown and proclaimed as God's eternal purpose for his people proved to be the indisputable truth through the evident work of God's Spirit among all the nations. Indeed, as Acts ends, the story continues to be told "without hindrance," and Gentiles continue to find salvation. The Jewish leadership and those who follow their misguided interpretation of Israel's story, on the other hand, remain in exile. Those who accept the interpretation detailed by Stephen and explicated throughout the book of Acts are filled with God's Spirit and included in God's new *ekklēsia* (church). Most of these are Gentiles—for "they will listen" (Acts 28:28)!

Chapter ten: Paul. The twist to the story of Israel that surfaces in the Gospels and in Acts continues and even culminates in the writings of Paul, which represent the most thoroughgoing attempt to demonstrate that the Deuteronomic blessings and curses as they relate to the sin–exile–restoration pattern in Israel's history have been reversed in Christ. Thus, Paul argues that those who attempt to adhere to the Mosaic code are in fact heaping upon their heads the covenantal curses, whereas those who believe in Jesus the Messiah—apart from the works of the law—in fact possess the Deuteronomic blessings, that long-awaited restoration of Israel.

Chapter eleven: General Epistles and Hebrews. But if the promised Messiah has already come, why are we still suffering? Where is the promised kingdom? The General Epistles write of this Christian paradox of living in an exile that is now and not yet over. Christians are not to settle down and make their homes in the exile any longer. They are sojourners in a land no longer their home. Because they are not yet in their home, they are still susceptible to suffering. For Peter, James and Jude, the restoration is not yet here. They speak from the viewpoint of an earlier Palestinian Jewish Christianity. The restoration is temporal (future but imminent) and probably expected in Palestine. Hebrews speaks from a different perspective. The restoration of Israel in Hebrews is seen in spatial ("heavenly") and atemporal ("rest") terms. Hebrews argues that the church is already experiencing in Christ at least some of the eschatological blessings of the restoration.

Chapter twelve: Revelation. This chapter shows how Revelation uses the central elements of the story of Israel—sin, exile and restoration—to transform its readers. The book addresses Christians who are being pressured to compromise with pagan powers. For those who are staying faithful to Christ and suffering for it, Revelation brings comfort and hope. For those who are compromising with the world in order to avoid persecution, Revelation conveys a formidable warning.

As a prophetic-apocalyptic letter functioning in the Old Testament prophetic tradition, Revelation creates a symbolic world for its readers. This visionary world of powerful images provides the heavenly perspective needed for God's people to live faithfully in a hostile world. More specifically, Revelation transforms its hearers by immersing them in God's story. Using colorful language and powerful imagery, John masterfully weaves together seven main threads or themes that amplify the traditional story of Israel by highlighting the main characters (Creator, enemies, Restorer, followers) and the central storyline (sin–exile–restoration). In these seven themes we see God's plan for reversing the curse of sin, restoring his creation and living among his people forever.

Chapter thirteen: Conclusion. In this final chapter we propose that we *can* have a biblical theology and that the story of Israel qualifies as such. We will review briefly the framework of that story and summarize how the sin–exile–restoration refrain runs throughout the biblical canon, encompassing such motifs as people of God, new covenant, promise/fulfillment, wisdom, kingdom of God, gospel, and new creation. In our view, the story of Israel represents a central theme of the biblical canon, allowing for both unity and diversity in the Bible.

Supplemental Reading in New Dictionary of Biblical Theology

Regarding the relationship between systematic and biblical theologies:
C. H. H. Scobie, "History of Biblical Theology," 11-20.
D. A. Carson, "Systematic Theology and Biblical Theology," 89-104.
Regarding the development of biblical theology:
C. L. Blomberg, "The Unity and Diversity of Scripture," 64-72.
Regarding the relationship between Old and New Testaments:
G. Goldsworthy, "Relationship of Old Testament and New Testament," 72-80.

Study Questions

1. What is the challenge of relating biblical and systematic theologies?

2. Why did the period 1787–1878 say "no" to the possibility of a biblical theology?

3. How did conservatives respond during that period to those who demurred from a biblical theology?

4. Why did the period between post-World War I and the 1960s assert that there is a biblical theology?

5. Discuss the five components of the story of Israel/Deuteronomistic tradition.

2

THE PENTATEUCH

Divine Will and
Human Responsibility

The Pentateuch begins with the creation of the world and concludes with the creation of a nation. Throughout the stories there is a struggle between divine will and human responsibility. The struggle for humans to be responsible often leads to sin, exile and restoration. This paradigm of sin–exile–restoration appears frequently in the Pentateuch in various forms. The stories from the Primeval History suggest that such a pattern stands outside of the story of Israel—it is the story of humanity. Yet the remainder of the Pentateuch indicates that this paradigm, while part of the story of humanity, can be traced in greater detail within the events surrounding the story of Israel.

Genesis 1—11: Prologue and Paradigm

Introduction to the Prologue. The opening eleven chapters of Genesis, otherwise known as the Primeval History, offer a collection of narratives and genealogies that move from the creation of the world to the identification of Abraham. Unfortunately, the traditional approach to reading Genesis is to divide the book between Genesis 1—11 and Genesis 12—50. This has resulted in an unfortunate bifurcation of the book (and the Pentateuch as a whole). The story of Israel is typically envisioned as beginning in Genesis 12, when in fact, the events that occur in the opening prologue are central to the story that follows. Such a division creates the illusion that what happens in the Primeval History is only peripherally related, at best, to what occurs in the remainder of the collection. Yet the events of the Primeval History are more than simply a prologue to the story of Israel. In many ways these events become paradigmatic in that they reflect the movement from sin to exile to restoration, as so often appears in the remainder of the Pentateuch (and the Old Testament as a whole).

Genesis 1–2: The blessing of creation. The opening chapters of Genesis are fertile ground for theological reflection. They have much to say about creation and the created order. But three blessings appear in these chapters that prove critical to reading the remainder of the Pentateuch. In the movement from sin to exile to restoration, these blessings are challenged, thus threatening the creative design of God.

The first blessing relates to the orderliness of creation. The highly poetic design of Genesis 1, with the repetition of numerous words and phrases, suggests that the author intended to present creation as an act of ultimate order.[1] The repetition of the phrase "and God saw that it was good" suggests that from the beginning creation fulfilled its creative design—the world was as it was intended to be. The remainder of the story of Israel and the story of the world in general, however, depicts a world gone awry—one that has long since faltered in maintaining its creative design. As John Walton has noted, Genesis 1 "is intended to show that the world was not always as it is now."[2] The chaos and disorder experienced in the stories that follow in the history of Israel only highlight the fact that the world is not as it was intended. Yet the function of Genesis 1 is to call people (and creation) back to its creative design—to fulfill those functions for which they were designed by God.

The second blessing pertains to the blessing of dominion and fertility. While dominion and fertility may be considered two distinct ideas, they can be subsumed under one theme. Through their appropriate use, humanity can continue the creative activity of God in the world. The two gifts of dominion and fertility were not given to be fanciful privileges of the human race; rather, they were given so that the human race might continue God's designs for his creation. The story of Israel, however, is fraught with stories where those creative designs are thwarted. The blessing to be fruitful and multiply is often challenged, threatening the future course of humanity. The oscillation between stories of barrenness and lists of genealogies suggests that the fulfillment of these blessings will be tenuous at best.

The final blessing is that of the presence of God. Although not specifically stated as a blessing, Genesis 2 alludes to God's close presence to the created order. The anthropomorphic language that pervades the chapter suggests a God who is near. He is one who "forms man" (Gen 2:7), "plants a garden" (Gen 2:8), and puts man in the garden (Gen 2:15). There is an apparent spatial relationship that the author intends for the reader to discover. In the Garden, the humans are near to God—it is paradise. But as Genesis 3 will demonstrate, outside the Garden indicates a certain separation from God. Thus, the remainder of the Pentateuch is about how Israel gets back to the Garden, not geographically but spatially. How do the people of God enjoy the blessing of being in God's presence?

Genesis 3—11: The curse of creation. Whereas Genesis 1—2 introduced the

---

[1]For literary features in Genesis 1, see John H. Walton, *Genesis*, NIV Application Commentary (Grand Rapids, Mich.: Zondervan, 2001), 66-67.
[2]Ibid., 65.

theme of blessing, Genesis 3—11 proves suggestive in determining the paradigm of sin–exile–restoration. The thesis first offered by Gerhard von Rad, and subsequently adapted by others, proves crucial for understanding the Primeval History and the story of Israel. Von Rad notes the dominant role of sin and its proliferation in the early chapters of Genesis and suggests that "the narrator's whole interest is . . . concentrated in showing a chain of actual events, a road which mankind took and the consequences of which could no more be undone by him."[3] Through these chapters the narrator highlights the unraveling of a blessed creation and offers a story of a creation once named "good" but now most certainly gone awry. And throughout Genesis 3—11 the story includes elements of sin, exile and restoration—it is the story of human responsibility and divine will.

Victor Hamilton has divided the Primeval History into six sections, alternating between narrative and genealogy:[4]

Gen 1:1–4:16	Narrative
Gen 4:17–5:32	Genealogy
Gen 6:1–9:28	Narrative
Gen 10:1-32	Genealogy
Gen 11:1-9	Narrative
Gen 11:10-32	Genealogy

Of the eleven chapters contained in the Primeval History, two chapters (Gen 5, 10) are composed of genealogy alone, with an additional two chapters (Gen 4, 11) containing both narrative and genealogy. Although the narrative portions typically receive the most attention from scholars, the genealogies serve a critical purpose in these chapters. The narrative portions of the Primeval History highlight the constant tension between divine will and human responsibility, manifested in the paradigm of sin–exile–restoration. And as Victor Hamilton notes, the genealogies "serve, as much as the narratives, as evidences of God's blessing upon these antediluvian figures and upon the eventual line that produces Abraham."[5] In essence, the genealogies serve as a visual representation of the restoration granted by Yahweh.

Scene 1. The first narrative involving the paradigm of sin–exile–restoration occurs in Genesis 3. While the sin of Adam and Eve needs no mention, a brief analysis of the results of their sin is critical to understanding the paradigm in Genesis 1—11. Following the disobedience of the primeval couple, God appears in the Garden both as interroga-

---

[3]Gerhard von Rad, *Old Testament Theology* (San Francisco: Harper & Row, 1962), 1:154. For a more recent adaptation of von Rad's thesis, see Walter Brueggemann, *Genesis,* Interpretation (Louisville, Ky.: Westminster John Knox, 1982), 11-22.
[4]Victor Hamilton, *The Book of Genesis: Chapters 1–17,* New International Commentary on the Old Testament (Grand Rapids, Mich.: Eerdmans, 1990), 248.
[5]Ibid.

tor and as judge. The sentences handed down in Genesis 3:14-19 represent a radical reorientation of creation—that which was blessed has now become cursed. In Genesis 1:24, God created "living creatures of every kind," including the "creeping things" which would presumably include the serpent. And following the pattern of the creation story, "God saw that it was good." Yet in Genesis 3 it is with the serpent, once blessed and deemed good, that the first occurrence of the word "cursed" (*'ārar*) appears.

Similar to the serpent, the man and woman experience the judgment of blessing turned to curse. While the word for curse does not actually appear in the judgment of the woman, there is little doubt that a curse is being issued. In Genesis 1:27-28 man and woman appear in tandem—as one flesh (cf. Gen 2:24). There is no sense of hierarchy in this initial description of man and woman. Simply put, both receive the blessing. This blessing involves a divine mandate, and this mandate for humanity is twofold: (1) Be fruitful and multiply; (2) and have dominion over the created order. Yet in the judgment of Eve the mandate is challenged. The blessing of being fruitful and multiplying turns to a curse when Yahweh proclaims "I will greatly increase your pangs in childbearing; in pain you shall bring forth children" (Gen 3:16). The second blessing of having dominion over the created order is complicated by the fact that she will experience the loss of a unified rule with Adam. Yahweh decrees, "Your desire shall be for your husband, and he shall rule over you" (Gen 3:16). The term for "desire" (*tĕšûqâ*) is the same word used later in Genesis 4:7 for sin's desire to overtake Cain. Thus, the curse for the woman involves not only her desire to overtake the male but also the claim that "he shall rule over you." As Hamilton suggests, "Far from being a reign of co-equals over the remainder of God's creation, the relationship now becomes a fierce dispute, with each party trying to rule the other. The two who once reigned as one attempt to rule each other."[6]

For the man, the curse appears somewhat innocuous, since it is not against him directly: "Cursed is the ground because of you" (Gen 3:17). But similar to the woman, due to sin that which was once a blessing has now become a curse. In Genesis 1:29, God announces, "See, I have given you every plant yielding seed that is upon all the face of the earth, and every tree with seed in its fruit." And while this blessing has not been revoked, it has clearly been altered. Just as woman will bring forth children and hence be fruitful and multiply, albeit in great pain or toil (*'iṣṣabôn*), so too must the man exert dominion over the land, but with great toil (*'iṣṣabôn*). For both man and woman, their disobedience has met with disastrous results.

The sin of the man and woman results not only in the reversing of the creation blessings but also in the exile, or expulsion, of the man and woman from the Garden. Presumably, they are sent out east of Eden, and to affirm the permanent expulsion,

---

[6]Ibid., 202.

cherubim and a flaming sword are placed on the east side of the Garden. Strikingly, however, the text does not mention the death of humans as their punishment for sin. Instead, in the paradigm established in the Primeval History, sin results in expulsion and wandering. Sin does not lead to death, but more ominously, to expulsion and wandering, to removal "from the safety of the Garden and exposure to a life of severity and uncertainty."[7] Thomas Mann explains, "Human beings are permanent exiles from the pristine space and time of Eden. There is no way back and the way ahead is uncertain. The plot of the Pentateuchal narrative, to its very end, will be concerned with the attempt to find another way human beings can live with integrity before God, at home on the earth, and within the security of divine blessing."[8]

Thus, the remainder of the Pentateuch will rehearse sins and the various exiles that will result. But the critical consideration is, how will humanity be restored into relationship with God? How will the curses now uttered, as well as those to follow, be reversed in an effort to ensure the blessings of God be restored?

The possibility of restoration begins in Genesis 4 with the birth of a child. Eve conceives and announces, "I have produced a man with the help of the LORD." Although this event seems far from an announcement of restoration, it serves as such. The disobedient couple has been exiled from the Garden—and presumably from God's presence. Yet Eve's claim asserts that even in their expulsion, God acted with humanity to continue the creation blessing: "Be fruitful and multiply." Thus, with the birth of Cain there emerges the possibility for a new generation, one that is obedient to the creation blessings.

Scene 2. Although the arrival of Cain offers some hope for a restored creation, those hopes are quickly dashed in the narrative. The sin of Cain does not stem from the type of gift offered. Instead, the question in the text is whether Cain can accept the circumstances around him, ambiguous though they may be, and "do well" (Gen 4:7). Sin is described in Genesis 4:7 using the same vocabulary as that used in the curse of the woman. In Genesis 3, the woman will have a desire for her husband and he will rule over her or master her. In Genesis 4, sin becomes the object of both verbs: "Its desire is for you, but you must master it." The creation blessing "to have dominion over the earth" is threatened by the possibility that sin will have dominion over Cain. The failure of Cain to master sin results in the murder of Abel, his brother.

The sin of Cain prompts exile and expulsion. Whereas the disobedient Adam causes the cursing of the once blessed ground, the cursed ground now curses Cain. And whereas Adam was still able to eat from the land, God announces that the ground

---

[7]Ibid., 204.
[8]Thomas Mann, *The Book of the Torah: The Narrative Integrity of the Pentateuch* (Louisville, Ky.: Westminster John Knox, 1988), 19.

"will no longer yield" its strength to Cain. And then Cain is told, "You will be a fugitive and a wanderer on the earth" (Gen 4:12). In addition to being exiled from the strength of the ground, Cain experiences two additional exiles, both far more ominous. In Genesis 4:16 the narrator indicates, "Cain went away from the presence of the Lord," followed by the statement that Cain settled "east of Eden." For the second time in as many scenes, the disobedient human is sent east—a symbolic reminder of the distance between the now-fallen humanity and the once-inhabited paradise of Eden.

The question of restoration in Genesis 4 is answered in the comparison of the offspring granted to Cain and Seth. With both there is offspring, and hence a possible restoration. Despite the sin of Cain, there is once again the hope of restoration with the birth of a child. Genesis 4:17 notes that "Cain knew his wife, and she conceived." Similar to Adam and Eve, this child offers the hope that God can restore humanity with the next generation. Yet the short genealogy of Cain (Gen 4:17-22) fails to reveal a restored humanity reflecting the paradisaical state of Eden. Instead, the genealogy concludes with a raucous taunt by Lamech, in which he claims the promises of Cain for himself. He has sought to make a name for himself, one greater than even Cain's.

The restoration really does not come to fruition until Genesis 4:25-26. In these two short verses, a hint of restoration appears. Eve bears a son, Seth, and similar to the proclamation made with Cain (Gen 4:1), she announces, "God has appointed for me another child instead of Abel." The attribution of life to God appears again in this short genealogy and makes its absence in Cain's genealogy even more striking—suggesting the hope of restoration lies with this line, the line of Seth. Enoch, the child of Cain, and the subsequent generations were associated with animal domestication (Gen 4:20), musical instrumentation (Gen 4:21), and metallurgy (Gen 4:22). Yet Enosh, the child of Seth, is only associated with religious practice: "At that time, people began to invoke the name of the LORD." As Walton has noted, "When people call upon the name of the Lord, this . . . constitutes a designation and recognition of Yahweh as God. This is the beginning of worship and shows that the development of civilization did not bring a total abandonment of the Lord."[9] With Enosh the hope of restoration emerges, suggesting that not all of humanity will follow the ways of Cain and Lamech.

Scene 3. Just as Genesis 4 concludes in a hopeful tenor, Genesis 5 opens with the prospects of a newly restored humanity. The genealogy of Adam proves critical to the story of Israel thus far. As mentioned above, the extended genealogies serve as a literary device to indicate the blessing of God. The narrator further stresses the significance of the genealogy by beginning Genesis 5 with language virtually parallel to Genesis 1:26-28: "When God created humankind, he made them in the likeness of God. Male and female he created them, and he blessed them and named them 'Humankind' when

---

[9]Walton, *Genesis,* 279.

they were created" (Gen 5:1b-2).

There are a number of similarities between the original creation story and the statement made in Genesis 5:

• Both texts mention that male and female constitute humanity.

• Both texts suggest that all humanity is created in the image/likeness of God.

• Both texts note that following his creative work, "God blessed them" (Gen 1:28; 5:1).

The short introductory comments to Genesis 5 reaffirm the blessing of God on all humanity *despite* the growing manifestation of sin in the lives of those blessed by God. In Genesis 5:3 the genealogy begins with similar creation language. Adam becomes a father of a son "in his likeness, according to his image." The implication follows that those who are listed in this genealogy have continued to experience the blessing of God while also exhibiting the image and likeness of their Creator (note that Cain is strikingly absent in this genealogy).[10] Thus, the reoccurring phrase "X became the father of Y" suggests more than a simple duplication of pattern embedded within a network of names. Rather, the phrase operates as a perpetual reminder of human identity—an identity cast in the image of God, lived out fully under the blessing of God.

At the conclusion of the genealogy, the narrator mentions the birth of Noah. In addition to serving as the link to the next series of narratives, the birth of Noah serves a critical function in the genealogy. Lamech proclaims that the son will be named Noah and explains, "Out of the ground that the LORD has cursed this one shall bring us relief from our work and from the toil of our hands" (Gen 5:29). Thus, Lamech anticipates that with the birth of Noah, there will be one who can reverse the curse first uttered in Genesis 3. Adam, the first name in the genealogy, prompted the cursing of the ground due to his sin, and now Noah, the last name in Genesis 5, holds out the hope as the one who may reverse the effects of the curse.

Scene 4. The hope expressed in Genesis 5 quickly dissipates in Genesis 6—9. While the flood story occupies the central focus of this pericope, the events recorded in Genesis 6:1-4 provide a critical introduction to the larger passage—offering a rationale for the catastrophe that is to follow. These enigmatic verses have prompted a number of interpretations—most with some merit. Yet within the scheme of sin–exile–restoration, there is little doubt that this story has been placed at the beginning of Genesis 6 to suggest that sin has now reached catastrophic proportions and deserves a catastrophic response.

The opening line of the chapter indicates that the scope of the narrative has extended. The story that began with a couple (Adam and Eve) and continued through

[10]Mann, *Book of the Torah*, 21.

familial lines (Cain, Abel and Seth) now effects all of humanity: "when people began to multiply on the face of the ground" (Gen 6:1). But the narrator extends the storyline one step further by including the "sons of God"—perhaps suggesting that the entire cosmos has been engulfed by, and enshrouded in, the destructive nature of sin. The emphasis on sin in the passage is intensified as language of Genesis 6:2 recalls the Garden scene in Genesis 3. The sons of God saw (*rā'āh*) that the daughters of men were good (*tôb*), just as Eve saw (*rā'āh*) that the fruit was good (*tôb*). And then just as Eve took (*lāqaḥ*) the fruit from the tree, thus disrupting the order established by God, so too the sons of God took (*lāqaḥ*) the women for themselves, suggesting once again a rupture in the divine order of creation.

Genesis 6:5 provides a summation and interpretation of Genesis 6:1-4 while also serving as a prelude to the flood narrative: "The LORD saw that the wickedness of humankind was great in the earth." In previous episodes in Genesis 1—11, sin has always prompted some type of exile—but in Genesis 6, the exile becomes an "uncreation" of sorts. The very categories mentioned in Genesis 1 (humans, animals, creeping things and birds of the air) appear in Genesis 6, but only to reiterate that which will be "blotted out" in this most severe of exiles.

The hope of restoration rests with Noah. Genesis 5 elicited a glimmer of hope with the announcement of Noah in Genesis 5:29, and a similar sentiment of hope is recorded in Genesis 6:8: "But Noah found favor in the sight of the LORD." And contrary to his primeval predecessors, Noah "did all that God commanded him" (Gen 6:22).

The obedience of Noah to the divine will results not only in a restoration but also in new creation. The Noachide covenant issued in Genesis 9:1-17 reclaims the original creation language but appropriates it for the family of Noah. In Genesis 9:1 God blesses Noah and his sons, just as humanity was blessed in Genesis 1. In addition they are given the mandate "be fruitful and multiply." An extended statement regarding dominion over the earth follows. The section concludes with Yahweh announcing the establishment of a covenant: "When the bow is in the clouds, I will see it and remember the everlasting covenant between God and every living creation of all flesh that is on the earth" (Gen 9:16).

The story of the Pentateuch hinges in part on covenants, both established and broken. In Genesis a covenant is made with Abraham and Sarah. A second covenant is established at Sinai in Exodus 19—24. And the Pentateuch concludes with the book of Deuteronomy, which is constructed in the form of an extended covenant treaty (see below). The covenant made with Noah serves as a precursor to the remaining Pentateuchal covenants—the covenants made between God and Israel are established because of the covenant made between God and all of creation in Genesis 9.

Scene 5. The final scene of sin–exile–restoration in Genesis 1—11 occurs in Genesis 11. The story of the tower of Babel moves the prologue back from the familial level to the scope of humanity: "Now the whole earth had one language and the same words"

(Gen 11:1). And they are said to be migrating eastward—thus recalling the expulsion and exile of Adam and Eve, along with that of Cain. In the earlier texts the movement eastward symbolized a distancing from the paradisaical qualities of Eden and from the presence of God. In this story, those in the land of Shinar are trying to return to the presence of God via a tower. Their language is reminiscent of Genesis 1:26, when God says, "Let us make humankind." Three times the people announce, "let us" (Gen 11:3, 4 [2x]) in an effort to make a name for themselves and to prevent their scattering across the earth. The punishment, however, begins in Genesis 11:5 when the narrator announces God's coming down to see the city. To their "god-like" language, God announces the final "let us," and he confuses the people and then scatters them abroad—in essence, in exile.

The Primeval History concludes with a genealogy—that of Shem (Gen 11:10-32). As with the other genealogies in this section, this one serves to signify that the blessings of God continue and that restoration will be possible. The genealogy concludes with the introduction of Abraham (Gen 11:27-32), who becomes the connection between the story of Israel and the history of the world.

Genesis 12–50: The Covenant with Abraham

The repeated theme of sin–exile–restoration that has played out in the Primeval History finds a new form of restoration in Abraham. In some sense, Abraham appears as a new type of Adam, with the Promised Land operating as the new Eden. The storyline of Genesis, previously played out within the history of the world, radically reorients itself to that of one family—and the interaction between divine will and human responsibility. Yet central to this interaction is the covenant made between Yahweh and Abraham (and his descendants).

Abraham is told that he will be a great nation (Gen 12:2). Genesis 10 had listed a number of the great nations in the genealogy found there, but Abraham is now assured that Yahweh will make him more than just a people, but in fact one of the great nations. Abraham is also told that Yahweh will make his name great. As opposed to the generation at Babel who failed to make their name great, Abraham will have a great name. Yet the text is clear: it will not be Abraham that makes his name great, but Yahweh. The affirmation of Yahweh's particular concern for Abraham and his descendants occurs in Genesis 12:3. Yahweh promises to bless those who bless Abraham and curse those who curse him.

At the center of the seven statements in Genesis 12:1-3 is the phrase "so that you will be a blessing." This suggests that Abraham must be both a receptacle and a transmitter of the blessings of Yahweh.[11] The significance of Abraham's operating as a trans-

---

[11]Hamilton, *Book of Genesis*, 373.

mitter of the blessings is indicated at the end of Genesis 12:3. Abraham is told that "in you all the families of the earth shall be blessed." The hope for the world and all humanity to return to its creative design rests with the obedience of this one family and its descendants.

Within these early chapters of the Abraham narrative, Lot appears as the foil to Abraham. Just as Abraham embodies the opportunities and possibilities once granted to Adam, Lot embodies the fate of the exiled individuals in the Primeval History. In Genesis 13, as Abraham and Lot prepare to part ways, Lot is offered the choice of land. He opts for the plain of the Jordan, which is described as "well watered everywhere *like the garden of the LORD,*" perhaps suggesting that Lot will enjoy the benefits expected from living in such a paradisaical setting. Yet such an expectation is quickly eradicated in the following verse (Gen 13:11). The text simply reads, "and Lot journeyed eastward." Similar to the fate of his primeval forbearers, Lot moves east—away from the presence of God.[12] The land that looks like the garden of the Lord will fail to produce the benefits of Eden. As a result of Lot's choice, Abraham is left with the land of Canaan. And in Genesis 13:14-16, Abraham is promised that God "will give it to you and to your offspring forever." The land that looks like Eden will fail to produce, while the land inhabited by Abraham will yield the prosperity of the Garden—the Promised Land is the new Eden.[13]

The remainder of Genesis 12—50 recounts numerous episodes in which divine will is met with human responsibility (Gen 15; 22; 32) as well as human irresponsibility (Gen 12:10—16; 38). And throughout, the story of Israel oscillates between the blessing of restoration and the threat of exile.

Exodus: The Divine Will and the Demand for Human Responsibility

The book of Genesis traces the story of Israel through one family, Abraham and his descendants. The Israelites as a nation, however, are not introduced until the book of Exodus. The faithfulness that Yahweh shows to the nation stems from his covenant loyalty, established first with the patriarchs. Frequently in the Exodus narrative, Yahweh is depicted as remembering the covenant with the patriarchs (Ex 2:24) or referencing the patriarchs in his self-identification (Ex 4:5). Thus, the story of Israel moves from one family to a nation, but the patriarchal elements serve as foundational to Israel's development. The first eighteen chapters of Exodus rehearse the story of Israel and their redemption from slavery in Egypt by Yahweh, the God of the patriarchs. It is this re-

---

[12]Walton, *Genesis,* 415. See also L. Helyer, "The Separation of Abram and Lot: Its Significance in the Patriarchal Narratives," *Journal for the Study of the Old Testament* 26 (1983): 77-88.

[13]Since Israel understood the Promised Land to be a new Eden of sorts, the experience of the Babylonian exile (once again an eastward movement) becomes a devastating rehearsal of the original expulsion of God's people from paradise.

demptive history that becomes central in the issuing of the divine will and the demand for human responsibility.

Exodus 19:3-6. At Sinai the nation gathers for the first time as a liberated people—free from the oppression of the Egyptians and free to become the people of Yahweh. Prior to the Book of the Covenant (Ex 20—23), Yahweh speaks to Moses, announcing his resolve for this group of freed slaves. The short speech by Yahweh begins with a historical recitation—the Egyptian experience is recounted: "You have seen what I did to the Egyptians, and how I bore you on eagles' wings and brought you to myself" (Ex 19:4). Yahweh appears as the active agent, working against the Egyptians, bearing up the Israelites and bringing them to him. There is no mention of what the Israelites did—the text clearly affirms that the divine will was to liberate *this* people to become *his* people.

By becoming his people, they will become a "treasured possession," "a priestly kingdom," and a "holy nation." Appearing in tandem with these descriptions is the assertion that Yahweh did not have to choose Israel. After all, "the whole earth is mine" (Ex 19:5). Thus the election of Israel affirms that Israel's status is dependent on divine will. Yet this status as God's treasured possession appears to be somewhat conditional. In Exodus 19:5 Yahweh announces, "Now therefore, if (*ki*) you obey my voice and keep my covenant, you shall be my treasured possession." Such a statement may appear contradictory to the graciousness of the divine will that rescued Israel from captivity. Yet as Walter Brueggemann has noted, "While Yahweh's initial rescue is unconditional and without reservation, a sustained relation with Yahweh is one of rigorous demand for covenant."[14] The demand for human responsibility remains coupled with divine will. Whereas it was divine will that initiated the relationship, it is the responsibility of the nation to be the people of God by obeying his words and keeping his covenant.

What follows in the Book of Covenant are laws stipulating what it means to "obey my voice." Except for the occasional reference (Ex 20:5-6; 20:12; 22:23-24), there are no extended statements of blessing or cursing within the actual Book of the Covenant. Those statements are reserved for the brief epilogue (Ex 23:20-33) to the Book of the Covenant. The epilogue contains a litany of blessings, but strikingly, only one warning or curse. In Exodus 23:20-21, Yahweh promises to send an angel before the people to protect them in their journey to the Promised Land. They are commanded to listen to the angel and be attentive to him. If they rebel against him, "he will not pardon your transgression" (Ex 23:21). The text is silent as to the implications of such a sin. A clue, however, may be deduced from Exodus 23:22. The verse begins "but if you listen attentively," suggesting that the blessings to follow are founded on the obedience of the people, and hence, any

---

[14]Walter Brueggemann, "Exodus," in *The New Interpreter's Bible* (Nashville: Abingdon, 1994), 1:835.

form of disobedience would result in the revoking of those blessings.

The apparent assumption is that those who have been rescued by Yahweh will respond appropriately and carry out the stipulations. The remainder of the passage focuses attention on blessings related to the Promised Land. If the Israelites are obedient, then Yahweh will enable them to "demolish the enemies" (Ex 23:24) and drive out those who are in the land (Ex 23:27-29). The land will be blessed with an abundance of bread and water (Ex 23:25), and their numbers will grow without anyone dying a premature death (Ex 23:26).

At the conclusion of the Book of the Covenant, Moses reads the stipulations and the people respond, "All that the LORD has spoken we will do, and we will be obedient" (Ex 24:7)—divine will and human responsibility.

Leviticus 26. The theme of obedience to "all that the Lord has spoken" continues through the Pentateuch and is surprisingly prominent in the book of Leviticus. Although the themes of sacrifice and ritual typically receive the most treatment in Leviticus, the theme of obedience to the statutes *(huqâ)*, the ordinances *(mišpāṭ),* and the commandments *(miṣwôt)* of Yahweh plays a critical role in the theology of the book. The key words, *statutes, ordinances* and *commandments,* appear more frequently in Leviticus than in any other book in the Pentateuch, with the exception of Deuteronomy.[15] The stress on these terms throughout Leviticus suggests that being the people of God is about more than just sacrifice and ritual, critical though they may be. Similar to Exodus 19, the stress appears to be on the ability of the people of Israel to listen attentively to the voice of Yahweh and to obey.

Leviticus 26 highlights the correlation of obedience and disobedience with blessing and cursing respectively—suggesting that obedience is critical if the community hopes to continue. The chapter itself can be easily divided into three sections: blessings resulting from obedience (Lev 26:3-13); curses resulting from disobedience (Lev 26:14-39); and the promise of restoration (Lev 26:40-45).[16] Although documents from other Ancient Near Eastern cultures do contain blessings and curses, the biblical texts differ at one significant point. As Gordon Wenham has noted, "Whereas the biblical texts are straightforward promises that God will respond to his people's behavior, the non-biblical texts are prayers to the gods to act."[17] The question for the nation of Israel, then, is not whether God will act, but whether they will be an obedient people.

---

[15]The majority of appearances are in Leviticus 17–26, which has traditionally been designated as the Holiness Code.
[16]In the Ancient Near Eastern documents, the number and length of curses typically exceeds the number and length of blessings. The blessings are typically understood as generalizations, but the curses are meant to deter, in rather graphic fashion, the hearer from disobedience. See Jacob Milgrom, *Leviticus 23—27,* Anchor Bible Commentary 3B (New York: Doubleday, 2001), 2286-87.
[17]Gordon J. Wenham, *The Book of Leviticus,* New International Commentary on the Old Testament (Grand Rapids, Mich.: Eerdmans, 1979), 327.

Blessings. The sense of conditionality that appeared in Exodus 19 also appears in Leviticus 26. The blessings begin, "If you follow my statutes and keep my commandments and observe them faithfully . . ." If the nation chooses to be obedient, there are five blessings listed in Leviticus 26: abundance, peace within the land, victory over the enemy outside the land, fulfillment of the covenant and God's presence in Israel. Each blessing presents a condition to be enjoyed *in the land*—thus the chief blessing to be enjoyed is their entry into the Promised Land. To that blessing, Yahweh will add those specifically cited in this chapter. And whereas Exodus 19 began with a short historical recitation of the Exodus events, Leviticus 26 concludes with the statement, "I am the Lord your God who brought you up out of the land of Egypt to be slaves no more." The historical reference serves as Yahweh's assurance that if Israel deserves the blessings, he is capable of providing them.[18]

Curses. The opening lines of the curse pericope emphasize the sheer weight of disobedience: "But if you will not obey me, and do not observe all these commandments, if you spurn my statutes, and abhor my ordinances, so that you will not observe all my commandments, and you break my covenant . . ." (Lev 26:14-15). The last phrase literally reads in the Hebrew "to cause my covenant to be broken." The implication is that if Israel fails to obey the "voice of Yahweh," then they have in fact broken, or at minimum violated, the covenant with Yahweh. The failure in human responsibility produces dramatic results with regard to the divine will. As Erhard Gerstenberger notes, Yahweh will "requite any breach in covenant . . . he will dissolve the covenant, and thereby also his promises of protection and blessing."[19] The withdrawal of protection and blessing from Yahweh results in a list of terrible curses.

There are five different curses announced in Leviticus 26, with the severity of the curses increasing as each is announced. These curses are in direct contrast to the blessings promised for obedience earlier in the chapter:

Blessing	Curse
Fertile land (vv. 4-5, 10)	Unproductive land (vv. 16, 19-20, 26)
God turns to his people (v. 9)	God turns against his people (v. 17)
Israel will destroy the enemies (v. 7)	Enemies will destroy Israel (vv. 17, 25)
Wild beasts will disappear (v. 6)	Wild beasts will devour them (v. 22)
No sword in the land (v. 6)	Sword will bring destruction (v. 25)
Obedience brings security (v. 5)	Disobedience brings exile (v. 33a)[20]

---

[18]Milgrom, *Leviticus 23–27*, 2303.

[19]Erhard Gerstenberger, *Leviticus: A Commentary,* Old Testament Library (Louisville, Ky.: Westminster John Knox, 1996), 412.

[20]Baruch Levine, *Leviticus* (Philadelphia: Jewish Publication Society, 1989), 276.

Disobedience, then, not only prevents Israel from receiving the blessings of Yahweh, but it ensures them of a future filled with the exact opposite of that which God has intended for an obedient people.

The last curse, and the most terrifying, serves as an ominous sign of the future of this people. If Israel remains disobedient, the last curse that Yahweh will bring upon his people will be exile. They will be reduced to cannibalism (Lev 26:29). The high places and altars will be destroyed (Lev 26:30-31). The land will be devastated by the enemies (Lev 26:32). And then Yahweh announces, "And you, I will scatter among the nations" (Lev 26:33a). So great will be the destruction that even the enemies will be appalled by it (Lev 26:33).

Restoration. Leviticus 26 concludes with the hope of restoration. If Israel fails to remain obedient and in turn becomes the recipient of Yahweh's curses, she still has a hope for restoration: "If they confess their iniquity and the iniquity of their ancestors . . . then I will remember my covenant with Jacob" (Lev 26:40, 42). The hope of restoration does not relieve Israel of its punishment. The sins of the people will necessitate punishment. The text is clear that because they rejected the ordinances and statutes of Yahweh they will be required to "make amends for their iniquity" (Lev 26:43). Hence, the exile serves as the means to making amends. Yet Yahweh assures his people that restoration is possible because he will not spurn them or destroy them utterly (Lev 26:44). Instead, he will remember the covenant he made with the ancestors that were brought out of Egypt.[21]

The paradigm revisited. The passages from Exodus and Leviticus illustrate that the story of Israel was predicated upon divine will and human responsibility. Yahweh established covenant demands, and Israel had to remain obedient in order to enjoy fully the blessings inherent in the covenant. The conditional statements in both passages suggest that obedience was not a given—there was room for disobedience and sin.

In Leviticus, the paradigm of sin–exile–restoration is clearly presented. If Israel remains disobedient (even through four curses), then Yahweh will scatter the people into exile. Yet even in exile, Yahweh yearns for his people and offers a means of restoration for "uncircumcised hearts" that become humble. The hope is that the nation will embrace the blessings and remain obedient—but should they sin, and should exile become necessary, there still remains the hope of restoration.

Deuteronomy: Call to the Covenantal Life

The book of Deuteronomy serves not only as the concluding book to the Pentateuch but perhaps more importantly as a hermeneutical key to the entire Pentateuch. Functionally, the book of Deuteronomy connects the stories of the patriarchs and the Sinai experience with what follows in the Deuteronomistic history. Theologically, however,

---

[21]On the concept of Yahweh "remembering," see Walter Kaiser, "Leviticus," in *The New Interpreter's Bible* (Nashville: Abingdon, 1994), 1:1181-82.

the book of Deuteronomy makes obedience to the words of Yahweh *the* central point in interpreting the history of God's people.[22]

Deuteronomy as covenant. Scholars have long recognized that the structure of Deuteronomy appears to resemble that of an Ancient Near Eastern vassal treaty. The various components of such a treaty appear in the outline of the book.

1. Preamble, 1:1-5, "These are the words which Moses addressed to all Israel . . ."
2. Historical Prologue, 1:6—4:49
3. General Stipulations, chapters 5—11
4. Specific Stipulations, chapters 12—26
5. Blessings and Curses, chapters 27—28
6. Witness to the Covenant, 30:19; 31:19; 32:1-43[23]

Such a structure reminds the reader that in some ways "we can understand Deuteronomy as the completion of a covenant-making process stretching back to the original events at Sinai."[24] Thus, the covenant established at Sinai comes to fruition in Deuteronomy. Deuteronomy is not the "second law" as the name implies; rather, it is the final giving of the law, which becomes incumbent upon the generations that will follow. In Exodus, the recipients of the law seem to be those located at the foot of Sinai; in Deuteronomy, the recipients are the present generation and all those to follow who call themselves the people of God. The book of Deuteronomy reminds the reader that the call to obedience is located within the domain of covenant.

Deuteronomy 1—11: Story as Torah. The first eleven chapters in Deuteronomy rehearse, in summary fashion, several of the key events in the nation's history. These stories function as more than anecdotes from the past. Instead, like the book of Deuteronomy, these stories are meant to serve as *torah*—they are meant to be instructive to the community.[25] The first eleven chapters are composed of stories that display Israel's failure as well as her triumphs as the people of God. Some of the key events include the following:

Deut 1	Rebellion and defeat at Kadesh
Deut 2–3	Journeys east of the Jordan

---

[22]The Hebrew title of Deuteronomy, "These are the words. . ." places the emphasis on the spoken demands of Yahweh. The words of Yahweh spoken through Moses, his mediator, become vitally important if Israel hopes to remain the people of God—they become binding.

[23]Debate has continued over whether the covenant formula adopted in the structure of Deuteronomy is a second-millennium or a first-millennium pattern. For arguments related to the second millennium, see Peter C. Craigie, *The Book of Deuteronomy,* New International Commentary on the Old Testament (Grand Rapids, Mich.: Eerdmans, 1979). For arguments in favor of the first millennium, see Ian Cairns, *Deuteronomy: Word and Presence,* International Theological Commentary (Grand Rapids, Mich.: Eerdmans, 1972); or Moshe Weinfeld, *Deuteronomy and the Deuteronomic School* (Oxford: Clarenden, 1992).

[24]Mann, *Book of the Torah,* 144.

[25]A strong pedagogical thrust permeates the book of Deuteronomy. The emphasis on teaching children the words of *torah* (4:10; 6:7) suggests that what is presented is for edification in matters of faith.

Deut 4–5	Horeb and the Ten Commandments
Deut 6:16	The events at Massah
Deut 8	Manna in the wilderness
Deut 9–10	Sinai and Horeb—The golden calf

In rather striking fashion the collection begins and concludes with a negative event (the failure at Kadesh and the golden calf). Both are incidents that depict the people of God on the brink of destruction—destruction resulting from their own disobedience. At Kadesh, Yahweh becomes so angered at their disobedience that he announces, "I am not in the midst of you" (Deut 1:42). In chapter 9, following the disobedience with the golden calf, Yahweh pledges to "destroy them and blot out their name from under heaven" (Deut 9:14). The lesson is clear—disobeying the covenant imperils the future of God's people.

In chapter 8 Moses urges the people to "take care that you do not forget the LORD your God by failing to keep his commandments, his ordinances, and his statutes" (Deut 8:11). Seven times in the opening chapters the people are asked to "remember." But the act of remembering is much more than a passive recollection of ancient history. Instead, these stories—the story of Israel—become catechetical in some sense. By remembering Yahweh and the stories of the Israelite people, faith is reaffirmed, commitment is redoubled and the covenant is maintained.

The "today" of Deuteronomy. Christopher Wright has noted that "while Deuteronomy is firmly grounded in the past events of election and redemption, it is predominantly a future-oriented book."[26] This orientation is facilitated by the repetition of the word *today*. The word occurs nearly one hundred times throughout, casting a certain sense of urgency on the book. For the writer of Deuteronomy, the future is the critical issue—whether or not they will receive the blessings of Yahweh—and "today" is the decisive moment in which they will seek Yahweh and be obedient or turn to the other gods in their disobedience.

Throughout the book, Moses summons the people to obedience "today." In Deuteronomy 11:26-28, Moses presents the people with a choice: "See, I am setting before you *today* a blessing and a curse: the blessing, if you obey the commandments of the LORD your God that I am commanding you *today;* and the curse, if you do not obey the commandments of the LORD your God, but turn from the way that I am commanding you *today.*"

The immediacy of the moment is clear in Moses' injunction to the people. For that generation and the generations to follow, "today" is always the time for obedience *or* disobedience—the future hinges on the decision.

Deuteronomic blessings. If Israel chooses to obey the voice of Yahweh, then certain

---

[26]Christopher Wright, *Deuteronomy,* New International Biblical Commentary (Peabody, Mass.: Hendrickson, 1996), 14.

blessings are promised throughout the book of Deuteronomy. In general, the blessings concern long life and blessings in the land.[27] In addition to their content, which will be addressed below, their location is critical in the structure of the book. The blessings appear as a type of inclusio to the Deuteronomic law code (the specific stipulations of the law), as indicated in figure 2.1.

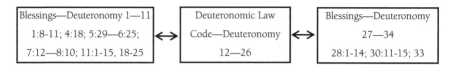

| Blessings—Deuteronomy 1—11
 1:8-11; 4:18; 5:29—6:25;
 7:12—8:10; 11:1-15, 18-25 | ⟷ | Deuteronomic Law
 Code—Deuteronomy
 12—26 | ⟷ | Blessings—Deuteronomy
 27—34
 28:1-14; 30:11-15; 33 |

Figure 2.1. Deuteronomic blessings

The structure emphasizes the connectedness between law and blessing—the two cannot be understood apart from each other. To read the law, one must be fully aware of the blessing, not just the demand. To read of the blessings, one must be fully cognizant of how obedience is manifested in the life of Yahweh's people.

The blessings in Deuteronomy appear to allude to the beginning of the Pentateuch. In chapter 5, the Israelites are urged to obey the ordinances of Yahweh "that you may live, and that it may go well with you, and that you may live long in the land that you are to possess" (Deut 5:33). The last generation to have "lived long" was that of Seth and his descendants in Genesis 4:25—5:32. As mentioned earlier in this chapter, the closing line of Genesis 4, "At that time, people began to invoke the name of the Lord," is critical, perhaps suggesting that their long life was due in part to their devotion to Yahweh. Similarly, the blessing of long life in Deuteronomy is predicated upon the present generation, somewhat like the Sethite generation, invoking the name of the Lord.

In addition to the blessing of long life, the Israelites are told that "the LORD will make you abound in the prosperity, in the fruit of your womb, in the fruit of your livestock, and in the fruit of your ground" (Deut 28:11). For an obedient people, the command to "be fruitful and multiply" will finally be realized in the new land, and the land which was once cursed (Gen 3, 4), will finally return to its paradisaical state.

Finally, the fate of an obedient people will differ drastically from that of the participants at Babel. Those at Babel sought to make a name for themselves by reaching up to the heavens—but their venture ended in failure. Yet in Deuteronomy Moses explains that for an obedient people, "the LORD your God will set you high above all the nations of the earth" (Deut 28:1). Those at Babel also wanted to make a name for themselves in an effort to be unified in their identity—yet they were scattered. Moses indicates that if the Israelites keep Yahweh's commandments they will be

---

[27]C. Marvin Pate, *Communities of the Last Days* (Downers Grove, Ill.: InterVarsity Press, 2000), 18.

unified as God's holy people (Deut 28:9) and they will in fact have a name for themselves: "All the peoples of the earth shall see that you are called by the name of the LORD" (Deut 28:10).

Obedience results in certain blessings. Yet the entry into the Promised Land and its subsequent blessings are more than simple rewards for obedience. They are the enacting of God's creative design upon a people that he has called out from all the nations of the earth. In essence, the entry into the land proves to be re-creational. Just as Abraham's entrance into the Promised Land is a return to the Garden of Eden, so too is the entry of the nation into the Promised Land. The captivity in Egypt in which the lives of the Israelites were "made bitter with hard service in mortar and brick and in every kind of field labor" (Ex 1:14) seems only a distant memory as the nation stands on the banks of Moab, preparing to enter a land filled with milk and honey. The new land, the Promised Land, will indeed be paradise for the obedient.

Deuteronomic curses. Just as obedience to Yahweh results in specific blessings, so too does disobedience yield specific curses. There are numerous curses presented throughout the book of Deuteronomy. Many of these curses fall under the ominous curse of Israel being defeated by her enemies and her subsequent exile into foreign lands. Just as the blessings served to create a future for Israel, the curses threatened to dismantle all that could have been Israel's.

In the structure of the book, the curses also surround the Deuteronomic law code, as indicated in figure 2.2.

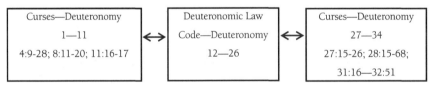

Figure 2.2. Deuteronomic curses

Similar to the blessings, the inclusio created by the curses reminds the people of God that law and curse appear in tandem and that they cannot be separated. Obedience to the law is paramount to the creation of Israel's future. Disobedience yields disastrous results.

Duane Christensen has suggested that a chiasm appears in Deuteronomy 28, which serves to emphasize the totality of these curses in the demise of the nation of Israel.[28] The central point in the chiasm reverses the blessings promised earlier in Deuteronomy 28:4, 8, 11:

---

[28]Duane Christensen, *Deuteronomy 21:10-34:12*, Word Biblical Commentary 6B (Nashville: Thomas Nelson, 2002), 680.

A   Triad of afflictions: curse, confusion, and cumbrance (Deut 28:20-22)

B   Agricultural Disaster (drought and hardening soil) (Deut 28:23-24)

C   War: defeat leading to Israel becoming an object lesson (Deut 28:25-26)

D   Boils of Egypt sent from Yahweh (Deut 28:27)

E   Madness and blindness (Deut 28:28-29a)

F   Oppressed and robbed all the days (Deut 28:29b)

X   **Undoing of the blessings** in 28:4, 8, 11 (Deut 28:30-31)

F'   Oppressed and crushed all the days (Deut 28:32-33)

E'   Madness from what one sees (Deut 28:34)

D'   Boils sent from Yahweh (Deut 28:35)

C'   War: exile leading to Israel becoming an object lesson (Deut 28:36-37)

B'   Agricultural disaster (crop-destroying pests) (Deut 28:38-42)

A' Economic collapse—impoverishment and debt (Deut 28:43-44)

The severity of the warfare and the subsequent exile is the theme of Deuteronomy 28:45-57.[29] Israel is promised that a nation "from far away, from the end of the earth" will swoop down and take the nation into exile. The siege upon the people will be so great that they will turn to cannibalism, mother and father eating in secret the flesh of their children (Deut 28:54-57). They will be taken away "in hunger and in thirst, in nakedness and lack of everything" (Deut 28:48).

The final pericope in Deuteronomy 28 is "a grand reversal of the epic story of Israel's exodus from Egypt."[30] The plagues that once visited Egypt will now visit Israel (Deut 28:58-61). The nation that once grew strong while in captivity (Ex 1) will now be decimated (Deut 28:62). The God that once protected Israel while destroying Egypt will turn upon Israel and "will take delight in bringing you to ruin and destruction" (Deut 28:63). The nation that once walked out of Egypt with the riches of the land on their backs will return to Egypt in ships to be sold into slavery—yet they will be such a despised people that no one will even purchase them (Deut 28:68).

The curses in Deuteronomy portray an ominous future for the nation—it will be the undoing of a nation and the blessings of its God.

Deuteronomic restoration. Central to the paradigm of sin–exile–restoration is the final element of restoration. This theme receives its most extended treatment in Deuteronomy. Although it was mentioned briefly in Leviticus, the idea of restoration dominates the discussion in Deuteronomy 30:1-10. And similar to the rest of the Pentateuch, the ideas of human responsibility and divine will undergird the discussion of restoration.

The text indicates that if Israel will return to Yahweh and obey with "all your heart

---

[29]The theme of exile as punishment for the breaking of the covenant also appears in Deuteronomy 29:21-27.

[30]Christensen, *Deuteronomy 21:10–34:12*, 609.

and all your soul," then Yahweh will restore the nation. This involves not only the restoration of their riches, but more importantly, the return of all those who have been exiled. Moses explains, "Even if you are exiled to the ends of the world, from there the LORD your God will gather you, and from there he will bring you back" (Deut 30:4).

The restoration extends beyond this to include the transformation of God's people. For those who are willing to turn to Yahweh, he will circumcise their hearts and the hearts of their descendants so that they may be able to love the Lord their God (Deut 30:6). The curses once placed on them will be placed on their enemies, and they will embody the creational design of being fruitful and multiplying.

For a nation that experiences the curses associated with disobedience, there is still hope—the hope of restoration if, and only if, the people return to Yahweh.

Conclusion

Following the announcement of a future restoration, Moses presents the people with a choice in Deuteronomy 30:15: "See I have set before you today life and prosperity, death and adversity." If the nation chooses to be obedient, then they will live and become prosperous—they will receive the blessings of Yahweh. But if they choose disobedience, then they will fail to receive the land promised to them—they will receive the curses of Yahweh.

Throughout the Pentateuch, the people of God have been presented with choices— a matter of divine will and human responsibility. These choices tie the end of the Pentateuch to its beginning. Thomas Mann notes:

> The Torah ends very much the way it began. Just as God placed the earth before Adam and Eve and offered it to them as their dominion, so God places the land of Canaan before Israel and offers it to them. Just as God provided for Adam and Eve a commandment, obedience to which would mean continued blessing, but disobedience to which would entail a curse, so God has blessed Israel as his special people, but warned them of the curse that leads to death. Just as Adam and Eve could be genuinely human only in responsibility to the divine will, so Israel can be God's holy nation only in responsibility to God's *torah*.[31]

Much like Adam and Eve, and much like the nation on the banks of Moab, future generations of God's people will be presented with the choices of life and prosperity or death and adversity. And the future of the nation of Israel will play out as it oscillates between obedience and disobedience. Similar to their primeval progenitors, future generations of Israelites will struggle with sin, attempt to overcome exile and, in the end, yearn for some type of restoration. "Today" will be the moment of decision for those that follow.

---

[31]Mann, *Book of the Torah*, 161.

Supplemental Reading in New Dictionary of Biblical Theology

T. D. Alexander, "Abraham (Abram)," 367-72.

M. J. Evans, "Blessing/Curse," 397-401.

P. R. Williamson, "Covenant," 419-29.

L. H. Osborn, "Creation," 429-35.

J. M. Lunde, "Repentance," 726-27.

Study Questions

1. Does the theme of exile–sin–restoration appear in the patriarchal narratives? If so, how?

2. The passages in both Exodus and Leviticus mentioned above indicate a certain conditionality related to the covenant. What stories in those books illustrate a failure to adhere to the covenantal demands? What are the consequences?

3. How do the stories from the wilderness period (i.e., the book of Numbers) affirm the conditionality of the covenant? How do they correspond to the sin–exile–restoration paradigm?

3

THE HISTORICAL BOOKS

Sin and Exile

This chapter will focus on the books of Joshua, Judges, Ruth, 1-2 Samuel, and 1-2 Kings. It will also touch briefly on the other books of Old Testament theological history, 1-2 Chronicles, Esther, and Ezra-Nehemiah.[1]

The "Deuteronomistic History"

A continuous story runs from Genesis 12 to 2 Kings 25. The first part of this story was discussed in chapter two above, ending with a description of Deuteronomy, the fifth book of the Pentateuch. Deuteronomy is a critical book, exerting a strong influence throughout much of the rest of the Old Testament. Indeed, the theology of Deuteronomy is tightly interwoven into the books that follow (Joshua, Judges, 1-2 Samuel, 1-2 Kings). Because of the tight thematic connection between these books, they are often viewed as a unit, described as the "Deuteronomistic history."[2]

---

[1]The Hebrew Bible arranges these canonical books in a slightly different location than do our modern English translations. In the Hebrew Bible there are three major units: the Torah, the Prophets, and the Writings. Joshua, Judges, 1-2 Samuel and 1-2 Kings are considered part of the Prophets, usually referred to as the Former Prophets. Ruth, 1-2 Chronicles, Ezra, Nehemiah and Esther, however, are included as part of the Writings. Thus, in the Hebrew Bible they come at the very end of the canon, in a slightly different order (1-2 Chronicles is last). Our English translations follow the canonical order of the Septuagint, the early Greek translation of the Old Testament that became the Bible of the early church.

[2]Usually when scholars use the label "Deuteronomistic history" they include the book of Deuteronomy along with Joshua, Judges, 1-2 Samuel, and 1-2 Kings. The exact relationship between Deuteronomy and the other books involves complicated issues of compilation and dating that are outside the scope of this book. For a discussion of these issues from an evangelical perspective, see J. Gordon McConville, *Grace in the End: A Study in Deuteronomic Theology,* Studies in Old Testament Biblical Theology, ed. Willem VanGemeren and Tremper Longman III (Grand Rapids, Mich.: Zondervan, 1993). The view underlying this chapter is similar to McConville's—Deuteronomy predates the other books, and they are dependent on it for their basic theological outlook. This is not to deny the probability of some literary development in Deuteronomy. For a discussion from an evangelical perspective of literary development within Deuteronomy, see Daniel I. Block, "Recovering the Voice of Moses: The Genesis of Deuteronomy," *Journal of the Evangelical Theological Society* 44 (2001): 385-408.

The story in the Pentateuch ends with a new generation of Israelites preparing to enter the Promised Land in fulfillment of the Abrahamic promises of Genesis. Before they enter, however, God calls them to covenant renewal, exhorting them to be faithful to the Mosaic covenant as presented in Deuteronomy. In the book of Deuteronomy, God tells Israel to obey the laws and decrees he has given to them. If they do obey, God promises that they will be blessed in the land that he is giving them. But if they fail to obey, God warns, and if they turn to other gods, then they will be cursed and will ultimately even lose the Promised Land. At the end of Deuteronomy, the people accept the Mosaic covenant with these terms clearly understood.

The central question that drives the story in the books that follow (Joshua, Judges, Ruth, 1-2 Samuel, 1-2 Kings) is this: Will Israel be faithful to following God in the Promised Land as spelled out in the book of Deuteronomy? The tragic but simple answer to this question is no.

Although Israel will have its ups and downs, accompanied by a few bright spots (Joshua, David), in general the Deuteronomistic history paints a bleak picture of Israel's rebellious downward slide toward the disaster of foreign invasion and exile from the Promised Land. The glorious blessings that God graciously gave to his people—the Promised Land and his presence among them—are squandered through sin and rebellion.

The contrasts between the opening chapters of Joshua and the closing chapters of 2 Kings underscore this point. In the early chapters of Joshua, the Israelites begin their victorious conquest of the Promised Land, laying siege to the city of Jericho and destroying this pagan city by the power of God. At the end of 2 Kings, however, it is the Babylonians who are the victorious conquerors of the land. They lay siege to Jerusalem and then destroy it completely. The Israelite king flees, only to be captured on the plains of Jericho (2 Kings 25:5), back where the whole conquest started. The Israelites are then driven from the Promised Land into exile (2 Kings 25:21). Another group of Israelites flees back to Egypt (2 Kings 25:26). Thus, they go full circle, returning to the place of bondage where the story of deliverance started back in Exodus.

Due to sin and rebellion, the people of God reverse the avenue of blessing in the Promised Land. Their rebellion moves them backward, away from blessing and into the punishment and curses described in Deuteronomy 28:15-68. The central theme of the Deuteronomistic history, therefore, is one of human failure to keep the Mosaic covenant.

In essence, the nation of Israel will live out the cycle of Genesis 1—11. The Deuteronomistic story begins with the creation of the nation and their establishment in the Promised Land (Joshua), which, like the Garden in Genesis, is blessed by the very presence of God. However, in Genesis 3—11, as in Judges and in 1-2 Kings, sin and rebellion destroy the relationship and the blessings (Noah and David are both exceptions, although both end up somewhat tainted). Ultimately, Adam and Eve are evicted from the Garden (Gen 3) and humankind is scattered across the earth (Gen 10—11). Likewise the children of Israel are driven from the Promised Land (2 Kings 17, 25) and scattered into Assyria (2 Kings 17) and Babylonia (2 Kings 25).

The disaster of Genesis 3—11, however, is quickly followed by the hope and promise of God's covenant with Abraham (Gen 12; 15; 17). The book of Deuteronomy likewise presents the hope of future restoration beyond the disaster and the curse (Deut 30:1-10). On the other hand, the history built upon Deuteronomy, the Deuteronomistic history of Joshua through 2 Kings, includes very little explicit hope of restoration. The unit ends with the destruction of Jerusalem and the exile. There are echoes of hope, especially from the victories of Joshua, as well as from the Davidic covenant of 2 Samuel 7, which promised that a descendant of David would rule forever. Hope also echoes from the narratives about the prophets Elijah and Elisha (1 Kings 17 through 2 Kings 9), from which the subtle theme of "individual deliverance in the face of national apostasy" emerges. Yet the final chapters of 2 Kings make no allusions to this hope. The story in this unit ends in exile and disaster.[3]

It will be the Prophets (see chapter five below) that preach the needed message of hope and restoration beyond the exile and disaster—a hope that is even beyond the national aspirations of Israel, a messianic hope for a new covenant and a new way of relating to God through the outpouring of his Spirit. It is also a hope that extends beyond the ethnic borders of Israel to include all peoples. Perhaps this is why the message of hope is absent from the end of 2 Kings. Within the Deuteronomistic history, the stress of the story is on Israel. There are allusions to the "blessings on the nations" of the Abrahamic promise, but these are weak at best. A message of hope and restoration within the context of the Deuteronomistic history perhaps would have been misconstrued into a strictly nationalistic understanding. In contrast, God's actual promise of future restoration as revealed in the Prophets is much broader and more glorious than a mere return to the situation described literally in Deuteronomy.

Of course, other theological themes emerge in these books as well. The books of Joshua, Judges, Ruth, 1-2 Samuel and 1-2 Kings are united by a common Deuteronomistic theology, contributing to a larger megastory of Israel, but they still reflect a certain degree of theological diversity that should not be overlooked.[4] That is, there are

---

[3]Some writers see hope expressed in the release of Jehoiachin in 2 Kings 25:27-30. However, Jehoichin remains in Babylon and receives his daily allowance from the king of Babylon, that is, he is still in total submission to Babylon. Furthermore, there is no mention of any repentance on Jehoichin's part. If there is hope being expressed here, it is very faint, and nothing at all like that expressed in the Prophets.

[4]See the discussion in Gordan J. Wenham, *Story as Torah: Reading the Old Testament Ethically*, Old Testament Studies, ed. David J. Reimer (Edinburgh: T & T Clark, 2000), 45-46.

small stories along the way that contribute in diverse ways to the bigger story.

Joshua. The book of Joshua follows close on the heels of the storyline in Deuteronomy. Deuteronomy 34 records the death of Moses. The Promised Land is in view, just across the Jordan River. In Joshua 1, Joshua becomes the new leader of Israel and leads the new generation across the Jordan and into the Promised Land. The story in Joshua unfolds in three basic units. Joshua 1—12 describes how Joshua and the Israelites, led by God and with his power, invade Canaan and shatter the major alliances that oppose them. Joshua 13—21 delineates the distribution of the Promised Land to the Israelites. Concluding the book is Joshua 22—24, a covenant renewal ceremony reminding the victorious Israelites of the importance of remaining faithful to God and his decrees.

Several related theological themes flow throughout the book of Joshua, moving the story forward while at the same time interconnecting with the Pentateuchal story that precedes it. One of the main themes is the movement toward the fulfillment of the Abrahamic promises (Genesis 12—22). Indeed, the fulfillment of God's promise to Abraham has been driving the story since Genesis 12. God promised Abraham that he would have numerous descendants, and the books of Exodus and Numbers describe the proliferation of the Israelites. God promised to make their name great and to curse those who cursed them; Exodus describes how God utterly destroyed the economy and military might of Egypt, which had enslaved them. God promised Abraham to be his God and the God of his descendants; the Mosaic covenant of Exodus, Leviticus, Numbers, and Deuteronomy define that relationship in detail. Yet God also promised that the descendants of Abraham would inherit the land of Canaan. The promise of the land was an important component of the Abrahamic promise, and at the close of Deuteronomy it remained unfulfilled. The book of Joshua describes in detail how Israel actually possesses the land that God promised to them.

The Promised Land theme is actually a broad umbrella that encompasses several other related subthemes. For example, the text stresses that the land was a gift from God. Both Deuteronomy and Joshua repeatedly cite (in various forms) the phrase "the land that I [God] am giving to you."

Closely interrelated with the land theme are the motifs of rest and blessing. Numerous times in Joshua, particularly at the beginning and at the end of the book, the promise and realization of rest is cited, usually in connection with the gift of the land (Josh 1:13, 15; 11:23; 14:15; 21:44; 22:4; 23:1). Indeed, the gift of the land and the rest associated with settlement within the land is one of the implied blessings of the Abrahamic promise. It is significant that out of the twenty-four chapters of Joshua, nine of them deal with the distribution of the land to the various tribes and families within the tribes. The land was an inheritance from God himself. Moreover, the equal distribution of land set up an egalitarian society in contrast to the societies that surrounded Israel. Theologically, the idea of being at rest in the land is the "restoration" toward which the story has been moving ever since Moses was called by God to deliver the Israelites from Egypt. In a sense it parallels life in the Garden. Near the end of the book, the narrator summarizes this fulfillment of land and rest: "Thus the LORD gave to Israel all the land that he swore to their ancestors that he would give them; and having taken possession of it, they settled there. And the LORD gave them rest on every side just as he had sworn to their ancestors" (Josh 21:43-44).

Another central element of the Abrahamic promise that surfaces in Joshua is Genesis 12:3: "I will bless those who bless you, and the one who curses you I will curse; and in you all the families of the earth shall be blessed." This text lies just below the surface in Joshua 2—7, combining with the Deuteronomic stress on faithfulness and obedience to God as the central requirement for being one of his people—that is, of obedience to the covenant, not ethnic identity, as the central requirement.[5]

Joshua 2–7 is a rather shocking unit. The main surface story describes the "siege" and destruction of Jericho. The amount of space devoted to this episode, combined with the placement of the material at the beginning of the book, underscores its importance. The Jericho episode, however, is bracketed by the stories of two individuals that encapsulate the Jericho story like bookends. In Joshua 2, Rahab the Canaanite harlot not only hides the Israelite spies but makes a profound statement of faith in the God of Israel. Thus, she is spared from the destruction of Jericho, and she becomes, in essence, an Israelite. In Joshua 7 another character, Achan, is the antithesis of Rahab. He arrogantly disobeys a direct command from God; thus, he dies like the Canaanites of Jericho. Rahab is blessed and Achan is cursed (cf. Gen 12:3). These two stories are important within the theology of Joshua, for they speak to the issue of who is included within the people of God that settle in the Promised Land and receive blessings. Rahab and Achan illustrate that faith in the promises of God is critical; ethnic identity is not.

The inclusion of Rahab into the people of God—she becomes part of the Davidic genealogy that leads to Christ—anticipates the fulfillment of the Abrahamic promise

---

[5]The promise of blessings on "all the families of the earth" in Genesis 12:3 reverberates throughout Scripture and serves as a corrective for the ethnocentric tendencies within the history of Israel. The inclusion of different ethnicities in the people of God is a fairly constant theme. Several of the patriarchs marry women of other nationalities (Aramean, Canaanite, Egyptian). In Exodus 12:38 a "mixed crowd" joins the people of the exodus, and in Numbers 12:1 Moses marries a Cushite. The inclusion of the Canaanite Rahab and her family, along with the addition of the Gibeonites (Joshua 9), appears to be an extension of this theme. The prophets will expand considerably on this theme, which will explode into a greater fulfillment in the New Testament era. Understanding Genesis 12:3 as pointing to the "restoration" from the sin and scattering in Genesis 3–11 underscores the multiethnic aspect of restoration theology. For a discussion that traces this theme throughout Scripture, see J. Daniel Hays, *From Every People and Nation: A Biblical Theology of Race*, New Studies in Biblical Theology, ed. D. A. Carson (Downers Grove, Ill.: InterVarsity Press, 2003).

of blessing on all the peoples of the earth (Gen 12:3), adding to the development of the restoration theme. In the Prophets, the theme of restoration will be broadened to include the nations of the world (Gentiles), tying the Abrahamic promise of Genesis 12:3 even more securely into the overarching theme of restoration. Rahab, who connects to David through genealogy and to Abraham through Genesis 12:3, foreshadows this development.

The fidelity of Joshua and the new generation of Israel to the covenant as formulated in Deuteronomy and restated in Joshua 24 is foundational to the success of the conquest of Canaan. Israel's faithfulness to the decrees of God brings his presence and power into the struggle to drive out the Canaanites. Thus, as long as they are faithful, they are victorious. In contrast to the disobedient generation that preceded them, the generation that died away from the Promised Land in the wilderness, and in contrast to the disastrous generations that come later in the book of Judges, the generation that follows Joshua into the land will be faithful to Yahweh. Thus, they are successful (Josh 24:31), enjoying God's powerful presence and blessing of rest. The culpability of later Israelites who slide into apostasy and lose the land is underscored by this generation that remained faithful.

However, even in the book of Joshua certain hints of foreboding foreshadow the disastrous future. The central tone of Joshua is upbeat and optimistic. In general, Israel is faithful and victorious. The promise to Abraham is being fulfilled. On the other hand, individuals such as Achan foreshadow the future disobedience of the nation. Likewise, the narrator quietly notes the times and places that Israel fails in her task to drive out the inhabitants (Josh 13:1-5, 13; 15:63; 16:10; 17:12). So even as Israel begins to enjoy the "rest" and the blessings within the garden of the Promised Land, the narrator reminds the readers that the seeds of sin, rebellion and apostasy have likewise been planted and are beginning to sprout.

Excursus: The Theological Problem of the Conquest

Many Christians are troubled by the severity of the conquest. God orders the Israelites to kill all of the Canaanites, including every man, woman and child. To some, this action conflicts with their sense of justice as well as with the compassion of God. In response, several points should be noted. First, the order to destroy all of the inhabitants of a conquered city applied only to the inhabitants in the Promised Land. It did not apply to battles and sieges outside its borders. Second, the Canaanite society that was to be totally destroyed is consistently depicted in the biblical record as exceptionally corrupt and immoral. The Sodom and Gomorrah episode (Genesis 19) presents a paradigmatic picture of Canaanite society. Likewise, Leviticus 18 connects sexual immorality and perversion to the inhabitants of the land of Canaan. Furthermore, in Genesis 9:25, Noah pronounced a "prophetic" curse on the Canaanites, a curse that finds fulfillment in the conquest.[6] Third, Genesis 15:16 implies that God was offended by the sin of the inhabitants of Canaan as early as the time of Abraham but that in his mercy he waited another four hundred years before judging them. So the judgment on the Canaanites in the book of Joshua was not a new idea; it had been growing throughout the pentateuchal period. Finally, it is ironic that the first major character in the story other than Joshua is an exception to the extermination rule. As mentioned above, the Rahab episode, placed at the beginning of the book and receiving considerable space in the compact story of the conquest, suggests that those inhabitants of the land that turned to the God of Israel could be delivered and incorporated into the people of God. The Gibeonites play a similar role in Joshua 9.

Judges. Although Joshua is an upbeat book of faith and victory, the story in the book of Judges is one of tragic human disaster. Judges 2:10—3:6 summarizes the main elements of the story. After the generation that conquers the land with Joshua dies, Israel forgets their God and turns to the local Canaanite deities. They quit trying to drive out the pagan inhabitants of the land. In fact, Israel settles among the Canaanites—and the Hittites, Amorites, and so forth—intermarries with them, and embraces their gods. This shocking behavior is the most serious violation of the covenant terms expressed in Deuteronomy that can be imagined. At the heart of the covenant between Israel and God is the threefold formula: I will be your God; you will be my people; I will dwell in your midst. In Judges the Israelites reject Yahweh, the God of Abraham, and turn to pagan gods. This action angers Yahweh, and he hands the people over to foreign domination and oppression.

Judges 2:10-19 describes the cycle that repeats several times throughout Judges. Israel sins and rebels against God, rejecting his gracious covenant and embracing instead the pagan gods of their neighbors. God therefore allows a foreign power to dominate and oppress Israel as punishment. The people groan and cry out in their suffering. God then has compassion on them and raises up a "judge"[7] who delivers them from the foreign domination. After the deliverance, the people of Israel return to their sin and idolatry again and the cycle repeats.

As the story described in this summary actually unfolds, a new wrinkle develops in the picture. Not only does the cycle (disobedience/idolatry, punishment, deliverance, disobedience/idolatry) repeat, but things get progressively worse as the story contin-

---

[6]Many scholars interpret the curse in Genesis 9:25 as a prophetic curse against the Canaanites, Israel's classic but future enemy. See, for example, Victor P. Hamilton, *The Book of Genesis: Chapters 1–17*, New International Commentary of the Old Testament (Grand Rapids, Mich.: Eerdmans, 1990), 324-27; and Allen P. Ross, *Creation and Blessing: A Guide to the Study and Exposition of Genesis* (Grand Rapids, Mich.: Baker, 1988). Ross (p. 217) points out that the euphemistic term used for sexual sin throughout Leviticus 18 (occurring twenty-four times) is the same term used in the Noah episode of Genesis 9:20-23.

[7]The term traditionally translated "judge" would probably be better translated as "leader." None of the judges other than Deborah appears to do any "judging."

ues. So the story is not so much a series of cycles as it is a downward spiral. This downward movement can be tracked along two lines. First, the people of Israel get more and more corrupt as the story progresses. Second, the judges (heroes?) themselves get worse and worse throughout the book.[8]

This negative assessment of the judges themselves is a critical aspect of the book and important to our theological understanding of this text. The first judge, Othniel, who overlaps with the faithful generation from the book of Joshua, is a fairly good hero—although his tribe of Judah fails to dislodge the chariot-driving inhabitants of the plain (Judg 1:19). But after Othniel all of the others except Deborah are tainted in some way. Ehud (Judg 3:12-30) delivers Israel by murdering the unarmed fat king of Moab, hardly the action of a real hero (contrast this story with David, who kills the heavily armed Goliath in one-on-one combat in 1 Samuel 17). While Deborah is the only flawless judge, she is in essence a foil for the timid and cowardly Barak (Judges 4—5). Furthermore, the unlikely "hero" and true deliverer emerging from this story is Jael, the woman who kills the Canaanite army commander.

Even Gideon (Judges 6–9) is a mixture of positive and negative virtues. Although many popular sermons have extolled his great faith—he defeats the huge Midianite army with only 300 men—a closer examination of the text reveals numerous negative aspects. Gideon is extremely reluctant to follow God's leading, and God has to give him miraculous sign after sign in order to get him to act. After the victory, rather than placing the gold taken as plunder into the tabernacle (as was done faithfully in the time of Moses and Joshua), Gideon takes some of it and makes a golden ephod for himself. Judges 9:27 clearly indicts him for this: "Gideon made an ephod of it and put it in his town, in Ophrah [instead of in the tabernacle]; and all Israel prostituted themselves to it there, and it became a snare to Gideon and his family." Finally, Gideon leaves a less-than-stellar legacy. His son Abimelech murders seventy of his brothers and tries to install himself as king.[9]

At the end of the list is Samson, who falls more into the category of "bum" than of "hero." Samson's parents dedicate him as a Nazirite (Num 6:1-12), but he continually violates the requirements of a Nazirite. Part of the vow, for example, is that he is forbidden to touch any dead animal. Yet Samson not only touches a dead lion, he eats honey out of the carcass (and gives some to his parents, thus defiling them as well). This action is an unimaginably blatant and disgusting violation of his Nazirite status. The only part of the vow that he appears to keep is the prohibition against cutting his hair, and yet even that he eventually gives up frivolously. Samson is selfish and self-

[8]Daniel I. Block states that by the end of the book there are only "antiheroes"; see *Judges, Ruth,* New American Commentary (Nashville: Broadman & Holman, 1999), 58.
[9]For a detailed discussion of the negative aspects of Gideon, see Wenham, *Story as Torah,* 119-27; and Daniel I. Block, "Will the Real Gideon Please Stand Up?" *Journal of the Evangelical Theological Society* 40 (1997): 353-66.

serving. He chases after Canaanite women, an action strictly forbidden in Deuteronomy. He cares nothing about Yahweh and about delivering Israel. He fights the Philistines only for personal revenge. In the end, he dies a tragic death.

The book of Judges allocates a considerable amount of text to the story of Samson, and the placement of his story at the end of the list of judges is suggestive. This selfish, disobedient judge, while no doubt a true historical character, probably also plays a symbolic role in the overall story. As such he would represent the nation of Israel itself. Note the parallels. God sets Israel apart to be holy. He empowers them to defeat the inhabitants of the Promised Land and commands them to drive out the Canaanites. Instead they fraternize with the Canaanites and intermarry with them. They squander their power potential and are subdued by foreign peoples like the Philistines. Samson likewise ignores his holy "set apart" status, chases foreign women, defiles himself and his parents, and is finally subdued by the Philistines, having squandered his God-given power.

An examination of the different nations that Israel fights in the book of Judges sheds light on another theme running throughout the book. In the book of Judges, the Israelites fight Arameans, Moabites, Ammonites, Amalekites, Canaanites, Midianites, and Philistines. Consider the irony of this list. During the exodus, Moses fought and destroyed the Amalekites, the Moabites, and the Midianites. The re-emergence of these once-defeated nations points to a reversal of Israel's story of restoration. By fighting them a second time, and by losing this time instead of winning as they did during the exodus, Israel demonstrates that she is moving backward in salvation history and not forward. The Philistines likewise play an interesting role in the story both here and in 1-2 Samuel. In the list of peoples that Israel fights, the Arameans, Moabites, Ammonites, Amalekites and Midianites all live outside the land of Canaan. They are merely raiders or invaders trying to expand their influence. The Canaanites, of course, are the original inhabitants that Israel is to drive out. The Philistines, however, are a new group, who, like Israel, have recently migrated into the region and have only recently settled. The theological irony, therefore, is that not only has Israel not driven out the Canaanites, but they now also are being attacked and oppressed by people that they had beaten earlier—and as an ultimate reversal, a new people (the Philistines) are challenging them for occupation of the Promised Land.

The irony only grows stronger as we progress through the book to the end. Not only do the Israelites fail to drive out the Canaanites, but they also start to fight each other. Thus, Abimelech destroys Shechem, an Israelite city (Judg 9), and Jephthah fights against the Israelite tribe of Ephraim (Judg 12). At the end of the tragic downward slide, it is the tribe of Benjamin, rather than the Canaanites, that is utterly destroyed by Israel (Judg 20:48).

The gruesome final chapters of Judges illustrate how Israel hits the bottom of the downward spiral with a morbid splash. The tribe of Dan leaves their inherited territory and migrates north, looking for an easier area to conquer. They convince a Levitical priest to lead them in worshiping local pagan household gods (Judg 17–18). In Judges 19 a Levite is attacked by the inhabitants of an Israelite city in Benjamin. In a scene that intentionally brings Sodom and Gomorrah (the prototypical sinful Canaanite cities of Genesis 19) to mind, the Israelite inhabitants demand to have homosexual relations with this Levite. Instead, he placates the mob by throwing out his concubine to them. They rape her and she dies. The Levite then calls out all Israel, and they annihilate the tribe of Benjamin.

Thus, by the end of the book the nation of Israel—whom God himself had brought up out of Egypt and called into covenant relationship—has degenerated to the same moral and theological level as the corrupt Canaanites. In fact, one of the central themes in Judges is the depiction of the "canaanization of Israel."[10] Note the irony of the story. One important aspect of Israel's invasion of Canaan was that the conquest was part of God's judgment on the Canaanites for the extreme moral and theological sinfulness of their society. By the end of Judges, however, Israel is no different than the Canaanites. By all of the terms laid down in Deuteronomy, God should sever his relationship with Israel and annihilate them completely. The fact that he continues to be patient with them, sending deliverer after deliverer, only underscores the depth of his grace toward his rebellious people.

At the end of Judges the reader is left with a certain apprehension. What will happen next? Will God destroy them completely? Or will someone like Moses rescue them again and deliver them again, returning them to a proper and obedient relationship with God? Who will that be? A new leader/hero is needed.

Ruth. Usually the book of Ruth is excluded from discussions of the Deuteronomistic history. In the Masoretic Text (the Hebrew Bible), the book of Ruth follows Proverbs instead of Judges, as it does in English Bibles. The probable connection for the Hebrew order in the canon is related to Proverbs 31:10-31, which describes the "wife of noble character" (NIV) or "capable wife" (NASB). The Hebrew phrase behind this translation is *ʿēšet ḥayil,* and it can refer to a "wife" or to a "woman." In Ruth 3:11 Boaz tells Ruth, "All the assembly of my people know that you are a *worthy woman.*" The Hebrew phrase translated "worthy woman" is *ʿēšet ḥayil,* identical to the phrase in Proverbs 31:10. Thus in the Hebrew canon, the book of Ruth appears to be connected to the "wife of noble character" in Proverbs 31 through this phrase.

The Septuagint (the Greek translation of the Hebrew text), however, placed the book of Ruth after Judges, thus associating this book with the story that runs from Genesis to 2 Kings. The Septuagint was embraced by the early church, and our English translations today continue to follow the Septuagint regarding the canonical order of the books.

Ruth does, in fact, fit very well into the story that we have termed loosely "the Deuteronomistic history." The book of Judges ended in disaster. The question echoing at the end of Judges is, "Who will deliver Israel from the terrible situation that they are

---

[10]Block, *Judges, Ruth,* 58.

in?" The answer, of course, is David. The book of Ruth introduces David into the story.

Although Ruth overlaps with the time period of Judges (Ruth 1:1), the characters and the story in Ruth stand in strong contrast to Judges. In Ruth there are no armies, battles or invasions. There is only the quiet story of a peasant Moabite widow and her grief-stricken Israelite mother-in-law trying to survive. God is at work in the book of Ruth, but he works quietly and behind the scenes. The manner in which God uses the Moabitess Ruth to bring about the deliverer and the restoration of Israel is instructive, for it points to a motif of strength through weakness. Indeed, throughout Scripture God often seems to delight in this motif of bringing a powerful deliverance or restoration through apparent weakness. This motif climaxes, of course, with the incarnation and the cross.

Besides bridging the story between Judges and 1-2 Samuel, Ruth also connects to Deuteronomistic theology. In Ruth 1 there is a famine in the land, a fulfillment of the punishment promised in Deuteronomy 28. A man and his two sons *leave* the Promised Land and journey outside of Israel to Moab. The land, however, is a gift from God, their inheritance and part of their covenant relationship with God. To leave the land has serious theological implications. These men apparently embark on a voluntary exile away from Yahweh and his Promised Land. Consequently, the men all promptly die, outside the land and without heirs. However, Naomi and Ruth, the main women in the story, return to Yahweh and the Promised Land and are thus blessed. The theme of reversing emptiness to fullness will be played out both in Naomi's life and in Ruth's life, connecting not only to the following story of Hannah in 1 Samuel but also to the story of Israel in general. As Naomi and Ruth turn to the God of Israel for protection, he responds not only with protection but also with rich blessing. Indeed, Ruth becomes the avenue through which the immediate deliverer, David—and the ultimate deliverer, Jesus Christ—will come.

The foreign ethnicity of Ruth is likewise significant. This aspect of the story connects to the inclusion of many peoples in the promise of Abraham, and it points to the further expansion of this theme that will appear in the Prophets. Relating to the big story of sin, exile and restoration, Ruth's entry into the people of God underscores that the ultimate restoration will have a multiethnic component.

1-2 Samuel. The books of 1 and 2 Samuel were originally part of one continuous book and therefore should be viewed together as a literary unit.[11] From a sociohistor-

---

[11]All Hebrew Bibles before the sixteenth century present 1 and 2 Samuel as a continuous work with no breaks. Prior to printed Hebrew editions, this material was presented on one long scroll, with no divisions marked. Hebrew, however, takes up less space than Greek, and when this book was translated into Greek (the Septuagint), it would no longer fit on one standard scroll. Thus it was divided into two books and placed on two scrolls. The Septuagint also connected 1-2 Samuel with 1-2 Kings, referring to the four books as 1-4 Kingdoms. The Latin Vulgate maintained the four-book connection, but revised the titles from "Kingdoms" to "Kings." Some Eastern Orthodox translations still use the Greek designation, and some older Catholic translations still follow the Vulgate's terminology.

ical point of view, this unit describes the transformation of Israel from a collection of unstable tribes (as described in Judges) to a strong, centralized monarchy.

The central human character in 1-2 Samuel is David. Although much of 1 Samuel deals with the prophet Samuel and the first king, Saul, these two serve primarily as transitions—or in Saul's case, as a foil for David, who is the focal point of the story.

As the story opens, the spiritual condition of Israel is terrible, similar to that portrayed in Judges. The high priest Eli is assisted by his two morally corrupt sons, who continually pervert the worship of Yahweh at the tabernacle. Climaxing the disaster that began in Judges, these two wicked priests of Israel are defeated and killed by the Philistines, who also capture the ark of Yahweh. The loss of the ark is one of the low points of Israelite history. The corrupt and immoral leaders of Israel trivialize the presence of God and thus they lose his presence through their foolishness.

Yahweh, however, remains a central character in 1-2 Samuel, and in 1 Samuel 4–6, he works alone to invade and conquer the Philistines. The Philistines have defeated the Israelites, but Yahweh, the God of Israel, has hardly been defeated by the Philistine god Dagon. In this "ark narrative," as Yahweh strikes down the idol of the god Dagon and smites city after city of Philistines, the story reads as if God is indeed invading and conquering Philistia. Yahweh returns to Israel by himself, loaded with tribute and plunder from the conquered Philistine cities that surrendered to him. This story makes a strong theological statement about God. He does not need Israel to protect him. He is not limited by human assistance. He is sovereign and carries out his designs whether or not Israel is obedient. In addition, this story is laying the theological groundwork for the fall of Israel in 2 Kings to the Babylonians. The ark narrative teaches that the defeat of a disobedient Israel is in no way a negative reflection on the power of Yahweh.

Concurrent with the disastrous leadership of Eli and his sons is the contrasting rise to power of Hannah's son Samuel. In spite of the blatant disobedience of Eli's sons, Yahweh works through the pious woman Hannah to raise up a transitional deliverer, Samuel, who, unlike the many tainted leaders in Judges, will be a righteous leader.[12]

However, as Samuel grows old, Israel demands a king so that they can be like the other nations. After warning them of the dangers that a monarchy poses, Yahweh and Samuel oblige them and Samuel anoints the first king, Saul.

---

[12]Hannah's song of praise in 1 Samuel 2 introduces the theme of "reversal of fortunes" that resurfaces several times in 1-2 Samuel. She sings: "The LORD makes poor and makes rich; he brings low, he also exalts. He raises up the poor from the dust; he lifts the needy from the ash heap, to make them sit with princes and inherit a seat of honor" (1 Sam 2:7-8). Note also that the opening song of Hannah (1 Sam 2) is paralleled by the closing song of David (2 Sam 22).

Although Saul is physically big and strong, and although he has Samuel to advise him and the Spirit of God to empower him, the new king has no depth of character, and he does not obey Yahweh faithfully. After Saul makes three serious mistakes—he fails to wait on Samuel to make sacrifices before a battle (1 Sam 13:5-15); he makes a foolish vow and tries to enforce it (1 Sam 14:24-46); and he disobeys Yahweh by keeping plunder he captured from the Amalekites (1 Sam 15:1-34)—Yahweh removes his power, presence and blessing from Saul and leads Samuel to anoint David as king. The power, success and blessing that the monarchy has potential to give are clearly tied to the monarch's obedience and faithfulness to Yahweh and his covenant.

David is contrasted with Saul throughout the narrative. He is everything that Saul is not—valiant, courageous and obedient to Yahweh.[13] The story in 1 Samuel 16—31 is driven by the contrasts between the two men. David grows stronger and stronger as Saul grows weaker and weaker (and more and more insane). Finally Saul dies, and after a time of political intrigue and civil war, David becomes the sole king over all Israel (2 Sam 1—5).

David then sets out to complete the conquest begun by Joshua, thus reversing the disaster of Judges. In contrast to the many defeats in Judges, David wins victory after victory over the Jebusites, the Philistines, the Moabites, the Arameans, the Edomites, and the Ammonites (2 Sam 5—10). He brings the ark of the covenant to Jerusalem and reestablishes it as the center of Israelite worship. He expands the borders of Israel very close to the limits that had been promised to Abraham.

At the peak of David's reign, and climaxing the restoration of Israel after the disaster of Judges, Yahweh makes an everlasting covenant with David (2 Sam 7), promising that a future heir of David's will reign forever. This Davidic covenant (promise of kingship) will combine with the Abrahamic covenant (promise of blessings on all the nations) to drive the biblical story throughout the rest of the Old Testament and into the New Testament toward Christ, who brings the ultimate monarchy and the ultimate restoration.

Yet David's life, both public and private, peaks in 2 Samuel 10. He is a great man and a great deliverer, but he is not perfect. He is but a man, and ultimately, as the story illustrates, he has feet of clay. The Bathsheba episode of 2 Samuel 11—12, chronicling David's sins of adultery, deceit and murder, is a critical episode in the 1-2 Samuel story. Until this point, everything in David's life is going well. His obedience to Yahweh allows him to finish the conquests of Joshua and to inaugurate many of the bless-

---

[13]Occasionally the narrator is rather subtle about the contrasts. For example, David is introduced as shepherding his father's sheep. Saul, by contrast, is introduced as wandering around aimlessly, looking for his father's lost donkeys. The contrast is clearest perhaps in the Goliath narrative (1 Sam 17), where the brave young man David fights the cowardly King Saul's battle for him.

ings promised to Abraham. After his blatant disregard of Yahweh and his abuse of kingly power in 2 Samuel 11—12, however, David's kingdom and his private life begin to unravel.

There are very few positive events in David's life after the Bathsheba affair. His eldest son, Amnon, rapes one of David's daughters and is in turn killed by another son, Absalom (2 Sam 13), who later usurps the throne from David (2 Sam 15). In shame, David is driven out of Jerusalem, the city he once conquered. Adding to the insult, along the road a man pelts him with rocks (2 Sam 16), contrasting with his earlier spectacular victory with rocks over Goliath. Eventually Absalom, whom David still loves, is killed, and the grieving David returns to the throne. Yet things in the kingdom are still unsettled. Another internal rebellion arises (2 Sam 20). Then, in 2 Samuel 21, David is once again fighting, this time with fatigue, against the Philistines, the enemy that he had defeated as he began his career so many years ago. At the end of 2 Samuel, David's action brings upon his people a plague from God rather than the blessings that he brought them in earlier days. David repents and offers a sacrifice, thus stopping the plague, but the negative tone of this final episode leaves a less than optimistic shadow over the reign of David.

What is the central biblical theology emerging from the narratives of 1-2 Samuel? In the overall scheme within the Deuteronomistic history, the events in 1-2 Samuel connect to the concept of "restoration." Yahweh placed Israel in the Promised Land and promised fantastic blessings on them if they would stay obedient and faithful to the covenant expressed in Deuteronomy. After a good start in Joshua, the Israelites in Judges snub Yahweh and become like the immoral, pagan Canaanites. According to the warnings in Deuteronomy 28, Israel deserves to be destroyed. Instead, Yahweh responds graciously to move them to restoration, raising up David and adding the Davidic covenant to his eternal promise. The rise of the monarchy, even though Yahweh opposed the reason and the manner in which Israel requested it (1 Sam 8), is incorporated into Yahweh's ultimate plan of restoration. From now on, all hope for restoration in the future will involve a descendant of David who rules as a king.

However, one of the main theological points emerging from the Davidic narratives is the sober reality that David is not the ultimate deliverer. For all of David's outstanding virtues—and the text stresses many—he nonetheless falters, stumbles and falls. As an individual, David's sin is forgiven by Yahweh. As the king, however, the leader of the people of God who was to usher in the blessings of the promise to Abraham, he suffers through the consequences of his unfaithful act. Just as the opportunity for establishing the consummate kingdom under Yahweh is within David's reach, the king gazes down at Bathsheba and the dream slips away out of his grasp . . . to await another, more qualified Messiah.

1—2 Kings. As mentioned above, 1 and 2 Kings were originally one book. It traces the tragic story of Israel from the death of David to the death of Jerusalem. The story is told through the analysis of the reigns of more than forty kings. The major issue, however, is simple—fidelity to the Mosaic covenant of Deuteronomy. The rise, decline, and fall of Israel and Judah are related directly to their obedience and disobedience to Deuteronomy. A few kings, such as Asa, Hezekiah and Josiah, will struggle to keep the covenant, but the majority will abandon Yahweh and his covenant and thus lead Israel and Judah into apostasy. In fulfillment of the judgmental promises of Deuteronomy 28, this results in exile and the loss of the Promised Land and all its associated blessings.

Structurally, the theological history of 1-2 Kings can be broken down into three basic units. The first unit, 1 Kings 1—11, describes the Solomonic kingdom. This story begins with the death of David and the succession of Solomon to the throne. It ends by stating bluntly that Solomon "did what was evil in the sight of the LORD," worshiping the foreign gods of his foreign wives. In the middle, the story describes the spectacular kingdom of Solomon, characterized by the wealth and wisdom that the king brought to the nation and epitomized by the construction of the magnificent temple of Yahweh that Solomon built.

Most scholars view this as the high point of Israelite history. They interpret Solomon as beginning well and as serving Yahweh well, but falling away in his old age, led astray by his foreign wives. While this continues, perhaps, to be the majority view, it has recently been challenged.[14] Although on the surface the narrator seems to be trying to impress the reader with the splendor of Solomon's kingdom, below the surface he drops numerous subtle hints that all is not well. Beneath the veneer of splendor, the narrator tells us that Solomon does not have the character of David and that something is not quite right about his heart. Solomon marries Pharaoh's daughter (bringing to mind all of the oppression of the Egyptian bondage). He does not dance with joy before Yahweh or show any of the humility that David personified. He does build the temple, but he seems equally concerned with the rest of his building program (including the house of Pharaoh's daughter), and he carries out this impressive building program with forced labor, which is the major cause of the civil war that erupts after his death.

Throughout the Solomon narratives, Deuteronomic warnings are frequently given to him, bidding him to follow the laws and decrees of Yahweh, one of the central things that he does not do. Note in particular the commandments in Deuteronomy 17:14-20 that are addressed specifically to the king. Three things are strictly forbidden: (1) he is

---

[14]Walter Brueggemann states that Solomon "is seen to be indifferent to Torah" and that the Solomon narrative serves as "an ominous critique of Solomon's disregard for Torah" (*1 & 2 Kings,* Smith & Helwys Commentary [Macon, Ga.: Smyth & Helwys, 2000], 3, 11). For an extensive discussion of the negative and ironic elements in the Solomon story, see J. Daniel Hays, "Has the Narrator Come to Praise Solomon or to Bury Him?" *Journal for the Study of the Old Testament* 28, no. 2 (2003): 163-88.

not to accumulate large numbers of horses, especially from Egypt; (2) he is not to accumulate large numbers of wives; and (3) he is not to accumulate a large quantity of silver and gold. The story of Solomon stresses how many horses and wives as well as how much silver and gold Solomon accumulated. The text boasts—ironically and sarcastically, it can be argued—about this accumulation (1 Kings 10:23-29). By 1 Kings 11, the narrator has dropped any subtlety and clearly states that Solomon is worshiping detestable foreign gods and has angered Yahweh through his disregard of the Deuteronomic covenant. The prophet Ahijah then announces judgment on Solomon's kingdom due to this disregard (1 Kings 11:29-39).

A very important theological point to observe in the Solomon narratives as well as throughout 1-2 Kings is the critical role that Yahweh's covenant with David (2 Sam 7) plays in maintaining the kingdom, the dynasty and the associated blessings. Twice Yahweh tells the wayward King Solomon that it is only due to this promise to David that judgment on him is delayed or muted (1 Kings 11:12-13; 11:34-39). Thus, the reason that Solomon reigns as long as he does and as prosperously as he does is due more to Yahweh's covenant with David than to Solomon's virtue or obedience. In fact, a certain tension develops, for Solomon's disobedience as described in 1 Kings 11 is extremely serious by Deuteronomistic standards. Indeed, he has fallen into the most serious apostasy, worshiping even the most detestable gods (those requiring child sacrifice). Deuteronomy requires that this be punished severely, but Yahweh's promise to David blunts the Deuteronomistic demands.

This tension continues into the next major section, 1 Kings 12 to 2 Kings 17, and indeed, even to the end of the book. After the death of Solomon, the nation erupts into civil war and divides into the two countries of Judah and Israel. Only Judah is ruled by the descendants of David. Although a few of Judah's kings (Asa, Josiah, Hezekiah) struggle to return the people to a true worship of Yahweh, many of David's descendants continue to lead Judah into devastating apostasy. Thus the tension within the story continues. Will Yahweh destroy them as Deuteronomy demands, or will he continue to give them a Davidic king as his promise to David demands? The fact that the southern kingdom Judah lasts much longer than the northern kingdom Israel is usually attributed to the intervention of the few good kings that rule. However, both the fact of their intervention and the long delay of Yahweh's judgment should perhaps be connected to Yahweh's promise to David.

In the northern kingdom a similar tension develops, but not in connection to the Davidic covenant. The northern kingdom passes through several dynasties, none of them Davidic and none of them approved by Yahweh. In fact, one of the first acts of the rebellious northern kingdom is to establish calf worship sanctuaries at Dan and at Bethel (1 Kings 12:25-33). In a clear connection to the horrendous golden calf episode of the exodus (Ex 32), the new king declares, "Here are your gods, O Israel, who brought you up out of the land of Egypt" (1 Kings 12:28). Few statements could be more blasphemous.[15] The northern nation of Israel will continue in apostasy throughout the 1-2 Kings story until their destruction by the Assyrians in 2 Kings 17. The tension arises over the long delay in Yahweh's judgment. The narrator of the story connects the delay back to the Abrahamic covenant. In the midst of Israel's apostasy, the narrator declares of the northern kingdom, "But the LORD was gracious to them and had compassion on them; he turned toward them, because of his covenant with Abraham, Isaac, and Jacob, and would not destroy them; nor has he banished them from his presence until now" (2 Kings 13:23).

Thus the story of 1-2 Kings places the demands of Deuteronomy in tension with the gracious covenants that Yahweh made with Abraham and with David. Deuteronomy demands judgment, but the covenants of Abraham and David promise restoration, blessing and an everlasting dynasty. This theological tension will be picked up and advanced by the Prophets. They will proclaim that the resolution of this tension will only be found through the coming of the Messiah and the inauguration of the new covenant. Indeed, this tension between Deuteronomy (the law) and the Abrahamic and Davidic covenants (grace) will not be resolved until the coming of Christ, and it will not be clearly explained until the apostle Paul explains it in Romans and Galatians.

The middle section of 1-2 Kings, dealing with the divided kingdom, extends from 1 Kings 12 to 2 Kings 17. Although most of 1-2 Kings focuses specifically on the actions of the monarchs, in this section the royal history is abruptly interrupted by "the prophetic counterforce in Israel's history."[16] Considerable attention is given to Yahweh's prophets (Elijah, Elisha, Micaiah). As the monarchy falls into apostasy, Yahweh speaks his word of warning and judgment to the kings through the prophets. Yet the Elijah/Elisha narratives are packed with other theological implications as well. Yahweh demonstrates through Elijah that the power of life is available to those of faith and is quite separate from the monarchy and the corrupted central temple complex (1 Kings 17). In 1 Kings 18, Yahweh uses Elijah to give clear evidence that Yahweh alone is God and that the Canaanite god Baal is nothing.

In 1 Kings 19 the concept of *remnant* is introduced. Even though practically it seems as if the entire nation has fallen into apostasy, Yahweh reveals to Elijah that seven thousand people have remained faithful to him. This remnant theology is part of a

---

[15]One of the most central descriptive phrases that Yahweh uses to define himself to Israel is, "I am Yahweh, who brought you up out of Egypt."

[16]Brueggemann, *1 & 2 Kings*, 207. Brueggemann continues, "Indeed, their presence in the narrative serves to expose the inadequacy and lameness of the kings as shapers of history, in order to assert that real authority and real energy for historical reality lie outside the legitimated claims of monarchy." This power lies, of course, with Yahweh and is found through obedience and faithfulness to him.

broader shift in thinking developed in the Elijah/Elisha narratives. For there is indeed a shift in these narratives from a national focus to an individual focus. In the midst of national calamity and national judgment due to sin and rebellion, there is individual salvation. Some will survive; some will be saved. There will always be a remnant.

Yet the bright hope inherent in the Abrahamic and Davidic covenants and the individual salvation suggested in the Elijah/Elisha narratives fade into the background as 1-2 Kings moves to the end of the story. The main event—indeed, the climax and focus of the Deuteronomistic story—is the destruction of Jerusalem and the exile of the rebellious, unrepentant Hebrews out of the Promised Land. Sin has its consequences, and God's judgment on sin is a part of the reality of the great megastory played out in human history.

In essence, the Deuteronomistic history ends by demonstrating that due to sin and stubborn rebellion God's people failed to find righteousness and blessing through keeping the law. The elements of hope and restoration fade at the end of this part of the story, for this phase of the story stresses the failure of sinful humankind. It points to the need for a king who is greater than David. It also suggests the need for a new covenant, one in which the promises of the Abrahamic and Davidic covenants can find ultimate fulfillment and thus lead to ultimate restoration and blessing. This theme of hope, merely a faint shadow of suggestion in the Deuteronomistic history, will be revived and expanded in the Prophets and will blossom into fulfillment in the New Testament with the coming of Christ.

The Other Historical Books

The Deuteronomistic story in Judges to 2 Kings, as discussed above, is apparently written from the viewpoint of one living in exile. That is, it implies that the reader lives after the final event described in 2 Kings 25 (the fall of Jerusalem in 586 B.C. and the exile). The Deuteronomistic story looks backward at the disastrous history of Israel and her relationship to Yahweh. It explains why Israel went into exile (failure to keep the Mosaic covenant). The other books of theological history (Esther, Ezra-Nehemiah, 1-2 Chronicles) likewise have an exilic perspective. Their point of view is different, however, for they look to the future more than to the past. These books seek to answer the exiled Israelites' questions such as: Where do we go from here? What happens next? What is our relationship with Yahweh?

The book of *Esther* takes place in Persia. No one in the book, including Esther, mentions God or shows any sign of repentance or any other theological awareness of Israel's history with Yahweh. However, in spite of this, Yahweh works to protect these exiled Jews, albeit behind the scenes. The point of the book from a biblical theology perspective is to show how God continues to protect a remnant of his people in exile, regardless of their attitude toward him. It implies that whether or not the exiled Jewish community is currently obedient to him, they (i.e., their descendants) will nonetheless play an important role in the ultimate future restoration.

Ezra and Nehemiah (originally one book) tell the story of the exiles that returned to the land after the Babylonian/Persian exile. The lesson learned from the Deuteronomistic story was not lost on them. In fact, Nehemiah 9 gives a very succinct summary of that theological history. At the conclusion of this summary, Nehemiah acknowledges that the return of the exiles that he has led is hardly the glorious restoration that was promised in the past: "Here we are, slaves to this day—slaves in the land that you gave to our ancestors to enjoy its fruit and its good gifts. Its rich yield goes to the kings whom you have set over us because of our sins; they have power also over our bodies and over our livestock at their pleasure, and we are in great distress" (Neh 9:36-37).

Thus, although the exiles do return to Israel in Ezra-Nehemiah and they do reconstruct the temple, they clearly do not reconstitute the Mosaic covenant arrangement with Yahweh as defined in Deuteronomy. Life in the land now does not resemble at all the description of the good life in the land promised in Deuteronomy. The Israelites remain under foreign domination, a small cog in the wheel of the huge Persian Empire. This fact is stressed in Ezra-Nehemiah. Likewise, although the temple is reconstructed, the presence of Yahweh does not come to fill it as it did in 1 Kings 7:10-11.[17] The ark of the covenant (presumed lost) is not even mentioned in Ezra's account of the temple dedication (Ezra 6:13-18), in contrast to the accounts in 2 Samuel 6 and 1 Kings 8. What is mentioned (and stressed) is the reign of Darius, the Persian king, a constant reminder that they are still under foreign domination and not under a Davidic king. Thus, although Israel is back in the Promised Land, they have not experienced the anticipated restoration. In essence, they are still in exile, awaiting the coming of the Davidic king who will ultimately restore them.

For those in the exile, the glorious situation described in Deuteronomy and brought close to fulfillment under David is gone. Ezra and Nehemiah are not returning Israel to that situation. What they are doing is reconstituting Israel as a people— a remnant that has survived the judgment—and providing them with guidelines for living in the interim period between the terrible exile and the coming, yet future, restoration. The political situation of power and domination described in Deuteronomy as well as the tremendous blessings described in the book are not available to Israel anymore, but nonetheless, in the meantime they are to live in obedience to the Torah.

---

[17]Ezekiel will describe the departure of the presence of God from the temple (see chapter five below). It is significant that none of the postexilic writers even allude to any return of God to the temple. In biblical theological terms, God does not return to the temple until Jesus Christ himself walks in through the gates.

In the Hebrew Bible, *1-2 Chronicles* comes at the very end of the canon, providing a final theological commentary on the history of Israel from a postexilic orientation. In some regards it is similar to 1-2 Kings. It covers many of the same events and much of the same time period as the Deuteronomistic account (although 1-2 Chronicles discusses only the Davidic kings of Judah). Theologically, the Chronicler comes to the same major conclusion as the narrator(s) in the Deuteronomistic story. Israel was unfaithful to Yahweh, breaking the laws and decrees of God in willful sin and rebellion. The exile came as a direct result of this disobedience.

However, there are also numerous significant differences, reflecting the differing theological purposes of the two works. The Chronicler begins his history with creation and carries the story into the exilic time of Persian domination. He seems to be stressing the consistency of God in his dealings with Israel. The Chronicler spends more than forty percent of his text on David and Solomon, but he does not mention any of the terrible negative events in their lives that the Deuteronomistic story revealed. This underscores one of the central differences in perspective between the two works. The Deuteronomistic story was looking back from the exile, explaining how Israel's sin and rebellion justly caused them to be in their present situation. The Chronicler, however, is looking forward, presenting his theology as a guideline for living during the postexilic period. Therefore, his concern with David and Solomon is to present their positive legacy—David's covenant and Solomon's temple/worship. From the stress on the Davidic covenant comes the hope of a future restored monarchy, even though the Persians rule at the present time.

The Chronicler stresses that obedience to God is an essential and timeless imperative for his people. Regardless of the political situation, he seems to be saying, worship of Yahweh continues. Added to Torah obedience, therefore, are the imperatives to seek God through worship and praise. The end of 2 Chronicles highlights this theology. Even though Cyrus the Persian is ruling, Yahweh is working through this foreign king to fulfill his promises; thus Cyrus exhorts the people of God to "go up!" (to Jerusalem in worship).

Summary and Conclusions

The Historical Books tell us the story of Israel's failure to live by the Mosaic covenant in Deuteronomy. The glaring and repetitive theological truth emerging is the sinfulness of humankind and their inability to obey God and live by his decrees. Thus, humankind squanders the presence of God and the wonderful blessings he offers and chooses instead a stubborn life of rebellion that leads to judgment.

These books also tell us much about God. Fortunately for humankind, God is patient and loving. He counterbalanced the demands of the law with the promises he made to Abraham and David. The tension created between these two aspects—iden-

tified as law and grace in the New Testament—creates hopeful expectation and anticipation, and drives the story of salvation through the Prophets and into the New Testament, where Christ appears as the resolution.

Supplementary Reading in New Dictionary of Biblical Theology

J. C. Laansma, "Rest," 729-32.
Regarding the consultation of the dead Samuel in 1 Samuel 28: P. S. Johnston, "Death
and Resurrection," 443-47.
R. J. McKelvey, "Temple," 806-11.
J. G. Millar, "Land," 623-27.
B. S. Rosner, "Idolatry," 569-75.
M. W. Elliott, "Remnant," 723-26.

Study Questions

1. Summarize the content and theology of the books that comprise the Deuteronomistic story (Judges to 2 Kings).

2. Does this chapter's explanation of the morality of the Conquest seem adequate to
   you? Summarize the arguments and critique the explanation.

3. Do you agree with the critique of Solomon? Summarize his argument and critique
   the position regarding Solomon. Is Solomon a good king or a bad king?

4. Trace references to the Davidic covenant from 2 Samuel 7 to the end of 2 Kings.
   Discuss how the Davidic covenant is used throughout the Deuteronomistic history.

4

PSALMS AND THE
WISDOM LITERATURE

Contested Story

The Psalms and Wisdom literature engage the story of Israel from two distinctively different perspectives. Both perspectives, however, do interact with the paradigm of sin–exile–restoration. The Psalms employ various historical events from the story of Israel, in part to create a didactic feature in Israel's liturgy. The historical psalms in particular rehearse the events in the life of Israel that best represent the movement from sin to exile and finally to restoration. The Wisdom literature, while devoid of specific references to historical events, does engage the sin–exile–restoration paradigm, but at a different level. The writers of the Wisdom literature explore the theological presuppositions at work in the paradigm, namely, Deuteronomistic theology. The sages wrestle with whether such a notion aptly represents Israel's history—and reality in general.

The Psalms

Historical motifs in the Psalms. The psalms are replete with images drawn from the history of Israel. These images are not relegated to one period of Israel's history alone. Instead, the psalmists freely drew from various periods in Israel's history.[1] As indicated below, references to each period of Israel's history appear in the Psalter:[2]

The Patriarchal Period—Ps 105; 107
The Exodus—Ps 66; 68; 77; 78; 81; 106; 114
The Wandering in the Wilderness—Ps 68; 78; 91; 95; 99
The Conquest—Ps 44; 68; 78; 80; 105; 107; 135
The Life in the Land—Ps 78; 83; 106; 107

---

[1] For a comprehensive treatment of historical motifs in the Psalms, see Erik Haglund, *Historical Motifs in the Psalms* (Stockholm: CWK Gleerup, 1984).

[2] The citations provided are only representative. Numerous other psalms fit within the historical divisions provided.

David—Ps 78; 89; 132; 144

Exile and Return—Ps 106; 107; 137

The motifs relating to the exodus and the wilderness period appear most frequently in the Psalter.[3] The purposes of the historical motifs are diverse, but in the historical psalms (Ps 78; 105; 106; 135; 136),[4] the primary purpose is to rehearse the major events in the relationship between God and his people.[5] The frequently occurring theme of Israel's sin is countered with the theme of God's mighty works. Thus it is little wonder that the periods of the exodus and the wilderness wandering dominate the historical motifs in the psalms. The former depicts the mighty works of God, while stressing his steadfast faithfulness to his people. The latter illustrates the willful disobedience of the nation.

The portrayal of Israel's history in the historical psalms often depicts, in truncated fashion, the history of Israel as played out in the sin–exile–restoration paradigm. As Gunkel has aptly summarized; "In each context where one encounters the narratives, either the deeds of YHWH are accented by themselves, or the sins of Israel which YHWH had to punish during this period are pushed to the foreground. However, YHWH did not allow these sins to dissuade him from bringing about his ultimate goal, leading his people to the Promised Land."[6]

While there are numerous motifs to be explored in the Psalter, the images of sin, exile and restoration will be explored below. Although one cannot say that the sin–exile–restoration paradigm is operating in every psalm, it does represent a constituent part of Israel's liturgy and worship.

The sin of the people. A dominant theme in the historical psalms is the failure of the nation to be obedient to the covenant made with Yahweh. In Psalm 78, the psalmist summarizes the failures of the people when he announces:

They did not keep God's covenant,
    but refused to walk according to his law.
They forgot what he had done,
    and the miracles that he had shown them. (Ps 78:10-11)

---

[3]Haglund, *Historical Motifs in the Psalms,* 102. Surprisingly, there is almost no mention of the events at Sinai.

[4]The dating of these psalms varies. Psalm 78 is typically dated to the preexilic period (see John Day, "Pre-Deuteronomic Allusions to the Covenant in Hosea and Psalm LXXVIII," *Vetus Testamentum* 36 [1986]: 1-12). The other four psalms are typically dated to the postexilic period (see Charles Fensham, "Nehemiah 9 and Pss 105, 106, 135, and 136: Post-exilic Historical Traditions in Poetic Form," *Journal of Northwest Semitic Languages* 9 [1981]: 35-51). The variance in dating suggests that a theological vision of Israel's history proved to be fertile ground for psalmic reflection throughout the history of Israel's worship.

[5]For a general introduction to the historical psalms, see Hermann Gunkel, *An Introduction to the Psalms,* trans. James Nogalski (Macon, Ga.: Mercer University Press, 1998), 247-49.

[6]Ibid., 247.

Throughout the remainder of Psalm 78, and in the historical psalms in general, the psalmists illustrate the rebellious nature of God's people. Central to the depiction of Israel's rebellion are allusions to the wilderness period. In Psalm 78 the psalmist proclaims:

How often they rebelled against him in the wilderness
   and grieved him in the desert! (Ps 78:40)

Psalm 106 provides the most extensive recitation of Israel's history in the wilderness. Nearly twenty-one verses are devoted to the topic of Israel's rebellion and provide ample anecdotal evidence of such. They put God to the test in the wilderness (Ps 106:14). They became jealous of Moses and of Aaron (Ps 106:16). The people made a calf at Horeb and "exchanged the glory of God for the image of an ox" (Ps 106:20). They despised the land and had "no faith in his promise" (Ps 106:24). The people worshiped the Baal of Peor and offered sacrifices to the dead (Ps 106:28). At Meribah, they angered the Lord (Ps 106:32). As Hans-Joachim Kraus has noted, "The entire history of Israel, which expresses itself in craving, oblivion, disobedience, and thoughtless exchange of gods, . . . is already basically present before the occupation of the land."[7]

Yet the sinfulness of Israel is greater than just the wilderness period. Once in the land, the nation "did not destroy the peoples" as commanded by Yahweh (Ps 106:34). Their actions were so abominable that the pristine land of the promise became a land polluted with blood, and the nation as a whole "became unclean by their acts" (Ps 106:39).

Exile. Psalm 78 and Psalm 106 indicate that sin cannot go unpunished and that some form of exile is required. The poet of Psalm 78 offers a unique perspective on sin and the resulting effect of exile. Drawing from the imagery in 1 Samuel 4—7, the psalmist rehearses Israel's loss to the Philistines and the subsequent loss of the ark of the covenant. Yet the psalmist clearly indicates that the blame rests with the nation of Israel, not with some failure of Yahweh to protect his people. Having listed the sins of Israel in Psalm 78:56-57, he then announces:

For they provoked him to anger with their high places;
   they moved him to jealousy with their idols.
When God heard, he was full of wrath,
   and he utterly rejected Israel. (Ps 78:58-59)

The last line reiterates the severity of punishment for sin, "he utterly rejected Israel." The Israelites experience the ravages of war in their loss to the Philistines. Fire devours their young men (Ps 78:63), priests fall by the sword (Ps 78:64), and the wid-

---

[7]Hans-Joachim Kraus, *Psalms 60-150* (Minneapolis: Augsburg, 1993), 322.

ows are so overcome by the losses that they have no lamentation (Ps 78:64). This punishment, however, is predicated on a far more devastating event. In Psalm 78:60, the psalmist explains:

> He abandoned his dwelling at Shiloh,
>> the tent where he dwelt among mortals.

Yet the exile is not with the nation of Israel—it is with Yahweh. The nation falls to the advances of its enemy but only because God has withdrawn his presence from among his people. James L. Mays has noted the theological undertones present in Psalm 78:

> By utterly rejecting Israel, the Lord cancels and dissolves the very manifestation of his sovereignty in the world achieved in redeeming a people as his possession, settling them as his people in his holy mountain and dwelling in their midst through the representation of his power in the ark at the sanctuary of Shiloh. The sovereign Lord is free to abandon the very achievements and institutions of his sovereignty.[8]

Simply put, sin threatens not only their physical security, but perhaps more damaging, it challenges their theological certainty.

The more traditional Deuteronomistic depiction of exile appears in Psalm 106. As Leslie C. Allen explains, "The present experience of exile is described deuteronomistically as punishment for a backlog of sins. . . . They are victims of their own and their predecessors' sins."[9] Similar to the statements made in Deuteronomy 28, the psalmist explains that the sin of the people inevitably led to the exile of the people—they were handed over to the nations (Ps 106:41). According to Psalm 106:42, they were oppressed by their enemies and brought under their power.

The details of a specific exile are left unstated, yet it is the theological thrust of the passage that proves most disconcerting. There can be little doubt that should a nation—even God's own people—choose to sin and become a rebellious people, they will be met with the destructive consequences of exile.

Restoration. The later historical psalms, especially Psalm 106 and Psalm 136, make explicit reference to some form of restoration. Following Deuteronomic theology (cf. Deut 30:4-6), the psalmists contend that while God justly punished a rebellious nation, he had not given up on them—even if they continued in their rebellious ways:

> Many times he delivered them,

[8]James L. Mays, *Psalms*, Interpretation (Louisville, Ky.: Westminster John Knox, 1994), 258.
[9]Leslie C. Allen, *Psalms 101–150*, Word Biblical Commentary 21 (Waco, Tex.: Word, 1983), 52. Hans-Joachim Kraus explains, "This general overview of the events between the occupation of the land and the loss of the land corresponds to the Deuteronomistic theology of history set forth in Judges 2" (*Psalms 60–150*, 321).

but they were rebellious in their purposes,
and were brought low through their iniquity. (Ps 106:43)

Yet like the events surrounding the Egyptian captivity (Ex 2:23-25) when the nation cried out to Yahweh, "for their sake he remembered his covenant" (Ps 106:45) with his people and caused the nations to pity Israel. Despite the previous failures of the nation, "he regarded their distress" (Ps 106:44), and he acted "according to the abundance of his steadfast love" (Ps 106:45).

Psalm 136 offers a continual praise of God for his mighty acts of deliverance in Israel's past. Yet the act of restoration from exile serves as the culminating event in this psalm:

It is he who remembered us in our low estate,
    for his steadfast love endures forever;
and rescued us from our foes,
    for his steadfast love endures forever. (Ps 136:23-24)

For those living after the exile, restoration was a powerful reminder of the steadfast love of Yahweh. "One subtext to the plot of God's eternal *hesed* ('steadfast love') is his self-binding oath or promise to provide. . .beneficence into the future."[10] The steadfast love of God assured Israel that God was at work in the world to create his people. Thus the repetition of the phrase "for his steadfast love endures forever" that appears throughout Psalm 136 does more than create some type of antiphonal reading. Rather, it is confessional: there is hope for Israel because God has not abandoned his people. Restoration in full may be delayed, but for those waiting, there is an assurance of its arrival.

Summary. Episodes from the history of Israel add to the theological witness of the Psalter. These episodes add a celebratory tone in some cases, while in others they offer a somber note to the continuing sinfulness of the nation. Yet in the historical psalms the story of Israel is the story of sin, exile and restoration. These motifs are intended to call the people to repentance but also to thanksgiving and praise. These psalms point beyond the mere history of Israel—they bear witness to the One who redeems Israel *despite* her history.

The Wisdom Literature

Engagement with the story of Israel. In the history of Old Testament theology, the function and message of the Wisdom literature has always proven difficult to cohere with the rest of the story of Israel. Brevard Childs notes that during the late nineteenth

---

[10]D. A. Baer and R. P. Gordon, "חֶסֶד," in *New International Dictionary of Old Testament Theology and Exegesis* (Grand Rapids, Mich.: Zondervan, 1997), 2:212.

and early twentieth centuries, "wisdom was thought to be a late post-exilic, and indeed foreign, importation into Israel. Since it had nothing to say about Israel's sacred history, her cult, or covenant, it was judged to be on the periphery of the Old Testament."[11] Although very little of the story of Israel can be found in much of the Wisdom literature, this does not suggest that it fails to engage the story. The writers of the Wisdom literature attempt to engage the story of Israel by wrestling with the theological tenets foundational to much of Deuteronomistic theology.

The primary assumption behind Deuteronomistic theology is that if one is obedient before God, one will be given the blessings of God. If, however, one is disobedient to the laws of God, then one will experience the curses promised to the disobedient (cf. Deut 28). In the book of Proverbs there is an echoing of this sentiment. Although the covenantal language found in the Deuteronomistic history is absent, the spirit of the theology is present. John J. Collins notes that "there is an underlying similarity between proverbial wisdom and covenantal Yahwism insofar as both posit a system of retribution."[12] The books of Job and Ecclesiastes, however, are more reluctant to embrace this view of reality, suggesting that the issue of blessing and cursing might be more complex. The language of covenant and the tenets of Deuteronomistic theology reemerge in a direct and forceful way in the Wisdom of Ben Sirach, thus suggesting a merger of Deuteronomistic and wisdom theologies.[13]

Proverbs. The language of Proverbs reflects an understanding of reality that closely resembles that present within the Deuteronomistic tradition. The similarities fall into two categories. First, the sage is careful to present a model of reality that presupposes a certain cause and effect relationship, often referred to as retributive theology. Second, the sage appears to have drawn not only from the ideas associated with the Deuteronomistic tradition, but also from the traditions associated within the book of Deuteronomy itself.

Retributive theology. The book of Proverbs stresses the significance of moral formation and character development, especially within the domain of the community. The frequent appeal to "my son" (e.g., Prov 1:8; 2:1; 3:1; 3:21) suggests that moral

---

[11]Brevard S. Childs, *Biblical Theology of the Old and New Testaments* (Minneapolis: Fortress, 1993), 187.

[12]John J. Collins, *Jewish Wisdom in the Hellenistic Age* (Louisville, Ky.: Westminister John Knox, 1997), 3.

[13]Although the Protestant canon does not include the Wisdom of Ben Sirach, it has been retained here in an effort to demonstrate the full range of theologies present within the wisdom tradition of Ancient Israel. More to the point, however, Sirach has been included to demonstrate how the story of Israel did receive attention within Israel's wisdom tradition, contrary to the caricature of Wisdom literature so often presented. Furthermore, Sirach is important for tracking the historical flow of ideas as they emerged from the Old Testament. This is especially the case in how Sirach reacts to the tension between Psalms/Proverbs and Job that pertains to the telling of the story of Israel. While that tension is resolved in the New Testament in the person of Christ, who was Wisdom Incarnate, it is anticipated in Sirach's fusion of the two wisdom traditions.

formation is, at its root, pedagogical.[14] Central to the pedagogy of character development is an understanding of behavior—and its resulting consequences. In the sin–exile–restoration paradigm, there is a clear sequence of thought. If one sins, that person can expect punishment, in some variety, for that sin. Similarly, the book of Proverbs suggests that negative behavior will result in some type of punishment. Note, however, that the paradigm has shifted from corporate identity to individual identity. The cause-and-effect relationships no longer play out at the national level, as depicted in Deuteronomy and the Deuteronomistic history. Rather, the object of the sage's message is the individual.

Wisdom poems comprise the bulk of Proverbs 1–9. This section concludes by offering the reader two choices: the simple, or unlearned, may choose to feast at the banquet of Woman Wisdom (Prov 9:1-6) or Woman Folly (Prov 9:13-18). In each case, the choice will dictate the subsequent response. For those who dine with Woman Wisdom, they will "walk in the way of insight" (Prov 9:6). For those who choose the way of Woman Folly, their fate is far more ominous. Those who feast there "do not know that the dead are there, that her guests are in the depths of Sheol" (Prov 9:18). There is little doubt for the sage that an unwise choice can reap disastrous results in the life of the individual.

Proverbs 10—22 is replete with numerous statements cast in the style of the proverb (*māšāl*). Many of the proverbs are presented in the antithetical style, suggesting what is appropriate and what is considered inappropriate. Yet these proverbs do more than simply list behaviors considered acceptable and unacceptable. The sage, recognizing the cause-and-effect relationship, offers a type of motive clause by suggesting possible outcomes for each choice. The following are illustrative of the cause and effect schemata developed by the sage:

> The righteous will never be removed,
>   but the wicked will not remain in the land. (Prov 10:30)[15]

> Those who guard their mouths preserve their lips;
>   those who open wide their lips come to ruin. (Prov 13:3)

---

[14]The phrase "my son," along with references to mother and father in Proverbs 1–9, suggests that at the core level of Israelite culture, the family and education occupied a central place. Michael V. Fox notes the significant roles that fathers played in the education of sons and concludes, "Even if Proverbs, or just Part I (Prov 1–9), was in fact composed for school-teaching, the terms 'father' and 'son' are meant literally. The terms do not display, but—at most—disguise a school situation" (*Proverbs 1–9*, Anchor Bible 18A [New York: Doubleday, 2000], 80).

[15]On the use of "land" in Proverbs, see Fox, *Proverbs 1–9*, 123-24. The chief issue that appears in the Wisdom literature is not concerning whether one inherits the Promised Land, necessarily, but concerning the length of one's life: "The righteous will live (long), the wicked will die (prematurely)" (123).

Those who are greedy for unjust gain make trouble for their households,
  but those who hate bribes will live. (Prov 15:27)

Proverbs 11:31 encapsulates the thought of the sage regarding the choices of the righteous and the wicked. According to the sage, there is punishment for those who choose incorrectly:

If the righteous are repaid on earth,
  how much more the wicked and the sinner!

Just as Deuteronomy indicates that punishment and curses will come to the disobedient, Proverbs announces the end of the wicked—the effective exile of those who choose to act contrary to the ways of God.

The influence of Deuteronomic theology in Proverbs. In addition to being influenced by the theology found in the Deuteronomistic tradition, the author of Proverbs appears to reflect on material found within the book of Deuteronomy itself. There are two texts in Proverbs that allude to passages in Deuteronomy. The first, Proverbs 3:1-12, appears to be an inner biblical allusion to the Great Shema in Deuteronomy 6:4-9.[16] The second passage is Proverbs 6:20-35 where the sage appears to allude to Deuteronomy 5:6-18 and Deuteronomy 6:4-9.[17] Both passages suggest that not only did the sage know the traditions in Deuteronomy, but he felt they were fully compatible with the worldview espoused by the wisdom writers.

There are several verbal links that suggest the writer of Proverbs was cognizant of the tradition associated with the Great Shema in Deuteronomy 6:4-9. Examples include:

The use of "bind"

| Deuteronomy 6:8 | "Bind them as signs on your hand" |
| Proverbs 3:3 | "Bind them around your neck" |

The use of "bind" in conjunction with "write"

| Deuteronomy 6:8-9 | "Bind them as signs on your hand. . .and write them on the doorposts" |
| Proverbs 3:3 | "Bind them around your neck, write them on the slate of your heart" |

The use of "heart" and "all"

| Deuteronomy 6:5 | "Love the LORD your God with all your heart" |
| Proverbs 3:5 | "Trust in the LORD with all your heart" |

---

[16]Paul Overlad, "Did the Sage Draw from the Shema? A Study of Proverbs 3:1-12," *Catholic Biblical Quarterly* 62 (2000): 424-41.

[17]Michael Fishbane, "Torah and Tradition," in *Tradition and Theology in the Old Testament,* ed. D. Knight (Philadelphia: Fortress, 1977), 275-300.

The idea of covenant love

Deuteronomy 6:5	"Love the LORD your God"
Proverbs 3:3	"Do not let lovingkindness and faithfulness forsake you"[18]

While none of these associations alone can prove that the sage alluded to the book of Deuteronomy, together they make a strong case that the sage was at least aware of that tradition and that it was formative in the writing and thinking at that time.

A second series of statements in Proverbs suggests, once again, that the sage has drawn from the book of Deuteronomy in the presentation of his material. Proverbs 6:20-35 makes references to material in Deuteronomy 5:6-18 and Deuteronomy 6:4-9.[19] There are at least seven connections between these texts:

Opening Vocative

Deuteronomy 6:4	"Hear, O Israel, what I command"
Proverbs 6:20	"Heed, my son, the commands"

Location Language

Deuteronomy 6:6	"When you dwell and journey, when you lie down and rise up"
Proverbs 6:22	"When you go about, when you lie down and awaken"

The Use of "Bind"

Deuteronomy 6:8	"Bind them on your hand"
Proverbs 6:21	"Bind them on your heart"

Father and Mother

Deuteronomy 5:16	"Honor your father and your mother"
Proverbs 6:20	"Heed . . . your father . . . your mother"

Adultery

Deuteronomy 5:18	"Do not commit adultery"
Proverbs 6:32	"Whoever had adultery with a woman"

Steal

Deuteronomy 5:19	"Do not steal"
Proverbs 6:30-31	"If [thieves] are caught, they will pay sevenfold"

---

[18] In this case, the link is conceptual. The concept to "love God" in Deuteronomy carries with it covenantal overtones. The words "lovingkindness" and "faithfulness," which appear often in Proverbs, are words that appear in relation to covenant language. Thus, as Overlad has suggested, "love in Deuteronomy 6:5 and 'lovingkindness and faithfulness' in Proverbs 3:3 both refer to covenant love" ("Did the Sage Draw from the Shema?" 427).

[19] For an extended treatment of how the Torah tradition influenced later biblical literature, see Fishbane, "Torah and Tradition," 275-300.

Neighbor's Wife

Deuteronomy 5:21   "Do not desire your fellow's wife"

Proverbs 6:25, 29   "Do not desire . . . your neighbor's wife"

The sheer number of allusions in Proverbs 6 to material in Deuteronomy further strengthens the argument that the writer of Proverbs drew from the traditions associated with Deuteronomy.

Summary. The frequent assertions by scholars that the Wisdom literature has no connection with the story of Israel appears somewhat lacking in its final analysis. While the traditional motifs related to the story of Israel are scarce, there is firm evidence that the theological presuppositions that guided the sage in his writing were Deuteronomistic in orientation. The direct allusion to texts in Deuteronomy, coupled with the use of retributive theology, suggests that the sage had adopted a view of reality that buttressed that found in Deuteronomic theology.

Reconsidering the tradition. Although Proverbs embraces the worldview generated through the Deuteronomistic tradition, not all of the Wisdom literature was so quick to follow. The view of reality espoused by the sage in Proverbs and the Deuteronomistic tradition in general is reconsidered in the books of Job and Ecclesiastes. Especially troublesome for the sages in these two books is the notion of cause and effect, sin and exile. Does all sin result in exile? Does every negative event necessarily presuppose sin? Is cause and effect the only way to create an authentic view of reality?

Job. The book of Job is quite complex, raising a number of theological issues throughout.[20] Arguably, the two chief themes in the book concern the motives of piety and the proper conduct of a suffering person. Yet both of these themes play out in dialog with the notion of retributive justice.

In Job 4—27, Job and his three friends engage in an extended discussion about the nature of reality and the certainty of cause and effect, or sin and exile. As opposed to Proverbs, where the sage embodies much of traditional Deuteronomistic theology, in Job it is the friends who have embraced this perspective, and it is Job, the quintessential sage, who is the challenger.

The speeches by the friends are replete with language reminiscent of the Deuteronomistic tradition. Leo Perdue notes that for the friends, "the dominant metaphor for God is that of divine ruler or judge whose edicts establish and carry out a retributive system of justice in which the wicked are punished and the righteous are rewarded."[21]

---

[20]Carol A. Newsome, "Job," in *The New Interpreter's Bible*, vol. 4, ed. L. Keck (Nashville: Abingdon, 1994), 334-38.

[21]Leo Perdue, *Wisdom and Creation: The Theology of the Wisdom Literature* (Nashville: Abingdon, 1994), 137.

Statements such as the one made by Eliphaz in Job 4:7-8 quickly alert the reader to Eliphaz's theological bias:

Think now, who that was innocent ever perished?
　Or where were the upright cut off?
As I have seen, those who plow iniquity
　and sow trouble reap the same.

And furthermore, Eliphaz presents suffering as divine punishment—that which is deserved as a result of disobedience:

How happy is the one whom God reproves;
　therefore do not despise the discipline of the Almighty. (Job 5:17)

For the friends of Job, the cosmos is mechanistic—it operates according to established norms, rooted in the perceived moral character of God.[22] If God is just, all sin must be punished and all righteousness must be rewarded. Moreover, no sinner would be rewarded and surely no righteous one would be punished—to do so would be contrary to the friends' perception of God's moral character. To this mechanistic notion of the cosmos, Job dares to offer a challenge. He defiantly announces:

I will not restrain my mouth;
I will speak in the anguish of my spirit;
I will complain in the bitterness of my soul. (Job 7:11)

Twice in Job 9 he protests, declaring his own innocence. Yet in his protestation of innocence, Job does more than seek an acquittal. Rather, he calls into question the notion of retributive justice and the mechanistic worldview that it creates. Job ultimately challenges the Deuteronomistic view, his friends, and even God, when he announces:

There are those who snatch the orphan child from the breast,
　and take as a pledge the infant of the poor;
They go about naked, without clothing;
　though hungry, they carry the sheaves;
between their terraces they press out oil;
　they tread the wine presses, but suffer thirst.
From the city the dying groan,
　and the throat of the wounded cries for help;
　yet God pays no attention to their prayer. (Job 24:9-12; italics added)

For Job, reality and theology do not match in a system governed only by retributive justice. To remedy this paradox of experience, Job continually challenges God to a

---

[22]Perdue notes that the entire system of retributive justice is grounded in the moral character of God (ibid., 138).

trial—to present his case before God. And through his sometimes caustic challenges, Job affirms not only his innocence but his integrity.

This challenge to the traditional view is vindicated in the divine speeches when Yahweh announces that Job has spoken rightly of him (Job 42:8). And in the same speech, God condemns the three friends (and their theological construction of reality) by announcing, "You have not spoken of me what is right" (Job 42:7). As Perdue has noted, "The false theology of retribution and the uncontested sovereignty of God are the twin features of the 'incorrect' views of the opponents of Job. The questioning of divine justice and the demand that God be attentive to the pleas of victims in ruling the universe are affirmed as the right theological posture."[23]

In the end, when God comes to Job in the whirlwind, he does not mention justice or injustice—God speaks only of order and chaos. God is not avoiding the attack by Job. Instead, God is extending the discussion. The God of Job is not one who "can be circumscribed by learned debate in the schools, or about whom calculations can be made, or with whom contractual arrangements can be drawn up."[24] God ultimately teaches Job that the belief in a universe built only on principles of rationality is in itself irrational and doomed to fail in the end.

Ecclesiastes. Similar to Job, Ecclesiastes (Qoheleth) offers a reading of reality slightly different from that presented in traditional wisdom theology. Gerhard von Rad has suggested that the theology in Qoheleth revolves around three themes: (1) a thorough, rational examination of life is unable to find any satisfactory meaning; everything is vanity; (2) God determines every event; and (3) humanity is unable to discern these decrees, these "works of God" in the world.[25] Von Rad's second tenet squares nicely with a theology of retribution. The first and third tenet, however, appear as a challenge to a rational world governed by a set of known principles.

The traditional sages contended that through observation and understanding one can predict the events to occur. Yet any hope of discerning a link between act and consequence is quickly dismissed by Qoheleth.[26] "I saw all the work of God, that no one can find out what is happening under the sun," Qoheleth states. "However much they may toil in seeking, they will not find it out; even though those who are wise claim to know, they cannot find it out" (Eccles 8:17). A similar view is adopted in Ecclesiastes 9:11-12, where Qoheleth suggests that "time and chance happen to them all. For no one can anticipate the time of disaster." Clearly, for Qoheleth experience had suggested just the opposite of what was suggested by the tra-

[23]Ibid., 182.
[24]Joseph Blenkinsopp, *Wisdom and Law in the Old Testament* (Oxford: Oxford University Press, 1995), 67.
[25]Gerhard von Rad, *Wisdom in Israel* (Nashville: Abingdon, 1972), 227-28.
[26]See Blenkinsopp, *Wisdom and Law in the Old Testament,* 75-76.

ditional sages. Although the earlier sages had suggested that reality (act and consequence) was knowable, Qoheleth suggests that such a reality is far from knowable—it is an enigma.

Summary. Both Job and Ecclesiastes refrain from drawing heavily on the story of Israel. There are virtually no statements employing the traditional historical motifs found elsewhere in the Bible. Yet the two books do interact with the biblical story. They offer a challenge to the notion of retributive justice presented in Proverbs and Deuteronomy. Job and Ecclesiastes suggest that reality is far too complicated to rely only on one perspective—hence they provide alternative readings of reality.

Sirach. The introduction of Sirach in the wisdom tradition produced a radical departure from the earlier literature. The universal thrust of the wisdom tradition as exhibited in Proverbs, Job and Qoheleth is tempered by the incorporation of the story of Israel into the theology of Sirach. As Martin Hengel has noted, "The universalistic attitude expressed in earlier Jewish wisdom tradition is necessarily qualified; wisdom and pious observance are identified, and the possibility of a profane wisdom disassociated from piety is excluded."[27] This shift in the wisdom tradition manifests itself in Sirach throughout but can be summarized in the following points: (1) the association of Torah and wisdom; (2) the use of retribution theology; and (3) the connection to the story of Israel.

The association of Torah and Wisdom. In Sirach, although the association between Torah and Wisdom appears throughout, a critical distinction should be noted. Whereas the word *torah* in the book of Proverbs (Prov 1:8) is usually translated as "instruction," the idea of *torah* in Sirach represents a more formalized notion of the law of Moses.[28] In Second Temple Judaism, the law of Moses was recognized as normative for the community of faith.[29] Thus, the plea of Sirach is not just to gain universal wisdom, but to gain wisdom grounded in the Law. The sage contends in 19:20:

> The whole of wisdom is fear of the Lord,
>   and in all wisdom there is the fulfillment of the law.

Yet lest the reader assume that Sirach has placed wisdom as a value higher than obedience to the Torah, he counters three verses later:

> Better are the God-fearing who lack understanding
>   than the highly intelligent who transgress the law. (19:24)

---

[27]Martin Hengel, *Judaism and Hellenism Studies in Their Encounter in Palestine During the Early Hellenistic Period* (Minneapolis: Fortress, 1974), 138.

[28]Ibid., 139. J. J. Collins notes, "When Sirach identifies wisdom and the law, however, he is in effect introducing the Torah of Moses into the wisdom school, and thereby attempting to combine two educational traditions" (*Jewish Wisdom in the Hellenistic Age*, 54).

[29]See Perdue, *Wisdom and Creation,* 250-51.

From the very beginning of the book, the sage is clear about the true source of wisdom. In Sirach 1:26, the sage writes,

> If you desire wisdom, keep the commandments,
>   and the Lord will lavish her upon you.

As indicated in chapter 3, wisdom is not universally shared, rather it belongs to God, and is given by God alone.

The poem honoring wisdom in chapter 24 emphatically announces that wisdom has in fact come only to one place, to the people of Yahweh. In autobiographical fashion, Wisdom announces:

> I took root in an honored people,
>   in the portion of the Lord, his heritage. (24:12)

This identification of the Law with wisdom suggests that the story of Israel has intersected with the wisdom tradition in a vitally important way. As will be demonstrated below, Jesus ben Sirach appears to have been steeped in the Law as expressed in the Deuteronomistic tradition. Thus what appears throughout the book is wisdom, but wisdom influenced by Law, and more particularly, Law as expressed in ideas associated with Deuteronomic theology.

The use of retribution theology. The concept of retribution theology is most clearly expressed in the Deuteronomic notions of blessing and cursing. The proverbs that appear throughout Sirach reflect a similar understanding of reality: obedience results in blessing, disobedience in cursing.[30] Such a view of reality appears in the following proverbs:

> Do good to the devout, and you will be repaid—
>   if not by them, certainly by the Most High. (12:2)

> Refrain from strife, and your sins will be fewer (28:8).

> The one who keeps the law preserves himself,
>   and the one who trusts in the Lord will not suffer loss. (32:24)

> Good is the opposite of evil,
>   and life the opposite of death;
>   so the sinner is the opposite of the godly. (33:14)

> All bribery and injustice will be blotted out,
>   but good faith will last forever. (40:12)

---

[30]See C. Marvin Pate, *The Reverse of the Curse,* Wissenschaftliche Untersuchungen zum Neuen Testament 114 (Tübingen, Germany: J.C.B. Mohr/Paul Siebeck, 2000), 28-30.

There are numerous other examples of proverbs that reflect retribution theology in the book of Sirach.[31]

One of the clearest examples of the influence of Deuteronomy on the book of Sirach appears in Sirach 15:15-20:

> If you choose, you can keep the commandments;
>> and to act faithfully is a matter of your own choice.
> He has placed before you fire and water;
>> stretch out your hand for whichever you chose.
> Before each person are life and death,
>> and whichever one chooses will be given.

The sentiments in Sirach 15 resemble the challenge Moses put before the nation in Deuteronomy 30, where Moses announces that he has put before them "life and prosperity, death and adversity." And then in Deuteronomy 30:19, he pleads, "Choose life so that you and your descendants may live." Similarly, the sage offers the people a choice—life or death, fire or water—and the choice must be made. But the sage is certain that one will receive what one chooses. This implies that disobedience will result in death, while obedience will yield life.[32]

The connection to the story of Israel. The particularist bent of Sirach becomes fully evident in his frequent use of, and allusion to, events and individuals within the story of Israel.[33] In addition to the mention of the Law, there are references to the covenants made between Israel and God (44:12; 45:5), as well as mention of Israel's election by Yahweh (45:4; 46:1). These references remind the reader of Sirach's movement from universal wisdom to a wisdom rooted in the story of Israel.

The reference to specific individuals from Israel's past not only roots the work of Sirach in the history of Israel but also demonstrates the radical shift proposed by the author. Chapters 44–50 offer a type of encomium, aptly entitled "Hymn in Honor of Our Ancestors." Yet the rehearsal of the lives of these great figures is intended to be didactic. These individuals and their lives are presented in such a way as to confirm the presuppositions related to Deuteronomic theology. The majority represent those who were obedient and as a result enjoyed the blessing of God. For example, Enoch is said to have pleased the Lord, and as a result "was taken up" (44:16). Phineas was praised for his zeal (45:23), and as a result established a covenant of friendship with God.

---

[31]For a listing of proverbs that correlate with Deuteronomic blessings and curses, see ibid., 30.

[32]The influence of Deuteronomy 30 on Sirach is further indicated by ben Sirach's use of the "law of life" in Sirach 17:11. In Sirach 45:5, Moses is said to have received "the law of life and knowledge" from God—thus suggesting that the law of life is synonymous with the Mosaic law. As Collins suggests, this notion of the life-giving capacity of the Law is expressed in Deuteronomy 30:11-20 (*Jewish Wisdom in the Hellenistic Age,* 59). See also Pate, *Reverse of the Curse,* 26.

[33]On the notion of Sirach's particularism, see Pate, *Reverse of the Curse,* 30-33.

Although most of the individuals mentioned do represent the notion of the Deuteronomic blessing, several that are mentioned reinforce the notion of the Deuteronomic
curse. All the kings except David, Hezekiah and Josiah are considered "great sinners,
for they abandoned the law of the Most High" (49:4). Dathan, Abiram and the com-
pany of Korah are mentioned as having angered the Lord, resulting in their destruction
by "the heat of his anger" (45:18-19).

Summary. Sirach represents a critical nexus in the history of Israel's thought: Wisdom merged with Law. The emphasis on gaining knowledge is tempered by a call to
Torah obedience. The ultimate test of wisdom comes in the ability of one to be obedient to the ways of Yahweh. Obedience will yield not only wisdom but life (15:17). Disobedience will yield a fate similar to that of Dathan, Abiram and the Korahites—it will
bring upon the apostates the Deuteronomic curses.

Conclusion

The Psalms and the Wisdom literature reflect a varied approach to the story of Israel
and its pedagogical value. The Psalms embrace the story of Israel and the theological
challenge that is sustained throughout. At various junctures the ideas associated with
Deuteronomic theology appear, reinforcing the necessity of obedience if the nation is
to enjoy the blessings of Yahweh.

Proverbs omits many of the direct references to the story of Israel while still embracing the central operating principle—retribution. The notion of retribution that appears throughout suggests the influence of the Deuteronomistic tradition. Yet the wisdom tradition was reticent to embrace fully such ideals. The books of Job and
Ecclesiastes mount a challenge to such a worldview, suggesting a more nuanced interpretation of reality.

Yet the book of Sirach suggests that Jewish theology came full circle. Law and wisdom merged to forge a powerful theological message. The story of Israel, rooted in
Deuteronomic theology, became the vehicle for understanding true wisdom. The wise,
then, are those who are committed to the Torah—and correspondingly, they are the
ones who enjoy the Deuteronomic blessings.

Supplemental Reading in New Dictionary of Biblical Theology

C. G. Bartholomew, "Wisdom Books," 120-22.

G. Goldsworthy, "Proverbs," 208-11.

G. W. Grugan, "Psalms," 203-8.

R. L. Schultz, "Ecclesiastes," 211-15.

E. J. Schnabel, "Wisdom," 843-48.

A. Viberg, "Job," 200-203.

Study Questions

1. What metaphors or images are used in the Psalms to convey the sin, exile and restoration of Israel?

2. How does the opening chapter of Proverbs contribute to the notion of retributive theology that seems to permeate the book?

3. Qoheleth is apparently responding negatively to the view of reality constructed in Proverbs. What kind of view of reality is he proposing? Give examples.

5

THE PROPHETS

Sin, Exile
and Restoration

The story of Israel (sin, exile, restoration) unfolds repeatedly across the pages of the literary prophets. Indeed, the Prophets probably present the entire message of sin, exile and restoration more powerfully and more clearly than any other portion of the canon.[1] Overlapping with the last days of the monarchies, the prophets proclaim boldly that the people of Israel and Judah have shattered the terms of the covenant in Deuteronomy and that without rapid and sincere repentance—which is not likely—judgment and exile is inevitable. This portion of the prophets' message repeats many of the implications we saw in the historical books. However, the prophets expand the message regarding the restoration, adding new material and nuances to the theme of hope and future restoration.

Thus far in our study we have seen two major story cycles. Genesis 3—11 is the cosmic, worldwide story of sin and scattering (exile from the presence of God). Genesis 12:3 presents the hope of restoration (blessings for the scattered nations in Genesis 10—11). The other story, which runs from Genesis 12 to 2 Kings 25, is about Israel. It parallels the first story and follows the same pattern of sin, exile and promised restoration. The remarkable theological contribution of the prophets is that they wed these two stories together. Sin will result in judgment on both Israel/Judah and on the nations. Likewise, the prophets proclaim, the true picture of future restoration is one that restores both Israel and the nations to God together. Thus, the prophets state, the specific theological story of Israel will merge with the cosmic universal theological story of Genesis 1—11 into a spectacular restoration that will bring Israel and the nations together in a true worship of God. This new people of God will be led by a glorious and righteous messianic Davidic king who will fulfill the Abrahamic promises

---

[1]Much of the material in this chapter is adapted from the chapter on Prophets in J. Scott Duvall and J. Daniel Hays, *Grasping God's Word: A Hands-On Approach to Reading, Interpreting, and Applying the Bible* (Grand Rapids, Mich.: Zondervan, 2001), 356-75.

both for Israel and for the nations. They will enter into a new covenant and will be empowered and enlightened by the very indwelling presence of Yahweh's Spirit.

The Nature of the Old Testament Prophetic Literature

The prophetic books in the Christian canon include the four *Major Prophets*—Isaiah, Jeremiah, Ezekiel and Daniel[2]—as well as the twelve *Minor Prophets*—Hosea, Joel, Amos, Obadiah, Jonah, Micah, Nahum, Habakkuk, Zephaniah, Haggai, Zechariah and Malachi.[3] The terms *major* and *minor* have nothing to do with importance. Rather, they refer to the length of the books. The first four prophetic books are much longer than the twelve that follow. For our analysis in this chapter, however, we will place the prophets in groups according to their themes and their historical context: (1) the standard preexilic prophets; (2) the nonstandard preexilic prophets; and (3) the postexilic prophets.

Many people assume that the word *prophecy* only refers to events of the end times and that the prophets of the Old Testament are primarily concerned with predicting the end times; however, only a small percentage of the prophetic literature deal with future events. In fact, Gordon Fee and Douglas Stuart write that "less than 2 percent of Old Testament prophecy is messianic. Less than 5 percent specifically describes the New Covenant age. Less than 1 percent concerns events yet to come."[4] Most of the material in the prophetic books addresses the disobedience of Israel/Judah (sin) and the consequential impending judgment (exile). The role of the prophet included the proclamation of this disobedience and the imminent judgment as much as it did the prediction of things to come in the far future.

The theological implications of the proclaimed future restoration are of immense value to our formulation of biblical theology, however, for it is the future restoration that ties New Testament fulfillment to the Old Testament, thus solidifying the continuity in biblical theology. As we strive to develop a biblical theology, the shorter sections in the Prophets that deal with the future restoration will tend to draw an unbalanced emphasis. As noted in chapter three, the historical books (Joshua through 2 Kings) present a clear message of sin and exile but are somewhat vague on the theme of restoration. The prophetic books, however, merge numerous themes and images

---

[2]In the Hebrew canon, the book of Daniel is not included with the Prophets, but rather is added to the Writings. Nowhere in the book is Daniel specifically called a prophet, and his message differs from that found in most of the rest of the prophetic literature. Yet the Christian canon, following the Septuagint, places Daniel with the Prophets, and he does "prophesy" about the future. Thus, we will include him in this chapter but will discuss his message separately.

[3]In the Hebrew canon these twelve books are often grouped together and called the "Book of the Twelve."

[4]Gordon D. Fee and Douglas Stuart, *How to Read the Bible for All Its Worth,* 2nd ed. (Grand Rapids, Mich.: Zondervan, 1993), 166.

into a grand vision of restoration. So although the prophets do spend more time dealing with sin and exile, their contribution to the theme of restoration is critically important to the overall biblical story. This importance has led some scholars to posit that
the prophets' major emphasis is actually on restoration.[5]

The prophets use *poetry* for much of their message, and it is the poetic aspect of
their message that is the most foreign to us. A central feature of Hebrew poetry is the
extensive use of figurative language. Their figures of speech are some of the main
weapons in the literary arsenal of the prophets. Indeed, figurative language is what
makes the prophetic books so colorful and fascinating. Amos does not simply say,
"God is angry." Rather, he proclaims, "The lion has roared." Isaiah does not analytically
discuss how terrible sin is and how wonderful forgiveness is; he announces, "Though
your sins are like scarlet, they shall be as white as snow." Jeremiah is disgusted with
the nation of Judah's unfaithful attitude toward God and wants to convey some of the
pain Yahweh feels because Judah has left Yahweh for idols, so throughout the book he
compares Judah to an unfaithful wife who has become a prostitute. "You have lived as
a prostitute with many lovers," Jeremiah proclaims, referring figuratively, but emotion-
ally, to Judah's idolatry.

The power of poetry lies in its ability to affect the emotions of the reader or listener. Without doubt, the prophetic literature is some of the most emotional literature in the Bible. The prophets express the deep love of Yahweh toward his people
and the intense pain he feels because of their rejection of him. On the other hand,
the prophets are also extremely explicit in their description of how horrible the coming judgment (invasion by the Assyrians or Babylonians) will be. They are scathing
in their critique and criticism of their society, especially of the king and the corrupt
priesthood. The emotional dimension is an essential part of the theology emanating
from these books.

Another important feature to note about the prophets is that their books are primarily
anthologies. By this we mean that the prophetic books are collections of shorter units,
usually oral messages that the prophets proclaimed publicly to the people of Israel or

---

[5]For example, Marvin A. Sweeney writes: "In general, prophetic books tend to focus on the punishment and restoration of Israel/Judah, with emphasis on the latter" (*Isaiah 1–39*, Forms of the Old Testament Literature XVI, ed. Rolf P. Knierim and Gene M. Tucker [Grand Rapids, Mich.: Eerdmans,
1996], 17). Ronald E. Clements notes that the New Testament writers certainly understood the prophetic message in this sense (Acts 3:18, 24; 1 Peter 1:10-12). He concludes, "Two things are immediately striking in this summary of Old Testament prophecy; the prophets are regarded as having proclaimed a unified message, and this message is regarded as one concerning the era of salvation which
the New Testament writers now regard as having dawned." Clements also notes that in the Dead Sea
Scrolls the prophetic message was viewed as dealing with both the destruction and the restoration of
Israel, but with an emphasis on the restoration. He suggests that "this was because this restoration
was still looked for in the future, while the destruction was believed to have already taken place" (*Old
Testament Prophecy: From Oracle to Canon* [Louisville, Ky.: Westminster John Knox, 1996], 191-93).

Judah. Other literary units such as narrative, oracles, and visions are mixed in. And sometimes the delivered oral message is the vision or oracle. However, it is important to note the *collective* nature of the books. Like a contemporary collection of a writer's poetry, the prophetic books are collections of relatively independent shorter units.

The units are not usually arranged chronologically, and often they do not appear to have thematic order either (see especially Jeremiah). Occasionally there is a broad overall theme (judgment, deliverance) that will unite a large section of text, but in general, tight thematic unity is absent. Because of this feature, most prophetic books are almost impossible to outline satisfactorily. By contrast, we can outline each of the New Testament letters, and our understanding of each book will be enhanced by the outline. Even the narratives of the Bible can be outlined beneficially. Outlines of the prophetic books, however, are normally useless. As anthologies they focus on a few major themes that they repeat over and over, so there is also quite a bit of repetition. This repetition, however, aids us in identifying the central themes. One of the most central of these that is repeated over and over in the Prophets is the story of Israel that we have been tracing—the theme of sin, exile and restoration.

The Standard Preexilic Prophets

Isaiah, Jeremiah, Ezekiel, Hosea, Joel, Amos, Micah, Habakkuk and Zephaniah are described as "preexilic" because their times are primarily located before the destruction of Jerusalem and the exile of 586 B.C.[6] They all stress the central theme of sin, exile and restoration. Because this group comprises a majority of the prophetic material, we have labeled this group as "standard" and the others as "nonstandard," although both groups reflect authoritative scripture. These standard prophetic books reflect a great degree of diversity in many details, but the central themes of sin, exile and restoration run throughout all of them. Moreover, they make up the majority of the prophetic material.

Historical/cultural and theological context of the standard preexilic prophets. As we have noted in earlier chapters, a continuous story runs from Genesis 12 to 2 Kings 25. In Genesis Yahweh calls Abraham and promises him descendants, a land and blessings—a promise that is repeated to Isaac and Jacob. However, by the end of Genesis, this special

---

[6]There were actually two Babylonian invasions of Judah. In 598 B.C. Judah surrendered to the Babylonian army and an elite group of Judahites were taken captive to Babylonia. In 587–586 B.C. another invasion occurred; this time the Babylonians completely destroyed Jerusalem, devastated the entire country, and took the majority of the people into captivity. Jeremiah's ministry occurred before, during and after these two invasions. Ezekiel's ministry occurred in between these two invasions. He was one of those taken in the first captivity, and his message is delivered while in Babylonia, so in one sense he can be called an "exilic" prophet. However, since he wrote prior to the terrible destruction of Jerusalem in 586 B.C. and the massive exile of the population, his message is similar in many regards to that of the other preexilic prophets.

family is in Egypt, away from the Promised Land. During the next four hundred years of life in Egypt, the Hebrews are forced into slavery by the Egyptians. In Exodus Yahweh comes and raises up Moses to miraculously deliver them from Egypt. God then enters into a covenant relationship with them, stating, "I will be your God; you will be my people; I will dwell in your midst." God presents them with the various laws of Exodus, Leviticus and Numbers, which define the terms by which they can live in the Promised Land with God in their midst and be blessed by him in the land. However, that first generation refuses to enter the land, and thus God allows them to die off in the wilderness. He takes the next generation back to the perimeter of the Promised Land and then recommits them to a renewed covenant relationship. As before, the terms of the covenant define how they are to live in the land with God in their midst. This relationship is defined specifically by the laws in Deuteronomy. The book of Deuteronomy clearly points out to the people that if they obey God and keep the Law, they will be immensely blessed. However, the book also stresses that if they disobey the Law and turn away from God, then they will be punished. Furthermore, if they do not repent of their sin, then they will eventually even lose the Promised Land.

The rest of the story up to the end of 2 Kings deals with the issue of whether or not the Israelites are going to keep the terms of this agreement. In Joshua the Israelites remain faithful to Yahweh, but in Judges they turn away from him and backslide into idolatry. Ruth introduces David, who dominates the story in 1-2 Samuel. David is faithful to God and brings the nation back to covenant obedience. However, even David is unable to stay completely faithful, as his sin with Bathsheba demonstrates. David's son Solomon is able to coast for awhile on his father's relationship with God, but soon Solomon turns to idols, setting the pattern for future kings and people alike. The books of 1 and 2 Kings tell the story of how the two nations of the Hebrews, Israel and Judah, continually fall away from Yahweh, turning instead to the idols of their neighbors. Ultimately, Yahweh punishes them, and they lose the right to live in the Promised Land. First, the northern kingdom, Israel, falls into idolatry and is destroyed by the Assyrians (722 B.C.). Later the southern kingdom, Judah, likewise turns away and is thus destroyed by the Babylonians (586 B.C.). The book of 2 Kings ends with the destruction of Jerusalem and the exile of the southern kingdom's inhabitants to Babylon.

The standard preexilic prophets preach primarily within the context of the latter part of this story. As Israel turns away from Yahweh, forgetting the covenant agreement they made with God in Deuteronomy, the prophets emerge as God's spokesmen to call the people back to covenant obedience and to proclaim the disastrous consequences if they refuse. So in regard to the historical setting, the prophets preach in one of two contexts: just prior to the Assyrian invasion, which destroyed the northern kingdom, or just prior to the Babylonian invasion, which destroyed the southern kingdom, Judah.

Theologically, the prophets proclaim their message from the context of the Mosaic covenant, primarily as defined in Deuteronomy.[7] The prophets tell the people to repent, to turn from idols and to return to the covenant that they agreed to keep in Deuteronomy. They warn the Israelites of the terrible punishments God promised them in Deuteronomy. The ultimate punishment, they announce with sorrow, is the loss of God's presence and the loss of the Promised Land (exile).

The basic preexilic prophetic message. As mentioned above, the prophets write in the theological context of Deuteronomy and in the historical context of an imminent invasion by either the Assyrians (against Israel) or the Babylonians (against Judah). But what is their message in this setting?

The prophets serve as Yahweh's prosecuting attorneys. They stand before Yahweh, accusing and warning the people of the consequences of covenant violation. While there are numerous nuances and subpoints to their proclamation, their overall message can be boiled down to three basic points: (1) You have *sinned* by breaking the covenant. Repent immediately! (2) No repentance? Then judgment and *exile*! (3) But yet there is hope beyond the judgment for a glorious future *restoration*.

In developing the first point, the prophets stress how serious the nation's covenant violation has become and the extent to which the people have actually broken the Deuteronomic (Mosaic) covenant. The prophets present a tremendous amount of evidence validating this charge. This evidence falls into three categories, all of which are explicitly listed in Deuteronomy. These reflect three major types of indictments against Israel: idolatry, social injustice, and religious ritualism.

Idolatry. This offense was perhaps the most flagrant violation of the covenant, and the prophets preach continuously against it. Israel, of course, was engaged in idolatry from their political beginning, with the golden calves in Bethel and Dan. But even Judah falls into serious idolatrous worship. Syncretization was in vogue with her neighbors; Judah likewise felt free to create a pantheon, worshiping Baal, Asherah and others along with Yahweh. They attempt to maintain the ritual of worshiping Yahweh in the temple while also sacrificing to the other regional gods and participating in their festivals.

This syncretistic idolatry climaxes in Ezekiel 8. In this chapter, the Spirit takes Ezekiel on a tour of the temple in Jerusalem. There he sees an idol at the entrance to the north gate, drawings and carvings of idols and unclean animals on the temple walls, women burning incense to the Babylonian vegetation god Tammuz, and the elders in the temple with their backs to the presence of Yahweh, facing the east and bowing to the sun. "This," Yahweh declares, "will drive me from my sanctuary." And indeed, in Ezekiel 10 the glory of Yahweh departs. In our opinion, the old Mosaic covenant as defined in Deuteronomy probably comes to an end with the departure of

---

[7]Ezekiel differs from the other prophets in that, in keeping with his priestly vocation and emphasis, he relies more on Leviticus than on Deuteronomy as the definition of the covenant.

Yahweh's presence in Ezekiel 10.

Idolatry was not merely a violation of the law. It struck at the heart of the relationship between Yahweh and his people. The central covenant formula in the Old Testament is the statement by Yahweh that "I will be your God; you will be my people; I will dwell in your midst." Idolatry was a rejection of this relationship. Several of the prophets stress the emotional hurt that God feels at this rejection. For God the issue is as much an emotional as a legal issue. To aptly illustrate this, several of the prophets use the faithful husband/unfaithful wife image. This is perhaps the central imagery that paints the seriousness of the idolatry charge. For example, the harlotry/unfaithful wife image runs throughout Jeremiah; indeed, it is one of the central images he uses. Ezekiel also uses this relational picture in Ezekiel 16. And poor Hosea lives out the heartbreaking drama in his own life.

The prophets not only proclaim that idolatry violates the relational and legal aspects of the covenant, but they also deliver scathing polemical diatribes against the idols, demonstrating how irrational and foolish it is to worship them. "Bring in your idols," Isaiah taunts, "to tell us what is going to happen. Tell us what the former things were . . . or declare to us the things to come . . . so that we might know that you are gods. Do something," the prophet challenges, "whether good or bad, so that we will be dismayed and filled with fear" (Is 41:22-24 NIV). Jeremiah too jeers at the idols and their impotence, mocking them with his imagery. "Their idols are like scarecrows in a cucumber field, and they cannot speak; they have to be carried, for they cannot walk" (Jer 10:5).

Social injustice. The second main indictment of the prophets against the people was social injustice. The covenant in Deuteronomy bound the people to more than just the worship of Yahweh. Relationship with God required proper relationship with people. Yahweh was concerned with justice for all, and he was especially concerned with how weaker individuals were treated. Deuteronomy demanded fair treatment of workers (Deut 24:14-15); justice in the court system (Deut 19:15-21); and special care for widows, orphans and foreigners (Deut 24:17-22).

As Israel and Judah turned from Yahweh, they also turned from Yahweh's demands for social justice. The prophets consistently condemn this and cite it as a central part of the covenant violation. They frequently cite the treatment of orphans and widows as examples of the social failure of the people. They also state that this lack of social justice invalidates the sacrifices. For example, in his opening salvo in Isaiah 1, Isaiah proclaims that, because of their social injustice, Yahweh will hide his eyes and not listen as they sacrifice. Likewise, Jeremiah proclaims, "They know no limits in deeds of wickedness; they do not judge with justice the cause of the orphan, to make it prosper, and they do not defend the rights of the needy. Shall I not punish them for these things? says the LORD" (Jer 5:28-29). In similar fashion Micah underscores that justice is more important to God than the ritual of sacrifice: "Will the LORD be pleased with thousands of rams, with ten thousands of rivers of oil? Shall I give my firstborn for my transgression, the fruit of my body for the sin of my soul? He has told you, O mortal, what is good; and what does the LORD require of you but to do justice, and to love kindness, and to walk humbly with your God?" (Mic 6:7-8).

Religious Ritualism. The Israelites were relying on ritual instead of relationship. They forgot that ritual was merely the means to the relationship, not the substitute for it. As Israel became more enamored with formalized ritual, they lost the concept of relationship with Yahweh. They trivialized the significance of his presence in their midst. They thought that only ritual was required of them. And they drew the illogical conclusion that proper ritual would cover over serious covenant violations like social injustice and idolatry. They rationalized their social injustice and their syncretism by focusing on the cultic ritual. This is hypocritical, the prophets declare, and not at all what God wants. Micah states this clearly in Micah 6:7-8, quoted above. Likewise, in Isaiah 1:11-12 Yahweh asks, "What to me is the multitude of your sacrifices? . . . Who asked this from your hand? Trample my courts no more; bringing offerings is futile."

Sacrifice was not the only cultic ritual that the prophets critiqued. The prophet Isaiah criticizes fasting as well: "You cannot fast as you do today and expect your voice to be heard on high." Isaiah quotes God: "Is not this the kind of fasting I have chosen: to loose the chains of injustice and untie the cords of the yoke, and to set the oppressed free and break every yoke? Is it not to share your food with the hungry and to provide the poor wanderer with shelter?" (Is 58:4-7 NIV).

Closely related to the prophetic proclamation of the broken covenant is the call to repentance. The prophets beg the people to repent of the sins listed in the indictments and to restore their relationship with Yahweh. Even after proclaiming that judgment is imminent, the prophets continue to plead for repentance. Jeremiah is the classic example, declaring the inevitability of the Babylonian conquest, but all the while saying that it can be averted if only the people will repent.

So the first central point of the prophets is concerned with sin, underscoring that Israel has broken, indeed shattered, the Mosaic covenant of Deuteronomy by their idolatry, social injustice and reliance on religious ritualism.

The second main point of the prophetic message is: *No repentance? Then judgment and exile!* The prophets plead with the people to repent and to turn back to covenant obedience. However, neither Israel nor Judah does repent, and the prophets acknowledge that obstinacy, proclaiming the severe consequences. Much of the material in the prophetic books delineates the terrible judgment that was about to fall on Israel or Judah. The major judgments predicted by the prophets are the horrific invasions— first, by the Assyrians, and later, by the Babylonians. The most serious aspect of this judgment is the loss of the Promised Land (exile) and the blessings associated with life in the land (such as the presence of Yahweh). Indeed, Yahweh is about to drive them out of the Promised Land as he had warned them he would in Deuteronomy.

The third and final central point of the prophetic message is: *there is hope beyond the judgment for a glorious, future restoration*. The messianic promises and future predictions of the prophets comprise a large portion of this point. As part of this portrayal, the prophets reveal how the major biblical covenants relate. Based on the conditional Mosaic covenant of Deuteronomy, the prophets proclaim judgment for sin committed. However, the prophets also reach back to the unconditional Abrahamic and Davidic covenants as the basis for their hope of a future restoration. The prophetic vision of the restoration merges the righteous king and shepherd image of the Davidic covenant with the promise of blessings on all the nations of the Abrahamic covenant.

Theologically, this interaction between the Mosaic covenant (resulting in judgment) and the Davidic/Abrahamic covenants (resulting in restoration) anticipates the New Testament discussion concerning law and grace. Thus, in the story of Israel, the Mosaic covenant (i.e., the Law) underscores the inability of God's people to live righteously by the Law. As a result of their willful disobedience and rebellion, judgment was inevitable. This is represented by the exile. However, the unconditional covenants (Davidic and Abrahamic) represent the undeserved grace of God toward his people and point clearly to the coming messianic age and to the restoration that Christ will bring.

The prophets, however, do not proclaim a restoration after the destructive exile that simply returns to the old Deuteronomic status quo. Their theological and relational picture of the future is different—and better. There will be a new exodus (Isaiah), a new covenant of forgiveness, written on hearts instead of stone (Jeremiah), and a new presence of Yahweh's indwelling Spirit within individuals (Ezekiel and Joel). Forgiveness and peace will characterize this new system. Relationship will replace ritual.

The wonderful prophecies of Christ are part of this portrayal of the glorious future restoration. The Coming One will be the humble Servant of Yahweh who will give himself up as a sacrifice for others (Isaiah). Unlike the terrible leaders that Israel had to endure in their history, the Coming One will be righteous, re-establishing the Davidic throne and epitomizing the ultimate good Shepherd of his people (Jeremiah, Ezekiel). Thus, the prophets merge the multihued prophecies of the coming Messiah with the promise of future restoration. Indeed, the prophets proclaim, the coming Servant/Messiah will be the means to the restoration, the channel through whom Yahweh will inaugurate a new covenant.

In Jeremiah 30—33, the prophet stresses how the new covenant time of restoration will reverse the negative elements of judgment and exile. With a touch of positive irony, Jeremiah picks up practically all of the negative images of judgment that he used in Jeremiah 1—29 and reverses them in Jeremiah 30—33 into positive images for the time of restoration: incurable sickness changes to healing; wailing and mourning change to singing and dancing; destruction of land and city changes to reconstruction; scattering changes to regathering; and the hardened prostitute changes to an innocent, young virgin.

The prophets also proclaim that Yahweh is the Lord of history and that all of the transpiring and coming events are under his sovereign control. Thus, the invasions by the Assyrians and the Babylonians are due to the fact that Israel and Judah have failed miserably to keep the Law and the Mosaic covenant. God has brought this calamity, using pagan nations as his tools to bring about this judgment. However, after the destruction, the prophets announce, in accordance with Yahweh's great plan, there will be a glorious restoration in which the Messiah will come and inaugurate a new and better covenant. The prophets stress that these events are not haphazard. Neither are they driven by chance or by the determination of world nations. Quite the contrary, they boldly proclaim, all of these events, the judgment and the restoration, are part of Yahweh's plan; and the unfolding of these events provide clear evidence that Yahweh is the Lord over history.

Another important facet of the prophetic message is the manner in which the prophets relate the fate of the nations to the story of Israel. As mentioned earlier in this chapter, the prophets will take the two parallel biblical stories—the story of the nations (Gen 3—11) and the story of Israel (Gen 12 through 2 Kings 25), both categorized by sin, exile and restoration—and merge these together into one story. Thus, as the prophets preach judgment on Israel and Judah due to sin and rebellion, they will also preach judgment on the Gentile nations that surround Israel and Judah (Egypt, Cush, Moab, Ammon, Philistia, Edom, Assyria, Babylonia) for their sin as well (idolatry, rebellion against Yahweh, oppression of Yahweh's people). However, the prophets in general, and Isaiah in particular, then include the foreign nations in their picture of future messianic restoration. They paint a picture of a multiethnic group mixed together with the remnant of restored Israelites streaming to Jerusalem to worship Yahweh. In the second half of the book of Isaiah, the prophet connects the coming Messianic Servant to this picture of restoration, stating that the task of being a "light to the nations" and of bringing salvation to all the peoples of the earth is assigned to the Messianic Servant of Yahweh (Is 42:6; 49:6).[8]

An example of how the prophets connect the vision of restoration to the cosmic story of Genesis 3—11 can be found in Isaiah 66:18-24. This closing unit of the book of Isaiah is a summary of major eschatological themes that run throughout the book. Isaiah 66:18 states, "And I, because of their actions and their imaginations, am about to come and gather all nations (*gôyīm*) and tongues (*lĕšōnôt*), and they will come and see my glory" (NIV). There is probably an intertextual allusion in this verse to Genesis 10—11. In Genesis 10 the division of the peoples of the world was structured by sum-

---

[8]For a detailed discussion of prophetic texts dealing with the multiethnic aspects of the inclusion of the nations, see J. Daniel Hays, *From Every People and Nation: A Biblical Theology of Race,* New Studies in Biblical Theology, ed. D. A. Carson (Leicester, U.K.: InterVarsity Press, 2003), 105-39.

mary statements employing the categories "families/clans, languages (*lĕšōnôt*), territories and nations (*gôyīm*)" (Gen 10:5, 20, 31).[9] Tightly connected to Genesis 10 is the tower of Babel story (Genesis 11), where God scatters the people across the face of the earth. The use of nation, language and gathering in Isaiah 66:18 suggests that the prophet is painting an eschatological picture in which the coming Messiah reverses the division described in Genesis 10—11 and brings about the promised blessing of Genesis 12:3 by gathering the peoples of the world to him in true worship.

A narrative section of Jeremiah foreshadows this future inclusion through the story of an individual foreigner (Jer 38—39). In this story, although all of Jerusalem rejected Jeremiah and his word from Yahweh and thus perished at the hand of the Babylonians, Ebedmelech the Cushite (KJV Ethiopian) believed the word of Yahweh through Jeremiah (Jer 39:17-18) and was saved (and saved Jeremiah as well). The African Ebedmelech will connect to the New Testament story of the Ethiopian eunuch (Acts 8), not only revealing the inclusion of Gentiles from the ends of the earth but also underscoring that this particular inclusion (both Ebedmelech's and the Ethiopian eunuch's) takes place precisely at the time when Israel rejects the message of God.

That the multiethnic aspect of the inclusion of the nations in the restoration is stressed is significant because this is one of the main areas of theology within the story of Israel that the Israelites distorted in Second Temple Judaism as the New Testament era drew near. Indeed, during this period the Jews misread and overstressed the ethnic implications of the postexilic prophets, as we will see below, and developed a rigid system of ethnocentrism that was contrary to the voice of the prophets. The New Testament writers, however, will bring this multiethnic aspect back into the story. Jesus will proclaim it; Paul will explain it and rebut Jewish objections; and John, in the Apocalypse, will highlight the multiethnic mix of God's people around the throne as he brings the story of Israel and the story of Genesis 1-11 together in the grand climax of history.

Most of the preexilic prophetic message can be summarized by the three points we have discussed. Isaiah, Jeremiah, Ezekiel, Hosea, Micah and Zephaniah contain all three. However, the diversity within the prophets cannot be denied. Some of them only stress certain aspects of this three-point summary. Amos, for example, focuses primarily only on broken covenant and judgment (points one and two). Not until Amos 8 does he mention any future hope and restoration. Joel, on the other hand, virtually skips point one, apparently assuming that the people understood that they had

---

[9]James M. Scott argues that Isaiah 66 alludes to Genesis 10 in several ways. He notes, for example, that Isaiah 66:19 references six groups of people from the Table of Nations in Genesis 10: Lud (following the LXX, i.e., Libya) from Shem; Put from Ham; and Tarshish, Tubal, Meshech, and Jarvan from Japheth (*Paul and the Nations: The Old Testament and Jewish Background of Paul's Mission to the Nations with Special Reference to the Destination of Galatians,* Wissenschaftliche Untersuchungen zum Neuen Testament 84 [Tübingen, Germany: J.C.B. Mohr/Paul Siebeck, 1995], 13-14).

broken the covenant. He goes straight into judgment (point two) and then into the future restoration (point three).

Likewise, the melding of the blessing for the nations into the restoration of Israel is not uniformly stressed in the Prophets. Isaiah is the premier champion of this theology, and this theme is presented clearly in both halves of the book of Isaiah. Likewise, although not all of the prophets make this connection, the image of the inclusion of the nations is also presented in Jeremiah, Amos, Micah and Zephaniah, making it an important theme for most of the standard preexilic prophets.

The Nonstandard Preexilic Prophets

Obadiah, Nahum and Jonah are preexilic prophets, but they do not present the standard three-point message discussed above. Obadiah and Nahum do not follow the typical pattern because they preach only against foreign nations (Edom and Nineveh, respectively) and not against Israel or Judah. Thus, they are similar in that they preach judgment on the nations, but they do not contain the standard message delivered by the other prophets to Israel and Judah (sin, exile and restoration). These two prophets, however, play minor roles in the overall prophetic message.

Jonah is much more important to the basic prophetic message, even though he also preaches against a foreign city (Nineveh) and not against Israel or Judah. Our understanding of Jonah is that while the actual preached message was to the Ninevites, the literary message was directed to Jonah's own people. Therefore, his story forms an indictment against Israel and Judah. In a literary sense, Jonah is a foil for the rest of the prophets. The repentance of the Ninevites stands in stark contrast to the obstinacy of the Israelites. What happens in Nineveh is what should have happened in Jerusalem but does not. For example, Jeremiah preaches in Jerusalem for decades, and the response is only hostility. No one repents, from the greatest to the least of them. Jonah, by contrast, preaches a short, reluctant sermon in Nineveh (of all places!), and the entire city repents, from the greatest to the least. The book of Jonah underscores how inexcusable is the response of Israel and Judah to the prophetic warning.

The Postexilic Prophets and Daniel

Typically Haggai, Zechariah and Malachi are identified as the "postexilic" prophets because they delivered their messages after the return of the exiles to Jerusalem following the Babylonian/Persian exile. This terminology is strongly entrenched in the vocabulary of biblical studies; however, it reflects a historical (and geographical) situation and not necessarily the theological one. While many Jews did return to Jerusalem and Palestine from Persia after the terrible destruction of Jerusalem and the exile, this return hardly signaled the inauguration of the glorious restoration that had been prophesied by the preexilic prophets. Indeed, the theological reality was that the Jews of the world, both those in Palestine and those throughout the dispersion, had not experienced restoration and were therefore still in exile.

During the Persian era some Jews were able to return to Jerusalem and begin to try to rebuild a Jewish community out of the ashes. Haggai, Zechariah and Malachi addressed this discouraged and disillusioned community. As this "remnant" returned and began rebuilding Jerusalem and the temple, the question in the minds of the community would have been whether or not this was the promised restoration. These three prophets answer this question with a sobering negative.

Both Haggai and Zechariah open with a reference to the reign of Darius the Persian, indicating from the very beginning that national and political restoration had certainly not been experienced. The dream of a Davidic king ruling over a strong and independent Israel appears to be dim indeed. Haggai focuses on the reconstruction of the temple. Practically and socially, the temple, regardless of its less-than-glorious construction, helped to galvanize the tattered Jewish remnant into a surviving religious community. At least it helped to keep the survivors focused on Yahweh and his promises. Yet in the book of Haggai, although Yahweh tells the people that he is with them, he does not come to fill the temple with his presence as he did so spectacularly in the time of Solomon. Instead, Yahweh points to the future, telling the Jewish inhabitants of the land that the coming of his glory to the temple still lies in the future (Hag 2:6-9). As mentioned earlier, the presence of Yahweh left the temple in Ezekiel 10 as the Babylonians drew near. Neither of the accounts of postexilic temple reconstruction in Ezra or in Haggai mentions the return of Yahweh's presence to the temple.[10] This absence is a clear indication that this return to the land did not result in a return to the Deuteronomic blessings of life in the land promised in Deuteronomy. The old covenant arrangement was gone.

The postexilic prophets look to the future restoration and strive to rebuild, but their message indicates that the return of a Jewish remnant to the land was not the true restoration that was promised. Paul House writes that these prophets saw their era as "preliminary and preparatory to complete renewal," which still lay in the future, and that they were "hopeful that the foundations that have been laid would be vital for the future."[11] Both Zechariah and Malachi contain "a mixture of hope and disillusionment,"[12] underscoring the fact that the restoration remained part of the future. This is clearest in the book of Zechariah, where the wonderful and glorious "not yet" is mixed

---

[10]As mentioned in chapter three, the presence of God does not return to the temple until Christ walks in through the gates in the New Testament era, thus underscoring the importance of that event.

[11]Paul R. House, *Old Testament Theology* (Downers Grove, Ill.: InterVarsity Press, 1998), 383.

[12]Donald E. Gowan, *Theology of the Prophetic Books: The Death and Resurrection of Israel* (Louisville, Ky.: Westminster John Knox, 1998), 170, 178.

in with the depressing and difficult "now," thus pointing to an ultimate final victory still future.[13] In this sense, from a theological perspective the people were still in exile. The restoration was still future, something to anticipate and hope for.

Also, although the Jews who returned to the land appear to have been cured of idolatry, the other two indictments of the preexilic prophets (social injustice and religious ritualism) resurface in the message of the postexilic prophets. Both Zechariah and Malachi mention the Deuteronomic issue of social justice for the widows, orphans and foreigners (Zech 7:8-10; Mal 3:5). All three books testify to the rising problem of religious ritualism, in which maintaining the rituals begins to take priority over relationship with Yahweh and the administering of social justice. This problem will continue to develop within Judaism even into the New Testament era, producing the legalistic Pharisaism with which the gospel collides.

The book of Zechariah also addresses the nations, merging them into the future picture in much the same fashion as the preexilic prophets did. Thus the prophet pronounces judgment on the nations due to their sin and rebellion, but he proclaims hope for their conversion as well. The nations are included in his vision of the ultimate restoration in which all of Yahweh's people come to worship him (Zech 2:11; 8:20-23; 14:16-19).[14]

The book of Daniel has been included in this section because both the context and the message of Daniel have points of similarity with that of the postexilic prophets. As mentioned above, in the Hebrew canon Daniel is placed in the collection known as the Writings, along with the wisdom books. In the Christian canon, the book is located with the Prophets because of its future-looking prophecies.[15] Goldingay suggests that these two different canonical locations reflect the two major theological "thrusts" of the book, one relating to wisdom and the other to eschatology.[16] Daniel 1—6 is narrative, relating how Daniel the Jew is able to remain faithful to God, living wisely even while under Babylonian and Persian rule. Daniel 7—12, however, focuses on visions of the future, including the restoration, and deals with all the nations of the world.

---

[13]I. M. Duguid, "Zechariah," in *New Dictionary of Biblical Theology*, ed. T. Desmond Alexander, Brian S. Rosner, D. A. Carson and Graeme Goldsworthy (Downers Grove, Ill.: InterVarsity Press, 2000), 258.

[14]Ibid., 259-60. See also Gowan, *Theology of the Prophetic Books*, 169.

[15]The literary genre of Daniel differs from that of the prophetic books, falling into the category of "apocalyptic" rather than "prophecy." Although scholars differ to some degree on what constitutes the genre of apocalyptic, House has summarized five basic components: (1) the use of highly symbolic language; (2) the periodization of future world history; (3) an emphasis on God's sovereignty; (4) the use of angels and visions to reveal the future; and (5) the ultimate victory of God and God's people over the forces of evil (*Old Testament Theology*, 498). For a comparison between Daniel and other Jewish apocalyptic literature, see John J. Collins, *Daniel: With an Introduction to Apocalyptic Literature*, The Forms of the Prophetic Literature 20, ed. Rolf P. Knierim and Gene M. Tucker (Grand Rapids, Mich: Eerdmans, 1984).

[16]John E. Goldingay, *Daniel*, Word Biblical Commentary (Dallas: Word, 1989), 333.

The book of Daniel makes a clear connection with the sin, exile and restoration story of Israel. The confessional prayer in Daniel 9 reflects a strong continuity with the Deuteronomistic story. Daniel confesses the sin of Israel, acknowledging that their punishment of exile and foreign domination was due to their covenant violation. His prayer is similar to Nehemiah's (Neh 1), and he prays for the restoration of the nation and of Jerusalem. Yet much of Daniel suggests that the ultimate restoration is still far off and that in the meantime the community of God will live under persecution.

Similar to the preexilic prophets, Daniel merges the story of Israel with the cosmic story of the nations begun in Genesis 1—11. The restoration of Israel is cast into the light of—indeed, perhaps subordinate to—God's ultimate plan for all of human history.[17] The restoration of Israel is swallowed up by the larger theme of the kingdom of God. The covenant name Yahweh practically disappears from the book of Daniel to be replaced with names carrying more of a universal significance for the nations: God in heaven, God of gods, and God Most High. In Daniel 7, perhaps the climax of the book, the messianic Son of Man comes into the presence of the Ancient of Days and is given power and authority, which evokes the worship of "all peoples, nations, and languages." This phrase is an allusion to Genesis 10—12 and shows that the fulfillment of the Abrahamic promise as a solution to the Genesis 3—11 problem will be carried out by the Son of Man in the eschatological future.

One of Daniel's major themes is that God is sovereign over all humankind and over all human kingdoms. Indeed, history moves forward toward the goal of establishing God's great kingdom. In the meantime, however, Daniel warns that for those still in the exile and awaiting the restoration, persecution can be expected. Like Daniel, God's people should face this persecution by remaining faithful and trusting in the power and current presence of God, ever looking forward to the future coming of the Son of Man and the establishment of God's kingdom, the true and ultimate restoration.

Conclusion

The story of Israel is integrally intertwined with the prophetic message. The prophets point to Deuteronomy and declare that Israel/Judah has sinned seriously, in violation of the Mosaic covenant. They call on Israel to repent and to return to the covenant, but alas, the people refuse. Therefore, the prophets announce, Yahweh will bring judgment on Israel through the invasions of the Assyrians and the Babylonians. This judgment will result in exile away from the land and away from the blessings described in Deuteronomy. However, the prophets then look beyond the exile and the judgment to

---

[17]Goldingay writes, "The prophets concern themselves with international history insofar as it affects the history of Israel; Daniel is closer to having a philosophy of international history in itself" (ibid., 331).

the glorious time of restoration when the Messiah will inaugurate a new covenant characterized by forgiveness and the indwelling presence of God's Spirit. Thus their message is one of sin, exile and restoration, paralleling and enhancing the story of Israel that runs from Genesis 12 to 2 Kings 25.

The prophets also announce judgment on the nations due to their sin. However, they proclaim that the time of restoration applies to the nations as well and that they will join Israel in worshiping Yahweh. Thus, the prophets merge the universal story in Genesis 3—11 with the story of Israel in Genesis 12—2 Kings 25.

Theologically, the postexilic prophets do not really live *after* the exile. Although a small and weak remnant returns to the land, the blessings and terms of Deuteronomy are not reinstituted. The story does not move back to the Mosaic covenant. Foreign nations still dominate the people of God, and the prospect of a Davidic king on the throne is maintained only by hope.

So the prophets look expectantly forward to the coming of Yahweh's Servant. Theologically, the postexilic people are still in exile, living back in the land but hardly enjoying the blessings associated with the promised restoration. The prophets challenge the people to look to the future and wait for Yahweh's Anointed One, the One who will come and bring the glorious time of restoration in fulfillment of the promises to Abraham and to David and in accordance with the prophetic word.

Supplementary Reading in New Dictionary of Biblical Theology

S. Dempster, "Prophetic Books," 122-26.

J. N. Oswalt, "Isaiah," 217-22.

J. R. Soza, "Jeremiah," 223-29.

I. M. Duguid, "Ezekiel," 229-32.

P. R. Williamson, "Covenant," 419-29.

I. M. Duguid, "Exile," 475-78.

B. S. Rosner, "Idolatry," 569-75.

W. S. Grudem, "Prophecy/Prophets," 701-10.

Study Questions

1. Trace the theme of sin-exile-restoration through Jeremiah 1—33.

2. Discuss the theme of sin–exile–restoration in regard to Israel and the nations in Isaiah 49.

3. Discuss the prophet's use of the marriage/unfaithful spouse/adultery theme.

4. Explain how the new covenant relates to the Mosaic covenant.

5. Explain how the prophets use the Abrahamic and Davidic covenants in their message.

6. What are the major differences between the message of the preexilic prophets and the postexilic prophets?

6

SECOND TEMPLE JUDAISM

Unity and Diversity
in the Deuteronomistic Tradition

The theme of the story of Israel—sin–exile–restoration, or the Deuteronomistic tradition—continues in the literature of Second Temple Judaism. These Jewish intertestamental materials, often labeled the Apocrypha[1] ("hidden" writings) and Pseudepigrapha[2] ("false" writings), were composed between ca. 200 B.C. and A.D. 100, though some books purport to have been written at the time of the fall of Jerusalem to the Babylonians (587 B.C.) or shortly thereafter at the rebuilding of the temple (519 B.C.).[3] Others deal with the persecution of Israel at the hands of Antiochus Epiphanes IV (171–167 B.C.).[4] Still others extend from the Hasmonean period[5] to Rome's takeover of Israel.[6] Finally, other Second Temple Jewish writings fall in be-

---

[1]The Apocrypha consists of some fifteen additional books in the Catholic Bible: 1 and 2 Esdras, Tobit, Judith, Additions to Esther, the Wisdom of Solomon, Ecclesiasticus, Sirach, Baruch, the Epistle of Jeremiah, the Prayer of Azariah and the Song of the Three Young Men, Susanna, Bel and the Dragon (these last three are supplements to Daniel), the Prayer of Manasseh and 1-4 Maccabees. Hermeneutically, the Apocrypha marks an important transition between the Old and New Testaments. Our usage of the Apocrypha is based on *The Apocrypha of the Old Testament, Revised Standard Version,* ed. Bruce Metzger (New York: Oxford University Press, 1977).

[2]The Pseudepigrapha is composed of approximately fifty Jewish intertestamental books (e.g., *1-3 Enoch, Jubilees, The Psalms of Solomon, 2 Baruch, Testaments of the Twelve Patriarchs, The Letter of Aristeas*) and is usually classified as either Palestinian (written in Aramaic in Israel) or Alexandrian (written in Greek in Alexandria, Egypt and beyond).

[3]For example, the Prayer of Azariah, Additions to Esther, 4 Ezra, *2 Baruch.*

[4]1-4 Maccabees are among those included in this category.

[5]Hasmonean is the family name of the Jewish freedom fighters (Mattathias, Judas, Jonathan, Simon) who regained control of Israel from Antiochus Epiphanes IV and his successors.

[6]Most notably, the Dead Sea Scrolls. For an overview of those materials and how they intersect with the Old and New Testament, see C. Marvin Pate, *Communities of the Last Days: The New Testament, the Dead Sea Scrolls, and the Story of Israel* (Downers Grove, Ill.: InterVarsity Press, 2000), and the bibliography cited there.

tween the above time frames.[7] But regardless of their precise date and origin, the evidence in this chapter will confirm N. T. Wright's claim that the fundamental question of Jewish intertestamental[8] literature was: How is it that Israel could be "restored" to her land but still remain in exile?[9]

Such a recurring theme in Second Temple Judaism is not uniform, however. There are, we suggest, at least four varieties of the leitmotif of the story of Israel:[10]

1. Theocratic: 1 Maccabees, Sirach, Baruch, *Psalms of Solomon*

2. Apocalyptic: *Testament of Moses, 4 Ezra* and *2 Baruch*

3. Apologetic: The Wisdom of Solomon, *The Third Sibylline Oracle, The Letter of Aristeas, The Testaments of the Twelve Patriarchs,* 4 Maccabees and Philo

4. Sectarian Apocalyptic: *1 Enoch, Jubilees* and the Dead Sea Scrolls

Because of the volume of this literature, we can only provide a survey of some of these writings, but one that will nevertheless establish our contention that the Deuteronomistic tradition runs deeply in early Judaism. We will offer a description of one representative book in each of the four categories and then provide charts to summarize a few of the other pertinent works. It will be seen that two common ideas characterize all four of the preceding constructs: *nomism* (the Law must be kept in order to remain in the covenant) and *particularism* (Jews, the elect people of God, are destined to rule the Gentiles).

Jewish Theocratic Writings

By "theocratic," we refer to those Second Temple Jewish works that, given the present status of Israel (sin and exile, even though she is regathered to her land), champion the conviction that only in returning to the entire Mosaic code (613 laws!) could Israel

---

[7]For example, Tobit, Sirach, Philo, Josephus (whose works *The Jewish War* and *The Antiquities of the Jews* describe the Jewish revolt against Rome from A.D. 66 to 73 but date to the 80s–90s).

[8]That is, 587 B.C. to A.D. 70, between the fall of the first and second temples in Jerusalem.

[9]This view has its detractors, for example A. T. Kraabel, "Unity and Diversity among Diaspora Synagogues," in *The Synagogue in Late Antiquity,* ed. Lee I. Levine (Philadelphia: American Schools of Oriental Research, 1987), 49-60, and Maurice Casey, "Where Wright is Wrong: A Critical Review of N. T. Wright's *Jesus and the Victory of God," Journal for the Study of the New Testament* 69 (1998): 77-94, 95-103. N. T. Wright responds in "Theology, History, and Jesus: A Response to Maurice Casey and Clive Marsh," *Journal for the Study of the New Testament* 69 (1998): 105-12. The evidence seems perspicuously in favor of the view that Israel perceived itself as still in exile after returning to her land in 539 B.C. For excellent support of this perspective, see James M. Scott, ed., *Exile: Old Testament, Jewish, and Christian Conceptions* (Leiden/New York: E. J. Brill, 1997). Our own argumentation in this chapter provides further documentation for Wright's thesis.

[10]For a more detailed investigation of these four constructs, see C. Marvin Pate, *The Reverse of the Curse: Paul, Wisdom, and the Law,* Wissenschaftliche Untersuchungen zum Neuen Testament 2/114 (Tübingen, Germany: J.C.B. Mohr/Paul Siebeck, 2000), part 1. Models are constructs that provide a grid through which to interpret a large and complex amount of data. As such, they are deductive and a bit artificial. Nevertheless, without these devices the task of interpreting multitudinous facts would be overwhelming.

hope to be delivered from her enemies and have God reenthroned as her king. The following materials can be classified under such a heading: 1 Maccabees, Sirach, Baruch and *Psalms of Solomon.*

1 Maccabees. The first of several books extolling the heroic efforts of the Maccabean family to restore Israel's land and the Law, 1 Maccabees was written after the death of John Hyrcanus, the first king and high priest of Israel[11] (104 B.C.; see 1 Macc 16:23-24, where it mentions the chronicles of John's reign), but before the Roman occupation of Israel when Pompey, the Roman general, entered and took over Jerusalem (63 B.C.; see 1 Macc 8; 12:1-4; 14:24, 40 and the positive references there to Rome).[12]

The author readily acknowledges Israel's sin in turning from the law of Moses in the face of Antiochus Epiphanes' attempt to force Hellenization on Palestinian Jews (1:11, 41-43, 52). Verse 52 summarizes his view of Israel's sin: "Many of the people [Jews] . . . forsook the law . . . and . . . did evil in the land." Consequently, God gave his people over to wrath (1:64), which, in light of 2:7-14, should be equated with judgment. Accordingly, Mattathias, father of the Maccabees, laments:

> "Alas! Why was I born to see this, the ruin of my people, the ruin of the holy city, and to dwell there when it was given over to the enemy, the sanctuary given over to aliens? Her temple has become like a man without honor; her glorious vessels have been carried into captivity. Her babes have been killed in her streets, her youths by the sword of the foe. What nation has not inherited her palaces and has not seized her spoils? All her adornment has been taken away; no longer free, she has become a slave. And behold, our holy place, our beauty, and our glory have been laid waste; the Gentiles have profaned it. Why should we live any longer?" And Mattathias and his sons rent their clothes, put on sackcloth, and mourned greatly.

In other words, Israel, though in her land, was still in exile.

But the tide changed for the Jews with the Maccabean revolt. Zealous for the Law (2:27, 50, 64-68; 3:21), Mattathias staged a rebellion against Antiochus's Hellenizing policy. His righteousness and that of his sons (Judas, Jonathan, Simon) turned away divine wrath by calling the people back to the Torah (3:8); thus, "they rescued the law out of the hands of the Gentiles and kings, and they never let the sinner gain the upper hand" (1 Macc 2:48; cf. 2:42-47). Subsequently, Judas rededicated the temple in 164 B.C. (4:42-51); and despite Judas's death in battle and Jonathan's death, by the time of the reign of their brother Simon, there was peace and rest in the land (14:4-18)—at least for awhile.

It is obvious that 1 Maccabees should be labeled "theocratic," for the marks of a true

---

[11]Elsewhere, Pate has defended the majority view that the authors of the Dead Sea Scrolls (probably the Essenes) separated themselves from the Hasmonean dynasty because of its combination of the roles of kingship and high priest into one; see Pate, *Communities of the Last Days,* chap. 2.

[12]George W. E. Nickelsburg, *Jewish Literature Between the Bible and the Mishnah* (Philadelphia: Fortress, 1981), 117.

Jew are championed by that author: circumcision (1:15; 2:45-46); Sabbath keeping (1:39; 2:38); and observance of the dietary laws (1:47). Little wonder it was the practice of these regulations that Antiochus forbade but that were reinstated under the Maccabean regime.

Clear in 1 Maccabees is the paramount importance of keeping the Mosaic code in order to experience renewal of the divine covenant (nomism). Furthermore, the anti-Gentile mentality (particularism) is readily identifiable (see 1 Macc 2:7, 48; cf. Pr Azar 20-21; 2 Macc 4:1—5:10; 3 Macc 6:10; 1 Esdr 8:68—9:55; Jdt 8—10).

Sirach, Psalms of Solomon, Baruch. Table 6.1 effectively summarizes the three earlier-mentioned works in the theocratic category.

Table 6.1

	Sirach*	*Psalms of Solomon*	Baruch
Israel's Sin	47:23-24; 49	1:5-6, 7-8; 2:3, 13b-15; 8:8-14, 29; 9:16; 17:6-8	1:17-19, 21
Israel's Exile	47:23-24; 49:5-6	1:1-2a; 2:1-2, 4-13, 16-23; 8:1-7, 15-24; 9:1-2a; 17:9-20	1:20; 2:1-4, 7-9, 20-21, 24-26; 3:4, 8
Israel's Restoration	36:1-17; cf. 15:15-20	2:24-30; 8:25-34; 9:6-10; 17	2:27-35

*See Pate, *Reverse of the Curse,* chap. 1, for a discussion of the Deuteronomistic influence on Sirach, *Psalms of Solomon* and Baruch, with attention given to wisdom, law and Israel's theocracy, and the nomistic and particularistic tendencies of these three works.

Jewish Apocalyptic Writings

The word *apocalypticism* has its etymological root in the Greek word *apocalypse,* which means "revelation" or "uncovering," with reference to the future and the heavenly world. Thus apocalypticism, like eschatology, often has to do with events at the end of time. During the period of Second Temple Judaism many Jews firmly believed that the age to come, or kingdom of God, was poised to descend to earth from heaven. Judaism expected certain events to precede the coming of God's rule on earth, especially the great tribulation (a time of unparalleled suffering that God's faithful were expected to endure at the hands of their enemies immediately before the arrival of the Messiah and the kingdom). It was thought that Israel's suffering, like a woman's birth pangs, would give birth to the Messiah (see Dan 12:1-3; *1 En* 80:4-5; 91:7; *Jub* 23:14-23; 4 Ezra 7:3) but not before the occurrence of religious apostasy, a large-scale turning away from God in the face of persecution (see, e.g., *1 En* 91:7; *Jub* 23:14-23; *4 Ezra* 5:1-2). The Messiah, or God's anointed one, would then come to earth to establish the kingdom of God, or the age to come.[13] At that time the resurrection of the righteous dead (Dan 12:2-3; *1 En* 51:1-2; *4 Ezra* 7:32; *2 Bar* 21:23); the judgment of the wicked (Dan 2:44; 12:2; *4 Ezra* 7:11; *2 Bar* 85:12); and cosmic renewal, or a new creation (Is 65:17-25; *1 En* 45:4; *Jub* 1:23; *4 Ezra* 7:75; *2 Bar* 32:6), were expected to occur. The controlling factor behind all these events was the belief that this age would give way to the age to come.

We will first analyze one apocalyptic work, *The Testament of Moses*, and then survey two others—*4 Ezra* and *2 Baruch*. The common theme of these writings is that the story of Israel is given an eschatological twist; that is, Jews are exhorted to obey the Mosaic law in this age of sorrow (Deuteronomic curses), which will give way to the bliss of the age to come (Deuteronomic blessings).

The Testament of Moses. The first draft of *Testament of Moses* was written during the persecution of Israel by Antiochus Epiphanes but before the rise of the Maccabean resistance.[14] Later, chapters 6 and 7 were added about A.D. 30 to update the events since the death of Herod the Great.[15] As Odil H. Steck has shown, *Testament of Moses* is indebted to the Deuteronomistic tradition. Steck identifies the following components of the story of Israel in *Testament of Moses:*

Chapter 2—Preexilic Israel's sin
Chapter 3:1-6—Nebuchadnezzar's defeat of Judah
Chapter 3:8—4:4—Exilic Israel's repentance and return to the Torah
Chapter 4:4-9—God's mercy and Israel's restoration under Cyrus the Persian[16]

But alas, by 171 B.C. Israel had once again plunged into idolatry, this time in the form of jettisoning Jewish convictions in favor of a Hellenistic lifestyle. Thus, according to Steck, the preceding cycle repeats itself:

Chapter 5—Israel's capitulation to Hellenism
Chapter 8—God's judgment on Israel in the form of the persecution of Antiochus Epiphanes
Chapter 9—The martyrdoms of Taxo and his sons because of their obedience to the Torah

---

[13]While many Jewish works anticipate the arrival of the Messiah—e.g. *T. Jud* 17:5-6; *Pss Sol* 17:23-51; *T. Levi* 18:2-7; 1QSa 9:11; CD 14:19—not all do; see *Jub* 31:18.

[14]See Nickelsburg, *Jewish Literature*, 80; cf. J. Priest, "Testament of Moses," in *The Old Testament Pseudepigrapha*, ed. James H. Charlesworth (Garden City, N.Y.: Doubleday, 1983), 1:919-26, esp. 920.

[15]George W. E. Nickelsburg, *Jewish Literature Between the Bible and the Mishnah: A Historical and Literary Introduction* (Philadelphia: Fortress, 1981), 213; cf. J. Priest, "Testament of Moses," 920-21.

[16]Odil H. Steck, *Israel und das gewaltsame Geschick der Propheten: Untersuchungen zur Überlieferung des deuteronomistischen Geschichtsbildes im Alten Testament, Spätjudentum und Urchristentum,* Wissenschaftliche Monographien zum Alten und Neun Testament 23 (Neukirchen-Vluyn: Neukirchener, 1967), 172.

and the turning of Israel back to the Law[17]

Chapter 10—An apocalyptic prophecy of God's future and final restoration of Israel[18]

George W. E. Nickelsburg is even more specific in his reading of the above two cycles in Testament of Moses, rooting them in the book of Deuteronomy itself, especially in Moses' farewell speech (see table 6.2). The story of Israel, then, dominates the narrative landscape of Testament of Moses.

Table 6.2

	Testament of Moses*		Deuteronomy	
1. Sin	2	5:1—6:1	28:15	32:15-18
2. Punishment	3:1-4	8	28:16-68	32:19-27
3. Turning Point	3:5—4:4	9	30:2	32:28-34
4. Salvation	4:5-9	10	30:3-10	32:35-43

*Nickelsburg, Jewish Literature, 81. Why Nickelsburg does not refer to Steck's work here and elsewhere is puzzling.

It seems that the view of the Law espoused by Testament of Moses is that of the theocratic perspective. Thus the authors (most probably Hasidic Jews[19]) lament Israel's defilement of the Torah, especially the sacrificial system (5:4-6) and circumcision (8:3[20]). Coupled with these concerns is the close affinity between Testament of Moses and the Maccabean literature (cf. the deaths of Taxo and his sons with the Jewish martyrs) and Daniel,[21] whose theocratic readings of the Torah appear to have influenced Testament of Moses.

But like 4 Ezra and 2 Baruch (see below), Testament of Moses places the Law in an apocalyptic framework. Thus Taxo's death (9:1-7) precipitates the messianic woes of the last days, after which God's kingdom will come and finally rescue the Jews (10:1-

---

[17]Taxo's martyrdom is in the same tradition of the martyrs of 1, 2 and 4 Maccabees.

[18]Steck, Israel und das gewaltsame Geschick der Propheten, 172; though Steck does not use the label "apocalyptic" for this chapter as we do. But the narrative is clearly cast as an end-time scenario.

[19]Priest's discussion of this possibility is helpful, "Testament of Moses," 921-22.

[20]This text reads, "And their wives will be given to the gods of the nations and their young sons will be cut by physicians to bring their foreskin." The first half of this verse refers to the coerced participation of Jews in pagan rites; cf. 2 Macc 6:7-9 (Priest, "Testament of Moses," 931). Perhaps the second half of the verse alludes to Hellenistically inclined Jews removing the marks of circumcision by surgery so as not to be offensive to Gentiles when they competed in the gymnasium (in the nude); cf. 1 Macc 1:14-15. Or perhaps it recalls Jewish involvement in pagan rituals that ridiculed circumcision. Either way, circumcision is being devalued.

[21]The intercessor for Israel in 4:1-4 may well be Daniel; see Priest, "Testament of Moses," 929.

10). Nicklesburg connects this end-time scenario with Deuteronomy 33:

> The author draws on the language of Deuteronomy 33 and describes God's final epiphany
> in terms of his ancient appearance on Sinai. God's victory will be complete. His reign will
> be evident throughout all his creation (10:1). Satan, the power of evil and the opponent
> of God, will be annihilated (cf. *Jub.* 23:29). The Gentiles—the persecutors of his people—
> will be punished, and their idols will be obliterated. And then the incredible—Israel will
> be exalted to the stars (10:9). The boundary between the mortal and the immortal will be
> transcended. Heaven will become the dwelling place of God's people while earth will be
> converted into the place of punishment for their enemies.[22]

In other words, the authors of *Testament of Moses* present the grim reality that Israel
will suffer for the Torah in this age but that, when the age to come arrives, she will be
eternally rewarded for her obedience to God, at which time Gentiles will be destroyed.
Such an attitude is obviously driven by nomistic and particularistic assumptions.

4 Ezra and 2 Baruch. We conclude this section by surveying in chart form the story
of Israel as it occurs in 4 Ezra and 2 Baruch (table 6.3).[23]

Table 6.3

	4 Ezra	2 Baruch
Sin	3:20-26; 7:129-30; 14:30-31	1:2-4a; 10:1—11:7; 13:9; 18:1-2; 19:3-4; 41:3; 44:3-4; 48:31-47; 77:2-3; 79:2-3; 84:2-6; 85:2-3
Exile (this age of covenantal curses)	3:3; 2:7-36; 7:129-130; 14:30-31	1:4b-5a; 4:1; 5:1-4; 6:1-8a; 7:1—8:5; 13:10a; 24:1-2; 29:1—30:5; 32:17; 44:5-6; 52:1—67:9; 77:4-5, 7-10; 78:2-6; 80; 85:3
Restoration (the age to come of covenantal blessings)	6:25-28; 7:14, 17-25, 36-37, 75-101; 8:1, 46-62; 9:1-8; 10:38-49; 11:13; 14:33-36	1:5b; 4:2-6; 6:8b-9; 12:1-4; 13:10b—158; 35:1—40:4; 41:1-8; 44:7—46:7; 48:48—51:16; 68:1±74:4; 77:6-8; 78:6-7; 82:1—84:2, 6-11; 85:4-15

Jewish Apologetic Works

The corpus of Jewish literature that has survived the Diaspora may be viewed as an
attempt to alleviate, or at least ameliorate, the dissonance a Jew experienced in be-

---

[22]Nicklesburg, *Jewish Literature,* 82.
[23]For detailed documentation of these writings' portrayal of the story of Israel as apocalyptic in orientation as well as their nomistic and particularistic mindset, see Pate, *Reverse of the Curse,* chap. 3.

ing caught between Judaism and Hellenism. Traditionally, these materials have been labeled "apologetic," since they were viewed as defending Judaism in Hellenistic categories and before Gentile audiences; or as "missionary," assuming they accompanied Jewish proselytizing efforts.[24] Victor Tcherikover, however, challenged these presuppositions, arguing instead that the intended audiences in Diaspora literature were Jewish.[25] Yet recent handling of this debate focuses, not on either Jew or Gentile, but on both/and, stemming from the growing realization that Diaspora literature emerged from the synagogue, where Jew and Gentile God-fearers worshiped together.[26]

The rather typical interpretation of these Diaspora writings has been to view them as reducing the Torah to its moral summation—love of God and neighbor—ideals compatible with the best of Hellenistic virtue. The point of such a "common ethic," to use John J. Collins's term,[27] was to commend Judaism to Hellenism. To accomplish this, the more offensive of the Jewish laws of self-identity—circumcision, dietary regulations, Sabbath worship—were downplayed.

Yet while Gentiles were expected to follow the moral summary of the Law, Jews were still required to keep the entirety of the Mosaic code.[28] It was the breaking of that standard that constituted Israel's sin and brought about her continuing exile; but Israel's return to that Law would ensure her restoration to the land and the covenantal blessings. Because we have detailed this theme in Jewish apologetic writings elsewhere,[29] we will simply summarize these works in table 6.4.

Philo. Perhaps the most celebrated example of a Diaspora Jew was Philo of Alexandria, Egypt. Philo (ca. 40 B.C.) is well known for his attempt to integrate the Old Testament with Greek philosophy, especially of the Platonic variety. While Philo related the Torah apologetically to Gentiles, that is, he offered a summary of the Mosaic law (virtue) as the standard by which non-Jews should live,[30] he nevertheless expected

[24]Good discussions of the nature of this genre can be found in M. Friedländer, *Geschichte der jüdischen Apologetik* (Zürich: Schmidt, 1903); P. Dalbert, *Die Theologie der hellenistisch-jüdischen Missionsliteratur unter Ausschluss von Philo und Josephus* (Hamburg: Reich, 1954); D. Georgi, *Die Gegner des Paulus im 2 Korintherbrief*, Wissenschaftliche Monographien zum Alten und Neuen Testament 11 (Neukirchen-Vluyn: Neukirchener Verlag, 1964), 51-53.
[25]Victor Tcherikover, "Jewish Apologetic Literature Reconsidered," *EOS commentarii societatis philologae polonorum* 48 (1956): 169-93.
[26]The reader is referred to Pate, *Reverse of the Curse*, chaps. 7–9.
[27]John J. Collins, *Between Athens and Jerusalem: Jewish Identity in the Hellenistic Diaspora* (New York: Crossroad, 1986), 137-74.
[28]See Pate's documentation of this point in *Reverse of the Curse*, chap. 2.
[29]See ibid. Despite a measure of openness to Gentiles and a "looser" handling of the Torah, nomism and particularism still prevail in Jewish apologetic literature.
[30]See for example, *Virtues and Migration of Abraham*. Everett Ferguson's survey of Philo's writings is helpful here: *Backgrounds of Early Christianity* (Grand Rapids, Mich.: Eerdmans, 1987), 381-83.

Jews to obey the complete Torah wholeheartedly (*Praem* 28 § 162-63). Indeed, it was for lack of commitment to the law of Moses that Israel was judged by God and sent into exile. Thus Philo declares:

> For even though they dwell in the uttermost parts of the earth, in slavery to those who led them away captive, one signal, as it were, one day will bring liberty to all. This conversion in a body to virtue will strike awe into their masters, who will set them free, ashamed to rule over men better than themselves. When they have gained this unexpected liberty, those who but now were scattered in Greece and the outside world over islands and continents will arise and post from every side with one impulse to the one appointed place,

Table 6.4

	Sin	Exile	Restoration
A. Wisdom of Solomon	1:2-5; 12:4-27	1:2-5; 12:4-27*	Cf. 4:6-18 with 12:21; 18:22; see also 8:14-17**
B. 4 Maccabees	4:15-20	4:21-26	5:1—18:24
C. *Third Sibylline Oracle*	vv. 265-81	vv. 265-81, 635-50, 657-702	vv. 574-600, 702-95
D. *Aristeas*	v. 131	vv. 4-5, 11-27	vv. 11-27, 52-120
E. *Testaments of the Twelve Patriarchs***	T. Sim 5:4a; T. Levi 10:13a, 14:1a; T. Jud 18:1-6; T. Iss 6:1-3; T. Zeb 9:5; T. Naph 4:1; T. Benj 9:1-2a	T. Sim 5:4b; T. Levi 10:3b-5, 14:1b—15:5, 17:9-10a; T. Iss 6:4; T. Zeb 9:6; T. Naph 4:2-3a; T. Benj 9:2b	T. Sim 6:1-4; T. Levi 17:10b, 18:1-14; T. Jud 22:2-3, 23:5b, 24:1; T. Iss 5:1-4, 6:4; T. Zeb 9:7-9; T. Naph 4:3b-5; T. Benj 9:2c-3

*Wisdom of Solomon seems to moralize the concepts of sin and exile and can therefore apply them to Israel (Wis 1:2-5) and just as well to the Canaanites (12:4-27); see Pate, *Reverse of The Curse*, 45-52, for further discussion.

**In Wisdom of Solomon the Deuteronomistic blessings are upon both the nation as a whole and the individual, in good proverbial fashion; see again Pate, *Reverse of The Curse*, 48-49.

***Collin's comments are helpful here: "The *Testaments of the Twelve Patriarchs* display a consistent pattern which involves three basic elements: (1) historical retrospective, in the form of a narrative about the patriarch's life (*T. Asher* is the only exception); (2) ethical exhortation; and (3) prediction of the future (these predictions often display the so-called sin-exile-return pattern, which is typical of Deuteronomic theology)." So the examples of the patriarchs (whether positive or negative) serve to motivate the audience to obey the law and thus receive the blessings of the covenant (*The Apocalyptic Imagination: An Introduction to the Jewish Matrix of Christianity* [New York: Crossroad, 1989], 108).

guided in their pilgrimage by a vision divine and superhuman unseen by others but manifest to them as they pass from exile to their home. (*Praem* 28-29 § 164-65)[31]

It can be seen from this key statement by Philo that he subscribed to the notion of
the story of Israel. First, in the future Israel's sin will give way to her wholesale conversion to the Torah; conversely, it is implied that Israel's past sin accounts for the present
state of her exile. Second, the dispersion and enslavement of Jews is indicative of God's
judgment upon them. Third, when Israel turns to God sincerely, he will restore her to
her land.

The story of Israel is quite clear in these remarkable comments by Philo: "Everything will suddenly be reversed, God will turn the curses against the enemies of these
penitents, the enemies who rejoiced in the misfortunes of the nation and mocked and
railed at them . . . then those of them who have not come to utter destruction, in tears
and groans lamenting their own lapse, will make their way back with course reversed
to the prosperity of the ancestral past" (*Praem* 29 § 169-70).

Jewish Apocalyptic Sectarian Writings

We turn now to Second Temple Jewish materials that are apocalyptic, but sectarian, in
their presentation of the story of Israel: the Dead Sea Scrolls, *1 Enoch* and *Jubilees*.[32] Because the literature under discussion is vast, we propose to treat one key Dead Sea
Scroll text (4QMMT) in depth. After that, we simply offer a chart on *1 Enoch* and *Jubilees*, surveying the relevance of the story of Israel for those writings.

Miqṣat Ma'aśê Ha Torah (4Q 394-99): Some Works of The Torah. 4QMMT is a
short text consisting of three parts: (1) a calendar, consisting of lines 1-20; (2) a section
of laws extending from lines 21-92a; and (3) an epilogue composed of lines 92b-118.
4QMMT is ostensibly Deuteronomistic in orientation. Thus, lines 92b-118 read:

> [And you know that] we have segregated ourselves from the rest of the poep[le and (that)
> we avoid] [93]mingling in these affairs and associating with them in these things. And you
> k[now that there is not] [94]to be found in our actions deceit or betrayal or evil, for concern-

[31]The translation is from F. H. Colson, *Philo* (Cambridge, Mass.: Harvard University Press, 1939), 341.
Craig A. Evans calls attention to these texts in Philo and their import for the story of Israel in "Aspects
of Exile and Restoration in the Proclamation of Jesus and the Gospels," in *Exile*, ed. James M. Scott
(Leiden: E. J. Brill, 1997), 315-16. For Philo's term for "exile," *phugē*, see Louis Feldman, "The Concept of Exile in Josephus," in Scott, *Exile*, ed. Scott, 146.

[32]We employ the label "sectarian" for Jewish materials prior to A.D. 70 advisedly, especially since that
literature was not monolithic in perspective. Nevertheless, to avoid even the term "Judaism" for the
Second Temple Period, preferring instead "Judaisms," as some scholars do, seems to us to an overre-
action (e.g., see J. Neusner, W. S. Green, and E. Frerichs, eds., *Judaisms and Their Messiahs at the Turn
of the Christian Era* (Cambridge: Cambridge University Press, 1987). In this section, our usage of "sectarian" refers to those minority Jewish communities at odds with the dominant religious parties of
their day.

ing [these things w]e give [. . . and further] [95]to you we have wr[itten] that you must understand the book of Moses [and the words of the pro]phets and of David [and the annals] [96][of eac]h generation. And in the book it is written [. . .] not to [97][. . .] And further it is written that [you shall stray] from the path and you will undergo evil. And it is written [98][. . .] and we determined [. . .] [99][. . .] And it is written that [100][all] these [things] shall happen to you at the end of days, the blessing [101]and the curse [. . .and you shall ass]ent in your heart and turn to me with all your heart [102][and with a]ll your soul [. . . at the e]nd [of time] and you shall be [. . .] [103][And it is written in the book of] Moses and in [the words of the prop]hets that [blessings and curses] will come upon you] which [. . .] [104][the bl]essings which c[ame upon] him in the days of Solomon the son of David and also the curses [105]which came upon him from the [days of Jeroboam son of Nebat right up to the capture of Jerusalem and of Zedekiah king of Judah [106][that] he should bring them in [. . .]. And we are aware that part of the blessings and curses have occurred [107]that are written in the b[ook of Mo]ses. And this is the end of days, when they go back to Israel [108]for [ever. . .] and not return [. . .] and the wicked will act wickedly and [. . .] [109]And [. . .] remember the kings of Israel and reflect on their deeds, how whoever of them [110]who respected [the Torah] was freed from his afflictions; those who sought the Torah [111][were forgiven] their sins. Remember David, one of the "pious" and he, too, [112]was freed from his many afflictions and was forgiven. And also we have written to you [113]some of the precepts [works] of the Torah which we think are good for you and for your people, for in you [we saw] [114]intellect and knowledge of the Torah. Reflect on all these matters and seek from him so that he may support [115]your counsel and keep far from you the evil scheming and counsel of Belial, [116]so that at the end of time, you may rejoice in finding that some of our words are true. [117]And it shall be reckoned to you as in justice when you do what is upright and good before him for your good [118]and that of Israel.

The sin–exile–restoration pattern is perspicuous in the epilogue. (1) Israel repeatedly sinned against the Lord from the time of Jeroboam to Zedekiah (lines 104-5); (2) consequently, God rained the Deuteronomic curses on the nation (lines 97, 101, 130-6); (3) but true Israel, the Essene community,[33] has repented of its sin (lines 101-2) by segregating itself from the rest of the people (lines 92-94). This has secured for the covenanters the Deuteronomic blessings (lines 100, 103-4, 106-8).

It is also obvious that 4QMMT reinterprets the Deuteronomistic tradition apocalyptically. Thus, all non-Qumranians belong to this age of Belial (100-101, 106, 116) and there-

[33]Of the numerous treatments of the Dead Sea Scrolls, James C. VanderKam's *The Dead Sea Scrolls Today* (Grand Rapids, Mich.: Eerdmans, 1994) is excellent, demonstrating both soundness and nuance; see also Lawrence H. Schiffman, *Reclaiming the Dead Sea Scrolls: Their Meaning for Judaism and Christianity*, Anchor Bible Reference Library (New York: Doubleday, 1995); and Pate, *Communities of the Last Days*, chaps. 1 and 2. We follow the translation by Florentino García Martínez, *The Dead Sea Scrolls Translated: The Qumran Texts in English* (Leiden: E. J. Brill, 1994). We assume here the traditional view that equates the writers of the Dead Sea Scrolls with the Essenes and that accepts a connection between the Scrolls and Khirbet Qumran.

fore are under the Deuteronomic curses, whereas the Essenes presently and incipiently enjoy the age to come and the Deuteronomic blessings (lines 99-102, 106-8, 110-18).

Furthermore, the laws required to be followed in order to experience the Deuteronomic blessings are the community's *halakah*,[34] which lines 1-92a are devoted to explaining. These consist of the covenanters' stringent reinterpretation of purity regulations and Sabbath-keeping. It is the sectaries' commitment to these rules that has caused them to separate from society (lines 92b-94). The Qumran community is thereby justified by God (line 117). The group's apocalyptic, sectarian reading of the Deuteronomistic tradition is clear in all of this.

Other Dead Sea Scrolls.[35] Space does not permit individual treatment of the other Dead Sea Scrolls that reinterpret the story of Israel in apocalyptic and sectarian fashion. But elsewhere we have summarized that data by classifying those materials under the following categories: (1) Wisdom as the sectaries' reinterpretation of the Mosaic law; (2) the realization of the eschatological Deuteronomic blessings in the Qumran community; and (3) the actualization of the Deuteronomic curses on nonsectarian Jews and Gentiles.

It is transparent in all of this that the Dead Sea Scrolls operate under the assumption that the Torah (more strictly defined) must be kept to remain in the covenant, a relationship that excluded Gentiles. A similar twofold perspective informs *1 Enoch* and *Jubilees* (see table 6.5).

Conclusion

These, then, are some of the Second Temple Jewish works that grapple with the story of Israel, confirming that the pattern of sin–exile–restoration was a pervasive feature in this literature. Yet the Deuteronomistic tradition, as we have also documented, is presented under four different categories: theocratic, apocalyptic, apologetic and apocalyptic sectarian. Moreover, we have seen that all of these constructs are informed by nomism and particularism. Ironically, these perspectives represent a break with the Old Testament prophetic tradition, which warned that a ritualistic obsession with the

---

[34]*Halakah* refers to a way of life. Eckhard Schnabel provides a helpful summary of the Qumran community's hidden/revealed laws relative to their sectarian rules, observing that with regard to the content of the law, two terms are to be noted. *Nigleh* designates the "revealed things," God's clear, revealed precepts in the Torah, which are known to everyone and which need no interpretation. On the other hand, the term *nistar* refers to the "hidden things," those precepts of the law (especially with regard to the calendar, the Sabbath and the festivals) for which only the community has the correct interpretation. These hidden things are known to the community as the result of (progressive) revelation or interpretation (*Law and Wisdom from Ben Sira to Paul,* Wissenschaftliche Untersuchungen zum Neuen Testament 2/16 [Tübingen, Germany: J.C.B. Mohr/Paul Siebeck, 1985], 172); cf. Lawrence H. Schiffman, *The Halakhah at Qumran,* Studies in Judaism in Late Antiquity 16 (Leiden: E. J. Brill, 1975), 22-32.

[35]The following summary comes from Pate, *Reverse of the Curse,* 122-24, as did the analysis of 4QMMT, ibid., 120-22. The same work analyzes two other Dead Sea Scrolls documents in terms of the story of Israel—The Community Rule (1QS) and The Damascus Covenant (CD), ibid., 109-19.

Torah did not, in fact, sustain the covenant with God. Neither did a xenophobic attitude square with the divine intention to convert the nations of the world. The same two concerns are reiterated in the New Testament, where grace in Christ replaces the

Table 6.5

*1 Enoch**		
	Unrighteous	Righteous
This Age: Sin	5:4	
Age to Come: Exile/Curses	5:5-7; 104:7-8	
This Age: Suffering for Righteousness's Sake		103:9-15
Age to Come: Blessings of Restoration		5:7-10; 104:1-6**

*First Enoch consists of an *Introduction* (chaps. 1—5); the *Book of Watchers* (chaps. 6—36); the *Similitudes* (chaps. 37—71); the *Astronomical Book* (chaps. 72-82); the *Dream Visions* (chaps. 83-90); and the *Admonitions of Enoch* (chaps. 91—105).

**Like the other apocalyptic works examined in this chapter, *1 Enoch* correlates the Deuteronomistic curses and blessings with this age and the age to come, respectively. Thus in this life, though sinners may seem to prosper, in the age to come they will suffer the Deuteronomistic curses eternally. Conversely, righteous Jews, because they are afflicted by their enemies in this age, will enjoy forever the Deuteronomistic blessings.

Jubilees	
Israel's Sin	1:7-11; 23:16-21
Prophets sent/rejected	1:12
Judgment and Exile	1:13-14*; 23:22-25
Restoration	1:15b-18, 27-31**

*The sectarian perspective of *Jubilees* is hinted at in 1:14, "They will err regarding the beginning of the month, the Sabbath, the festival, the jubilee, and the decree." *Jubilees* is a reworking of Genesis 1—Exodus 12, and claims to be a secret revelation from God to Moses via angels. Like *1 Enoch* and the Dead Sea Scrolls, *Jubilees* adheres to the solar, rather than the lunar calendar (*Jub* 6:35), thus throwing off the traditional times of the Sabbaths and feasts.

**This outline of the Deuteronomistic tradition in *Jubilees* is indebted to James C. Vanderkam, "*Exile* in Jewish Apocalyptic Literature," in *Exile,* ed. Scott, 103-4; and Nickleburg, *Jewish Literature,* 77. The latter calls attention to the apocalyptic tone of *Jubilees* 23:16-22, which projects the Deuteronomic blessings into the future age to come (76-78).

Torah and the inclusion of Gentiles into the people of God is the order of the day.[36]

Supplemental Readings in New Dictionary of Biblical Theology

R. T. Beckwith, "Canon," 27-34.

M. J. Evans, "Blessing/Curse," 397-401.

I. M. Duguid, "Exile," 475-78.

J. G. Millar, "Land," 623-27.

C. K. Kruse, "Law," 629-36.

A. J. Köstenberger, "Mission," 663-68.

Study Questions

1. Define "Apocrypha" and "Pseudepigrapha" and discuss the importance of that literature.

2. How does the story of Israel (sin–exile–restoration) inform Jewish theocratic writings of the intertestamental period?

3. How is the story of Israel reflected in Jewish apologetic intertestamental works?

4. How does the story of Israel influence Jewish apocalyptic intertestamental works?

5. How is the story of Israel manifested in Jewish apocalyptic sectarian writings?

6. In general, what is the role of Gentiles in the preceding literature?

---

[36]E. P. Sanders has argued that Jewish intertestamental literature should be labeled "covenantal nomism" (one enters the covenant by faith and remains in it by obeying the Torah) and thereby is free of legalism (salvation results from faith plus the works of the law); see *Paul and Palestinian Judaism: A Comparison of Patterns of Religion* (Philadelphia: Fortress, 1977). To this observer, although Sanders's term is quite correct as a descriptor, nevertheless the writings we have investigated in this chapter smack of an ultimate reliance on human works as the means to salvation, that is, legalism; see Pate, *Reverse of the Curse*, Part I for further documentation.

7

THE SYNOPTICS

The Gospel Story and the Story of Israel

In a very real sense, the Gospels are written as Christian accounts of God's active presence in the world. As such, they are *heilsgeschichtliche* (salvation-historical) portrayals of the history of God's dealings with his people. From the climactic point of the experience of God's visible reentrance into the life of Israel through Jesus Christ, the Gospel writers cast their description of the coming of God's kingdom in language and with emphases that parallel Old Testament stories of God and Israel. They are descriptions of the fulfillment of God's promises, and they therefore function as the explanation for how Israel *should have* understood God's history with his people and the nations all along. Beyond being theological biographies of Jesus, the Gospels give content to the old prophetic message of God's new covenant relationship. Because of this, their recounting of "kingdom events" in Jesus' ministry stand as corrective reinterpretations of God and Israel.

History of Israel and the Gospel Genealogies

Although both Matthew and Luke follow Mark's structure and outline for their Gospels, they both move beyond Mark with powerful genealogies that not only connect to the history of Israel, but set the stage for their particular account.

Matthew 1:1 proves almost titular in its significance for the Gospel itself. The genealogy of Jesus can be reduced to two key connections—he is the son of David and the son of Abraham. His direct connection to Abraham, the father of Israel's faith and the recipient of God's promise of blessing to himself and to the multitudes of all following generations of Abrahamic faith (Gen 12:3), yields credence to Matthew's description of Jesus as the fulfillment of all God's promises. His direct connection to

David, the messianic king of old Israel—a man after God's own heart—who brought the promise of the Abrahamic covenant as close to fulfillment as Israel had ever known it, allows Matthew's readers to understand Jesus as God's messiah sent to establish God's kingdom among the people. The Gospel account that follows this introduction will evidence how God has remembered his covenant with Abraham and is now going to bring his history with Israel to its fulfillment. The story of Matthew's Gospel clarifies the meaning of the history between God and Israel. What God has been about all the time in his relationship with Israel is now made evident.

Luke's genealogy of Jesus, although given much less prominence than Matthew's (it does not occur until Lk 3:23), has much the same function for Luke's Gospel.[1] Having used the first several chapters to firmly establish the connection between the worship of God (Lk 1:8), the preparatory steps of God (Lk 1:17), the new and direct entrance of God into human history (Lk 1:35; 2:11), the recognition of this deed by devout people (Lk 2:25-26, 36-38), the amazement of scholars of Judaism (Lk 2:46-47), and God's visible and vocal declaration of Jesus as his son (Lk 3:21-22), Luke now (Lk 3:23-38) roots his description of God's *heilsgeschichtliche* work in a genealogy that not only focuses on David and Abraham but continues through Adam to God. In Luke's description, God's work must be understood in its universal significance (Matthew's inclusion of the visit by the magi from the East may function to give a similar universal perspective to the significance of the Jesus event). The history of Israel, which is the focus for the Old Testament description of God's dealing with humanity, has significance precisely because of the role it plays in God's universal plan for *all* of his creation. As Luke will show later in his account of Stephen's speech in Acts 7, Israel misunderstands the purpose of God's actions in their history. God will not be limited to a house in Jerusalem designed for national worship (Acts 7:47-48). From the beginning, Yahweh is God of all the nations (Acts 7:49 // Is 66:1-2). What unfolds in Luke's two-volume work shows that the history of Israel is meaningful because of the role it plays in God's universal plan. Although this might not have become evident to Israel earlier, it is now in God's revelation of himself through Jesus and the following expansion of the church.

The Story of Israel and the Structure of Mark's Gospel

Mark chose to begin his Gospel at the beginning of Jesus' public ministry, at his baptism rather than at his birth. In spite of this difference between the two other Synoptic

---

[1]See Luke Timothy Johnson's remark on Luke's purpose: "The clear function of Luke's genealogy of Jesus is therefore, like that of the infancy account as a whole, to root his narrative in the story of the entire people as recorded in the birth records of Torah" (*The Gospel of Luke*, Sacra Pagina, no. 3, ed. D. J. Harrington [Collegeville, Minn.: Liturgical Press, 1991], 72).

Gospels and Mark, the structural significance of Mark's Gospel for Matthew and Luke has been agreed upon by most scholars for about a century.[2] Mark's basic outline for the story of God's renewed presence among his people through Jesus clearly suggests that the Gospel writers saw this story as pivotally important for the story of God and Israel.[3]

The absence of a reference to Jesus' miraculous birth in Mark does not suggest that he chose to disconnect the story of Jesus from Israel's story. The rooting of the gospel story in God's purposes for Israel cannot be missed even if Mark is read alone. The prominence in all the Gospels (Mk 1:7; Mt 3:11; Lk 3:16; cf. Jn 1:27) of John the Baptist as the "obvious" fulfillment of Isaiah 40, and John's direct pronouncement of Jesus as the "one to come," sets the stage for the unavoidable conclusion that the Jesus story inseparably connects to God's dealings with Israel. There can be little doubt that the Gospel writers saw Jesus as *the* central figure for God's new covenant relationship with Israel and the nations.[4]

In his helpful 1936 book *The Apostolic Preaching and Its Development,* C. H. Dodd notes that the earliest Christian preaching primarily concerned itself with the declaration of God's mighty acts in relation to Israel in a way that is similar to Old Testament passages like Joshua 24 and the historical psalms.[5] Mark's intentions are evident in his opening use of the word *gospel,* which is a term "virtually equivalent for *kerygma.*"[6]

Mark desires to describe the significance of the gospel *news* for the whole event of

---

[2]Although earlier attempts had been made to affirm the priority of Mark's Gospel, it was H. J. Holzmann's *Die Synoptischen Evangelien* (1863) that convincingly argued for what is now called "The Two-Document Hypothesis." Though the arguments for this theory have been refined since Holzmann, the basic argument that Mark is the more primitive of the Gospels and that it functions, along with another document, Q, as the major source for Matthew and Luke has stayed the same. An earlier theory proposed by J. J. Griesbach in 1783, claiming Matthew to be first and Mark to depend on both Matthew and Luke, has been revived by W. M. Farmer (see *The Synoptic Problem,* 1964) and others. Still, it would be fair to say that most scholars by far hold Mark to be earliest.

[3]The freedom of Matthew and Luke to add and rewrite some of Mark's material without changing the basic Gospel storyline may be due to a common perspective on Mark that follows the description Papias claims to have received from John the Presbyter: "Mark, having become the interpreter of Peter, wrote down accurately whatever he remembered of the things said and done by the Lord, but not however in order" (quoted from Eusebius, *Hist. Eccl.* III.xxxix).

[4]Although this parallels N. T. Wright's claim that "Jesus saw himself as the leader and focal point of the true, returning-from-exile Israel" (*Jesus and the Victory of God* [Minneapolis: Fortress, 1996], 477), a slightly broader formulation seems helpful.

[5]Dodd argues for a sharp distinction between preaching (*kērygma*) and teaching (*didachē*) in the early church. The *kērygma* focused on God's mighty deeds, while the *didachē* concentrated on the ethical implications of these deeds. The Gospels are *kērygma;* for, as Dodd notes, "it was by *kerygma,* says Paul, not by *didache*, that it pleased God to save men" (*Apostolic Preaching and Its Development* [reprint; Grand Rapids, Mich.: Baker, 1980], 8).

[6]Ibid., 47.

God.[7] No sooner does he name his account gospel (*euangelion*) than he quotes Isaiah (Mk 1:2). What follows must be seen in light of God's promise of old, and God's promise of old can only be understood in light of the *news* brought in Mark's Gospel. The connection between Mark's opening emphasis on John the Baptist and Isaiah 40 may further implicate the restoration motif as the deliberate structure of his Gospel. Arguably, the unapologetic reference to Isaiah 40 as a stage-setter for God's actions, as recognized by Mark's portrayal of God's *euangelion,* may well function as a reminder to his readers of the *euangelion* presented by Isaiah in the chapters that follow. This certainly is true if Isaiah 40:1-8 function as a preamble or prologue to the rest of Isaiah.[8] God's announcement of his will to bring about a new time of forgiveness, peace and restoration for Israel (Is 40:1-8) includes, then, in Mark's thought, the specific restorative proclamations given in the following chapters of Isaiah (see esp. Is 41; 52; 61).

Mark follows the pattern of the early church *kērygma* found throughout the New Testament. One example of this would be Peter's speeches in Acts. First, Old Testament prophecy is being fulfilled (cf. Acts 2:16; 3:18, 24). Second, fulfillment took place through the ministry, death and resurrection of Jesus, which happened according to the predetermined plan of God (Acts 2:22; 3:22). Third, resurrection delivers the evidence that Jesus is indeed the messianic head of the new Israel (Acts 2:33-36; 3:13; 4:11 // Ps 118:22). Fourth, the presence of the Holy Spirit in the church signifies Christ's power and glory (Acts 2:17-21 // Joel 2:28-32). Fifth, the imminent return of Christ shows the brevity of the messianic age now experienced and its predetermined nature (Acts 3:21: "Jesus, who must remain in heaven until the time of universal restoration that God announced long ago through his holy prophets"). Sixth, the proclamation of this *kērygma* leads to an appeal for repentance and the offer of forgiveness and endowment with the Holy Spirit, which is the evidence of salvation and the age to come (Acts 2:38-39 // Joel 2:32 and Is 57:19; 3:19, 25-26 // Gen 12:3).

Mark is almost breathtaking in the pace and vividness with which he presents the gospel message. What Matthew and Luke use a few chapters to depict, Mark handles in a few verses. Not only does he reduce Jesus' baptism and temptation to a few terse sentences, but everything is described as happening *euthys* (immediately, or at once). In chapter 1 alone, *euthys* is used eleven times (Mk 1:10, 12, 18, 20, 21, 23, 28, 29, 30, 42, 43) out of forty times in the whole Gospel. Furthermore, action verbs and quick scene changes fill Mark's description. He avoids long teaching sections almost

---

[7]Although Dodd may have overstated the difference between *kērygma* and *didachē*, the Gospels' focus on the Christ event's significance for the understanding of God's dealings with Israel and the nations is unmistakable (cf. John B. Polhill, "Kerygma and Didache," in *Dictionary of the Later New Testament and Its Developments,* ed. Ralph P. Martin and Peter H. Davids [Downers Grove, Ill.: InterVarsity Press, 1997], 626-29).
[8]Many, if not most, modern scholars see Isaiah 40–55 as a manuscript that originally was separate from Isaiah 1–39.

completely with the notable exception of the Olivet discourse in Mark 13, which in itself is action-packed speech. God is again active in the history of his people—in ways even more climactic than the days of old. Everything Israel's history has pointed to now finds fulfillment in the "gospel of God."

The Story of Israel and Jesus' Teaching on the Presence of God's Kingdom

Mark's first reference to the teaching of Jesus is a quick summary statement that functions as a transitional sentence connecting the prophetic message of the Old Testament to the ministry and message of Jesus—the gospel news from God: "Jesus came preaching to Galilee, proclaiming the good news [or gospel] of God, and saying, 'The time is fulfilled, and the kingdom of God has come near; repent and believe in the good news [or gospel]'" (Mk 1:14-15).[9]

The coming of God's kingdom,[10] the active, unequivocal, reign of God among his people which had been promised by all the prophets, was now a reality in Jesus. The power of Jesus' statement on the nearness of the kingdom was not found in its proleptic quality, announcing that it would break through soon, but in its radical claim that it was here *now*.[11] Jesus brought it! Beyond merely proclaiming *with* the prophets that the time when God will restore his people and bring them back to preexilic experiences of God's presence was near, Jesus announced that it had come. "Near" means spatially close. It can be felt and seen. The whole point of Jesus' ministry and message was to say and show that the time of waiting was over. What Judaism understood to be the age *to come* had now broken into their present reality.

Jesus' announcement of the kingdom's nearness had a spatial focus. God's presence could be seen and experienced. "But if it is by the Spirit of God that I cast out demons," Jesus said, "then the kingdom of God has come to you" (Mt 12:28 // Lk 11:20). A predominantly temporal reading of Jesus' kingdom announcement misses the point of the gospel. John the Baptist, frustrated in jail, sent his disciples to ask Jesus if he truly was the one to come or if they should expect another. Jesus' answer evidences the gospel perspective, "Go and tell John what you have seen and heard: the blind receive their sight, the lame walk, the lepers are cleansed, the deaf hear, the dead are raised, the

---

[9]In the heydays of *ipsissima vox/verba* studies (form critical approaches to determining the "exact words" of Jesus), scholars would agree that even if nothing else could be shown to be unique to Jesus, Mark 1:15 had to be. It was too radical to have been made up by the early church.

[10]Nothing should be made of Matthew's consistent use of *kingdom of heaven* as opposed to Mark's *kingdom of God*. This is due simply to a Matthean reverence for God's name. Exceptions are Matthew 12:28; 19:24; 21:31, 43.

[11]W. G. Kümmel states quite boldly that the literal meaning of *engus* in the New Testament is "completely unambiguous: it denotes nearness in space" (*Promise and Fulfilment: The Eschatological Message of Jesus*, 2nd ed., trans. Dorothea M. Barton, Studies in Biblical Theology, no. 23 [London: SCM Press, 1961], 19). Paradoxically, he then uses the bulk of his book to argue for a temporal use of the term.

poor have good news brought to them" (Lk 7:22 // Mt 11:4-5). The connection between the gospel story and the story of Israel is at the point of fulfillment, not at the
point of parallel anticipation. The kingdom is here now, and it is unequivocally visible.
The things that happen through the ministry of Jesus are God-things that portray the
very character of the kingdom. Said differently, Jesus' proclamation of the *nearness* of
the kingdom has less to do with the time for the kingdom and more to do with the
character of the kingdom.[12]

It may be that a correction needs to be made to the traditional "already/not yet" language for God's kingdom. The Gospels' focuses are not primarily on the early beginnings of the inbreaking of God's kingdom, like an overture before a concert or a com-
mercial before a movie. The point made is that the real thing has come. The future
aspect of Jesus' announcement of the kingdom is better understood as "not fully" than
as "not yet." The kingdom of God—the real thing—is here already, though not fully.
What comes in the future, when Christ fills all in all, is not something different, just
more of what Christ brought. The kingdom is *already* because God's kingdom is near;
it is *not fully* because the kingdom of this world still reigns (Mt 24:9-14).[13]

The spatial significance of Jesus' kingdom announcement becomes even more evident when seen in context. People are to "repent and believe" because of it. This repentance is not a preparatory act for something that will happen later, but rather a prerequisite for participation in what has already come to pass. In fact, in the Gospel
description, the power of God's kingdom is not only a special endowment belonging
to the person of Jesus. It was also distributed to and through those who belonged to
the one who brought it (cf. Mt 10:7-8 and Lk 10:9, 11). It overflowed to all who came
in contact with it. The redeeming power of the kingdom is effective because of its spatial closeness, not because of an anticipatory nearness of the future. In other words,
what the prophets had preached and the people had longed for was now a reality.[14]

When Jesus teaches his disciples to pray, the same emphasis is clear. The second
petition requests the coming of God's kingdom (*elthetō hē basileia sou* "may your
kingdom come"). Had the emphasis of this petition primarily rested on the temporal

---

[12]This, of course, is not to say that Jesus' language had no future perspective. As W. D. Davies and Dale
C. Allison correctly note, "Only overly skeptical dissection or misinterpretation can remove from
Jesus' preaching of the kingdom either its future or its present elements" (*The Gospel According to Saint
Matthew 8–18*, International Critical Commentary 2, ed. C. E. B. Cranfield [Edinburgh: T & T Clark,
1991], 389).

[13]For a contemporary Jewish description of God's kingdom as breaking into history prior to a time of
judgment and salvation, see, for example, *Jubilees* 23:26-28, 23:30ff.

[14]Kümmel's stress that the lesson of the fig tree shows that Jesus expected the kingdom to come in the
immediate future does not convince (*Promise and Fulfillment,* 20ff.). The point Luke makes is that just
as leaves on a fig tree reveal that it *is* summer, the signs happening through Jesus reveal the visible
presence of God's kingdom.

aspect of the coming, one would expect the use of *parachrēma* ("immediately" or "soon"). Instead, the petition succeeds the petition *may your name be made holy,* and precedes the petition *may your will be done.* Both of these petitions focus on the desire for the *recognition* of God's presence among people, not for a future coming of it.[15] The same holds true for the petition for the coming of the kingdom.

The Gospels' emphasis on the spatial nearness of the kingdom does not deny a future consummation; it simply focuses on the arrival of the kingdom in Jesus. The distance between God and his people caused by sin and experienced as exile has been eliminated. God is again near. The nearness of the kind of power that unquestionably belonged to the kingdom of God proved that Jesus brought the divine presence. Furthermore, the ability of the disciples (and the subsequent church as portrayed in Acts) to *demonstrate* the kingdom in ways similar to Jesus intensified this experience. What Israel's history had pointed toward—and looked for as the age to come—had now broken into history.

Different from a realized eschatology, the Gospels' affirmation of a present eschatology does not suggest that the kingdom of God is fully realized in this age. Rather, it suggests that the kingdom breaks into the sphere of history in a way that underscores the relational character of God. God's presence now dwells dynamically among people. It is here already, though not fully. It follows from this that present manifestations of the kingdom cannot exegetically be given mystical or merely symbolic interpretations. The kingdom of God is ontologically a part of history. *Heilsgeschichte* is a historical rather than a philosophical category. God actively and dynamically involves himself in the redemption of history.

Kingdom of God thus functions as an overarching theological motif in the Synoptic Gospels. Concluding the prophetic message of sin, exile and restoration, the Gospel writers champion God's restoring act through Jesus Christ. The time promised by Jeremiah,[16] Ezekiel[17] and Joel,[18] where God's prophetic spirit is poured out upon all the

---

[15]Again, the connection to Israel's history and her prayers is clear. See Billerbeck's claim that in rabbinical literature *"sagt man nicht: Gottes Königsherrschaft möge 'kommen', sondern: möge 'offenbart werden' oder 'sich offenbaren' oder 'erscheine'"* (rabbinical literature does not say: God's kingly rule may 'come,' rather: may 'be revealed' or 'may reveal itself' or 'shine') (Paul Billerbeck and H. L. Strack, *Kommentarzum Neuen Testament aus Talmud und Midrash,* vol. 1, *Das Evangelium nach Matthaus erläutert aus Talmud und Midrasch* [München: C. H. Beck'sche Verlagsbuchhandlung, 1922], 418).

[16]Jeremiah 31:31-34: "But this is the covenant that I will make with the house of Israel after those days, says the LORD: I will put my law within them, and I will write it on their hearts; and I will be their God, and they shall be my people" (Jer 31:33).

[17]Ezekiel 36:26ff.: "A new heart I will give you, and a new spirit I will put within you; and I will remove from your body the heart of stone and give you a heart of flesh. I will put my spirit within you, and make you follow my statutes and be careful to observe my ordinances" (Ezek 36:26-27).

[18]Joel 2:28-29: "Then afterward I will pour out my spirit on all flesh; your sons and your daughters shall prophesy, your old men shall dream dreams, and your young men shall see visions. Even on the male and female slaves, in those days, I will pour out my spirit."

"citizens" of his kingdom, allowing them *all* to see, understand and speak prophetically, has come. Without exactly making Israel's history the storyline for the Gospels, the significance of the life of Jesus is explained in ways that consistently touch on pivotal events in God's redemptive history. As will become evident, these "touch-points" to Israel's story speak both ways. Pointing backward, they speak with evangelistic force, showing that the presence of God's kingdom is now as powerfully as ever an observable part of Israel's history. Pointing forward, they speak with prophetic force, showing that God is in the midst of fulfilling his promises of old. What happens presently, the Gospels proclaim, is what God has planned from the beginning. Prophets of old, filled with God's Spirit, saw it dimly; followers of Christ, new members of God's kingdom, now see it clearly.

As mentioned above, this approach to the story of Jesus enables a subtle rereading of who God and his people are—a reading that becomes full-blown and up-front in Luke's account of Stephen's speech in Acts 7. The story of the Gospels clarifies the meaning of the story of God and the purpose of Israel. What God has been about all the time in his relationship with Israel and the nations is now made evident in the gospel story.

The Story of Israel and the Gospel Fulfillment of Isaianic Prophecy

As has been mentioned, Mark begins his Gospel tersely with a summary statement that points to the preparatory work of John the Baptist as foreseen by Isaiah. This is followed by a brief but exceedingly important account of Jesus' baptism. Unmistakably, and in spite of the lack of details compared to Matthew's account, the baptism of Jesus includes a declaration of God that conspicuously refers to Isaiah's Servant Song in Isaiah 42. The scene in Isaiah is a theophany that includes an audible voice from heaven proclaiming the coming fulfillment of Isaiah's prophecy that God intends for his covenant with Israel to have significance for all the nations. Mark's baptismal scene proclaims that Israel's history and national purpose find this fulfillment through the one for whom the way was prepared according to Isaiah 40. God himself inaugurates Jesus' mission by a purpose statement from Isaiah 42.[19]

Mark's point can hardly be overemphasized. The application to Jesus of the unmistakable connection in Isaiah 42 between the outpouring of God's Spirit upon his servant and the fulfillment of Israel's purpose as a light to the nations that comes from this seems impossible to miss. Luke picks up on this in an even stronger way. After reducing his baptismal account to an absolute minimum and delaying the Spirit endowment

---

[19]Indeed, if the claim that this deliberately holds a threefold OT reference proves correct, it only strengthens Mark's case. "This is my son" makes reference to Psalm 2:7, part of a royal psalm, thus identifying Jesus as a sovereign messianic king in the line of David. "Whom I love" refers to Genesis 22:2, identifying Jesus as the son to be sacrificed. "With you I am well pleased" references Isaiah 42, identifying Jesus as the suffering servant.

and divine inauguration to a following prayer session, Luke launches into a genealogy that moves beyond Abraham to Adam and ultimately to God. The plan God ordained, and endowed Jesus to fulfill, had to be understood in universal terms. God's plan was not just for Israel (Abraham), but for all God's creation (Adam). As the Spirit-endowed servant of Isaiah 42, Jesus came to lead God's people to fulfill its eternal purpose.

That Luke makes such a strong connection between Israel's purpose as declared by Isaiah and Jesus' ministry becomes even more evident in his sequencing and narrative focus of the early events of Jesus' ministry. Like Matthew, he follows Mark's basic outline: baptism, temptation, early Galilean ministry and calling of the disciples. His interjections to this outline, however, elucidate his focus. Beyond the placing of a genealogy of Jesus that goes back to Adam right after the baptismal announcement, Luke includes in his description of Jesus' earliest Galilean ministry a teaching event from the Nazareth synagogue that neither Mark nor Matthew include.[20]

According to Luke, Jesus begins his teaching ministry, following the temptation in the desert, in his childhood synagogue in Nazareth (Lk 4:16-21). As Luke details this event, Jesus receives the scroll to read and chooses a passage from Isaiah 61—a passage that resonates the theme from Isaiah 42.[21] He closes the scroll and interprets the passage by saying: "Today this scripture has been fulfilled in your hearing" (Lk 4:21).

No reader of Luke could be in doubt. Jesus had come to point Israel to the purpose of her history, which was to be God's instrument to bring light to the nations. The time had come; the kingdom of God was now among them. The *good news* of the gospel would be preached to all peoples through God's anointed servant. What may have been isolated incidents in the past, when prophets like Elijah went on God's command to Zarephath in Sidon to feed a widow (Lk 4:25-26) or when Elisha was empowered to give healing to a leprous Syrian, would now become the normal pattern (Lk 4:27). Indeed, according to Luke, God's calling and re-calling of a people governed by his dynamic presence is for the purpose of bringing to fulfillment the historical relationship between God and his people for the salvation of the whole created order.

The Story of Israel and the Gospel Wilderness Motif

That God is in the process of doing an extraordinary work proves evident also from Jesus' forty days of testing in the desert. All three Synoptic Gospels place the tempta-

---

[20]Mark 6:1-6 and Matthew 13:53-58 give reference to the same event but without detail and allusion to any reading of Isaiah.

[21]Luke 4:18-19, "The Spirit of the Lord is upon me, because he has anointed me to bring good news to the poor. He has sent me to proclaim release to the captives and recovery of sight to the blind, to let the oppressed go free, to proclaim the year of the Lord's favor."

Isaiah 42:6b-7, "I have given you as a covenant to the people, a light to the nations, to open the eyes that are blind, to bring out the prisoners from the dungeon, from the prison those who sit in darkness."

tion narrative immediately following Jesus' baptism. In a way that parallels other giants of God's covenantal history, God tests Jesus in the wilderness before launching his ministry. This obvious connection to Abraham and Moses—and even to Israel herself—shows once again how the Jesus event has magnificent scale in God's plan.

From the very beginning of Israel's history, God used the wilderness experience to prepare his servants for pivotal covenantal moments. No one knowledgeable of the history of the relationship between God and Israel would miss that. Abraham, the father of faith, had to leave Ur for a wandering into the wilderness. It was this journey, filled with tests, traps and temptations that refined Abraham's understanding of God and his mission and defined Abraham as God's chosen servant. The climactic point, of course, was God's call and covenantal promise of land, descendants and blessing (Gen 12:2-3; 15:5ff.; 17:4-8; 22:17-18), the so-called Abrahamic covenant.

The next giant covenantal personality, Moses, would likewise spend forty years in the desert before God launched his ministry. It is hardly coincidental to Israel's history that Moses' burning bush experience happened in the desert. Neither is the close connection between Moses' call at the bush in Exodus 3 and God's wrath toward him for not having circumcised his son in Exodus 4. The whole event of the Mosaic covenant is wrapped in this wilderness focus.

Pivotal as Moses is for God's history, it is the giving of the law at Sinai that towers as the primary focus for the story of the Mosaic covenant. Before Israel could enter the Promised Land, they too needed a defining period in the wilderness. Much can be said of the length of this experience as a period of judgment for refusing to enter the land (Numbers 14), of course, but to miss the theological significance of Israel's wilderness experience would be a mistake. It was in the wilderness that God gave Israel the law that defined them as a people and a nation. It was in the wilderness that they learned to worship the one true God. It was the length of their wilderness journey (forty years, like Moses) that created a people who had grown up under God's care, devoid of Egyptian experiences. The relationship between God and his people is refined though wilderness experiences.

Carrying through on the description of the significance of wilderness experiences for covenantal figures, 1 Samuel makes a point of noticing that David was prepared for his task by tending sheep in the wilderness (1 Sam 16:11; 17:28, 36-37). Many of David's psalms likewise speak to God's forging and preparatory use of the wilderness.[22]

It seems clear that the Synoptic Gospels use the forty-day testing experience of Jesus in the wilderness as evidence that God is renewing his covenant with his people through Jesus. Indeed, one may claim that the consistent Gospel references to John the Baptist as a "voice crying in the wilderness" function to show the Jesus story as a cov-

---

[22]This survey aims only at giving a quick reference to a few major events. The wilderness motif is found throughout Scripture and can easily be traced through the major biblical characters and events.

enantal event from the very outset. In other words, the story of Jesus' temptation in the wilderness is a Gospel touch-point to the story of Israel that allows the evangelists to retell the story of God and his purpose.[23]

Although Mark seems little interested in the temptation narrative beyond this wilderness touch-point,[24] Matthew and Luke seem eager to elaborate on the obedience motif in Jesus' temptation (Mt 4:1-11 // Lk 4:1-13). Unlike the Israelites, who spent most of their time in the wilderness proving their disobedience and lack of trust in God, Jesus never wavered. Unlike disobedient Israel that complained against God when they were hungry (Ex 16:3; Deut 8:3), Jesus answered this temptation by a quote from one of the warning sections of Deuteronomy (Deut 8:3). A careful reader of Matthew and Luke will recognize that the forty days of Jesus' fast in God's presence correspond exactly to Moses' fast while receiving the law at Sinai (Ex 34:28) and to Elijah's fast at Mount Horeb (1 Kings 19:8).

Jesus' two other temptations, to show disobedience by trusting in powers beside Yahweh and to put Yahweh to the test, are both rebutted by quotes from the Great Shema in Deuteronomy 6. Matthew and Luke include descriptions of Jesus' temptation experience in the wilderness that aim to show how Israel failed at the very pinnacle of their own experience with Yahweh. From the chapter that most Jews would recite daily as their confession of faith comes the evidence that Jesus was the true messenger of God who was to remind Israel of her purpose in God's plan—to be God's obedient messenger of salvation among the nations.

The Story of Israel and Jesus' Twelve Disciples

The Gospels' emphasis on Jesus' special appointment of exactly twelve disciples is of great significance for their "new" presentation of Israel's history as well.[25] Not only do each of the Gospels place this calling in conjunction with Jesus' wilderness experience, but the consistent emphasis on twelve in a story that details several other groups of disciples[26] is hardly a mere historical fact devoid of theological importance. Quite to

---

[23]For a study on the use of the wilderness motif in the New Testament, see Ulrich W. Mauser, *Christ in the Wilderness*, Studies in Biblical Theology 39 (London: SCM Press, 1963).

[24]In his two short verses on this event, he mentions wilderness (*erēmos*) twice and includes a reference to wild beasts (*thērion*).

[25]Craig A. Evans ("Jesus and the Continuing Exile of Israel," in *Jesus and the Restoration of Israel*, ed. Carey C. Newman [Downers Grove, Ill.: InterVarsity Press, 1999], 91) calls it the "single most important datum that attests to the presence of exile theology in Jesus' thinking."

[26]Contrary to Strecker's claim that the term "disciples" exclusively refers to the Twelve, the evidence for an understanding of "disciples" that has multiple references is overwhelming. Used only by the Gospels and Acts, the word occurs 261 times in multifarious contexts referring to individuals and groups. For example, see Matthew 9:36-37, where the word is used right before the listing of the twelve. In Luke 6:13, Jesus calls his disciples to himself and chooses among them twelve; in Luke 6:17 Jesus teaches "a great crowd of his disciples." In Luke 10, although the term *disciple* is not used, the reference is clear. Jesus appoints 70 (or 72, see discussion below) and sends them out two by two.

the contrary, the Synoptics parade the Twelve as significant pillars in God's restoration of Israel's purpose. The Twelve became a symbol tightly intertwined with Jesus' ministry of restoration. Already in Pauline texts that predate the Gospels, *the Twelve* had become a technical term. When Paul, in 1 Corinthians 15:5, recounts the postresurrection appearances, he lists without hesitation a post-Judas appearance to the Twelve. This is noteworthy, as E. P. Sander claims, because "the church would not have invented the appearance to the *twelve*" after Judas's betrayal.[27] Historically, Judas was not present, but his absence made no difference to the fact that Jesus appeared to his "group of twelve." Thus, *twelve* was not a mere count of a number of especially devoted disciples; it was a reference to a group of disciples who were theologically significant for Jesus' message and ministry.

Jesus' call of *twelve* disciples at the outset of his ministry proclaims loud and clear that God was calling Israel back to her purpose. Matthew forefronts the theological importance of this even more through a Jesus saying that directly relates the purpose of the twelve disciples to the future destiny of Israel: "Truly I tell you, at the renewal of all things, when the Son of Man is seated on the throne of his glory, you who have followed me will also sit on twelve thrones, judging the twelve tribes of Israel" (Mt 19:28).

This understanding of the eschatological rule of Jesus' disciples was well established and found expression outside the Gospels as can be seen in the Revelation of John (Rev 3:21; 20:6). The point in this connection, however, is the special symbolic force of the twelve disciples who represent the true Israel. They will sit on thrones judging unbelieving Israel as they are being restored and reconstituted into twelve tribes.[28] The point was hard to miss. The reference in the first century *Psalms of Solomon* to a coming judgment of Israel's tribes (17:26) hints that such ideas were familiar and at least somewhat accepted and understandable to Jesus' audience.[29] *Testament of Judah's* claim (25:1) that the twelve patriarchs would reign in the New Age[30] makes an almost direct parallel to Jesus' claim for his disciples. The gospel storyline connects to Israel's story, and it does so with reinterpretative force.

The number twelve, then, represents the call to restoration—the return from exile—for all of Israel. Although the list of the disciples differs slightly between the Gos-

---

[27]E. P. Sanders, *Jesus and Judaism* (Philadelphia: Fortress, 1985), 99; italics mine.

[28]As Donald A. Hagner notes, at the time of Jesus, nine and a half of the tribes were considered lost (*Matthew 14–28*, Word Biblical Commentary 33B [Dallas: Word, 1995], 565).

[29]See James H. Charlesworth, *Old Testament Pseudepigrapha* (Garden City, N.Y.: Doubleday, 1985), 2:667.

[30]See James H. Charlesworth, *Old Testament Pseudepigrapha* (Garden City, N.Y.: Doubleday, 1983), 1:801.

pels, a snapshot picture of the group can be taken.[31] The striking assembly of average, mostly unschooled people from an incredibly diverse background underscores the radical nature of Jesus' message. In the new and restored Israel God is creating, Roman hirelings (Matthew) will work side by side with Jewish Zealots (Simon).

Even more conspicuous is the absence of anyone from recognized Jewish piety. There is no mention of anyone one from the Sanhedrin, although some show interest in Jesus; and no one is mentioned from the parties of the Pharisees and Sadducees, although the Pharisees engage in conversation with Jesus on a consistent basis. The newness of God's kingdom, or God's restoring power, was of such character that the "wise" were dumbfounded and the ignorant were "wise." Teachers of Israel do not understand (Jn 3:10), but unschooled men speak with the power of God's Spirit (Acts 4:8, 13). The prophetic announcement about God's restoration is being fulfilled for all to see.

Rather than being taught by the teachers of Israel, God himself will teach his people (Jer 31:33-34); they will all be guided by God's Spirit like their forefathers (Ezek 36:27-28), and they shall be like a nation of prophets (Joel 2:28-29). What could look like a simple historical recounting of a rabbi and the call of his disciples is portrayed in the Gospels in such a way that it becomes an announcement of restoration and divine presence.

The Story of Israel and the Sending Out of Seventy Disciples

One more comment needs to be made concerning the significance of specific groups of disciples for the gospel message and portrayal of Jesus' ministry. In an account exclusive to Luke, Jesus sends out seventy disciples in groups of two (Lk 10:1-10). Why seventy? And why do some manuscripts have seventy-two? Most likely the background for this should not be sought in Moses' choosing of seventy elders (Num 11:16-17) as Luke Timothy Johnson, for example, seems to suggest.[32] In light of Luke's universal perspective, a background in Genesis 10 and the listing of the nations seems more probable. This corresponds with the textual difficulty of the passage. Without getting into text-critical evaluations that do not yield conclusive evidence in this passage anyway, suffice it to say that "seventy" would have its reference in the Masoretic Text where Genesis 10 lists seventy nations of the earth, whereas seventy-two would

---

[31]An attempt can be made at an harmonization. Besides the difference in sequence, which proves less interesting for this discussion, Luke's preference for "Zealot" rather than "Cananean," like Mark and Matthew, can probably be explained as a translation. Zealot is Greek for the Aramaic Cananean. It proves more difficult to explain why Matthew and Mark chose Thaddaeus for Luke's Judas, son of James. It might not be too much of a stretch to suggest that Mark and Matthew referred to Judas as Thaddaeus to avoid any confusion with Judas Iscariot. Why Luke did not do so is hard to tell.

[32]Johnson, *Gospel of Luke,* 167.

have its reference in the Septuagint where Genesis 10 lists seventy-two nations of the earth. In other words, Jesus sends out a number of disciples that symbolically represents the number of nations of the earth.

Luke's mention of this becomes even more powerful, considering its context in rabbinical teaching. Karl Heinrich Rengstorf's remark proves helpful at this point: "Since the Rabbis were firmly convinced that the Torah had been offered to all nations before Israel became the one people of the Law, there was a widespread view that it was given to the human race in seventy languages (Sota, 7, 5; T. Sota, 8, 6 etc.)."[33] In Luke's mind something important was proclaimed by this deed of Jesus. When the Law was given, it was offered to all the nations—yet only Israel accepted. Now, when the new covenant is offered, it too is offered to all the nations. The twelve disciples were sent to the tribes of Israel (Mt 10:5), the seventy (seventy-two) to the nations of the earth. What God had desired from the beginning, that all the earth should know him, was coming to a fulfillment—not through the teachers of Israel, but through the disciples of Jesus. The good news of the gospel created a new, almost reverse situation. Now Israel would reject the covenant with God, while the nations would accept it.[34] The purpose of Israel's history with God would be fulfilled whether Israel understood or not (Mt 21:43).

The numbers "seven" and "ten" are repeated throughout Scripture with high frequency, and although they clearly have symbolic significance, one must be careful not to overinterpret their use. Having said that, Matthew's omission of this sending narrative does not necessarily militate against such a strong reading of Luke 10. The only other Synoptic use of seventy is found in Matthew's church passage in Matthew 18. Peter asks how many times he should forgive—seven? Jesus answers, "No, seventy times seven." Could it be that the only Gospel passage dealing with the church and the struggles between members has a subtle (if indeed, not direct) reference to forgiveness that parallels God's forgiveness of his creation?

The context seems to suggest just such a reading.[35] The incident is preceded by Matthew's abbreviated version of the lost sheep (the shepherd leaves the flock to go find the lost), and it is succeeded by the parable of the unfaithful servant (a man has been forgiven a huge sum but is not willing to forgive his own debtor's small amount). Could readers of Matthew miss this as a reference to their own stubbornness in relation to the nations? Again, the Gospels present a touch-point to Israel's

---

[33]TDNT, s.v. "Hepta," 634.

[34]Cf. Richard Bauckham's remarks in *The Climax of Prophecy: Studies on the Book of Revelation* (Edinburgh: T & T Clark, 1993), 326ff.

[35]The common suggestion that "seventy times seven" simply indicates the superior strictness of Jesus' righteousness in comparison to the Rabbis, who only required forgiveness three times, does not convince. Cf., Hagner, *Matthew 14–28*, 537.

story that forces the readers to rethink God's purpose for his people.[36]

As already mentioned and argued, Mark presents the Gospel, the good news of God's kingdom, in a very succinct and direct way. His first four chapters tell the story of the significance of Jesus as the Son of God sent to fulfill God's purpose for his creation. Jesus' message is that God's kingdom has come near and been made visible through God's power in the healing of human misery and the exorcism of demons. Questions raised concerning issues of the Law are answered by a proclamation of Jesus' authority over God's law. With symbolic force Jesus calls twelve disciples, and when charged for being in league with the devil (Beelzebub), Jesus uses the event to show that Israel's teachers did not know the difference between God's kingdom and Satan's kingdom—a sin that is likened to unforgivable blasphemy (Mk 3:28-30).

The Story of Israel and Jesus' Parables

Mark's brevity compared to the other Gospels is to a large degree due to his lack of much teaching material. With a few exceptions, Mark collected Jesus' parabolic teaching in Mark 4. The exceptions are quickly listed. In Mark 2:19-20, 21, 22, Jesus uses three brief illustrations to answer a question about fasting. In Mark 3:23-27, Jesus counters a charge that he is demon possessed by using an illustration. Chapter 7 uses the word "parables" (Mk 7:17) when the people ask him what he meant by saying humans cannot be defiled by anything external (Mk 7:15). Mark gives the parable of the vineyard and the tenants in Mark 12:1-12—a story that functions as an allegory on Jesus and his reception by the Jewish leadership.[37] Chapter 13 explains the withered fig tree (Mk 13:28-29) and illustrates the uncertainty of the eschaton (Mk 13:33-37).

Mark 4, Mark's parable chapter, functions as a summary statement on Jesus' teaching. Except for the Olivet Discourse (Mk 13), Mark 4:1-34 is the only sustained teaching section of Jesus. The chapter sets the stage by declaring that Jesus "began to teach beside the sea" (Mk 4:1) and that he "began to teach them many things in parables" (Mk 4:2). Mark portrays Jesus' proclamation of the arrival of God's kingdom among the people in two major ways: he performs miracles as evidence of God's presence, and he teaches in parables to convey the consequences of this presence. In other words, in Jesus' preaching the miracles function as dramatized parables on the king-

---

[36]If the background for Jesus' use of "seventy times seven" rather should be found in Genesis 4:24, where Lamech, one of Cain's descendants, brags that he would revenge an attack of a man "seventy times seven" times, the above reading of Jesus' saying may still stand. Genesis uses the story to bring the Cainite genealogy to an abrupt conclusion. The next verse (Gen 4:25) talks about the birth of Seth, Adam's child to replace Abel. What Jesus hints, then, is that God's purpose for his people is a complete reversal of the spirit of Cain. The nations shunned from God's presence will be forgiven and filled with God's Spirit.

[37]Morna D. Hooker, "Mark's Parables of the Kingdom," in *The Challenge of Jesus' Parables,* ed. Richard N. Longenecker (Grand Rapids, Mich.: Eerdmans, 2000), 81.

dom. Although a few of the parables narrated may lack the traditional formula for the so-called kingdom parables, ("the kingdom of God is like . . ."), they all have a clear kingdom perspective.

The parable of the sower (Mk 4:3-9) gives a picture of a farmer liberally spreading his seeds even on soils and grounds that yield no fruit. Mark 4:11, then, relates this picture to the kingdom of God. The seed is the prophetic word of God being propagated among God's people—yet much is wasted. Some reject this word, some receive it and reject it later, some receive it without bearing fruit, and some receive it bearing much fruit. Even as God liberally spreads his word about his restoring presence, his message is wasted on many of his people. That Jesus clearly had Israel's rejection of his mission and message in mind is evident. That his explanation (Mk 4:13-20) focuses on fulfillment likewise seems plain (Mk 4:20).[38] That he attempted to retell the whole of Israel's story, showing that their rejection had left them in exile, seems less certain.[39] Such a claim, however, may be accurate as a broad summary statement for Mark's theological purpose when putting Mark 4:1-34 together the way he did.

The most baffling statement concerning Jesus' use of parables to teach kingdom truths comes in the opening line of his explanation. Speaking to the disciples, he says (Mk 4:11), "To you has been given the secret of the kingdom of God, but for those outside, everything comes in parables; in order that 'they may indeed look, but not perceive, and may indeed listen, but not understand; so that they may not turn again and be forgiven.'" The parallel text in Matthew 13:10-17 elaborates this notion even further, including the specific reference to Isaiah (Is 6:9-10) about hearing without understanding and looking without seeing, followed by a seemingly exclusivist statement, "For to those who have, more will be given, and they will have an abundance; but from those who have nothing, even what they have will be taken away" (Mt 13:12).[40] Are we to conclude that Jesus used parables to confuse his message rather than to clarify it?

Not likely! Jesus spoke in parables to make his point clear—even (or maybe especially) to "simple" uneducated people. The point being made is that the Pharisees and the scribes had made up their minds about God's plan for Israel to such a degree that they were unable to "hear" and "see" God's actions in their midst. The charge was not against ignorance on the part of those not understanding. The meaning of

---

[38]Robert A. Guelich, Mark 1—8:26, Word Biblical Commentary 34A (Dallas: Word, 1989), 197: "Readily see that it makes a statement about God's eschatological activity or more specifically about the outcome of God's eschatological activity in history, an outcome that is more complex than the common Jewish expectation of a final harvest. God's eschatological activity does not consist in one grand harvest of deliverance and/or judgment."

[39]See N. T. Wright's intriguing discussion (Jesus and the Victory of God, 230-39).

[40]Luke follows the brevity of Mark.

the parables was clear enough for Jesus' opponents to realize that Jesus used parables to speak against them (Mt 21:45). The blinding effect came, not from the obscurity of the parables, but from the firmness with which Israel had misinterpreted God's plan for his people. Presuppositions had made teachers of Israel deaf and blind to God's true purpose as seen through his present work in their midst (cf. Jesus' rebuke of Nicodemus, Jn 3:10). It is indeed likely, as Edward J. Malley notes, that Jesus by his statement joins the scribes and Pharisees to the ranks of the sinners. It was a rather common notion that God withheld his revelation from sinners while revealing it to the righteous.[41]

Jeremias's suggestion, therefore, that *mēpote* (NRSV: "so that"; NIV, NASB: "otherwise") in Mark 4:12 should mean "unless" does not convince.[42] The point is specifically that their hardness hinders a change in their understanding and leaves them in darkness. Matthew's use of Psalm 78:2 as a fulfillment interpretation of this "darkness" crystallizes this point (Mt 13:34). Psalm 78 deals with Israel's early history, repeatedly reminding the singing congregation that beyond the mere events of their history, God's involvement in his people's history revealed truth about God that they too often forgot. Because of their inability to remember and their refusal to heed God's call, they walk in darkness and his plan remains hidden to them. They look without perceiving and listen without understanding. In contrast, the disciples, those who follow Jesus and recognize the presence of the kingdom, receive the revelation and understand the meaning. What should have been evident to Israel is now made plain to those who believe in the good news of the gospel.

Mark follows the parable of the sower with something that reads as much like a saying as it does a parable. He leaves out all references to the audience, giving the clear indication that this, like the explanation of the sower parable, is for the disciples rather than for the crowd. The tight connection between the sower and the light under a bushel saying may be seen in Mark's and Matthew's use of Jesus' statement about giving to those who have and taking from those who have nothing. Mark uses this statement as a summary statement of the light under a bushel saying (Mk 4:25). Matthew uses it to conclude Jesus' purpose statement on parables (Mt 13:12).[43]

If nothing else, most certainly in the case of Matthew, these usages show that the evangelist considered the revelation of God's plan to be self-evident to all those who had ears to hear. That is, people who may have been "blind sinners" but who now, as followers of Jesus, are beginning to "see," will become the true receptors of God's revelation. Those

---

[41] *The New Jerome Biblical Commentary*, 42:26. Cf. Num 12:8; 2 Esd 12:36-7; 1QS 9:17; 4:6.

[42] Joachim Jeremias, *The Parables of Jesus* (London: SCM Press, 1978), 17.

[43] Notice also the conceptual connection between light, seed and word in, for example, Ps 43:3; 119:105; Prov 6:23. Cf. Zech 14:7.

who thought themselves to be God's lightbearers will find that even the little light they had, dimmed as it was from being hid under a bushel, will be taken away. God does not hide his revelation; his purposes are made clear—but only to those who recognize the presence of his kingdom, that is, those who see what historical Israel should have seen.

The parables of the growing seed (Mk 4:26-29) and the mustard seed (Mk 4:30-32) run parallel. They both emphasize God-given growth that is not caused, influenced or directed by humans. Once planted, the seed grows without the farmer's knowing how. It happens "automatically" or "by itself," caused by God's plan for the created order. The mustard seed may seem like the smallest of all seeds, but it will grow large and spread its branches. So it is, Jesus taught, with the kingdom of God. God's kingdom will grow night and day without the farmer (Israel) understanding why. Furthermore, what Jesus and his followers were sowing at the moment may seem small and insignificant, but it will grow large and give rest and protection for the nations.[44] In other words, God's plan for his creation cannot be stopped or kept hidden—even by Israel's unwillingness to accept the gospel of God.

Mark's brief summary statement in Mark 4:33-34 only functions to strengthen this emphasis. All that Jesus taught was in the form of parables—that is, it remained incomprehensible to "the blind." Opposite these "blind" opponents of God's news, Jesus' followers received the explanation necessary to understand God's restoring presence. What Israel had expected at the return from the Babylonian exile, the gathering of God's true people and the restoration of God's kingdom in their midst, was happening now. It happened, however, in a way that was incomprehensible and unacceptable to Israel's leadership and teachers, who therefore would be left in exile without the awareness of God's blessed presence.

The kingdom parables individually and collectively proclaim the already/but not fully of God's presence. Revelation has already come; nothing is hidden—yet God's kingdom must and will grow to cover the earth and include the nations. Those who can "hear and see" will understand and be participants; those who do not will be left outside—in exile—missing the blessings that flow from God's presence. What God had been about since the beginning, throughout his history with Israel, unfolds now in their midst. What Ezekiel prophesied (Ezek 17:22ff.), in very similar language, about the sovereign restoration God is now being fulfilled.[45] Yet Israel herself does not understand.

---

[44]It may seem like an allegorical stretch to interpret "birds" as nations or Gentiles. But in light of the context Mark gives this parable, such an interpretation flows rather naturally (cf. Luke's context, Lk 13:18-19).

[45]The reference to Ezekiel 17:23 is unmistakable. God himself will plant a small shoot that will grow large enough for every kind of bird to find a dwelling place. Cf. George R. Beasley-Murray, *Jesus and the Kingdom of God* (Grand Rapids, Mich.: Eerdmans, 1987), 123.

The Story of Israel and Jesus' Miracles

To remove any doubt about the truthfulness of this parabolic teaching, Mark ends his teaching chapter with a powerful teaching crescendo. The one who explains everything to his disciples is indeed God's chosen one. With a show of power that can come only from the Creator himself, the stilling of a violent storm, the stage is set for a rebuke of those who lack faith (Mk 4:40). Although Jesus directs this rebuke toward his disciples, the Markan context forces the reader to understand this broadly. The question "Have you still no faith?" in context means "Are you still like the blind who cannot see?" What Jesus taught in parables is proven true by his miracles.

The whole question of historicity and whether one understands the miracles as factual accounts is a question that relates to one's philosophical suppositions. D. E. Nineham exhibits the problem created by modern historiography: "It is of the essence of the modern historian's method and criteria that they are applicable only to purely human phenomena, and to human phenomena of a normal, that is non-miraculous, non-unique, character. It followed that any picture of Jesus that could consistently approve itself to an historical investigator using these criteria, must, a priori, be of a purely human figure and it must be bounded by his death."[46]

Most of the suppositions of modern historians build to a smaller or larger degree on Ernst Troeltsch's historiographical principle that past experiences do not differ essentially from the present.[47] The means "by which criticism becomes possible at all is the use of analogy. The analogy to what happens before our eyes and to what happens in us is the key to our criticism."[48] Carl L. Becker affirms the principle of analogy in a similar way, "History rests on testimony, but the qualitative value of testimony is determined in the last analysis by tested and accepted experience. . . . The historian knows well that no amount of testimony is ever permitted to establish as past reality a thing that cannot be found in present reality."[49]

Wolfhart Pannenberg, however, has argued persuasively for a transposition in the understanding of the principle of analogy. Agreeing in principle with the concept of analogy, without which history cannot be evaluated or even studied, he holds that analogy can only be used positively: "That a reported event bursts analogies with otherwise usual or repeatedly attested events is still no ground for disputing its facticity. It is another matter when positive analogies

---

[46]D. E. Nineham, "Some Reflections on the Present Position with Regard to the Jesus of History," *Church Quarterly Review* 166 (January 1965): 6.

[47]Ernst Troeltsch, "Über historische und dogmatische Methode in der Theologie," in *Gesammelte Schriften, zweiter band, "Zur religiösen Lage, Religionsphilosophie und Ethik,"* ed. Ernst Troeltsch (Berlin: Scientia Verlag Aalen, 1962), 729-53.

[48]Ibid., 732; author's translation.

[49]Carl L. Becker, in *Detachment and the Writing of History: Essays and Letters of Carl L. Becker,* ed. Phil L. Snyder (Westport, Conn.: Greenwood Press, 1972), 13.

to forms of tradition (such as myths and even legends) relating to unreal objects, phenomena
referring to states of consciousness (like visions) may be found in the historical sources. In such
cases historical understanding guided by analogy can lead to a negative judgment about the
reality of the occurrences reported in the tradition."[50]

That miracles function as teaching devices and proofs, or confirmations, of kingdom presence can be observed throughout the Gospels.[51] The preaching of the kingdom of God was fleshed out in the miraculous deeds of Jesus, presenting both as
God's revelation of his presence. To relegate reports of the deeds of Jesus to a lower
level of revelatory significance than reports of the sayings of Jesus would be a serious
hermeneutical mistake.[52] Miracles validate Jesus' message. The evangelists consistently use Jesus' deeds to affirm the truth value of his teaching. It is because the presence of God's kingdom cannot be denied due to the obedience of nature, demons
and powers that Jesus' teaching has authority beyond compare. The power of restoration, the overcoming of the results of sin, proves evident in the miracle/parable
teaching of Jesus. As Jesus said to the disciples of a frustrated John the Baptist who
had become unsure if Jesus indeed was the anticipated Messiah, "Go and tell John
what you hear and see: the blind receive their sight, the lame walk, the lepers are
cleansed, the deaf hear, the dead are raised, and the poor have good news brought
to them" (Mt 11:5).

---

*The theological discussion of the relationship between narrative and teaching (**didachē**) is im-*
portant because of the narrative nature of the passages dealing with the miraculous. Conser-
vatives and liberals have gone hand in hand in their eagerness to reject the contingency of
miracles. Liberals and existentialists have argued that the biblical miracles were either liter-
ary myths or simply natural phenomena that ancient man in his naiveté experienced as mir-
acles.

The conservatives, holding to the actual intervention of God in the biblical miracles, have ar-
gued that the miracles have ceased to exist, declaring that teaching concerning the miracles

---

[50]Wolfhart Pannenberg, "Redemptive Event and History," in *Basic Questions in Theology: Collected Essays*,
trans. George H. Kehm (Philadelphia: Westminister Press, 1970), 48-49.

[51]For a concise historical summary of the interpretation of miracles, see William Lane Craig, "The Problem of Miracles: A Historical and Philosophical Perspective," in *Miracles of Jesus*, ed. David Wenham
and Craig Blomberg (Sheffield: JSOT Press, 1986), 9-48; see also Colin Brown, *Miracles and the Critical Mind* (Grand Rapids, Mich.: Eerdmans, 1984).

[52]Cf. Paul J. Achtemeier's emphasis ("The Lucan Perspective on the Miracles of Jesus: A Preliminary
Sketch," *Journal of Biblical Literature* 94 [1975]: 550) that Luke balanced Jesus' teaching with the miracles "in such a way as to give them equal weight."

cannot, and should not, be gleaned from narratives.[53] *The crux of the discussion may be best illustrated by a reference to the existential search for meaning. Traditionally, conservative scholars have been keen in their affirmation of the historical reliability of the Gospels. This has at times resulted in a minimizing of the existential quality (necessity) of Scripture, almost to the point of exclusion. Ironically, this was precisely the presuppositional mistake of the old liberal scholars of the First Quest.*[54]

   The theological problem in disregarding the existential question is, of course, that historical events can only be eternally meaningful if they are also existential. The problem historic Christianity has with the existentialists, on the other hand, is that they have so emphasized the eternality of central truths that history has lost all importance. A lack of stress on the historical foundation for Christianity will ultimately degrade the Gospels. It becomes impossible to qualify the real difference between the Christian scriptures and existential fairy tales from people like Hans Christian Andersen—or even the brothers Grimm. It is, however, the sovereign feature of the Christian religion that even its metaphysical elements are anchored in history.

   Mark's placing of the healing of the Gerasene demoniac immediately following his only sustained teaching section by Jesus, along with the flow of following events, emphasizes this understanding as well. The subtlety of Mark's storytelling can easily be missed, but it is extraordinarily profound.[55] In Mark 4:35-41, Jesus calms the stormy sea. Mark 5:1-20 tells the story of an exorcism of a legion of spirits from a demoniac.[56] These spirits confess the authoritative power of Jesus as the Son of God after which Jesus sends them into a herd of swine. Upon being demon possessed, the swine throw

---

[53]The debate has often centered on Acts and Pentecost. See Frederick Dale Bruner, *A Theology of the Holy Spirit* (Grand Rapids, Mich.: Eerdmans, 1970), and the popular book by John R. W. Stott, *The Baptism and Fullness of the Holy Spirit* (Downers Grove, Ill.: InterVarsity Press, 1964).

[54]For a survey of quests for the historical Jesus see W. G. Kümmel, *The New Testament: The History of the Investigation of Its Problems,* trans. S. Mclean Gilmour and Howard C. Kee (Nashville: Abingdon, 1972), 120ff.

[55]If *didachē* (theology) is intrinsic to Gospel narration, and if the historic nature of these narratives can be affirmed, the exegesis of such passages must be intensely influenced by this. A consistent application of the special relationship in the Gospels between history and faith (which scholars generally agree on) may require a change in the understanding of biblical miracles. The essence of evangelical understanding is not orthodoxy (a clinging to traditional interpretations), but the ratification of the authority of a correctly interpreted text. In other words, if Gospel miracle stories are theological and not just historical, their teaching is as important as narrative and epistolary texts.

[56]In relation to the historicity of exorcisms in Jesus' ministry, James D. G. Dunn says, "We need not labor the point. Jesus' reputation as a successful exorcist is as firmly established as a historical datum as we could hope for. The only obvious explanation for that reputation is that it was born of a ministry in which successful exorcisms were at least a significant part. In other words, here we certainly have what can properly be called "an indisputable fact" ("Matthew 12:28/Luke 11:20—A Word of Jesus?" in *Eschatology and the New Testament,* ed. W. H. Gloer [Peabody, Mass.: Hendrickson, 1988], 33).

themselves into the very water Jesus has just calmed. The word gets out, and great crowds now follow him. Great signs follow, and some believe, while others reject him.

The next time Mark mentions water (Mk 6:45) the sea is again stirred. What caused that? The demons? The disciples struggled with the sea, but Jesus walked on top of the stirred water (tramples on the demons?). They mistook him for a ghost, but he proved to be God's Son.[57] As he got into their boat, the wind ceased and the waters calmed. As they landed on the other side, every sick person brought to Jesus was healed.

Subtleties abound also in other areas of Mark's miracle accounts. After the healing of the demoniac who had spent his life disfellowshipped from his people, Jesus tells him to go home and let everybody know what "the Lord has done for you." This in itself is remarkable in light of Mark's repeated emphasis on Jesus' request for keeping messianic pronouncements silent. In this connection, however, the point is that everyone in Decapolis, a predominantly Gentile area, marveled when they heard his story.

Another revelatory miracle follows upon this story, and this time at the heart of Jewish faith. A synagogue leader, Jairus, whose daughter is ill, recognizes Jesus' healing powers and asks for his help. In light of the flow of Mark's Gospel, the absence of even a hint of confession or faith is conspicuous. As all the Synoptic Gospels recount the event, the daughter dies before Jesus gets there. The synagogue leadership, still blind to God's restoring presence, concludes that it is too late for Jesus to do anything. In contrast, a woman shunned from worshiping Israel's God because of a twelve-year flow of blood exhibits a faith that goes far beyond what was found in the leadership of the synagogue. Mark's sandwiching of these two stories forcefully portrays the teaching quality of Jesus' miracles. Notice the comparisons and contrasts made by Mark (see table 7.1 below).

Again, in the flow of Mark's storytelling, the bleeding woman of faith stands as a corrective to the synagogue leader, a symbol of righteous Israel, who did not understand and recognize that the power of God's kingdom was among them. This kind of blindness among worshipers in the synagogues (righteous Israel) claims even more prominence in Mark's Gospel when he lets the story of Jesus' rejection in his home synagogue follow the Jairus story. In complete ignorance, and bereft of insight into God's revelation, they disable God's power in their midst (Mk 6:5).

With storytelling finesse, Mark concludes with a compelling statement of inversion. In language parallel to repeated statements about people being amazed or awed at Jesus' miracles (Mk 1:27; 2:12; 4:41; 5:20; 5:42), Jesus is now amazed, even awed, at their unbelief (Mk 6:6). To the readers of Mark's Gospel there is no doubt: Israel

---

[57]Notice the differences between Mark's account and Matthew's more elaborated account in Matthew 14:22-33. More directly than Mark, Matthew includes details about lack of faith, worship of Jesus and confession of him as Son of God.

Table 7.1

Jarius	Bleeding Woman
Blessed man	"Cursed" woman
Prominent and well known	Common and unknown
Leader of Israel's worship	Unclean, shunned from synagogue
Daughter 12 years old	Bleeding for 12 years
Fell at Jesus' feet	Fell at Jesus' feet
Healed immediately by words	Healing immediately by touch
Jesus touched to heal	Woman touched Jesus to be healed
Private healing	Public healing
Approached from the front	Approached from behind
Father asked for his daughter	Woman asked for herself
Daughter	"Daughter"
Was told to believe	Had faith on her own
Jesus ridiculed by crowd	Jesus ridiculed by the disciples

misunderderstood and remained in sin and exile; restoration was coming to those who believed and thereby were given revelation to see the presence of God's kingdom.

Indeed, the power of restoration belonged to those who acknowledged the nearness of God's kingdom. Mark followed the story of the disabling unbelief of Nazareth with a story portraying restoration power at the disposal of the disciples. What Israel used to know by the hand of their most powerful prophets, they can now know by the hands of Jesus' disciples. Jesus gave his disciples authority to act as representatives for God's kingdom, enabling them to perform the very miracles that proved its presence. As God's Son, it was Jesus who brought the kingdom; but those who by faith accepted God's present work would experience themselves as participants in God's eschatological plan. What the prophets had proclaimed was indeed being fulfilled.

Nowhere in the Gospels is the connection between Jesus' ministry and Israel's history with God made more evident than in the miracle of the feeding of the five thousand.[58] If any doubt was still left in the readers of the Gospels, it would now be removed. The repeated emphasis on the setting as a lonely place (Mk 6:31, 33, 35) is a clear reference to the desert setting of Sinai during Israel's wilderness wandering.[59] The lack of food for throngs of people and God's miraculous power to provide it when they need it is almost repetitive of the feeding episode by manna in Sinai's desert (Ex 16:31ff.).[60] This is an eschatological feast celebrating God's renewed presence among his people. As William Lane suggests, here is even more than Moses; this event affirms afresh Isaiah's prophecy that "the Messiah will feast with men in the wilderness (Is 25:6-9)."[61] The Gospel readers should not miss that this event was for God's new people. The Gospel writers make sure to include even the detail that twelve baskets were filled with leftovers. A good measure for God's eschatological people! Again, the story of Israel is reinterpreted through a Gospel story of God's fulfillment of his plan for his people.

The Story of Israel and the Defenders of Second Temple Judaism

Following this stirring and, for the reader, convicting list of evidence for God's presence, Mark gives the strongest contrast possible. Opposite Jesus, who has just "proved" that his interpretation of God's plan is true, the Pharisees show their ignorance and misinterpretation of God's purposes. With reference to their own righteousness in following God's command—keeping the purity laws—they question the very validity of Jesus' ministry and the kingdom message. However, this only sets the stage for Jesus to use a quote from Isaiah to expose the defenders of Second Temple Judaism as fraudulent interpreters of God's revelation (Mk 7:5-8).

The scribes and Pharisees had become hypocrites, with an external appearance of piety that lacked the inner awareness of God necessary to know and interpret his work and will correctly. In Mark's narrative structure, this disclosure of Pharisaic misunderstanding of God's purpose for his people is hardly a coincidence.[62] The contrast with Jesus' miracles, which result in awe and amazement leading to worship, is passionately highlighted through Jesus' use of Isaiah—the prophet of divine presence par excellence—to show that Pharisaic worship of God was in vain (*matēn*, 'worthless'). In fact, they had turned things around to such a degree that they, the self-proclaimed "defend-

---

[58]This is the only miracle of Jesus that is recorded in all four of the Gospels: Mk 6:30-44 // Mt 14:13-21 // Lk 9:10-17 // Jn 6:1-14.

[59]Notice also the "sheep without shepherd" reference (Mk 6:34) which echoes Num 27:17.

[60]For other parallels to Israel's history, see 2 Kings 4:42-44.

[61]William L. Lane, *The Gospel of Mark,* International Commentary on the New Testament (Grand Rapids, Mich.: Eerdmans, 1974), 232.

[62]G. Salyer, "Rhetoric, Purity, and Play: Aspects of Mark 7.1-23," *Semeia* 64 (1993): 139-69. For a note on "Corban" and a possible Markan grouping of these sayings, see discussion in Ben Witherington III, *The Gospel of Mark: A Socio-Rhetorical Commentary* (Grand Rapids, Mich.: Eerdmans, 2001), 226-27.

ers of God's law," in reality were breaking God's commandments in order to keep their own rules (Mk 7:13). Editorial discussions on the radical nature of this saying notwithstanding,[63] Mark clearly uses this event as a turning point for his narrative. What has been implicitly apparent to the reader from the beginning is now stated openly. External and forensic expressions of allegiance to Second Temple Judaism had blinded God's people to his relational purpose and power in their midst.

Throughout Israel's history God had pleaded with his people to listen to his voice and look for his hand. The prophets, in the midst of their indictment of Israel, had looked for a time of a new covenant when God's law would be internalized and written on his people's hearts, enabling them to understand his purpose and plan without confusion (Jer 31:33ff.)—a new covenant time, when all God's people would be like prophets, filled with and purified by God's Spirit (Ezek 36:26-27), and enabled to hear his voice! Jesus' ministry was the evidence that God's plan for his people would be fulfilled as promised through his prophets. The defenders of Second Temple Judaism were blinded to this by their own rules, but Jesus would reveal God's kingdom to those who would believe.

Open confession of faith now takes the front seat in Mark's narrative. The Pharisees have been exposed as false interpreters of Israel's story. From now on Mark concentrates on the confession and revelation of Jesus as God's Son. The purpose of Israel's story, and the presence of God's kingdom in her midst, is revealed by Jesus and not by Israel's leadership. The few confrontations between Jesus and the Pharisees that follow (Mk 8:11; 10:2; 12:13; Sadducees in Mk 12:18) all function to reveal their ignorance and lack of insight contrasted to Jesus' wisdom and understanding.

The Story of Israel and Confessions of Jesus as the Christ

Following this discussion of external versus internal purity, a Syrophoenician woman (hence, a Gentile) exhibits a faith worthy of God's kingdom power that enables the healing of her demon-possessed daughter.[64] From here, the Gospel story moves to a healing episode that gives hearing and speech to a deaf mute. The gospel proclamation here is loud and clear: Isaiah 35:5-6 is being fulfilled.[65] The promise given to Israel by her prophet about what was to happen when the redeemed returned from exile was being fulfilled before their very eyes. The divine announcement is now evident and can be both heard and spoken. Indeed, the astonishment

---

[63]Witherington, *Gospel of Mark,* 228-30.

[64]Cf. Mt 15:21-28, where a Canaanite daughter is healed of demon possession.

[65]*"Then the eyes of the blind shall be opened, and the ears of the deaf unstopped; then the lame shall leap like a deer, and the tongue of the speechless sing for joy."* Morna Hooker notes that this is the first healing of a deaf person in the Gospel story (*The Gospel According to Mark* [Peabody, Mass.: Hendrickson, 1991], 184-85).

was beyond measure (*hyperperissōs*), and the collective conclusion was inescapable: "He has done everything well; he even makes the deaf to hear and the mute to speak" (Mk 7:37b). Contrary to Pharisaic rejection, the people rejoice in God's evident work.

William Lane's observation that Mark's eighth chapter recycles the argument he just made through his narrative stringing of Jesus episodes in chapters 6 and 7 provides even more evidence for Mark's theological purpose. Lane charts these episodes (table 7.2).[66]

Table 7.2

Mark 6:31-44	Feeding of the Multitude	Mark 8:1-9
Mark 6:45-56	Crossing of the Sea and Landing	Mark 8:10
Mark 7:1-23	Conflict with the Pharisees	Mark 8:11-13
Mark 7:24-30	Conversation About Bread	Mark 8:14-21
Mark 7:31-36	Healing	Mark 8:22-26
Mark 7:37	Confession of Faith	Mark 8:27-30

As discussed above, the feeding of the multitudes in Mark 6 manifested God's presence to Israel with clear reference to the exodus wandering. It allowed Israel to see Jesus as a prophet even greater than Moses. In Mark 8, the feeding miracle has an expanded focus. Now the miracle of God's providing presence includes Gentiles. Mark 8 contains no allusion to Moses but stresses that some came from far away (Mk 8:3)—a phrase often used in the Greek Old Testament to describe Gentile areas and in Old Testament promises of a future ingathering of the people of God from such distant lands, according to Larry Hurtado.[67] Rather than being an example of "Markan redundancy," this second and different feeding miracle[68] allows Mark another touch-point to the story of Israel that establishes God's eternal plan to bless the nations.

---

[66]Lane, *Gospel of Mark*, 269.

[67]E.g., Is 60:4, 9; Jer 46:27; and passages found only in the Greek versions of Jer 26:27 and Jer 38:10. Larry W. Hurtado, *Mark*, New International Biblical Commentary (Peabody, Mass.: Hendrickson, 1983), 122.

[68]See discussion in Robert H. Gundry, *Mark: A Commentary on His Apology for the Cross* (Grand Rapids, Mich.: Eerdmans, 1993), 398-400.

The placing of this second feeding miracle after a discussion redefining clean/unclean (Mk 7:1-23) enables Mark, once again, to show the error of the interpretation given by the defenders of Second Temple Judaism. Their inability or unwillingness to understand God's actions leads to another confrontation between Jesus and the Pharisees that gives Jesus a chance to refute their corruption and warn the disciples against becoming like them (Mk 8:11-21).

With illustrative force, Mark contrasts the stubborn "blindness" of the Pharisees with a story of a blind man who through Jesus' touch gradually gets his sight back. Striking parallels to the healing of the deaf-mute in Mark 7:32-37 aside, the details and the progressive character of the healing in Mark 8:23-25 seem powerfully parabolic in its Markan setting. Followers of Jesus may be still be "blind" or short of full understanding (cf. Mk 8:21), but their eyes will gradually be opened, and they will soon come to understand and see everything clearly *(eneblepen tēlaugōs hapanta)*. Indeed, the next episode climaxes the first half of Mark with Peter's crescendo confession, "You are the Christ!" Some may not have had their eyes opened yet—suggesting Jesus to be John the Baptist, Elijah or one of the prophets (Mk 8:27-29)—but followers of Jesus can "see" and will proclaim with interpretative force, "You are the Christ, the Son of the living God!" (Mt 16:16).

As the reader has followed the Gospel story, she or he has answered Jesus' probing question, "Who do you say that I am?" even before they "hear" Peter's conclusion. Through their reading of the *euangelion,* the good news of the gospel, they have been gradually moved from "blindness" to clear vision. Some, like the defenders of Second Temple Judaism, will not be healed from blindness, but followers of Jesus will be. God's purpose for his people will be apparent as their blindness is removed.

To clarify the meaning of the confession just given by the disciples, which they themselves clearly did not fully comprehend (Mk 8:32), the rest of the Gospel story focuses on presenting the content of Jesus' messiahship. Jesus accepted their confession proclaiming him to be the Christ (Messiah) and hence the fulfillment of God's plan for Israel. His messiahship, however, could not be understood in the framework of traditional first-century Judaism. He was different from the kind of Messiah inspired by popular Jewish belief, which had found and would continue to find outlet in various self-proclaimed messianic figures. As N. T. Wright puts it, "It was a claim to a Messiahship which redefined itself around Jesus' own Kingdom-agenda, picking several strands available within popular messianic expectation but weaving them into a striking new pattern, corresponding to none of the options canvassed by others at the time."[69]

---

[69]Wright, *Jesus and the Victory of God,* 538.

Jesus now began to teach them (Mk 8:31) with prophetic power about his passion and resurrection. The use of *dei*, "it is necessary," to explain his death and resurrection informs his statement and makes it a declaration of God's plan. When Peter objected, Jesus denounced his objection as coming from Satan and being an attempt to thwart God's plan. His objection followed the thinking of men, the traditions of the defenders of Second Temple Judaism, and had to change in order for him or anyone to see God's *necessary* plan.

There can be no question that Jesus spoke truthfully about this "necessity" of God. Peter got the confession right but missed its content. Jesus redirects their thinking in a highly controversial way, but no sooner has he refuted Peter's and all other disciples'—and for Mark, all other Gospel readers'—objection than God himself "confesses" Jesus to be the fulfillment of his plan and shows Jesus' interpretation of messiahship to be true. Mark's recounting of the events on the Mount of Transfiguration (Mk 9:2-12) at one and the same time brings the reader back to Jesus' anointing at his baptism, thereby renewing the validity of everything proclaimed thus far, and sets the stage for the disciples to understand everything that comes as the fulfillment of God's plan for Israel.

The parallelism between the first part of God's speech at the baptism and the transfiguration—*you are/this is my Son, whom I love*—breaks for the second part. Whereas the baptismal announcement—*with you I am well pleased*—has anointing and inaugurating force, the announcement at the transfiguration—*listen to him*—has affirming force and gives divine correction to Peter's objection in the preceding section. When Jesus speaks of his passion and resurrection, followers of Jesus should listen to him. God is confirming both the disciples' confession and Jesus' interpretation of God's plan for his people. The disciples (and Mark's readers) become aware beforehand that the "scandal" of the cross belongs to God's predetermined plan. Even the suffering that they themselves will come to experience belongs to God's plan, as does their following compensatory participation in glory.

The whole scene has reinterpretive power and functions as a declarative event parallel to Sinai and illustrative of eschatological fulfillment. The mountain is high and enveloped in a cloud (Ex 24:15-16; 19:9), symbolizing the power and glory of God's presence (Ex 40:34-38; Num 9:15-16; Is 4:5). Israel's story and her glorious experiences in the past, now lost in the judgment of exile, are being restored among Jesus' followers, God's new people (cf. Is 4:5). Jesus' prediction that some would see the kingdom of God come with power before their death was now being fulfilled in the experience of three disciples (Mk 9:1-2). Indeed, the disciples share their experience of Jesus' transfiguration into glory with Moses and Elijah. The Old Testament prophets of God's presence join Jesus' followers in the cloud to hear God speak. Any interpretation of God's story with Israel that ran contrary to Jesus' teaching militated against God himself and the teaching of his prophets.[70] The ultimate Word of God had been revealed, and everyone should heed God's call to "listen to him."

The Story of Israel and Jesus' Reinterpretative Teaching

After this climactic statement from God, the storyline of the Gospels presents Jesus in a series of teaching situations that collectively give a picture of God and Israel that effectively reinterprets the misinterpretations of Second Temple Judaism (Mk 9:30ff; Mt 17:22ff; Lk 9:43ff). Opposite from what they had anticipated, God's Messiah would come as a suffering servant. He would bring an end to the exile, but the forgiveness this end required would come about through the Messiah's suffering. The forces of evil that held Jerusalem captive would be defeated, and God's kingdom would be restored; but both the process and the scope of this would run against the current of the traditional teachings of contemporary Judaism. The Son of Man would be killed, but through his death he would defeat the powers of evil that held God's people in captivity, and on the third day he would rise again to proclaim victory. The disciples were left dumbfounded, unable to understand this "new" teaching (Mk 9:32; Mt 17:23b; Lk 9:45).

The series of snapshot teachings that follows radically reinterprets Israel's understanding of God. In line with his proclamation that the greatest prophet, the Messiah, must suffer and be humiliated, Jesus, now in the authoritative position of a teacher (Mk 9:35a), explains how the very structure of God's kingdom negates the common understanding of greatness and position. In God's kingdom, it is those who reveal a heart of servanthood and faith who are placed first. A child, who in antiquity was held in little regard, best exemplifies someone of position in God's kingdom. Israel wanted prominence for herself, but those who understood God's story with his people would know that God gave prominence to the humble—those who did not expect it. His kingdom would establish a new order that would be brought about by a Messiah whose character and purpose should be sought in the suffering servant motifs of Isaiah rather than in the militant notions of Second Temple Judaism (Mk 9:37).

In a radical statement on maiming, Jesus continues this reinterpretative teaching by

---

[70]Notice here the immediate correction of Peter, James and John's misunderstanding of the role of Elijah in connection with the coming of Messiah (Mk 9:11). Still caught in the web of "scribal teaching," these disciples needed to be retaught in order to understand the necessity of messianic suffering. Jesus' answer (Mk 9:13), connecting Elijah to John the Baptist, a murdered prophet (Mk 6:14ff.), stood as an incredible contrast to the traditional teaching about the heavenly Elijah who never died. A suffering Elijah who had already come and even been killed? (See contrast in *Mekilta on Ex 16:33*). Elijah proclaiming the coming of a *suffering* "Son of Man"? These disciples had understood that Jesus was God's Messiah, but until they truly listened to and understood Jesus' teaching on God's purpose and the place of Israel's story within this purpose, they would not see what God was about to do or know the power of God's kingdom (cf. the following section, Mk 9:14-29).

focusing on the relational character of God's purpose. What matters is not external cleansings but internal purity. External cleansings by themselves will cast people into eternal exile, while internal purity will bring believers into God's eternal kingdom (Mk 9:42ff.). God's kingdom will consist of those who consider a relationship with him of primary importance. Anyone (Jew or Gentile) who causes a believer (Jew or Gentile) to sin would be better off dead. It is better to be maimed on the outside than scarred on the inside. External disfigurement may cause contemporary Judaism to desocialize a person from the congregation, but internal marring caused by sin could desocialize a person from God's eternal kingdom (cf. Mt 10:28; Lk 12:4). God purposed to bring his people out of exilic judgment and into his kingdom, but those going in will be those who avoid the corruption of those blinded to Jesus' message (Mk 9:50).[71]

In his following teaching on divorce, Jesus again shows himself to be the corrective interpreter of Moses. His opponents' misunderstanding of Moses' comments on divorce exhibits, once again, their misunderstanding of God's purposes—a misunderstanding that made them turn God's prohibition into permission. Hardness of heart brings judgment and exile; submission and humility bring kingdom and presence. Indeed, the kingdom of God must be received with a childlike dependence upon God.

That this point is at the core of the Gospels' teaching becomes evidently clear from their joining of the "blessing of the children" event with the "rich young man" story. Contrary to the children, who had nothing to give in themselves, the rich young man/ruler (Mk 10:17-31 // Mt 19:16-30 // Lk 18:18-30) had everything to give. He was righteous in all the externals. Yet, unlike the children, who belonged to the kingdom, this man remained outside because he refused the very thing the kingdom required—a heart of humility that depended on God for its survival.

The force of this reinterpretative teaching about God's plan for his people was so dramatic that the disciples (along with the Gospel readers) found their own interpretative framework challenged: "Who, then, can be saved?" Jesus' teaching did not just adjust the peripherals of their learning; it restructured their understanding of God and Israel.

These brief "teaching bites" function as touch-points to Israel's story that allow the readers to understand Jesus' teaching as correctives to the errant interpretation of Israel's teachers. In God's kingdom the first shall be the last and the last the first (Mk 10:31). Those whose teaching had kept Israel in spiritual exile will be last, while those who trusted Jesus himself to be God's messiah, and his gospel to be God's message, would be the first to leave this exile and enter the promised and present kingdom.

As a fitting climax to this section, Mark recounts a healing episode in which a blind

---

[71]That is, "those who have lost their saltness." Salt's purifying qualities were well recognized. (See Lev 2:13 and Ezek 43:24 for examples of salt being sprinkled on the sacrificial flame to purify it.)

man, Bartimaeus, who had heard about Jesus and concluded that he was the Son of David, received his sight. This is Mark's only account where the messianic title Son of David occurs. The crowd rebukes the blind man for saying this, but his persistent faith in Jesus releases the power of God's kingdom. As Eduard Schweizer comments, "Only those who are like the blind man will share in the miracle of enlightenment."[72]

The Story of Israel and Their Rejection of God

No event in Jesus' life gives greater evidence of the corrective interpretation given by the Gospel story to the contemporary understandings of the story of Israel than the triumphal entry and the cleansing of the temple. Provoked by the misunderstanding of Second Temple Judaism, the triumphal entry is at one and the same time a fulfillment of prophecy (Zech 9:9) and a rejection of contemporary messianic expectations. Excited and rapturous, the crowd saw in Jesus a Davidic king restoring Israel to political power. To them, the kingdom of David and the kingdom of God were synonymous. The story of Israel was approaching the point where God would bring them out of exile—set them free from the captors.

The Gospels show such interpretation to be completely misguided, however. Instead of evidencing a proper understanding of the prophetic promise, it exhibited a complete ignorance of God's plan for Israel. Unaware of what Mark shows to be God's true purpose, Israel was about to miss the new covenant promised by their own prophets.

Mark's placing of the temple cleansing in the midst of the cursing of the fig tree story casts the whole event as an expression of God's rejection of Israel's worship. The presence of God, which had filled Solomon's temple but which had not come back to fill the Second Temple, was now about to enter through the person of Jesus. And when it did, it came with a cleansing fury that exposed Israel's worship as cursed and dead—or put differently, as remaining in exile under judgment and shunned from God's presence. In the flow of Mark's narrative, the fig tree incident gives a grim picture of God's pronouncement on Second Temple Judaism. It no longer bears fruit and has withered away to its roots. Just like Jesus looked for fruit on the fig tree but could find nothing (Mk 11:13), so also God could find no fruit in Israel's worship.

Indeed, contemporary Judaism had moved so far away from God's purpose that they could be compared to unfaithful tenants of a vineyard (Mk 12:1-12). The owner of the vineyard left his property in the hands of tenants, who violated the rights of the owner. When he sent his servants to check on the field, the tenants wounded and killed them. When finally he sent his own son, they killed him as well. They left the owner with no choice but to come and destroy the tenants and give the vineyard to

---

[72]Eduard Schweizer, *The Good News According to Mark,* trans. Donald H. Madvig (Richmond, Va.: John Knox Press, 1970), 225.

others (Mk 12:9). To the Gospel readers (and those listening to Jesus telling this parable) there could be no doubt that Israel was completely unwilling to recognize God's will and purpose, and was cursed because of it. They were, as the readers would soon learn, still killing their prophets.

This climactic reinterpretation of the very heart of Second Temple Judaism, their worship and their ability to hear God's voice and know his will, moved to new heights in confrontations with Pharisees (Mk 12:13-17), Sadducees (Mk 12:18-23) and their learned scribes (Mk 12:28-34), who all fell under the same judgment of Jesus, "Is not this the reason you are wrong, that you know neither the Scriptures nor the power of God?" As the whole leadership of corporate Jewish worship is now exposed, Jesus can give a direct reinterpretative challenge to their understanding of the story of Israel. Those who are worshiping God in truth and Spirit are those who, like the poor widow, put their whole living in God's hand (Mk 12:44). They are the ones who will experience the blessings of God's promise. Those considered blessed by Jesus' adversaries—those of position, wealth and extroverted piety—will be cursed rather than blessed.

The eschatological discourse in Mark 13 fits completely into this reinterpretation of the story of Israel's relationship with God (cf. Mt 24). Discussions on this "Little Apocalypse" aside, and various interpretative difficulties notwithstanding,[73] Mark's use of this account at this point in his discourse clearly exposes the Gospel's eschatological perspective. The temple, the pivotal center for Israel's self-understanding, would be destroyed as a part of God's eschatological plan. The eschatological purpose for God's history with Israel was not to restore the Mosaic covenant or the temple worship from the monarchial period, as Second Temple Judaism so desperately had tried to accomplish. God was not looking for a people who worship on "this or that mountain," but for those who worship "in spirit and in truth" (cf. Jn 4:21, 24). The promise of the exilic and postexilic prophets would soon come to fulfillment. God's Spirit would be poured out upon all true believers, and the Son of Man would show his glory and power. Faithless Israel will remain in spiritual exile, while faithful followers of Jesus, the true believers in God's eschatological purpose, will be restored and saved.

The Second Temple misinterpretation of Israel's story resulted, as Mark's narrative explains it, in grotesque situations. Opening his fourteenth chapter with an unmistakable anointing of Jesus as God's suffering servant (Mk 14:8; cf. Mt 26:6-13), Mark shows how the leading Jews were now actively plotting to remove God's anointed one from their midst. Not only that, but they were asking Rome to help

---

[73]For a survey of interpretations on this chapter, see George R. Beasley-Murray, *Jesus and the Last Days: The Interpretation of the Olivet Discourse* (Peabody, Mass.: Hendrickson, 1993), 32-79.

them do it. In the words of Stephen (Acts 7:39), "in their hearts they had turned back to Egypt." Or to put it differently, they were asking "Babylon" for help to "keep them in exile." They were actively and effectively rejecting Israel's God. Rather than serving God, they turned themselves into servants of Caesar, who by means of crucifixion proclaimed Rome's sovereignty to the entire world.[74] Contrary to God's purposes, as promised by the prophets and revealed by Jesus, to bring an end to the exile through a renewal of the covenant by an outpouring of the Spirit, Jesus' challengers solidified their place in the exile by rejecting God's power and affirming Caesar's.

The Story of Israel and the Restoration of God

Like a crescendo to the Gospels' interpretation of the story of Israel, Jesus' resurrection proclaims the victory of God. It establishes Jesus' teaching on the presence of God's kingdom as true, and it verifies the defeat of the enemies of God's eschatological purposes. As far as the Gospels' interpretation of God's purposes is concerned, the story of Israel had come to its point of fulfillment. God's eternal purpose of using Israel as a hinge to open the door for his salvation to all nations had been accomplished. God's people were now free to return from their exile.

That YHWH's presence returns means that the exile is over. Evil is defeated, sins are forgiven, God's reign is restored, and his glory is returning to his temple. Zion is being restored—not in terms of narrow geography, but in terms of the restoration of YHWH's presence and power on the earth. The valley of the dead bones is coming back to life (Ezek 37); God's Spirit is poured out upon people who trust in the message and deeds of his Son. Such believers are now the living evidence of God's eschatological purposes and of his restoring power that calls his creation together from all nations of the earth under his kingship.

Supplemental Readings in New Dictionary of Biblical Theology

D. A. Hagner, "Synoptic Gospels," 127-29.
D. L. Bock, "Luke-Acts," 129-31.
D. A. Hagner, "Matthew," 262-66.
C. A. Evans, "Mark," 267-73.
D. L. Bock, "Luke," 273-80.
I. H. Marshal, "Jesus Christ," 592-602.
G. Goldsworthy, "Kingdom of God," 615-20.
K. E. Brower, "Eschatology," 459-64.

---

[74]See Wright, *Victory of God*, 543.

Study Questions

1. What was Jesus' main message?

2. How does Jesus' main message relate to the story of Israel?

3. How does the Gospel story explain God's eschatological purposes for Israel?

4. What is the significance of Jesus' sending of the seventy disciples?

5. How does the Gospel story portray the leadership of Second Temple Judaism?

6. Explain Mark's sandwiching of the withering fig tree and the cleansing of the temple.

7. In terms of the "exile" motif, how does the Gospel story portray the significance of Jesus' message and deeds? How does the Gospel story understand "restoration"?

8

JOHN

Signs of the Restoration

First and foremost, the Gospel of John, like the Synoptics, is the story of Jesus. The Jesus story overshadows and overwhelms all other themes, but it is not a change of stories. For John, the story of Israel is the interpretive grid for his understanding of Jesus. As N. T. Wright put it:

> This is the story of Jesus *told* as the true, and redeeming, story of Israel, *told* as the true, and redeeming, story of the creator and the cosmos. John's gospel … tells the recognizably Jewish story of Israel and the world, but, like Paul and the synoptics … draws the eye on to Jesus as the fulfillment, and hence the subversion, of that story.[1]

A separate chapter on the Gospel of John is not meant to imply that John stands apart from the other Gospels in his use of the story of Israel. In many ways, John presents the same story, although he often used different events or sayings to tell it. We will first look at the way John tells his story, his narrative structure. Then we will look at the major themes John shares with the Synoptic Gospels by reviewing the major conclusions of the previous chapter, this time citing stories from John. The commonality between the Synoptics and John arises from the shared story of Jesus. Finally, after seeing John's continuity with the Synoptics, we will look at some uniquely Johannine emphases and how these fit in the story of Israel.

The Narrative Structure of John

The Gospel of John is composed of four distinct parts: the Prologue (Jn 1:1-18); the Book of Signs (Jn 1:19—12); John's version of the Passion Narrative (Jn 13—20); and the Epilogue (Jn 21).[2] It appears that John had a source (perhaps material he himself

---

[1]N. T. Wright, *The New Testament and the People of God* (Minneapolis: Fortress, 1992), 416-17.

[2]John has woven the material together so tightly that it is not clear if the Signs Source ended with John 11 or John 12. Scholars of the last century sought underlying sources as an attempt to get closer to the "authentic story." We do not consider the Gospel of John to be secondary to its sources. Rather, we are merely identifying blocks of preformed material. Nevertheless, not all scholars see distinct sources or see any reason to discuss them; see for example, Wright, *People of God,* 411, n. 134.

had written[3]) that described the "signs" Jesus did.[4] John also had an account of the passion (the last week of Jesus' earthly ministry) that was no doubt formed from years of retelling. As the end of his life neared, John wanted to prepare a written account: "Now Jesus did many other signs in the presence of his disciples, which are not written in this book. But these things are written so that you may come to believe that Jesus is the Messiah, the Son of God, and that through believing you may have life in his name" (Jn 20:30-31).

John took the material from the Signs Source and joined it with his story of the passion. He composed the prologue to highlight themes he intended to develop throughout this new Gospel, and then he wrote a resurrection account that connected back to the prologue.[5] The themes highlighted in the prologue were woven across the entire original draft of the Gospel (Jn 1—20). After John's death, his disciples published the Gospel. As part of the publication process, they wrote and appended John 21 as an epilogue. John 21 has two stories that they had heard many times from John, their teacher (see Jn 21:25). These stories were added to clarify both the death of John and John's relationship with Peter, two problems that had arisen after John's death. The Epilogue ends with a validation subscription (Jn 21:24-25).

A writing process using a large block of preformed material produces several telltale signs. The themes introduced in the prologue appear in the background of some stories, in several added comments throughout the Gospel, and again in chapter 20. These overarching themes, however, are not underscored in every individual episode in the Gospel. It is to be expected that the major themes would appear throughout but not in every place. On the other hand, the Signs Source originally had some of its own themes and motifs. These run throughout the stories of John 2—12, but are not significant in the Passion Narrative. For example, the Prologue describes Jesus as the Light. The story of Nicodemus (Jn 3) is part of a "witness" motif that runs through

---

[3]The material is consistent with John but has some interesting peculiarities. For example, love is not a dominant theme, Judea rather than Galilee takes a major role, and there seems to be a deep familiarity with the temple cultus.

[4]Scholars generally agree that John identifies six signs. Köstenberger sees a preformed "signs" document and presents a compelling case for the temple cleansing as a sign, making the raising of Lazarus the seventh and greatest sign. See Andreas Köstenberger, *The Missions of Jesus and the Disciples According to the Fourth Gospel* (Grand Rapids, Mich.: Eerdmans, 1998), 60-71.

[5]Parallels between the prologue and John 20 are, for example: (a) "light overcomes the darkness of the early morning," (b) "Jesus gives the right to share his status: 'I am ascending to my Father *and your Father*, to my God *and your God*'" (Jn 20:17), and (c) Thomas repeats the affirmation of John by announcing Jesus as "My Lord and My God" (Jn 20:28) (Wright, *People of God*, 417, and in Wright, *The Resurrection of the Son of God* [Minneapolis: Fortress, 2003], 667-75). Thomas's wording "my Lord and my God" also accomplishes a secondary purpose for John: he repeats the title ascribed to Caesar but directs it solely to Christ. John is seeking to encourage his readers to stand firm in the face of mounting pressure from the imperial cult.

the Signs Source; however, John adds the comment that Nicodemus visited Jesus at night (Jn 3:2), an insignificant part of the Nicodemus story, but a part of the "Light" motif John is weaving across the whole Gospel. John paints a picture of Nicodemus coming out of the darkness to Jesus the Light—a point not made in the actual Nicodemus story. Then "light" shows up in scattered comments throughout the Signs Source: Nicodemus comes at night (Jn 3:2); judgment comes to those who love darkness rather than light (Jn 3:19); Jesus announces in the temple that he is the light of the world (Jn 8:12); Jesus heals the man born blind (Jn 9); and finally, Jesus announces in the temple that the light is with them only a little longer (Jn 12:35-36). Later, when Judas leaves the Last Supper in order to betray Jesus, John adds the observation "and it was night" (Jn 13:30). While this is an insignificant part of the Last Supper story, John is painting a picture of Judas leaving Jesus the Light to go into the darkness, in contrast to Nicodemus.

Aside from the reference in the betrayal of Judas, the Passion Narrative is missing the Light theme, even though there were several good opportunities: the arrest in the garden at night, Peter's denials at night, Annas (mentioned only by John) questioning Jesus at night, and the omission of the story of the sun going dark during the crucifixion.[6] The Light motif is picked up again in John 20. Mary goes to the tomb while it is still dark (Jn 20:1) but as light dawns. When Jesus visits the disciples for the first time after the resurrection, it is evening and they are huddled in a locked room, afraid (Jn 20:19).

We see therefore that John wove his material into a tightly knit narrative, adding themes to reach across all sections, but he did not necessarily weave all his themes into every section. Thus, Jesus as the paschal lamb shows up in John 1 and again in John 19, but not in between. This paschal lamb theme was introduced when John wrote the Gospel. He did not bother to weave it into the individual stories of the signs material. John also did not delete original thematic material, for instance, from the Signs Source. Its independent themes were left to enrich further the Gospel story.

We saw in the Synoptics that themes often ran across multiple stories: Jesus calmed the stormy sea and walked on the water. Jesus then calmed the stormy, demon-possessed man and then cast the demons into the water (symbolically under his feet). In John, the Signs Source has several themes of its own that remained intact when woven into the completed Gospel. There is the obvious theme of signs indicating who Jesus is. The miracle in Cana was "the first of his signs" (Jn 2:11). The "signs that Jesus did" are also acknowledged by seekers (Jn 3:2; 4:48; 9:16; 10:41), disciples (Jn 6:14; 20:30), crowds (Jn 2:23; 6:2, 14; 7:31; 12:18, 37) and opponents (Jn 11:47). John also

---

[6] It is possible that John is making the very subtle point of the overtaking darkness of the passion by not mentioning the light, but it is then very subtle.

mentions requests for a "sign" by the crowd (Jn 6:30) and by his opponents (Jn 2:18). But signs are not the only themes that run through this material. Two other themes that illustrate this trait are "water" and "witness."

The Signs Source shows a persistent theme of water: John baptizes with water (Jn 1:26); water is turned to wine (Jn 2:9); Nicodemus must be born of water and the Spirit (Jn 3:5); the Samaritan woman comes to draw water and Jesus offers another kind (Jn 4:10); a man is healed by Jesus rather than by the stirring of the water (Jn 5:7-8); Jesus walks on the water (Jn 6:19); Jesus offers living water in the temple (Jn 7:38); Jesus spits and makes mud, and the man washes in a pool to be healed (Jn 9:6-7). Finally, the motif fades away in John 10-12 with only a reference to Jesus crossing the Jordan (Jn 10:40).

The prologue (Jn 1:7, 8, 15) introduces the theme of witnessing (*martyreō*) and testimonies (*martyria*). After the temple incident in John 2, "many believed in his name because they saw the signs that he was doing" (Jn 2:23). John then adds that Jesus did not need witnesses/testimonies. In John 2:24, John states that Jesus did not need anyone to testify (*martyreō*) about man (*anthrōpos*) because he knew the heart of man (*anthrōpos*). Then in the next verse we are told that a man (*anthrōpos*) of the Pharisees named Nicodemus comes. Yet Jesus knows his heart and does not need his testimony. In John 4, Jesus knows another's heart, and yet the Samaritan woman is introduced as the positive antithesis of Nicodemus: a female, Samaritan, low status, immoral, needy, but believing, in contrast to the male, Jewish, ruler, Pharisee, teacher, but still unbelieving (in the story).[7] Jesus does not need Nicodemus's testimony (Jn 7:50-52). The Samaritan woman testifies about Jesus and many come, but Jesus also does not need her testimony (Jn 4:42). In John 5, a man is miraculously healed, but Jesus does not need his testimony (5:15-17). Later in John 5, Jesus does not need the testimony of the Baptist (Jn 5:31-34). In John 6, the crowd witnesses the miraculous multiplication of bread and fish, but Jesus does not need their testimony (Jn 6:14). In John 7, the witness motif builds in volume, with multiple groups bearing witness about Jesus (his family, the Pharisees, various groups in the crowd, the temple police and Nicodemus). John tells the story in such a way that the testimony of each is immediately disproved. The crowd testifies that no one was trying to kill Jesus (Jn 7:20); yet others then testify to the contrary (Jn 7:25). The crowd testifies that Jesus cannot be the Messiah because no one will know where the Messiah comes from (Jn 7:27). Then the leaders reject Jesus because they know the Messiah must come from Bethlehem (Jn 7:42). The issue

---

[7] In the previous chapter, we saw that in Mark's story of Jairus's daughter and the bleeding woman, the supposedly unclean woman stood as a corrective to the supposedly clean synagogue leader. She had the faith and recognized God at work. John makes the same contrast with Nicodemus and the Samaritan woman.

of testimonies reaches a crescendo in the controversy over Jesus testifying about himself (Jn 8:12-59) and the testimonies of the man born blind, his parents, and the Jewish leaders (Jn 9). Throughout the Signs Source, the point is made that Jesus does not need any of their testimonies, and yet testimonies keep piling up. The testimony motif peaks in the Lazarus story when the Jewish leaders sought to silence the testimony of Lazarus (Jn 12:9-11) and ultimately the testimony of Jesus himself (Jn 11:53).

These themes, original to the Signs Source, add to the beauty of the Gospel but are not the overarching theme that John intended when he wrote his story of Jesus. When the Gospel was formed by John, any themes from the Signs Source (or from his original story of the passion) are subsumed. John, like the Synoptics, interpreted Jesus' words and deeds against the backdrop of the story of Israel.

The Story of Israel: Shared Themes from the Synoptic Gospels and John

Like the Synoptics, John saw Jesus as the true story of Israel.[8] This shared understanding is revealed in the repetition of themes in both the Synoptics and John. Although John's Gospel stands quite apart from the Synoptics in the way the Jesus story is told, shared themes arising from the story of Israel can be seen in John as well. A brief review of the major themes outlined in the previous chapter will show how John shares the same viewpoint even though he is making his point with a different story (and sometimes with a distinctly Johannine twist).

The history of Israel and the Gospel genealogies. As discussed in the previous chapter, genealogies connect Jesus to the history of Israel (Matthew/Luke) and ultimately to all of creation (Luke) as part of God's *heilsgeschichtliche* (salvation-history) work. John has a very different type of genealogy, announcing that "in the beginning was the Word" (Jn 1:1), rooting Jesus as the author and sustainer of *Heilsgeschichte* (God's saving actions in history). For John the Jesus story starts with the creation. John brings creation language to the Jesus event through his word choice in the prologue ("In the beginning"), which connects God's creative actions in the world with his actions in sending Christ: "He was in the world, and the world came into being through him; yet the world did not know him. He came to what was his own, and his own people did not accept him" (Jn 1:10-11).

What the Creator has and is doing in the world (*kosmos*) has become focused to the point of what Jesus is doing in Israel. The activities of Jesus in Palestine have *cosmic* repercussions. It is the culmination of God's saving activity, stretching back through Israel's history, through Abraham, back to creation itself.

John the Baptist and the story of Israel. The work of the Baptist is the "obvious fulfillment" (in the Synoptics) of Isaiah 40. The Fourth Gospel carries this same theme,

---

[8]Wright, *People of God,* 416-17.

using the Baptist as the link between the Old Testament story of Israel and the ministry of Jesus and again showing that God is active in the history of his people.

The presence of God's kingdom. The previous chapter demonstrated that in the Synoptic Gospels, the kingdom is here now. This position was carefully delineated in the previous chapter because a surface reading of the Synoptics can leave an impression of only a future (coming) kingdom. The Gospel of John, however, speaks clearly of the presence of the kingdom *now*. Often scholars speak of John's "realized eschatology," meaning that John often describes believers as presently experiencing (currently realizing) blessings that were expected in the future age, the eschaton.[9]

Jesus' hearers were to "repent and believe" in order to *enter* the kingdom now, not in order to *prepare* for a coming kingdom.[10] There is no call for disciples to prepare the way. Thus Jesus tells Nicodemus, "No one can enter the kingdom of God without being born of water and Spirit" (Jn 3:5). One's belief about Christ in this life produces results normally expected at the eschaton: "Those who believe in him are not condemned; but those who do not believe are condemned already" (Jn 3:18). Eternal condemnation is usually the result of a decision made at the Last Judgment, but John tells us that "this is the judgment, that the light has come into the world, and people loved darkness rather than light" (Jn 3:19).

Nevertheless, John is not presenting the judgment as fully realized in this present age. There is an eschatological (end of time) dimension as well. In a passage stressing the present aspect of judgment, Jesus says, "The hour is coming, *and is now here,* when the dead will hear the voice of the Son of God, and those who hear will live" (Jn 5:25). We find also a clear reference to the eschaton: "The hour is coming when all who are in their graves will hear his voice and will come out—those who have done good, to the resurrection of life, and those who have done evil, to the resurrection of condemnation" (Jn 5:28-29). As in the Synoptics, the kingdom is described by John as both present and future.[11]

---

[9]For example, eschatological feasting (Jn 2:7), life in the kingdom (Jn 3:5-6), judgment (Jn 3:18), no longer thirsting (Jn 4:14), and freedom from death (Jn 6:50; 11:26). This term "realized eschatology" is used only in this general sense and is not meant to imply the over-realized theology of C. H. Dodd. Jesus clearly understood his words to have a present and a future dimension. For example, he promises those who eat of this bread will not die but will live forever (Jn 6:50-51) but then immediately says, "and I will raise them up on the last day" (Jn 6:54).

[10]John does speak of the kingdom. His more customary term is "eternal life." By life, John means "life in the kingdom" as seen in John 17:3, "This is eternal life, that they may know you, the only true God, and Jesus Christ whom you have sent." This is the language of the restoration. See the discussion of the kingdom in John in C. C. Caragounis, "Kingdom of God/Heaven," in *Dictionary of Jesus and the Gospels,* ed. J. B. Green, Scot McKnight and I. H. Marshall (Downers Grove, Ill.: InterVarsity Press, 1992), 429.

[11]Luke tells of Jesus' experience in Nazareth, where he reads from Isaiah 61 and announces, "Today this scripture has been fulfilled in your hearing" (Lk 4:21).

The story of Israel and Jesus' disciples. E. P. Sanders noted that Jesus' use of twelve disciples was a symbol of "restoration."[12] Wright adds that Jesus' calling of the Twelve was a call to be part of "remnant-theology," a "return-from-exile theology," a sign that God was restoring his people.[13] The Synoptics make much use of the theme of the twelve disciples. As demonstrated in the previous chapter, this theme is not about the number of actual disciples, but rather to connect them with the story of Israel. John, however, does not use the symbolism of twelve disciples in his Gospel (although he will make use of this symbol in the Revelation). John speaks frequently of the disciples, but he leaves them unnumbered, giving each hearer the impression that he or she too could be counted among them. "Twelve" baskets of leftover bread (Jn 6:13) do not produce faithful followers (Jn 6:66). When John mentions the Twelve, it is usually not an image of completeness or faithfulness. Jesus states, "Did I not choose you, the twelve?" (Jn 6:70). Then he immediately adds a comment indicating that they were not complete, "Yet one of you is a devil" (Jn 6:70). John then further elaborates this connection, "He was speaking of Judas son of Simon Iscariot, for he, *though one of the twelve,* was going to betray him" (Jn 6:71).

At the cross where the Twelve are conspicuously missing (except John), we are told of the brave actions of "Joseph of Arimathea, who was a disciple of Jesus" (Jn 19:38). The first resurrection appearance is to Mary of Magadala, not one of the Twelve. Later that day, Jesus appears to "the disciples" (Jn 20:19). John avoids numbering the disciples, for he wants his readers to join the group. John specifically mentions the Twelve, but does so by indicating that not all were witnesses to the resurrection, for Thomas was missing (Jn 20:24). When Thomas is present the next week, the group is again called only "his disciples" (Jn 20:26), leaving room for others. The story then ends with a special blessing announced upon those who were *not* one of the Twelve, "Blessed are those who have not seen and yet have come to believe" (Jn 20:29). For John, "disciples" were all those willing to believe and be witnesses.[14]

The Synoptics emphasize the lack of disciples from the Sanhedrin, Pharisees or Sadducees. John likewise shares this emphasis. Nicodemus is specifically called a leader (Jn 3:1) and teacher (Jn 3:10), but as we saw, he is used by John as an example of how Jesus does not need the testimony and assistance of these people. As in the Synoptics, God himself will teach his people. The Samaritan woman asserted that when the Messiah came, he would teach them, and Jesus announces that he is the one (Jn 4:25-26). God is present and working among his people. Unlike the Synoptic empha-

---

[12]E. P. Sanders, *Jesus and Judaism* (Philadelphia: Fortress, 1985), 98.
[13]N. T. Wright, *Jesus and the Victory of God* (Minneapolis: Fortress, 1997), 430-31.
[14]At the time his Gospel was published, the role of the Twelve was a moot issue. Apostolic authority had given way to the next generation of disciples. It was better for John's audience to minimize the role of the Twelve and to broaden the general understanding of "disciple."

sis, John is stressing that God himself (Jesus) is leading his people directly.

The story of Israel and the sending of the seventy. The previous chapter described how the "sending of the seventy" was symbolic of reaching the nations. The Synoptics have a clear theme of the gospel reaching outside the nation of Israel. John shares this emphasis, although he does not recount the sending of the seventy. As just seen, the Synoptics emphasize the Twelve as leading the way and teaching the people, while John stresses Jesus leading the way and teaching the people. In the Synoptics, the seventy symbolize the disciples of Jesus reaching out to the nations. In John, it is Jesus himself. The Son was sent into the *world* (Jn 3:17) and will draw *all people* to himself (Jn 12:32). To illustrate this irresistible draw, John tells us that some Greeks, representing the nations, suddenly appeared and said, "We wish to see Jesus" (Jn 12:21).

The story of Israel and Jesus' miracles. We saw that in Mark the miracles function as dramatized parables on the kingdom; they validate Jesus' message. John makes this connection more explicit. He does not refer to these actions as "miracles" or "wonders"; rather, he calls them "signs." As modern readers we have grown up with this nomenclature, and now in Christian terminology, "sign" is a synonym for "miracle." "Signs and wonders" is a common English expression indicating the same thing. We picked this up from John's Gospel. He does mean "miracle," but we should not miss his point. In John's day, a "sign" (*sēmeion*) meant what we mean by a road *sign*, a door *sign*, a store *sign*. It points to something else. These "miracles" were *signs* of who Jesus is. However, just as parables did not always result in genuine faith in the Synoptics (Mt 13:10-17), so also in John, signs did not always produce disciples, as seen in his expansion, in chapter 6, of the story of the bread and fishes. Jesus said (Jn 6:26) the crowd did not seek him because they saw a "sign" (the miraculous multiplication of bread) but because they ate their fill (from the miraculous multiplication of bread). Were these not the same event? Yes, but the crowd only saw a miracle; they did not see the miracle as a *sign* pointing out who Jesus was. Therefore, when they found his teaching difficult (Jn 6:60), they no longer followed him (Jn 6:66).

The defenders of Second Temple Judaism. In the Synoptics, the Pharisees and scribes had made up their minds about God's plan for Israel, so they could not "hear" and "see" God at work in their midst. Thus in the Synoptics, parables meant outsiders could look but not see, hear but not understand. Likewise in John, the Jewish leadership could not understand Jesus (Jn 3:10-12) and were "blind" to his saving actions (Jn 9:40-41). Mark's parables of the growing seed (Jn 4:26-29) and the mustard seed (Jn 4:30-32) lead to his conclusion that Israel's leadership was unwilling and thus unable to "see" what Jesus was doing and remained "blind" to the kingdom of God and therefore were left in exile apart from the presence of God (Jn 4:33-34). John makes this same point in his story of the man born blind. The healed man grows in his awareness of who Jesus is: at first he does "not know" who Jesus is (Jn 9:12), then he declares Jesus "a prophet" (Jn 9:17) and "from God" (Jn 9:33), then he "sees" Jesus (Jn 9:37) and pronounces him "Lord" (Jn 9:38); whereas the Pharisees grow more blind to who Jesus is: they declare that he is "not from God" (Jn 9:16) and that he "is a sinner" (Jn 9:24); they announce "we do not know where he comes from" (Jn 9:29), so they are "blind" (Jn 9:39) and Jesus pronounces them "sinners" (Jn 9:41). The healed man *sees* the Lord (Jn 9:37-38), the quintessential form of the Deuteronomic blessing of having God in their midst (Moses sees the Lord, Ex 33:20-23), whereas the Jewish leaders remain in sin (Jn 9:41), which in Deuteronomic law means being put outside the community (Deut 13:1-5). By attempting to get the man born blind to deny the miracle, these leaders were "misleading a blind man" and under the Deuteronomic curse (Deut 27:18), which has as its punishment "madness, blindness, and confusion of mind; you will grope about at noon as blind people grope in darkness, but you shall be unable to find your way" (Deut 28:28-29). Thus, these leaders became blind and unable to find the Way, that is, Jesus, according to John (Jn 14:6). Ancient Israel was held accountable with the blessings and curses of Deuteronomy 28 because they had "seen all the LORD did before [their] eyes" (Deut 29:2). In the same way in John, these leaders were accountable because they saw (and did not deny) the miracle, but failed to see the "sign."

The story of Israel and confessions of Jesus as the Christ. John continues the Synoptic emphasis on the clear proclamation of faith. As the Syrophoenician woman expressed clear faith (Mk 7:24-30), so also does the Samaritan woman (Jn 4:29). In Mark (Mk 8:23-25), a blind man gradually is able to see, symbolizing how the disciples gradually came to see who Jesus was. So also in John, the man born blind, although immediately given physical sight, gradually came to see who Jesus was. In Mark's story (Mk 8:27-29), some disciples did not "see" who Jesus was (some thought he was Elijah or one of the prophets); yet Peter believed. So also in John's story, some did not believe, while one did (Jn 9:34-39).

Jesus' reinterpretation of the kingdom. The Synoptics use a series of short parables and teaching segments to describe how God's kingdom negates the world's understanding of greatness, position and authority (e.g., Mk 9:33-40). Mark summarizes, "Whoever wants to be first must be last of all and servant of all." John drives this point home powerfully, telling how Jesus washed the feet of his disciples. This enacted parable is then explicitly explained, "So if I, your Lord and Teacher, have washed your feet, you also ought to wash one another's feet" (Jn 13:14). This servant motif is then immediately tied to suffering: "The one who ate my bread has lifted his heel against me" (Jn 13:18), thus continuing the Synoptic tradition of connecting messiahship to the suffering servant of Isaiah rather than to the militant Davidic image of Second Temple Judaism.

In both the Synoptics and John, the triumphal entry symbolized the fulfillment of prophecy (Zech 9:9), Jesus' public announcement of his messiahship (Jn 12:13) and his rejection of the contemporary militaristic messianic expectations. John adds to this image by describing Jesus as "anointed" before his entry into Jerusalem (Jn 12:1-8) but not anointed by the Jewish leadership. Yet the leadership indirectly acknowledged his anointing, "Look, the world has gone after him" (Jn 12:19), a point then demonstrated by the Greeks wanting to see Jesus (Jn 12:21). Yet as in the Synoptics, ultimately Second Temple Judaism rejected Christ. John describes the final sign, raising Lazarus from the dead (Jn 11:38-44). The leaders see and acknowledge the *miracle* but reject the *sign* (Jn 11:47). They reject Jesus, who raised Lazarus from death, by planning his death (Jn 11:53), and they even seek to destroy evidence of the sign by killing Lazarus (Jn 12:9-11). God's people were still killing their prophets. John's story of the public ministry of Jesus ends on this note. In the chapters that follow (Jn 13—19), John tells the passion story of Christ.

The Story of Israel and John's Story of Jesus

As we have seen, John shares many themes with the Synoptics; however, he also brings his own uniqueness to the discussion. John has one overriding purpose in writing his Gospel: *to share that God himself was finally redeeming Israel from her exile.*

John concludes his story, "But these are written so that you may come to believe that Jesus is the Messiah, the Son of God, and that through believing you may have life in his name" (Jn 20:31). John's purpose is not merely to recount the life of a significant figure of his time; he is not writing biography. Rather, John wants to engender faith in his hearers. The events John chooses to recount are to convince his audience that God had returned to restore his people from exile. Jesus not only announced that the exile was ending but that he himself was to bring this about.[15] To do this, John demonstrates that in Jesus, God was again living among his people, that God was working to restore them from exile, and that Jesus was the Messiah who would bring this about.

Jesus announces the arrival of the kingdom, demonstrating the return from exile and the return of Yahweh to Zion.[16] In Christ, God has returned to dwell among his people. John shows this in two ways: first, Jesus is portrayed in Old Testament Wisdom language; and second, Jesus is shown in John to be exercising divine rights and actions.

God (Wisdom) "tabernacled" amidst his people. In Jewish writings, Wisdom described herself as having "[come] forth from the mouth of the Most High" (Sir 24:3) and made her abode among men. She pitched her tent among the Jewish people:

> My Creator chose the place for my tent (tabernacle, *skēnē*)
> He said, "Make your dwelling in Jacob" (Sir 24:8).

---

[15]Wright, *Victory of God,* 126-27.
[16]Ibid., 481.

In the holy tent (tabernacle, *skēnē*) I ministered before him
And so I was established in Zion. (Sir 24:10)

John tells us that the "Word" was made flesh and "tabernacled" (*eskēnōsen*) among us (Jn 1:14). John's use of a wisdom motif has elsewhere been clearly demonstrated[17] and does not need to be reargued here. Instead, we will briefly outline the way Wisdom was treated in Jewish writings before John and then demonstrate that John was quite familiar with Jewish Wisdom literature but that he stands apart from this material in several ways.

For most readers of Scripture, our first clear encounter with Wisdom is Proverbs 8, where Wisdom is personified as a woman calling out to all who will hear, encouraging them to seek the path of wisdom (Prov 8:1-5). Yet Wisdom is further described as being the first thing created and as having been present at the rest of creation: "The LORD created me at the beginning of his work, the first of his acts of long ago. . . . When he established the heavens, I was there . . . when he marked out the foundations of the earth, then I was beside him, like a master worker" (Prov 8:22-30). From this tradition, three subsidiary themes arose in later Jewish writings: (1) Wisdom as the firstfruit and hence supreme over creation; (2) Wisdom as an agent of God in creation; and (3) the quest for Wisdom to find a "home" among creation.

Since Proverbs 8 describes Wisdom as first among God's creative acts, it is connected to the first creative act described in Genesis 1, "And God *said,* 'Let there be light.'" Thus, Wisdom is described as coming forth from the mouth of God.[18] This position as firstborn carried rights of inheritance over creation. Thus, Wisdom is described as ruling over creation:

I dwelt in the highest heavens . . .
Alone I compassed the vault of heaven . . .
Over all the earth, and over every people and nation
I held sway. (Sir 24:4-6)

The image of Wisdom working beside the Creator (Prov 8:27-30) was developed by later Jewish writers to where she becomes the agent of God in creation. Solomon (in the apocryphal Wisdom of Solomon[19]) declares, "for Wisdom, the fashioner of all things, taught me" (Wis 7:22) and "O God . . . who have made all things by your word,

---

[17]For a concise presentation, see Marvin Pate, *Communities of the Last Days: The Dead Sea Scrolls, the New Testament and the Story of Israel* (Downers Grove, Ill.: InterVarsity Press, 2000), 226-29, or Wright, *People of God,* 413-16.

[18]Ancient near eastern "wisdom" was connected primarily with speech; a wise man demonstrates his wisdom by what he says. Thus, wisdom comes out of the mouth of the wise man.

[19]This work was written in Greek by a Hellenized Jew, most likely living in Alexandria, Egypt. It was written at about the same time as the New Testament.

and by your wisdom have formed humankind" (Wis 9:1-2).

One of the more unusual developments in Wisdom literature was the theme of Wisdom seeking a home. In the apocryphal *The Wisdom of Jesus, Son of Sirach*[20] Wisdom is given a home by the Creator. Wisdom found her home among the Jewish people, perhaps dwelling in the temple itself:

> Thus in the beloved city he gave me a resting place,
> And in Jerusalem was my domain. (Sir 24:11)

In a later Jewish writing, *1 Enoch*,[21] Wisdom does *not* find a place to dwell among men:

> Wisdom could not find a place in which she could dwell;
> But a place was found (for her) in the heavens.
> Then Wisdom went out to dwell with the children of the people,
> But she found no dwelling place.
> So Wisdom returned to her place
> And she settled permanently among the angels. (*1 En* 42:1-2)

This section of *1 Enoch* dates to the first Christian century. It is possible that the destruction of the temple in A.D. 70 caused the writer to describe Wisdom as not finding a home here, instead returning to the heavenlies.

It is quite clear that John and his readers were familiar with these more popular traditions about Wisdom. John draws parallels between his telling of the Jesus story and popular Wisdom literature. James Dunn argues that John is presenting Christ as the Wisdom of God rather than Torah as the Wisdom of God. John cites critical parallels to the Wisdom material, but in each case he demonstrates that it is Jesus who actually is the true manifestation of the Wisdom of God. These contrasts show up most clearly in two places: the Prologue (Jn 1:1-18) and the "I AM" sayings.[22]

Craig Evans has shown that the Prologue to the Gospel of John describes Jesus in figurative terms that are strikingly parallel to the way "Wisdom" is described (see table 8.1).[23]

---

[20]This title is the Greek rendering of the Hebrew: Joshua ben Sira. This work is often cited as *Sirach* and as *Ben Sira* and even as *Ecclesiasticus*. The book is a collection of wisdom sayings from this famous Jerusalem scribe and is commonly dated 180 B.C.

[21]This large book is actually a compilation of (probably) five books. The passage cited here is from the Book of the Similitudes (*1 En* 37—71) and dates to the first Christian century.

[22]James Dunn, "Let John Be John: A Gospel for Its Time." In *Das Evangelium und die Evangelium*, Wissenschaftliche Untersuchungen zum Neuen Testament 28, ed. Peter Stuhlmacher (Tübingen, Germany: Mohr, 1983), 333. He actually argues for three places of parallelism, adding John's description of Jesus as the "Revealer" who descended from heaven and has now ascended back, finding this in Sir 24:3-17; Wis 9:10, 17; and *1 En* 42. I agree but chose not to describe this third parallel here.

[23]Craig Evans, *Word and Glory: On the Exegetical and Theological Background of John's Prologue*, Journal for the Study of the New Testament, Sup. Ser. 89 (Sheffield: JSOT, 1993), 84-92. The material in the chart was modified from Pate, *Communities of the Last Days*, 227.

Table 8.1

Description	"Word"	"Wisdom"
was in the Beginning	Jn 1:1	Prov 8:22-23; Sir 1:4; Wis 9:9
was with God	Jn 1:1	Prov 8:30; Sir 1:1; Wis 9:9
was a co-creator	Jn 1:1-3	Prov 3:19; 8:30; Wis 7:22; 9:1-2
is light	Jn 1:4, 9	Wis 7:26; Bar 4:2
contrasted to "darkness" (evil)	Jn 1:5	Wis 7:29-30; 18:4
came to this world	Jn 1:10	Sir 24:7-12
was rejected by its own	Jn 1:11	*1 En* 42:1-2; Bar 3:20-23
dwelt ("tabernacled")	"tabernacled" among us (Jn 1:14)	"tabernacled in Israel" (Sir 24:10); did not "tabernacle" here but returned to the heavenlies (*1 En* 42:1-2)

Jewish readers were familiar with the promises offered by Wisdom. According to later Jewish writings, for example Sirach and Baruch, Wisdom was found in the Torah. According to Baruch, God found Wisdom and

> gave her to his servant Jacob
> and to Israel, whom he loved.
> Afterward she appeared on earth
> and lived with humankind.
> She is the book of the commandments of God,
> the law that endures forever.
> All who hold her fast will live,
> and those who forsake her will die. (Bar 3:36—4:1)

John, however, argues that Wisdom dwelt no longer in the Torah (as Baruch argued) but rather in Christ, and no longer in the temple (as Sirach argued) but rather in Christ.

Readers of the Gospel of John quickly note the "I AM" sayings play a significant role in the Gospel. An "I AM" statement was often teamed with a sign to illustrate it: "I AM the Bread of Life" and the one who multiplies the loaves and fishes, or "I AM the Light of the World" and the one who heals the man born blind, or "I AM the Resurrection and the Life" and the one who raises Lazarus from the dead. The "I AM" statements share descriptions with Wisdom (see table 8.2).[24] Wisdom promised the Jewish people light, sustenance, protection, life. For John, Christ provides these things.

Table 8.2

Description	"Word"	"Wisdom"
is the Bread and Water	Jn 6:35; 7:37-38	Prov 9:5; Sir 15:3; 24:21; Wis 11:4
is Light	Jn 8:12	Wis 7:26-30; 18:3-4
is the Door	Jn 10:7, 9	Prov 8:34; Wis 7:25
is the protecting Shepherd	Jn 10:7-15	Wis 7:25 (?)
gives life	Jn 11:25-26	Prov 3:18; 8:35; Wis 8:13
is the Way	Jn 14:6	Prov 3:17; Bar 3:20, 27-28

John, however, does not merely attribute descriptions of Wisdom to Jesus. The description of Wisdom made a trajectory from Proverbs through Sirach/Wisdom of Solomon to 1 Enoch. John builds on the image of Wisdom in Proverbs, but he corrects several aspects of the image in the later Jewish writings of Sirach, Wisdom and 1 Enoch.[25] Like Wisdom in Proverbs, Jesus was present at creation and was the agent of creation: "He was in the beginning with God. All things came into being through him" (Jn 1:2-3). Like Wisdom in Sirach, he is the Word, coming from the mouth of God (Jn 1:1). And like Wisdom in Sirach, Jesus describes himself as a flowing river, refreshing all who come to him (Jn 7:37-38). Yet John usurps the story. He takes Wisdom away from the Torah and the temple. Wisdom (and her promises) no longer "tabernacles" in the temple, as promised by Sirach. The "way of truth" is no longer found in the Law (Torah), as promised by Baruch (3:9—4:1): "The law indeed was given through Moses; grace and truth came through Jesus Christ" (Jn 1:17). The path ("way") that Moses took did not lead to seeing the face (*kabod*, "glory") of God. Imme-

[24]See Martin Scott, *Sophia and the Johannine Jesus,* Journal for the Study of the New Testament, Sup. Ser. 71 (Sheffield: JSOT, 1992), 116-30. The material in the chart was modified from Pate, *Communities of the Last Days,* 228. Jesus as the Giver of Rest, a theme in Matthew (11:29) is also a Wisdom trait: Wis 8:16; Sir 6:28.

[25]N. T. Wright prefers to say that John is "a subversive retelling of the story of Wisdom" (*People of God,* 415).

diately after contrasting Moses and Christ in John 1:17, John adds, "No one has ever seen God. It is God the only Son, who is close to the Father's heart, who has made him known" (Jn 1:18). "Wisdom" in Sirach promised, "Those who eat of me will hunger for more. / And those who drink of me will thirst for more" (24:21). In contrast, Jesus as Wisdom promised, "Whoever comes to me will never be hungry, and whoever believes in me will never be thirsty" (Jn 6:35).

The most striking way in which John usurps the Wisdom tradition is in the story of Wisdom finding a home to pitch her "tent" (tabernacle). In Sirach, Wisdom dwelt in the temple among the people of Israel. In *1 Enoch*, Wisdom found no place in this world to make a permanent home and left to dwell among the angels. In John, the Word (Wisdom) became flesh and lived (tabernacled) among them and they saw his glory (*doxa*), a glory full (*plērēs*) of grace (Jn 1:14), as Israel once saw the glory (*doxa*) of the Lord fill (*eplēsthē*) the tabernacle (Ex 40:34 LXX).

God at work: Divine activities and rights. The act of the incarnation—when the Word became flesh—forces humanity to decide between light and dark (Jn 3:17-21). For John, bringing the kingdom (through the incarnation) is tied to revealing the kingdom: "The one who comes from heaven is above all. . . . He testifies to what he has seen and heard. . . . He whom God has sent speaks the words of God, for he gives the Spirit without measure" (Jn 3:31-34). To those in the kingdom Jesus promised "eternal life" (Jn 3:36). For John, "eternal life" was more than merely everlasting years; he was speaking of "life in the kingdom." Jesus' actions (and words) were not just announcements of the kingdom but were the actual means of *bringing* the kingdom.[26] Jesus was there to restore God's people from exile. To restore his people meant to define his relationship with them; it is the meaning and purpose of covenant. As N. T. Wright has demonstrated, Jesus sought to redefine Israel by focusing on how Israel defined herself.[27] To redefine the covenant and the "people of God" is a divine prerogative.

The traditional Jewish symbols of national identity and Israel's righteousness—land, temple, law (especially Sabbath and food laws), kinship and blessing (meaning material possessions)—were the focus of Jesus' criticism. For example, Jesus was critiquing the entire temple system.[28] He was pronouncing judgment on the temple, which was nevertheless an integral and necessary part of the old covenant. Jesus was not seeking to reform or purify these institutions, but rather to announce a new covenant and thus the end of the exile, which had been God's judgment on his people for breaking the old covenant.

John demonstrates Jesus as exercising divine rights, pronouncing the covenant of

[26]Wright, *Victory of God,* 170-76.
[27]Ibid., 369-442.
[28]Wright, *People of God,* 417.

Moses as broken and offering the promised new covenant of Jeremiah. Jesus as the divine critic of the old covenant is a theme that runs subtly through the Gospel of John. In chapter 1, the Baptist announces that there is one standing among the Pharisees *whom they did not know* (Jn 1:26). This one would take away the sin of the world (Jn 1:29), something not even promised in the old covenant. Jesus fills the dry, empty pots of ceremonial Judaism to the brim with new wine (Jn 2).[29] Jesus continues in this same vein by immediately critiquing the temple (Jn 2:13-22):

> As the Davidic Messiah—and as such invested with the authority to appraise the temple and its activities—Jesus has complained of the failure of the ruling priests. Instead of becoming a place of prayer for Gentiles and a place for the regathering of Israel's exiles, the temple fosters oppression and neglects the needy (as seen in many of the pericopes that make up Mk 12).[30]

After critiquing the temple,[31] Jesus establishes the requirements for leaving the exile and entering the restoration (kingdom): one must be born from above (Jn 3:3). Jesus then announces a new way of worship, replacing the old temple system: "But the hour is coming, and is now here, when the true worshipers will worship the Father in spirit and truth" (Jn 4:23). Such radical claims require a sign (verification). John then provides several examples of Jesus exercising divine rights. Jesus heals a man with a statement that simultaneously heals him and violates Sabbath law: "Stand up, take your mat and walk" (Jn 5:8).[32] To claim such a right required a sign: Jesus provided bread in the wilderness, a divine sign, because it was God not Moses who provided the manna, as Jesus reminded them (Jn 6:32). Again, Jesus provides a sign by conquering the sea, something only Yahweh does.[33] Jesus claims to be the springs of life (Jn 7) and the light of the world (Jn 8) and to predate Abraham. Such

---

[29]This is clearly the point John wishes to make since he emphasizes the jars were currently unusable by Jewish law (Jn 2:6). Yet Jesus likely was making the same point in the original event. He was not merely using available containers, for obviously there were plenty of freshly empty wine containers, and the ancient Mediterranean world with its heightened sensitivity to clean/unclean did not make casual selection of containers (see Jn 4:9).

[30]Craig A. Evans, "Jesus and the Continuing Exile of Israel," in *Jesus and the Restoration of Israel: A Critical Assessment of N. T. Wright's "Jesus and the Victory of God,"* ed. Carey C. Newman (Downers Grove, Ill.: InterVarsity Press, 1999), 97.

[31]Most scholars see John moving the temple incident from Passion Week to early in Jesus' ministry. While this is possible, a strong case can be made for two distinct temple incidents.

[32]Jesus was not laying the foundation for mothers to insist that their children make their beds in the morning. Everyone involved (Jesus, the healed man and the Pharisees) saw the miracle and the Sabbath violation as interconnected (Jn 5:11, 16). A theological crisis ensued: only Yahweh was permitted to work on the Sabbath (Jn 5:17).

[33]See Ps 89:9. This is the reason the disciples worship Jesus in Matthew 14:33. Jesus is also contrasting himself to Moses. It is noteworthy that Jesus refers to Moses (Jn 5:45-47) and then immediately provides bread (Jn 6:1-15) and then crosses the sea (Jn 6:16-21).

unbelievable claims were demonstrated by healing a man born blind, something no man, including Moses, had ever done (Jn 9:29-32). Finally, Jesus' critique of the old covenant culminates in his allusion to Ezekiel 34. Through this prophet Yahweh announces that all the current Jewish leaders are poor shepherds, abusing the flock.[34] Yahweh himself will come and be the Good Shepherd (Ezek 34:1-22). In Jesus' condemnation of the Jewish leadership because they refused the sign of healing the man born blind, Jesus announces that he himself is the Good Shepherd (Jn 10:11). John makes Jesus' claim clear by tying the sheep image to Jesus' claim that "the Father and I are one" (Jn 10:26-30). This final and most outlandish claim requires the final and greatest sign: the raising of a man who has been dead four days (Jn 11:1-44). The new covenant in Christ has produced life: "Those who believe in me, even though they die, will live, and everyone who lives and believes in me will never die" (Jn 11:25-26).

"Signs" and the end of the exile. "Israel's exile was still in progress," writes N. T. Wright. "Although she had come back from Babylon, the glorious message of the prophets remained unfulfilled. Israel still remained in thrall to foreigners; worse, Israel's God had not returned to Zion."[35]

First-century Jews expected that a messiah who would bring Israel out of exile would be attested by "signs and wonders." There was a problem with Jesus' messiahship: "Jesus came announcing the 'end of the exile,' for which almost all Jews longed, in his own person and work, yet without producing most of the characteristic signs that were expected to accompany that end (most notably, ridding the land of the Romans)."[36] Jews were willing and ready (many were even eager) to accept a messiah attested by signs and wonders. The problem was that Jesus did not produce the "right" signs and wonders.

The Messiah will be recognized by "signs and wonders." Among the Dead Sea Scrolls, it was announced that the eschatological restoration would be marked by "the sign": wickedness would be banished by righteousness "as *darkness* in the presence of *light* . . . *True knowledge* shall *fill* the *world*" (1Q27 frag. 1, 1:5-7).[37] John used similar language. The Messiah was expected to be verified by "signs." Two other Jewish men of the first century claimed to be the Messiah and preached that they would prove their

---

[34]The theme of Israel as lost sheep while in exile is picked up in intertestamental literature (e.g., *1 En* 90:33).

[35]Wright, *People of God,* 268-69.

[36]This is the primary thesis of N. T. Wright, as ably summarized by Craig Blomberg, "The Wright Stuff: A Critical Overview of *Jesus and the Victory of God,*" in *Jesus and the Restoration of Israel,* ed. Carey C. Newman (Downers Grove, Ill.: InterVarsity Press, 1999), 20.

[37]Translation by Michael Wise, Martin Abegg and Edward Cook, *The Dead Sea Scrolls: A New Translation* (San Francisco: HarperCollins, 1996), 176; italics added, highlighting words that are in distinctive Johannine idiom.

claim by a miraculous sign.[38] Signs were an important part of the Exodus story.[39] Since the Messiah was often connected with the Deuteronomic promise that Yahweh would one day raise up a prophet like Moses (Deut 18:15), the people expected the Messiah also to do signs like Yahweh did through Moses (Num 14:22). Josephus and the Dead Sea Scrolls give independent evidence that the people expected signs.[40] When Sirach appeals for the restoration, for Yahweh to "gather all the tribes of Jacob, and give them their inheritance, as at the beginning" (Sir 36:13-16), he calls upon Yahweh to "Give new signs (*sēmeia*), and work other wonders" (Sir 36:6).[41] Thus, many people accepted Jesus rather than John the Baptist as the Messiah because the Baptist "performed no sign" (Jn 10:41). For these first-century Jews, the deciding issue was the "signs." A generation later, Josephus detailed how misreading the "signs" led to many Jews falsely (in his mind) supporting the Jewish revolt. He did not dismiss the importance of signs, but rather argued that the people had misread them. "The point of all this," according to Evans, "is to underscore how important signs were to Jews, even to a sophisticated and skeptical person like Josephus. Paul is not guilty of an unfair generalization when he asserts that 'Jews demand signs' (1 Cor 1:22)."[42] Promises of signs (as was done by messianic pretenders) or demands for signs (in the case of Jesus' opponents) are "symptomatic of a society in which many of its members hoped for and anticipated national deliverance."[43] Jesus' hearers expected one of the signs, if not the main sign, to be deliverance from Rome. They were disappointed. Yet John was arguing that Jesus did indeed provide the "signs" that he was the one.

In John's temple incident, Jesus does not quote the judgment pronouncement of Isaiah 56:7 (and Jer 7:11). Rather, he quotes Zechariah 14:21. He was calling Israel to fulfill the eschatological expectations for the ingathering of the nations into Zion, part of the restoration hope, for "all those who survive of the nations . . . shall go up year after year to worship the King, the LORD of hosts" (Zech 14:16). The Jews (in John) ask for a sign to validate that he had the authority to cast out the "traders," for according to Zechariah, only when the Lord becomes king over all the earth will there no longer be traders in the house of the Lord (Zech 14:21). Jesus' opponents recognized

---

[38]As ably demonstrated by Evans, "Continuing Exile," 78-82.

[39]For a concise but well-balanced discussion of signs in John, see Köstenberger, *Missions of Jesus and the Disciples*, 54-74.

[40]See Evans, "Continuing Exile," 93.

[41]Sir 33:6 LXX. The two major Greek recensions and the Hebrew recension from Qumran do not always agree, and chapters 33–38 have the most relocations (see Richard Coggins, *Sirach*, Guides to Apocrypha and Pseudepigrapha series [Sheffield: Academic Press, 1998], 30-31). Furthermore, Sirach 36:1-21 is likely a later addition to the book (Coggins, *Sirach*, 24) but is still earlier than the time of Jesus.

[42]Evans, "Continuing Exile," 94.

[43]Ibid., 91.

his actions as making a messianic claim. Such a claim needed a sign. John's Gospel gives many. John concludes his Gospel by saying that Jesus did many other signs, "but these [signs][44] are written [to show] that Jesus is the Messiah" so that they might have life—life in the kingdom, life in the restoration (Jn 20:30-31).

Because of the signs, there is no need of witnesses. Concurrent with his description of the signs that Jesus did was John's argument that Jesus did not need witnesses. He did not need others to "testify" that he was the Messiah; his "signs" did so. Why would John want to downplay the role of "witnesses"? Part of the explanation is found in the historical situation of John. All the eyewitnesses were dying. Signs remain, even when witnesses disappear. Yet John is ultimately not dismissing the importance of witnesses. John gives multiple witnesses while all the time asserting that Jesus did not *need* them. John himself will appeal to the importance of witnesses in a letter, "We declare to you what was from the beginning, what we have heard, what we have seen with our own eyes" (1 Jn 1:1). Nevertheless, his emphasis is on "signs." As in Second Temple literature, the end of the exile was brought by the Messiah, attested by signs. John's signs show that God (in Jesus) was restoring his people.

Restoration: People (Land/Law), Spirit, Temple and Presence of God. The promised restoration has come. God is dwelling again amidst his people: "Jesus quite self-consciously came not merely to announce the kingdom but to enact and embody the return from exile, the defeat of evil and the coming of Yahweh to Zion."[45]

The restoration promised that God would dwell again amidst his people. The covenant established that Yahweh would be their God and they would be his people. As the Mosaic covenant was broken, the question became, who really are the sons of Abraham, the inheritors of the promise of the Abrahamic covenant?[46] John answers in ways apart from national Judaism. It is not those who possess the land or keep the Law, but those to whom Jesus gives the right: "He came to what was his own, and his own people did not accept him. But to all who received him, who believed in his name, he gave power to become children of God" (Jn 1:11-12). The prophets promised that in the restoration God would pour out his Spirit on his people. In John, Jesus pours out the Spirit (Jn 3:34; 4:14; 6:63; 7:38-39; 14:16; 16:7; 20:22). The tabernacle symbolized the presence of God, especially the "glory" that indwelt the tabernacle. John redefines the presence of God. Only John records the statement in which Jesus equates the

---

[44]Although "these" is often used substantively (in the neuter) to mean "these things," the antecedent of "these" *(tauta)* here is signs.

[45]Blomberg, "Wright Stuff," 35.

[46]The "debate about Abraham and his true children in John 8 is crucial to the whole story: part of the question at issue in the book is precisely whether Jesus or the Judaeans of his day are the true children of Abraham" (Wright, *People of God,* 411). The questions about Abraham (Jn 8:31-39) or about Moses (Jn 6:30-31) are questions about who represents the true succession. Note that John 7:16-19 connects "glory" and "Moses" as is done in the prologue.

temple with his own body (Jn 2:19-22).[47] God now "tabernacles" among his people in Christ. Finally, the Last Supper symbolized in John (as in the Synoptics) the ending of the old covenant by the establishment of the new covenant.[48]

Yet in John, the restoration comes in ways not foreseen in the old covenant. Righteousness in John is described without references to the Law.[49] In fact, the national Jewish symbols are missing: "land" and "law" are central elements in the old covenant but are missing from John's description of life in the kingdom. "The law indeed was given through Moses; grace and truth came through Jesus Christ" (Jn 1:17).

Secondary purposes: To correct some misunderstandings. John's primary purpose was to show that Jesus was the Messiah who was ending Israel's exile, but that does not preclude his handling a few other issues with his Gospel.

Polemic against disciples of the Baptist. There are indications that some disciples of the Baptist had not joined the ministry of Jesus (Lk 7:18) or even disbanded with the Baptist's imprisonment (Mt 11:2; 14:12) and death (Acts 18:25). After the fall of Jerusalem, at least some of these disciples relocated to Ephesus and possibly even opposed Christians.[50] John, writing from Ephesus, is seeking to win these disciples over. He is never critical of the Baptist; he does not repeat the comments of Jesus that could be seen as critical (Mt 11:2-11; Lk 7:18-28); he does not mention John's arrest (Mt 4:12; Mk 1:14). In fact, he portrays the Baptist as the ideal prophet. Yet in subtle (and not so subtle) ways, John places the Baptist in his proper place. John does not discuss Jesus' baptism, for it could suggest a secondary or derivative tone to the ministry of Jesus. Rather, he emphasizes statements of the Baptist showing his own secondary nature (Jn 1:6-35; 3:27-30; 5:33-36). John mentions Jesus having more disciples than the Baptist, but even more subtly he mentions that Jesus himself did not baptize; rather, his disciples did, placing the Baptist on their level (Jn 4:1-2). Likewise, John does not mention the Baptist's execution (Mt 14:1-12; Mk 6:14-29; Lk 9:7-9), which might suggest equal status with Jesus as a comartyr. John's message is clear: as a true and faithful prophet, the Baptist proclaimed the message given to him: announce the arrival of Jesus the Messiah (Jn 1:29-34).

The death of the apostle John. When the Gospel was published, John 21 was added to address the death of the beloved apostle, for a tradition had developed that John

---

[47]In Tobit 14:5, the people will rebuild the temple, but in John, Jesus himself will rebuild it in the form of the resurrection of his body.

[48]John uses three different images: he pronounces that the disciples have no place in the kingdom apart from his work (Jn 13:8); he declares the disciples clean (Jn 13:10); the meal sets the process in place for Christ to be the paschal lamb (Jn 13:27-30).

[49]Wright, *Victory of God*, 218, argues this for all four Gospels.

[50]That Jesus and John separated their ministries is clear from the New Testament. Later conflict is debated among church historians. See Scot McKnight, "John the Baptist," in *New Dictionary of Biblical Theology* (Downers Grove, Ill.: InterVarsity Press, 2000), 604.

would not die before the return of Christ. A story from their teacher John needed to be told to clarify this popular misunderstanding with the ensuing crisis that occurred after John's death (and after the Gospel, i.e., John 1—20, was drafted). The story explains the origin of the mistaken tradition: "So the rumor spread in the community that this disciple would not die" (Jn 21:23). The disciples of John, however, do not show his subtlety. Rather than leaving the point understated, they overstate it: "Yet Jesus did not say to him that he would not die, but, 'If it is my will that he remain until I come, what is that to you?'" (Jn 21:23).

John's relation to Peter. The community of John also wanted to tell the story they heard from John that explained the relationship between John and Peter. The two are fishing together in John 21 when they see Jesus. Each brings his own gift: John is first to recognize that it is Jesus, and Peter is the first to act (Jn 21:7). The community wanted to defend Peter's place of authority (in spite of his denial of Christ) but also not diminish in any way the role of their own teacher, John. Thus, they recount Peter's restoration by Jesus (Jn 21:15-19) and then the independent nature of John's ministry (Jn 21:23).

Conclusions: The Story of Israel in the Gospel of John

For John, the story of Israel (the end of the exile with the reversal of the Deuteronomic curses, and the restoration) is seen in the ministry of Jesus.[51] There are numerous connections in John to the story of Israel. John mentions the Jewish festival calendar more than the Synoptics: Passover three times (Jn 2:13; 6:4; 11:55), Tabernacles (Jn 7:2), Dedication (Jn 10:22) and an unnamed feast (Jn 5:1). John's repeated reference that "the time of the Passover was near" (three times) may indicate a subtle play that the time of deliverance for Israel was near, particularly in light of John's equally subtle portrayal of Jesus as the final Passover lamb (Jn 1:29; 19:14, 31, 42),[52] protecting his followers from the angel of death (Jn 11:25-26). The Feast of Tabernacles celebrated God's provision for his people in the wilderness by providing bread (manna) and water (from the rock). So in John, Jesus provides water and bread for his people (Jn 4—6) before announcing who he is at the Feast of Tabernacles (Jn 7—8). The Feast of Dedication commemorates God's restoring access to the temple and providing light for seven days. So Jesus reopens the temple to a man (by making him whole) and shows he is the light of the world by healing his blindness (Jn 9) before announcing who he is at the Feast of Dedication. In this way we are prepared for Passover. Jesus delivers

---

[51]Paul draws these conclusions even more strongly than John. See chapter ten on Paul.

[52]Wright, *Victory of God*, 412, also sees John portraying Jesus as the Passover lamb. For a full argument, see Nils Dahl, "The Johannine Church and History," in *The Interpretation of John*, ed. J. Ashton (Philadelphia: Fortress, 1986), 128-32.

Lazarus from death (Jn 11) before announcing who he is (Jn 12—20).

In his use of the story of Israel, John shares many points in common with the Synoptics. Yet he also brings his own unique contributions. John usurps later Jewish Wisdom tradition and rewrites aspects of it to show Jesus as Wisdom that has tabernacled among us. Jewish Wisdom tradition had been "retelling Genesis and focusing it on a particular point. Sirach was claiming that Jerusalem and the Torah were the focal points of the entire cosmos, the place where the creator's own Wisdom had come, uniquely, to dwell. John claims exactly this for Jesus."[53]

Isaiah describes the return from exile:

These I will bring [LXX: gather] to my holy mountain
and make them joyful in my house of prayer;
    their burnt offerings and their sacrifices will be accepted on my altar;
    for my house shall be called a house of prayer for all peoples. (Is 56:7)

Jesus' citation of this passage during the synoptic temple incident shows his understanding of the restoration. John demonstrates it in a different manner. The identification of the holy mountain was being argued by the Samaritans of Jesus' day.[54] On which holy mountain will the restored people pray? The Samaritan woman tells Jesus that it is not agreed which mountain is the place to worship (Jn 4:20) but that the Messiah will make the answer clear (Jn 4:25). Since the Messiah will gather the exiles together, it will be clear to all which holy mountain is the place to pray. Jesus, as the Messiah, does resolve the conflict, but not in a way that either group expected (Jn 4:21-24).

John's story is that God has returned to his people, as promised in the restoration. *First Enoch* 90:33 speaks of the restoration, "All those [sheep] which had been destroyed and dispersed . . . were gathered together in that house; and the LORD of the sheep rejoiced with great joy because they had all become gentle and returned to his house." So Jesus now seeks, in John 10, to regather the lost sheep. The theme of lost sheep in the Synoptics implies that the scattered Jews of the Diaspora would be gathered together again. John makes the same point explicit. Hireling shepherds did not guard the sheep but fled. As a result, the sheep were scattered (Jn 10:13). Jesus is the Good Shepherd, and he will make one flock (Jn 10:16), a regathering and restoration image. This image is enhanced because of the reference to including Gentiles in the flock (Jn 10:16), a common restoration image. This story is immediately juxtaposed to the temple during the Feast of Dedication (Jn 10:22). What this festival was supposed to commemorate—the restoration of Israel and the renewed presence of God in Zion—was actually being done by Christ as the Good Shepherd. John emphasizes the

---

[53]Wright, *People of God*, 416.
[54]The Aramaic Targum reads "to *the* holy mountain" instead of "to *my* holy mountain," an indication in the text of the dispute over the location.

connection of the Good Shepherd discourse with the temple by repeating again the reference to sheep (Jn 10:26-27). The contrast of the "gentle sheep" returning to God's house in *1 Enoch* 90:33 with the Jews picking up stones (part of the temple) to kill Jesus is dramatic irony.

Jesus brings the restoration of Israel, not through new covenant faithfulness to Torah, but through his own sacrifice. The restoration of Israel, then, has cosmic repercussions: *Greeks* want to see Jesus. Jesus answers their request by saying that his hour had finally come and that, when he is lifted up, he will draw *all people* to himself (Jn 12:20-32). Jesus then challenges his hearers with exhortations previewed in the Prologue: light has come into the world (Jn 12:35; 1:9); do not be overtaken by darkness (Jn 12:35; 1:5); therefore, believe and become children of God (Jn 12:36; 1:12). John weaves a tightly knit narrative of the story of Jesus.

The story of Israel is, for John, the story of the world.[55] When John makes his case for Jesus as "God in our midst," he does not use Greco-Roman or gnostic imagery. He uses the story of Israel. As God dwelt among his people in the tabernacle as evidenced by signs and wonders, so also now God in Jesus is present with his people. As the presence of God was an abiding glory in the tabernacle, so also God as the Word "tabernacles" among us, and we behold his glory—not the glory of Shekinah and Torah but the glory of the only unique Son (Jn 1:14, 17).

Supplemental Readings in New Dictionary of Biblical Theology

D. A. Carson, "Johannine Writings," 132-36.

A. Köstenberger, "John (Gospel)," 280-85.

G. H. Twelftree, "Signs and Wonders," 775-81.

R. G. Maccini, "Testimony/Witness," 811-14.

D. T. Tsumura, "Water," 840-41.

B. M. Fanning, "Jesus as the Word," 852-53 in "Word," 848-53.

T. Renz, "World," 853-55.

For additional reading on particular items in John, see also the following articles in the *Dictionary of Jesus and the Gospels* (Downers Grove, Ill.: InterVarsity Press, 1992):

Ben Witherington III, "Birth of Jesus," §§7-8, 70-73.

C. D. C. Howard, "Blindness," §1, 81-82.

W. L. Kynes, "New Birth," 574-76.

J. Painter, "Bread," §5, 85-86.

G. M. Burge, "I AM Sayings," 354-56.

---

[55]Wright, *People of God,* 416-17.

M. M. Thompson, "John, Gospel of," 368-83.

Ben Witherington III, "John the Baptist," 383-91.

R. H. Stein, "Last Supper," 444-50.

R. W. Paschal, "Lazarus," §1, 461-62.

G. R. Osborne, "Resurrection," §4, 684-87.

H. G. M. Williamson, "Samaritans," 724-28.

D. H. Johnson, "Shepherd," §2, 751-53.

W. R. Herzog, "Temple Cleansing," 817-20.

R. A. Whitacre, "Vine," 867-68.

G. M. Burge, "Water," 869-70.

D. F. Watson, "Wine," §6, 873.

Study Questions

1. In the previous chapter, we saw that the Synoptics use "the Twelve" as a theme. Contrast John's use of "disciples" with that of the Synoptics.

2. Compare and contrast how John's description of Jesus parallels the traditional Jewish image of Wisdom.

3. Make a case for or against John 21 as added by John's disciples when the Gospel was published.

4. Discuss John's use of "signs."

5. Trace through the Gospel of John these various themes: light/darkness, know/believe, water, witnesses.

9

ACTS

The Nations Will Listen

The nature of the book of Acts as the second volume of Luke's description of the Christian movement and faith seems to imply that Acts is a mere sequel to the story told in Luke's Gospel.[1] In spite of recent arguments that the unity of authorship does not automatically require unity of narrative and theology, and that Luke and Acts are independent narratives that should be dealt with as Luke *and* Acts rather than Luke/Acts,[2] it still seems evident that Luke's understanding of the story as outlined in his Gospel has not changed.

The change of focus from Christology in Luke's Gospel to ecclesiology in Acts is not as significant for each of these stories as one might think at first. There is no clear evidence that Luke saw an essential distinction between the divine acts of the human Christ in the Gospels and the divine acts of the resurrected Christ in Acts. In fact, one may well argue with Roger Stronstad that the deeds of the Spirit of Christ in Luke's presentation in Acts of the Apostles parallel the deeds of Jesus in his Gospel presentation.[3]

Before looking specifically at Luke's interpretation of the story of Israel in the book of Acts, it will prove useful to consider some general characteristics of Luke's historiography—the conventions that guide his understanding and recounting of historical events. These will form the hermeneutical foundation for Luke's ability to portray God's actions in history.

Luke's use of a historiographical model that has close affinity to the Septuagint al-

---

[1]Almost without exception, biblical scholars accept the unity of authorship in Luke/Acts (see Acts 1:1-2).

[2]See Mikeal C. Parsons and Richard I. Pervo, *Rethinking the Unity of Luke and Acts* (Minneapolis: Fortress, 1994): "Acts does not continue the story of Jesus, whose departure makes its story possible. It is thus best understood as a sequel rather than a second chapter or simple continuation" (123).

[3]Roger Stronstad, *The Charismatic Theology of St. Luke* (Peabody, Mass.: Hendrickson, 1984). See also the 1927 work by Henry J. Cadbury, *The Making of Luke-Acts,* 2nd ed. (Peabody, Mass.: Hendrickson, 1958).

lows him to use historical events as a vehicle for teaching[4] without losing the integrity of the historical events themselves. This purposeful use of history for the sake of teaching makes the traditional distinction between teaching (*didachē*) and history impossible to particularize and makes Grant Osborne's and Clark Pinnock's remarks somewhat superfluous:

> Didactic portions of Scripture must have precedence over historical passages in establishing doctrine. We ought to move here [when dealing with teaching on the Holy Spirit] from the teaching of First Corinthians to the narrative of Acts rather than the reverse.[5]

The continuing emphasis on time in the New Testament[6] is an indication that theology was not seen as the antithesis of history. It is not possible to hide either under the cover of the other. Rather, Luke's selective choice of events that would expose God's renewed historical presence[7] underscores the necessity of considering the theological content of the narrative material.[8]

The Broader Structure of Luke's Presentation

Typology and narrative material. To establish the relationship between narrative (history telling) and theology even further, attention must be turned to typology.[9] This is to some extent what Gordon Fee calls the "pattern" value of a narrative. The principle of

---

[4]Martin Hengel, *Acts and the History of Earliest Christianity,* trans. John Bowden (Philadelphia: Fortress, 1979): "Once again we may single out Luke, as being the most significant historian of the New Testament. A comparison of his work with that of Josephus or the books of Maccabees . . . shows his particular proximity to Jewish Hellenistic historiography. Luke is evidently influenced by a firm tradition with a religious view of history which essentially derives from the Septuagint" (51-52). In the same vein I. Howard Marshall (*Luke: Historian and Theologian* [Grand Rapids, Mich.: Zondervan, 1970], 55) affirms that Luke's style, "which is frequently reminiscent of the Septuagint, demands that he also be compared with Jewish historians." For a list of septuagintisms in Lukan Greek, see Joseph A. Fitzmyer, *The Gospel According to Luke (I-IX),* Anchor Bible 28A (New York: Doubleday, 1970), 114-16.

[5]Clark H. Pinnock and Grant R. Osborne, "A True Proposal for the Tongues Controversy," *Christianity Today* (October 1971): 8.

[6]See for example, Oscar Cullmann, *Christ and Time* (London: SCM Press, 1965), 38.

[7]Part of the reason for Luke's selective approach is found in the practical fact that he wanted his writings to fit on one roll of papyrus. See for example Hengel, who qualifies this by saying, "The earliest Christian communities were poor, and did not have large libraries at their disposal; furthermore, too long a book presented problems for liturgical readings. Its content had to be restricted to the most important details, and other less essential features were omitted" (*Acts,* 8).

[8]Gordon D. Fee's remark that "historical precedent, to have normative value, must be related to *intent*" goes without saying, although the difficulty in determining the didactic intent in a narrated episode indicates that Fee's underlying understanding of a separation between history and *didachē* is unattainable ("Hermeneutics and Historical Precedent—A Major Problem in Pentecostal Hermeneutics," in *Perspectives on the New Pentecostalism,* ed. Russell P. Spittler [Grand Rapids, Mich.: Baker, 1976], 126).

[9]The use of Old Testament events as "types" for New Testament fulfillment, e.g., the salvation of God's people in the exodus event is a typological precedent to the cross.

analogy falls into place as one narrative is understood in the light of a former. How this ties in with the theological use of narratives can been seen, for example, in Luke 13:33 where Luke's description of Jesus' words, "I must go on my way today and tomorrow and the day following; for it cannot be that a prophet should perish away from Jerusalem," indicates that Jesus' death in Jerusalem was patterned after former episodes.[10]

This approach to history, where the dialectic of the imperative and the indicative is held in tension is an integral part of Luke's historiography. The existence God gives always occurs in a history that by nature is nonrepetitive and unprecedented in detail, yet is didactic in significance. Salvation historical events thus become teaching moments and at times even imperative instructions.

The use of typology as the hermeneutical scheme for the New Testament's interpretation of the Old Testament gives ground for believing that the same hermeneutic is used in the reporting (and interpretation) of Jesus' earthly ministry and of the Acts of the Apostles. If this is so, the teaching of the narratives is in no way subordinate to other *directly* didactic texts in the New Testament. E. Earle Ellis, finding support from Birger Gerhardsson, seems to agree: "Indeed, they [the narrative episodes] are a teaching by historical narration as much as Jesus' *meshalim* (i.e., parables) are a teaching by illustrative stories and sayings."[11]

It follows from this that the teaching from the biblical narratives must be read in light of the author's Christology.[12] The narrative structure aligns itself to christological intentions that are tied to a teaching on discipleship (e.g., Lk 14). If this is indeed so, it follows naturally that the purpose of Luke's narrative material moves beyond a mere display of the power of Jesus as the Son of God (whether in human form as in the Gospel or in Spirit as in Acts) to become a forward-looking typology for how God works in the world.

Programmatic Narrative Teaching

Eduard Lohse's position that Luke in his description of past events intended to teach

---

[10]E. J. Tinsley (*The Imitation of God in Christ: An Essay on the Biblical Basis of Christian Spirituality* [London: SCM Press, 1960]) finds the same use of typology in the Old Testament: "In the Book of Deuteronomy there is a continual oscillation between *derek* meaning the actual historical way which Israel has traversed from Red Sea to Promised Land, and *derek* meaning the 'way of life' to which the people are consequently summoned. . . . Deut 8.1f. is a good example of the ambiguity which arises from the Deuteronomic style of writing where there is reference both to the historical past and the existential present. . . . The image of the 'Way' is never detached from the historical journey once taken" (34-35).

[11]E. Earle Ellis, *The Making of the New Testament Documents* (Boston: Brill Academic, 1999), 350.

[12]As also Ellis seems to affirm in *Prophecy and Hermeneutic in Early Christianity: New Testament Essays* (Grand Rapids, Mich.: Eerdmans, 1978), 166: "New Testament typology is thoroughly Christological in its focus. Jesus is the 'prophet like Moses' (Acts 3,22f.) who in his passion brings the Old Covenant to its proper goal and end (Rom 10,4; Hb 10,9f.) and establishes a New Covenant (Lk 22,20,29)."

the church of his day how it should live and preach the gospel[13] is plausible only if the Gospel episodes not only point typologically backward but also programmatically forward. That these happenings gain theological significance from analogous theological events in the past can only be important to the reader of Luke's Gospel if this significance is programmatically carried into the future. In other words, what Jesus did was to Luke not just consequential for the historic moment in which it happened, but for future ministry patterns (Lk 6:40).

This is seen most vividly in Luke 4:18-19 where the program for Jesus' ministry and Luke's Gospel is laid out as an introduction for the ministry that followed Jesus' baptism. Likewise, Acts 1:8 gives the blueprint for both Luke's account of the beginning of the Christian church *and* the program for its continuation.

In both of his writings, Luke thus utilized the recounting of events as teaching models. Theologically, this is even more apparent in the overlapping of the Gospel ending and the Acts introduction. The ministry of Jesus in the Gospel continues programmatically in the ministry of the church. As Jesus preached, they preached; as Jesus healed, they healed; as Jesus engaged in exorcism, they engaged in exorcism. Filled with his Spirit, they continued his ministry.[14] It is difficult to overlook the similarity between the coming of the Spirit at the beginning of Jesus' public ministry and the coming of the Spirit at the beginning of the disciples' ministry.[15] What God told Israel through the ministry of Jesus, he now tells the world though the ministry of Jesus' Spirit.[16] The purpose of God's story with Israel as taught through the words and deeds of Jesus in Luke's Gospel continues to be explicated through the words and deeds of God's Spirit throughout the book of Acts.

Parallel Structures in Luke and Acts

Luke's use of narrative to explicate the pattern of God's story with Israel and the nations becomes even more evident when comparisons are made between certain emphases in the Gospel of Luke and Acts. Although caution is important when conclusions are drawn from such studies, it is difficult to avoid the suggestion that Luke quite deliberately shaped his narratives with tremendous finesse. Beyond the selection and recounting of specific stories, Luke puts his narrative together in such a way that the Gospel accounts of Jesus' ministry typologically precede the ministry of the

---

[13]Eduard Lohse, "Lukas als Theologe der Heilsgeschichte," *Evangelische Theologie* 14 (1954): 256-75.

[14]John Drury sees this as well, saying, "There comes a point when the Spirit takes Jesus' place on the historical scene. He leaves it and continues to influence it, not by mystical indwelling, but by the strictly historical means of the telling of his life-story" (*Tradition and Design in Luke's Gospel: A Study in Early Christian Historiography* [London: Darton, Longman & Todd, 1976], 176).

[15]Both in the case of Jesus' baptism and on the day of Pentecost, the coming of the Spirit is reported as a visible and audible event.

[16]Notice here also John's emphases in Jesus' high-priestly prayer, John 17:18.

Spirit-empowered church. The narrative locale and details change, but the story remains the same.

Early on, Matthias Schneckenburger, following F. C. Baur[17] and Karl Schrader,[18] developed the thesis that the miracles of Paul were deliberately paralleled with the miracles of Peter by the author of Acts. Schneckenburger contended that

> Acts is directed towards Jewish Christians in Rome and has a twofold apologetic purpose:
> (1) to defend the Apostle Paul in his apostolic dignity, in his personal and apostolic behavior, especially in the matter of the Gentiles, against all attacks of the Judaizers, the same charges against which Paul defended himself in his Epistles; (2) to demonstrate to these same Jewish Christians the political legitimacy of Paul. . . . Luke, by recounting Paul's acquittals in other cities, assures the Jewish Christians of Rome that their security will not be endangered by Pauline universalism.[19]

Some scholars took this Paul-Peter parallelism even further and used it to argue for a mediating purpose of Acts.[20] The contention that Peter and Paul were at enmity, however, no longer has any serious support and is rightly rejected as an old Hegelian approach to history that fits the historiography of Luke poorly.

The parallels are massive and persuasive and cannot be rejected as coincidental. John A. Hardon lists them (see table 9.1) and notes that "not only are the miracles of Peter and Paul susceptible of parallel classification, but once so paralleled, we have practically covered all the miracle passages reported in the Acts about the two apostles."[21]

Conclusions from Luke's use of such a cognizant style of presentation need not speak to a tension between history and theology, as suggested by earlier scholars.[22] The affirmation of current scholarship that Luke combines history and theology in a dis-

---

[17]F. C. Baur, in an essay on the Christ-party in the Corinthian church, used what became known as *Tendenzkritik* to show the theological tendency of the Christian writings, arguing for a Petrus-party that rejected the teachings of Paul. Later, in an article on Romans, striving to present the letter to the Romans as an anti Jewish-Christian tract, he launches the argument that Acts was written by a "Paulinist" to defend the mission of Paul to the Gentiles.

[18]Karl Schrader noted in 1836 that the Paul of Acts was presented as a miracle-worker in order to give him the same rank as Peter. On this see F. Neirynck, "The Miracle Stories in the Acts of the Apostles," in *Les Actes des Apôtres: Traditions, Rédaction, Théologie, Bibliotheca Ephemeridum Theologicarum Lovaniensium 48,* ed. J. Kremer (Leuven: University Press, 1979), 173, n. 10.

[19]A. J. Mattill, "The Purpose of Acts: Schneckenburger Reconsidered," in *Apostolic History and the Gospel,* ed. W. Ward Gasque and Ralph P. Martin (Grand Rapids, Mich.: Eerdmans, 1998), 108.

[20]While Schneckenburger saw Acts as an apologetic script written by Paul's friend Luke before A.D. 70 to the Judaizers, Tübingen scholars took it to be a second-century device to mediate between two hostile fractions in the church, namely the Petrine and the Pauline factions.

[21]John A. Hardon, "The Miracle Narratives in the Acts of the Apostles," *Catholic Biblical Quarterly* 16 (July 1954): 308-9, 310.

[22]This does not mean, of course, that the quality of the parallels is without problems. Healings of lame people, for example, seem to be rather frequent, making a comparison between Acts 3:1ff. and Acts 14:7ff. a possible interpretive stretch. The lack of parallel sequencing between the Peter and the Paul ac-

play of the character of salvation history is much more likely and falls in line with what
has been shown above. In fact, these parallelisms arguably find further significance in
how they parallel the events of Jesus. They are not Luke's attempt to defend Paul
against attacks from Jewish constituencies in a comparison to Peter. Rather, these parallelisms give credence to the continuous effects of God's work as fulfilled in Jesus and
his Spirit (Acts 28:30-31).

Table 9.1

Miracles in the Life of St. Peter	Miracles in the Life of St. Paul
Many signs and wonders (2:43)	Many signs and wonders (14:3)
Healing of a lame man (3:1ff.)	Healing of a lame man (14:7ff.)
Rebuke of Ananias and Saphira (5:1ff.)	Rebuke of Elymas suddenly blinded (13:8ff.)
Shaking of a building by prayer (4:31)	Shaking of a building by praise (16:25ff.)
Healing by the shadow of Peter (5:15)	Healing by the handkerchiefs of Paul (19:12)
Sudden healing off a paralytic at Lydda (9:33ff.)	Sudden healing of dysentery (28:7ff.)
Resuscitation of Tabitha (9:36-44)	Resuscitation of Eutychus (20:9ff.)
Removal of chains in prison (12:5ff.)	Removal of chains in prison (16:25ff.)

In 1850 Bruno Bauer drew the radical conclusion that the "original behind the Peter and Paul from Acts was the Jesus of the Synoptic Gospels."[23] Without this extreme
and negative conclusion as to the historical reliability of Luke, Charles Talbert[24] and
A. J. Mattill[25] pick up on the significance of the parallels between the ministry of Jesus
and of Peter/Paul for Luke's description.

---

counts likewise places into question the possibility of drawing major conclusions regarding Luke's
desire to compare Paul to Peter. Furthermore, if Luke's purpose was to show that Paul "matched up"
to Peter, the significance of divine events caused by other disciples like Philip become unintelligible.

[23] Bruno Bauer, *Die Apostelgeschichte: Eine Ausgleichung des Paulinismus und des Judenthums innerhalb der
christlichen Kirche* (Berlin: Verlag von Gustav Hempel, 1850), 12; author's translation.

[24] C. H. Talbert, *Literary Patterns, Theological Themes, and the Genre of Luke-Acts,* SBL Monograph Series
20 (Missoula, Mont.: Scholars Press, 1975), esp. pp. 15-65.

[25] A. J. Mattill, "The Jesus-Paul Parallels and the Purpose of Luke-Acts: H. H. Evans Reconsidered," *Novum Testamentum* 17 (January 1975): 15-46.

Mattill concludes from this that Luke's major themes are the "Unity of the Christian Church with the Traditions of Israel," "God's Plan of Salvation" and "The Journey Toward Jerusalem and Passion." According to Mattill, Luke wanted to exhibit how God approved the ministry of Peter and Paul by giving them the power for miracle working in a way very similar to Jesus (see table 9.2).[26]

Table 9.2

Miracles of Jesus	Miracles of Paul
Casting out demons (Lk 4:33-37, 41; 8:26-39; 11:20. Cf. Acts 10:38)	Casting out demons (Acts 16:16-18)
Healing of a lame man (Lk 5:17-26)	Healing of a lame man (Acts 14:8-14)
Healing of many sick (Lk 4:40; 6:17-19)	Healing of many sick (Acts 28:9)
Curing of fever, in consequence of which the sick stream in and are healed (Lk 4:38-40)	Curing of fever, in consequence of which the sick stream in and are healed (Acts 28:7-10)
Raising of dead (Lk 7:11-17; 8:40-42, 49-56)	Raising of dead (Lk 20:9-12)
Affirming that the person is not really dead (Lk 8:52)	Affirming that the person is not really dead (Acts 20:10)
Physically imparted healing power (Lk 5:17; 6:19; 8:46)	Physically imparted healing power (Acts 19:6, 11-12)
Those healed by Jesus gratefully supply the necessities of life to theirr healer (Lk 8:2-3)	Those healed by Paul gratefully supply the necessities of life to their healer (Acts 28:10)

These parallels obviously hold the same problems and should be read with the same caution as the Peter-Paul parallelisms described above. Yet as above, the evidence cannot be overlooked as insignificant.

Although the structure of these parallelisms may be comparable, one distinction

---

[26]Beyond these parallels, Mattill also finds some correspondences in the form of the miracle stories: Lk 3:38-40 // Acts 28:7-10; Lk 5:18-26 // Acts 14:8-10; Lk 8:35-37 // Acts 16:38-39; Lk 4:35 // Acts 17:18. "Each is recognized by demons (Lk 4:34-35, 41; 8:28; Acts 16:17; 19:15): Lk 8:28 // Acts 16:17: *tou theou tou hypsistou.* Then Luke lets an evil spirit with supernatural knowledge make the parallelism explicit: Jesus I know, and Paul I know (Acts 19:15)" (ibid., 28-29).

needs mentioning. Since it is impossible to hold that Luke attempts to "match up" Paul and Peter to Jesus, the lack of chronology and the exact form and number of miracles are not quite as critical in the parallels between Jesus and Paul/Peter. The point here is that Luke, in a subtle but sedulous manner, attempts to show that the pattern of Jesus' ministry and the power from his Spirit continues in the early church. God continues to implement his story with Israel and the nations.

Mattill's suggestion that the person of Paul (and/or Peter) is the case in point for the parallelisms does not persuade. By telling the story of Peter and Paul, Luke narrates the spread of the gospel to the Gentiles. As such, they were early and primary vehicles from Israel's soil. Yet there is no suggestion of anything beyond this. Even in Paul's (and Peter's) own time, new leadership came to the fore, continuing in Jesus' (and Paul/Peter's) footsteps.[27] It seems natural, therefore, that if one allows for an evaluation of the parallelisms within the category of the kingdom of God, the issue of personality (Paul and Peter) becomes subordinate to the greater question of church. God's purpose for Israel's assembly (*qahal*) as shown in the Gospel of Luke is being fulfilled in the Christian church (*ekklēsia*) as becomes evident in Acts.

Outlining the Acts of the Apostles

Approaching Acts as an historical/theological manuscript that connects to Luke's Gospel as a sequel that purports to retell the story in a new locale with new details and with an even greater emphasis on fulfillment gives room for a look at the structure of Acts that moves beyond the traditional outlines. It clearly can be claimed, of course, that Acts 1:8 forms an outline for Luke's description of the geographical expansion of the gospel. It moved in ever-expanding circles from Jerusalem, to Judea,[28] to Samaria,[29] and to the ends of the earth.[30] It is not altogether certain, however, that Acts 1:8 is a

---

[27] 1 Cor 11:1, "Be imitators of me, as I am of Christ."

[28] Southern part of Palestine as distinct from other parts (cf., Lk 1:65; 2:4; Acts 8:1; 9:31; 11:1, 29; 12:19; 21:10).

[29] The region south of Galilee (Acts 8:2, 5, 9, 14; 9:31; 15:3; cf., Lk 17:11). The question, however, is whether the Samaritan reference is a geographical reference at all. Philip's ministry in Samaria in Acts 8, caused by the scattering of Christians due to Stephen's stoning, is a gigantic move for the gospel *beyond* the "borders" of Judaism (not just Judea). More than a geographical reference, this likely speaks to a *new ethnic reality*. People of all ethnic backgrounds come to faith. See J. Daniel Hays, *From Every People and Nation: A Biblical Theology of Race,* New Studies in Biblical Theology, no. 14, (Downers Grove, Ill.: InterVarsity Press, 2003), 167.

[30] This phrase may be a direct reference to Isaiah 49:6, "I will give you as a light to the nations, that my salvation may reach to the end of the earth" (cf., Acts 13:47; Lk 2:32). Based on a reference in *Pss. Sol.* 8:15, F. J. Foakes-Jackson (*The Beginnings of Christianity* [London: Macmillan, 1922], 2:79), Conzelmann and others hold the "end of the earth" refers to Rome and thus explains why Acts ends where it does. Others argue that the phrase refers to Spain (E. Earle Ellis, "'The End of the Earth' [Acts 1:8]," *BBR* 1 [1991]: 123-33) or Ethiopia (Henry J. Cadbury, *The Book of Acts in History* [New York: Harper

geographical statement. In light of Luke 24:47 and Acts 2:5, it is quite likely that the phrase has as much ethnic and sociological content as it does geographical.[31]

In terms of leadership and church life, the emphasis on Peter in Acts 1—12 and on Paul in Acts 13—28 likewise seems a natural claim for Luke's outline. Combining the two and emphasizing Luke's historical purpose, some have claimed that Luke's primary purpose was to give a progress report for the early church.[32] However, as will be shown later, other approaches to the Acts of the Apostles may yield a better and clearer understanding of Luke's purpose for writing and the story he wants to tell.

The suggestion that Luke wrote Acts as an apology has already been touched upon above.[33] Those who practice *Tendenz* criticism (attempting to discern an author's bias) have argued this most every possible way: Luke wrote to defend Paul against Peter, or to make a mediating statement between two major factions in the church. Acts was, in other words, the synthesis between the thesis, Peter, and the antithesis, Paul. The same argument has been used to claim that Acts was an apology for Jews and Jewish Christians against a growing presence of Gentile Christians in the early church. The other way around, others have argued that this was an apology for Gentile Christians who were "questionable" members of the new "Christian" expression of Judaism. Arguing from the mentioning of Theophilus in Acts 1:1, others have claimed that Luke primarily attempted to convince Theophilus that this new Christian sect presented no political threat to Rome.

Although the fact that both the Gospel of Luke and Acts are directed to the Roman official (or at least the quite prominent Roman citizen) Theophilus may yield credence to the argument that the purpose of Luke and Acts is to present the story of Jesus and its consequence, the spread of this new movement, in a positive light, there is nothing that indicates that Luke saw his documents as decidedly defensive apologetic pieces. It is more likely that Theophilus was Luke's patron and a leader of a Roman house-church.

Dedicating his manuscripts to such a leader does not suggest that they were meant for his private reading only. Rather, Luke told the story so that it would be taught in all the house churches, that God's original purpose for his creation was now being fulfilled. Just as Luke's Gospel is the story of Israel and her misunderstanding of God's

---

& Bros., 1955], 15). Again, this might be an ethnic or sociological phrase more than a geographical one (e.g., Ethiopian eunuch, Acts 8).

[31]Cf. Thomas S. Moore, "'To the End of the Earth': The Geographical and Ethnic Universalism of Acts 1:8 in Light of Isaianic Influence on Luke," *Journal of the Evangelical Theological Society* 40, no. 3 (September 1997): 389-99.

[32]Acts 1:1—6:6, The Earliest Church in Jerusalem; Acts 6:8—9:31, The First Geographical Expansion; Acts 9:32—12:24, The First Expansion to the Gentiles; Acts 12:25—16:5, The First Geographical Expansion into the Gentile World; Acts 16:6—19:20, The Gospel Reaches Europe; Acts 19:21—28:31, The Gospel Reaches Rome.

[33]See note 18.

eternal purpose, so Acts is the story of God's fulfillment of this eternal purpose in spite of Israel's misunderstanding. Just as the historical Jesus reveals God's original plan and enables its fruition, the Spirit of Jesus reveals and enables God's plan to be fulfilled throughout his creation. God's purpose for Israel to be a light to the nations through the power of his presence is now accomplished through the new Israel, Jesus' disciples, who are empowered by the presence of God's Spirit.

Rather than approaching Acts from a perspective of geographical expansion, or from leadership issues being resolved through the presentation of Peter and Paul as equally significant personalities, or from the presupposition that Luke had apologetic purposes of some kind, it will prove more fruitful to investigate how Luke treats the story of Israel in Acts. As became clear in the study of the Gospels, Luke's presentation of God's story with Israel stood as a correction to the traditional interpretations of first-century Judaism. Any informed first-century reader of Luke would understand that according to Luke, Jesus came to enable the fulfillment of God's original purpose for his creation. *This same story is now retold in Acts.*

Approaching Acts from this perspective can be done in various ways. However, the significance of the speeches in Acts for Luke's theological purposes places them in the forefront of such investigation.[34] Moreover, it seems that the way Luke uses these speeches as anchor-points for his narrative allows the material connecting the speeches to reiterate the teaching/preaching proclaimed in the speeches themselves. In other words, the individual pericopes making up the Acts narrative, the speeches, summaries and narrative enforcers, both individually and collectively parade Luke's message that God's story with Israel is now coming to its climactic fulfillment and conclusion. In terms of historical narrative, the speeches may function as summary statements of sorts, but in terms of theology they are the pillars to which the narrative sections connect.[35] The narrative material affirms the speeches, not the other way around.

In terms of the story told through the speeches, Acts 2 begins with an exhibition of the fulfillment of Joel's prophecy. From this grand display of God's presence, Peter's first public speech moves the readers to an awareness of Israel's wickedness and need for repentance (Acts 2:22-40). Sounding the prophetic message once again, Peter's sec-

---

[34]W. Ward Gasque's survey ("The Speeches of Acts: Dibelius Reconsidered," in *New Dimensions in New Testament Study,* ed. Richard N. Longenecker and Merrill C. Tenney [Grand Rapids, Mich.: Zondervan, 1974]) of the various approaches to the speeches in Acts gives a helpful perspective on their theological significance *and* a strong affirmation of their historical authenticity. See also the introduction in Marion L. Soards, *The Speeches in Acts: Their Content, Context, and Concerns* (Louisville, Ky.: Westminster John Knox, 1994).

[35]Luke sprinkles major and minor speeches throughout Acts: Jesus—Acts 1; Peter's speeches—Acts 1; 2; 3; 4; 5; 10; 11; 13; James's speeches—Acts 15; 21; Stephen's speech—Acts 7; Paul's speeches—Acts 13; 14; 17; 20; 22; 23; 24; 26; 28. Other speeches: Gamaliel, Acts 5:35-39; an Ephesian, Acts 19:35-40; Tertullus, Acts 24:2-8; Festus, Acts 25:14-21, 24-27.

ond speech beginning in Acts 3:12 focuses on the need for Israel to repent and turn from her sins. This moves in Stephen's speech to the Jewish leadership in Acts 7 to an all-out charge of being stiff-necked (Acts 7:51). As Stephen retells the whole flow of Israel's story, it becomes evident that Israel has misinterpreted God's actions in their midst and missed the purpose of her calling and her history with God.

Indeed, it is the Gentiles, not Israel, who are calling upon God and being visited by his Spirit (Acts 10). Peter is invited to speak in the home of a devout and God-fearing Gentile and is convinced by God himself to accept the invitation (Acts 10:9-23). This leads to an outpouring of God's Spirit upon Gentiles, who are now marked by the very evidence of YHWH's presence, the Holy Spirit (Acts 10). Peter can conclude nothing other than that "God shows no partiality, but in every nation anyone who fears him and does what is right is acceptable to him" (Acts 10:34).

Paul's speech in Acts 13 takes this even further. Beginning with a recounting of God's history with Israel (Acts 13:16), the emphasis now falls on restoration and forgiveness of sin (Acts 13:38). God's justification goes far beyond any justification that could come from Moses' law. In fact, God's final work in Jesus forgives specifically "all those sins from which you could not be freed by the law of Moses" (Acts 13:39).

As a crescendo to the Acts narrative, Luke ends with Paul's speech to the Roman guard (Acts 28:17ff.), where an Isaiah quote (Is 6:9, 10) makes it evident that although Israel's story had been intricately tied to God's plan for the nations, God's plans are now being fulfilled in spite of Israel's obstinacy. Israel would not listen, but the Gentiles will (Acts 28:28). Israel missed her appointment and forfeited the purpose of her calling, yet God's plan for his creation moves unhindered toward its completion (Acts 28:31).

Analyzing the Text of Acts

Transitioning from the Historical Jesus to the Spirit of Jesus. Luke uses the first eleven verses of Acts to summarize his Gospel account. Beyond allowing Acts to stand on its own as a manuscript that can be read without the Gospel, this enables Luke to transition and connect everything that happens in the following story to the teaching and work of the historical Jesus. As seen in the comparisons above, there is no essential difference between what Jesus does through his physical presence and through his spiritual presence. Acts is not about what individual apprentices of Jesus did, but about how Jesus' ministry continued through his Spirit even after he had physically ascended from the earth. The disciples were completely powerless without his presence and had to delay their ministry until they had been baptized with the Holy Spirit (Acts 1:5).

Although clairvoyance did not exactly characterize the disciples in most of the Gospel stories, they now clearly understood that Jesus' ministry was about the fulfillment of God's plan for Israel and the nations. Although they understood this in political terms, as Luke portrays it in Acts 1:6, their question, which most likely was the question of many of Luke's readers as well, gave an opportunity to reiterate that God's plan would be accomplished only through the enabling power of God's Spirit. The restoration of this enabling presence among his people was not for Israel's national restoration, but for the purpose of completing God's original creation purpose among all peoples of all ethnic groups (Acts 1:8). Luke does not reject Israel's role, but understands it to be fulfilled only in connection with its universal mission to be a light to all the Gentiles.

The connection between Jesus' spiritual presence after the ascension and the living presence of the resurrected Lord before his ascension is further emphasized in the parallelism of language used to describe the befuddled disciples at the empty tomb (Lk 24:4)[36] and the confounded followers at the scene of Jesus' ascension.[37] Such use of "resurrection language" could hardly be missed as an indication that just as the death of Jesus did not end his ministry, neither would his ascension. Although his historical presence as they had known it changed, his "living" presence would be restored among them "in not many days" (Acts 1:5).

Peter's speech to the 120 in the upper room. After making the connection back to the historical Jesus, Luke moves the story forward through a detailed account of the selection process for Judas Iscariot's replacement. The actual replacement seems almost an aside to Luke—a choice was made between two who fulfilled the criteria (having accompanied the historical Jesus, Acts 1:21-22)—while the theological interpretation of the event receives complete prominence. The two chosen for the selection process are unknown, and neither is mentioned in Luke's Gospel or other places in Acts.[38]

Everything in this account rests on the necessity for Scripture to be fulfilled (Acts

---

[36]This may further point back to the experience on the mount of transfiguration (Lk 9:30). Notice the connection between the transfiguration and ascension. Elijah ascended in 2 Kings 2:11-12. See also Philo's description of Moses' ascension: "For when he was now on the point of being taken away, and was standing at the very starting-place, as it were, that he might fly away and complete his journey to heaven, he was once more inspired and filled with the Holy Spirit, and while still alive, he prophesied admirably what should happen to himself after his death, relating, that is, how he had died when he was not as yet dead, and how he was buried without any one being present so as to know of his tomb, because in fact he was entombed not by mortal hands, but by immortal powers" (*On the Life of Moses* 2:291).

[37]Parallelism of language does not, of course, suggest that the historical event of the resurrection is not clearly distinguishable from the ascension. See James D. G. Dunn (*Jesus and the Spirit: A Study of the Religious and Charismatic Experience of Jesus and the First Christians As Reflected in the New Testament* [London: SCM Press, 1975], 143) who argues in favor of a distinctive event of Pentecost but rejects a distinct forty-day period of postresurrection appearances of Jesus concluding with the ascension.

[38]Matthias and Joseph are mentioned only here in Acts unless Joseph Barsabbas is the same as Judas called Barsabbas in Acts 15:22. The only other disciple mentioned in Acts called Joseph is Barnabas (Acts 4:36). It would be easy to understand how the name Barnabas (Son of Encouragement) could be given to one whose real name was Barsabbas when he encouraged the church with a large gift.

1:16). Judas was numbered among the Twelve and therefore allotted his share. This reference to Judas's "allotment of share" draws its language directly from the distribution of the land among the twelve tribes in Numbers, which also was "apportioned by lot" (Num 26:55; 33:54).[39] The conclusion seems clear: Judas needed to be replaced because God was bringing about his original purpose for the twelve tribes of Israel now represented by the twelve disciples of Jesus. Israel's exile was over, their "number" was reestablished, and their story was coming to the fulfillment God had promised David.

To affirm this specific event as a theological necessity anticipated by David (Acts 1:21), Luke includes Peter's midrash (rabbinic interpretation) on two Psalms (Ps 69:25 and Ps 109:8). The application of one of Hillel's exegetical rules, *qal wahomer* (light to heavy),[40] to Judas's situation makes this clear. What was asserted by David about false companions and wicked men in general "applies specifically to Judas."[41] Moreover, not only did this necessitate a replacement of Judas, but Judas became symbolic of, or even a typological interpretation of, faithless men. The stage is now set for Luke's readers to understand the new events of the Spirit as the necessary (Greek *dei*, Acts 1:21) completions of Israel's own history.

Pentecost. That God is reversing the curse, or even restoring the consequences of the Fall, now becomes clear from Luke's highlighting of the Pentecost event. Not only are the disciples the community that represents God's restoration of his people; they are boldly proclaiming the actions of God with a power that reverses Babel (Gen 11:6-9). Opposite Babel, where people were scattered throughout the earth and cursed with language barriers that disabled community and communication, Pentecost parades a gathering of people from "every nation under heaven" (Acts 2:5) who all understood the same speech as if spoken in their own language (Acts 2:6). It is not that God undid what he had done at Babel—rather, he reenabled what was possible before Babel—that God-fearing people (Jews, Acts 2:5) of all languages could understand God's actions. Israel's exile was coming to an end; God's presence was again evident in Jerusalem.

The outpouring of God's Spirit during the Jewish celebration of Pentecost makes the connection to, and reinterpretation of, Israel's history even more self-evident on

---

[39]The connection of the allotment to service should most likely be understood in light of the allotment of service rather than land to the Levites (Num 18:21-24). The Levites were supported by a tithe from the land-allotted tribes (Num. 18:25-26).

[40]Or lesser to greater. What applies in a less important case applies also in a more important case and vice versa. Hillel, a famous rabbi, developed seven major rules of interpretation. *Qal wahomer* is one of these. See further Richard N. Longenecker, *Biblical Exegesis in the Apostolic Period* (Grand Rapids, Mich.: Eerdmans, 1975).

[41]Ibid., 97. This may even be understood as a *Pesher* interpretation—a typological interpretation enabled by a presupposition about historical correspondence (ibid., 100).

several points. Pentecost was a thanksgiving banquet or a harvest feast, celebrating God's providence. Its origin in the Exodus account (Ex 23:16)[42] gives what happens an immediate context of presence, provision and historical purpose (Deut 16:9-12).[43] God's people have come from far away (Egypt/Diaspora/exile?) to celebrate their deliverance from captivity and God's dwelling among them (Deut 16:11). It is hardly possible for Luke's readers to miss the point of Exodus's true fulfillment in this Pentecost event. What Israel had been moving toward since the time of Egypt was becoming a reality before their very eyes. God was in their midst guiding by his Spirit.

Indeed, the remarkable language of Luke's account adds a literary context to this event that allows its historical setting to be understood even more powerfully as God's fulfillment of his history with Israel. The language of the Spirit coming with "the sound like the rush of a violent wind" (Acts 2:2) conjures up images of Old Testament theophanies like Elijah (1 Kings 19:11-12; 2 Kings 2:11) and the Exodus account of the law-giving at Sinai (Ex 19:16-19). Interestingly, Philo's interpretation of the law-giving at Sinai, an interpretation most likely known to many of the listeners (and Luke's readers), reads like a parallel to the experience at Pentecost:

> And a voice sounded forth from out of the midst of the fire which had flowed from heaven, a most marvelous and awful voice, the flame being endowed with articulate speech *in a language familiar to the hearers,* which expressed its words with such clearness and distinctness that the people seemed rather to be seeing than hearing it.[44]

Luke's explicit use of Philo's conjunction of fire and communication from God at Sinai enables him to implicitly suggest that the giving of the Spirit not only parallels but fulfills the giving of the Law.[45] The Law, God's word and covenantal revelation, which the Talmud taught was intended for all the nations of the world, claiming that it was given in the seventy languages that made up the nations of the world,[46] was now

---

[42]Pentecost was one of three major feasts in the Jewish calendar: "You shall observe the festival of harvest, of the first fruits of your labor, of what you sow in the field. You shall observe the festival of ingathering at the end of the year, when you gather in from the field the fruit of your labor" (cf., Ex 34:22; Lev 23:15-21; Num 28:26).

[43]"You shall count seven weeks; begin to count the seven weeks from the time the sickle is first put to the standing grain. Then you shall keep the festival of weeks to the LORD your God, contributing a freewill offering in proportion to the blessing that you have received from the LORD your God. Rejoice before the LORD your God—you and your sons and your daughters, your male and female slaves, the Levites resident in your towns, as well as the strangers, the orphans, and the widows who are among you—at the place that the LORD your God will choose as a dwelling for his name. Remember that you were a slave in Egypt, and diligently observe these statutes."

[44]*Decalogue* 46; emphasis mine.

[45]Luke Timothy Johnson sees Luke's use of Moses' typology to be so strong that "it would be surprising if the use of sound and fire and languages here did not allude to the Sinai event" (*The Acts of the Apostles,* Sacra Pagina, no. 5, ed. D. J. Harrington [Collegeville, Minn.: Liturgical Press, 1992], 46. See also the connection between wind and future restoration of Israel in Ezekiel 37.

[46]*b.Shab.* 88b.

demonstratively fulfilling its goal. Pentecost was the celebration of covenant renewal—now no longer a mere commemoration of past renewals,[47] but a divine fulfillment of the promised New Covenant (Ezek 36:27-29; Jer 31:33-34). Laden with historical symbolism and wrapped in literary parallels, Luke's Pentecost presents a strong rein-terpretation of God's story with Israel.

Peter's speech at Pentecost. The stage is now set for Peter's speech. The people in Jerusalem and Luke's readers are ready for an explanation. Babel is reversed and Exo-dus' true purpose, that God would dwell among his people, leading and guiding them by his Spirit, has been fulfilled—God's people have returned from exile and God's word is being proclaimed in all languages! God's re-creative power evidently hovers over Israel![48] The promised new covenant has replaced the old in a setting of historical celebration and with a display that recalls the foundational covenant experience at Si-nai. The people are not sure what to make of all this—"What does this mean?" (Acts 2:12), but Peter's speech gives the answers—"let me explain this to you" (Acts 2:14).

The connection to God's actions in Israel's history is immediate. With next to no introduction, Peter draws a direct line to the prophetic promise for the end times and declares it to be fulfilled in this new covenant Pentecost event. With a slight change in the introductory formula—Joel 2:28 introduces the prophecy by "after these things"; Peter says "in the last days"—the fulfillment of Joel's prophecy seem indisputable. The parallels between what the listeners had just heard and seen (and readers have just read) and God's promises of old are too obvious to miss. The anticipated fulfillment of Israel's story, where God's Spirit rests not only on a selected few, but on all regardless of age, sex, rank and nationality, has come. Even a simple fisherman from Galilee (Acts 2:7) is now empowered to expound on the words and acts of God. God would now, as he promised, turn every individual among his people into a prophet. The Spirit has come, not just on the group, but explicitly on *each* of them (Acts 2:3), giving them pro-phetic ministry like Joel had promised.[49]

The connection between Israel's story and the inclusions of all nations comes force-fully to the forefront in Joel 2:32 (par. Acts 2:21) and receives full clarification through

---

[47]*Jubilees* explains Pentecost as a covenant-renewal feast: "Therefore, it is ordained and written in the heavenly tablets that they should observe the feast of Shebuot [weeks] in this month, once per year, in order to renew the covenant in all (respects), year by year. And all of this feast was celebrated in heaven from the day of creation until the days of Noah, twenty-six jubilees and five weeks of years. And Noah and his children kept it for seven jubilees and one week of years until the day of the death of Noah. . . . And you, command the children of Israel so that they might keep this feast in all of their generations as a commandment to them" (*Jub* 6:17-21).

[48]Beyond the references given above, the "sound" and "wind" language as an expression of God's pres-ence may even conjure up images from the creation narrative among the readers.

[49]The references to dreams and visions (Acts 2:17) refer to prophetic insight and are not to be thought of as expressions of utopian fantasies (cf. Johnson, *Acts,* 49).

Peter's citation in this context. The link between the international gathering exposed in Acts 2:9-11, the obvious presence of God in the disciples, and the resulting conversion of three thousand leaves little to the imagination. Clarity from God's side reigns. This is for all of Israel to understand. Peter's repetitive mention of Israel is not accidental (Acts 2:14, fellow Jews; Acts 2:22, men of Israel; Acts 2:29, brothers; Acts 2:36, let all Israel be assured). The very purpose of Peter's speech is to show that those who did not recognize that what happened was God's fulfillment of Israel's story were rejecting what God had been planning from the beginning, remaining ignorant of Israel's purpose.[50]

As clearly proclaimed by the Gospel story, the significance of Jesus' death and resurrection for God's plan cannot be exaggerated. He was accredited by God through deeds of power, wonders and signs (Acts 2:22)—an attestation now given to Peter and the apostles—and his death, though caused by the Jewish leadership who evidently did not understand God's purpose for Israel, happened "according to God's definite plan and foreknowledge" (Acts 2:23).

That this claim by Peter was the truth was apparent from Jesus' resurrection (Acts 2:24). David saw this; the contemporary Jewish leadership missed it. Indeed, if Israel had paid attention, they would not have missed it either, since David, who was a prophet who knew God (Acts 2:30), spoke about it in Psalm 110:1 (Acts 2:34). Moreover, they should have recognized that David in his highest moments of inspiration was a type of what would come through Christ (Acts 2:25-28 // Ps 16:8-11). David's words were not about himself but about Christ, the fulfillment of the promise given to him that his dynasty would be eternal though one of his descendants. As the listeners (and readers) could see, hints to God's purpose and point of fulfillment had been dropped throughout Israel's history.[51]

The new community that fulfills the prophetic call to Israel. The response was immediate; the evidence was overwhelming. Three thousand people now recognized God's purpose and repented. When they did, they were baptized into the community of those who accepted this fulfillment of God's purposes for his people. Their sins were forgiven, and the evidence was the gift of the Spirit. God was restoring his people, enabling the

---

[50]Notice Paul's use of Joel 2:32 in Romans 10:13, where he argues the removal of any distinction between Jew and Gentile among believers (Rom 10:11-13).

[51]Peter's use of common *midrashic* rules of interpretation brings home his proof for the resurrection. The rule used here is called *Gezerah Shewa*: the use of the same words in two separate cases enables the application of the same interpretative considerations. Here the use of "right hand" in Ps 16 and Ps 110 supports the argument for the resurrection: "For David says concerning him, 'I saw the Lord always before me, for he is at my *right hand* so that I will not be shaken; therefore my heart was glad, and my tongue rejoiced; moreover my flesh will live in hope. For you will not abandon my soul to Hades, or let your Holy One experience corruption.' . . . David spoke of the *resurrection* of the Messiah, saying, 'He was not abandoned to Hades, nor did his flesh experience corruption.' . . . [34] For David did not ascend into the heavens, but he himself says, 'The Lord said to my Lord, "Sit at my *right hand*, until I make your enemies my footstool" '" (Acts 2:25-35).

new believers to experience the fulfillment of the blessings first promised to Abraham.

That Israel's purpose had been fulfilled found conclusive argument in Luke's follow-up to Peter's speech. Beyond the Spirit's verification of the inauguration of God's eschatological work among his people and beyond Peter's explanation of this event as he evidenced its consistency with God's promises of old, the community created by this Spirit proved to be a complete answer to the prophetic call.

The prophets consistently brought three serious charges against Israel as they warned them against breaking their covenant with God: (1) idolatry—the breaking of the first commandment; (2) religious formalism—the disconnect between external ceremony and inner devotion; and (3) social injustice—the lack of concern for the poor. The prophetic new community of Acts 2 embodied the correction to these charges. Opposite a community that could be charged with idolatry, this new community, guided by God's Spirit, gave their constant attention *(proskarterountes)* to the presence of God (Acts 2:42). The teaching, the fellowship, the breaking of bread, and the prayers together expressed the undeviating focus on God that Israel had been called to throughout her history. The "teaching" has direct reference to the study of God's word likewise encouraged throughout the Old Testament. The "fellowship" has a direct parallel to God's covenantal community. The "breaking of bread" stays the focus on God's pivotal action for his people, the Passover, which reminds the reader of the repeated Old Testament reference to God as the one who brought them out of Egypt— an event that Christ now had brought to its intended fulfillment. The "prayer" brings devotion, intimacy and thanksgiving to the forefront. The call of God through his prophets has been heard and heeded by this new community that fulfills the call of the prophets. Opposite historical Israel, their focus stays on God and God alone.

Religious formalism has no room in this new community. Their devotion *(proskarterountes)* was much more than ritualism or a system of worship and sacrifice that belonged to the cultic expression of religion. Rather, this was a genuine cry from the heart that, over and beyond the participation in the temple services (Acts 2:46a), came to expression every time and everywhere they met—even in their private homes (Acts 2:46b). The externality of formalism had been replaced by a sincerity of heart that was filled with the constant praise of God (Acts 2:46c).

If the evidence from the outpouring of the Spirit and the speech of Peter had left anyone unconvinced, Luke's summarizing of the life of the Christ-following community brings a powerful crescendo to his storyline. Even the prophetic charge that Israel did not take care of the poor is answered by this text (Acts 2:44-45). Again the connection this text makes to the prophetic charge is too close to miss. This cannot be relegated to a discussion of utopian visions of society as some commentators try to do. Nor should this be read as a call to all followers of Christ to sell all their possessions as others have argued. The emphasis here is on the new community that answers the call of the prophets and makes sure no one has needs (Acts 2:45b). The true Israel, a community living the life God's prophets described for Israel, has emerged.

Peter's speech at Solomon's Portico. As if to give an illustration of Israel's exilic situation in Second Temple Judaism and to contrast this with the power of God's new covenant, Luke chooses to begin his recording of the new covenant community work with a miracle in the context of temple worship. A lame man is placed by the temple gate every day (Acts 3:2) to beg. This setting itself exposes the impotence of Israel's worship. With less drama than the temple cleansing recorded in the Gospels, the misinterpretation of what God's presence was supposed to mean to Israel shines though with full clarity in Acts 3:1-10. With no expectation of God's restoring power, the crippled man is left *outside* God's presence to beg his way through poverty from "money changers."

The contrast to the response given by the community who were experiencing God's restorative power is razor sharp. Rather than accepting the beggar's misguided call, which would have left him outside the temple and outside the community, Peter and John offer him the experience of Israel's promise. The limbs that had disabled his entrance into the temple of God were given strength and enabled him to walk, even jump, and to participate in the praise of God *inside* the temple gate (Acts 3:8). God's presence in the temple was again obvious—at least to Luke's readers. The temple had been changed from a place for the "money changers" to a true "house of prayer." The purpose of Israel's relationship to God was made manifest.

Again, Luke uses his narrative sections as stage-setters for the proclamation of the speeches. It is hardly sufficient to see in Luke's narrative flow the explication of "an atmosphere of charity and growth."[52] Rather, the purpose is to show how this connects to Israel's history. Peter gets up to give answer to the bewilderment this obvious act of God had caused among the people. "Men of Israel, why does this surprise you?" (Acts 3:12). As Peter will demonstrate, this is what Israel's history has pointed to from the beginning. They had missed it, but God was now giving them an opportunity to repent and get it right.

The reference to "the God of Abraham, Isaac and Jacob" should not be dismissed as a mere idiomatic title for God, but should be seen, along with "the God of our fathers" (Acts 3:13), as a deliberate joining of God's previous covenant to his new covenant. The allusions from this phraseology go back to the burning bush event where Moses received his call to lead Israel out of slavery.[53] The connection to Jesus, then, is made explicit by an allusion in the statement "glorified his servant" to Isaiah's Servant

---

[52]Marion Soards, *Speeches in Acts,* 38.

[53]"Remove the sandals from your feet, for the place on which you are standing is holy ground." He said further, "I am the God of your father, the God of Abraham, the God of Isaac, and the God of Jacob" (Ex 3:5-6). God also said to Moses, "Thus you shall say to the Israelites, 'The Lord, the God of your ancestors, the God of Abraham, the God of Isaac, and the God of Jacob, has sent me to you': This is my name forever, and this my title for all generations" (Ex 3:15).

Songs, especially Isaiah 52:13 ("See, my servant shall prosper; he shall be exalted and lifted up, and shall be very high"). What God had been about since Abraham, and what the call of Moses had affirmed, had not been hidden but was plain for all to see. Isaiah had prophesied about it—as had all the prophets (Acts 3:18)—and his prophecy about Israel as God's servant had now come to fulfillment in Jesus.

God's willingness to forgive Israel of her ignorance (Acts 3:18) had led to their misinterpretation of his action and purpose and resulted in their murdering Jesus, his Holy and Righteous One (Acts 3:14-15). God, however, had raised this Jesus from the dead and enabled salvation for all who would repent and trust that what God had done through Jesus was a crucial event for the fulfillment of Israel's purpose as foretold by Moses and the prophets (Acts 3:22, 24-25). Israel's spiritual exile was over; times of refreshment were upon the people (Acts 3:19).

Peter and John before the Sanhedrin. To move the story and the argument forward, Luke now highlights an encounter between Jesus' two most prominent disciples and the Jewish leadership. The reinterpretation of Israel's story has moved from the discussion on streets to the assembly of the Jewish leadership, the guardians of Israel's story and faith. The direct mentioning by name of the high priests, Annas and Caiaphas, parallels Peter and John's summit with Jesus' encounter and inquisition during his trial (Lk 22:66 // Mt 26:57 // Jn 18:13). The context is set for the reader to understand that Caiaphas and Annas had miscalculated the situation when they attempted to portray Jesus as yet another blasphemous Messiah wannabe. As Luke's description of this encounter will prove, it is not "right in God's sight" to obey the chief priests rather than God (Acts 4:19).

In terms of the larger story line, just as the Sanhedrin thought they had shut down Jesus' teaching and claims, they found that the opposite had happened. Luke's capitalization of this point should not be missed. Almost like an insert to the flow of his narrative, he mentions that the number of men who followed this new understanding of God's work now had risen to five thousand. As the account reads, it is evident that no one can hinder or thwart the plans and purposes of God (Acts 4:4). Using one of Israel's great hymns of thanksgiving as evidence of the Sanhedrin's mistake (Acts 4:11; Ps 118), a hymn Jesus had used to argue this same point (Lk 20:17-19), Peter repeats the indictment that the Sanhedrin's interpretation of Israel's tradition militates against God's original purposes.

Acts 4 exhibits the contrast between the Spirit-empowered disciples (Acts 4:8) and the Spirit-depleted Sanhedrin with ridiculing force. God's restoring power and presence, which had so apparently been Israel's blessing and salvation (Deut 28) until her breaking of the Mosaic covenant left her in exile, was now on trial before Israel's leadership (Acts 4:9). What they rejected was nothing less than the prophetic promise of Israel's fulfillment in the new covenant (Acts 4:12). Luke's recounting of this incident celebrates the distinction between Israel's people and her leadership. Peter and John cannot be silenced because they do the will of God. Israel's leaders stand in opposition to this, but the people understand and praise God (Acts 4:21-22).

That Luke speaks to the story of Israel in his recounting of this event becomes even clearer in what follows. The attempt to silence the proclamation of God's Spirit (Acts 4:20) is contrasted to the unified prayer of the believers, "who raised their voiced together" to extol God's plan laid down since of creation (Acts 4:24) and to acknowledge that even its opposition by Gentiles and Jews alike (Acts 4:27) was part of God's foreordained plan (Acts 4:28) as indeed Israel's greatest leaders had always recognized (Acts 4:25-26).[54] The Sanhedrin's lack of authority and their inability to decide what to do (Acts 4:21) comes to the fore even more starkly when compared with the believers, who, in what reads like another Pentecostal moment, pray for more boldness and power and are answered by God's visible approval (Acts 4:31). The prophetic charge has now been answered; idolatry, religious formalism, and social injustice have been overcome (Acts 4:32-37). The Spirit is again present. There can be no doubt that the Sanhedrin was wrong and the believers were right. Even the Levites were now joining them (Acts 4:36).

Pressures from within and without. Acts 5—6 sets the stage for the most detailed and pivotal reinterpretation of Israel's history given in Acts—the speech of Stephen in Acts 7. The purpose of these chapters is to continue to build the case that regardless of the pressure to return to the "old ways," the believers would be empowered to show that the presence of God's Spirit did inaugurate a new time and covenant. When Ananias and Saphira tried to introduce lying and hypocrisy (religious formalism) to the new fellowship, it was a revolt against the Holy Spirit himself (Acts 5:3). The effects of this divine presence are felt in the land even without a direct word or prayer (Acts 5:15), causing restoration from the curse of sin (Acts 5:16). Israel's leaders are powerless! When they try to silence and jail the apostles, God's angel sets them free (Acts 5:19) and they are found teaching in the temple. When they are captured again, they claim that God sent Jesus to make possible Israel's repentance and forgiveness (Acts 5:31). Those who obey God will experience the presence of God's Spirit; when the Sanhedrin does not, the only possible conclusion is that they do not obey (Acts 5:32-33). That the Sanhedrin is wrong becomes even more obvious when one of their own, Gamaliel, argues that this new teaching will die on its own unless it is from God—a line that gives even more force to Luke's conclusion that "they did not cease to teach and proclaim Jesus as the Messiah" (Acts 5:42).

The inclusion of the selection of seven deacons to help solve the practical issues of

---

[54]Their use of Psalm 2, a royal psalm whose *Sitz im Leben* (use in the life of Israel) may have been the royal enthronement festival for a king—or even for YHWH himself. At any rate, the content of the psalm is rather straight forward: YHWH is unassailable and invincible; whoever tries to threaten his will is doomed to fail. Cf. Hans-Joachim Kraus, *Psalms 1-59: A Commentary,* trans. H. C. Oswald (Minneapolis: Augsburg, 1988), 126.

community (Acts 6:1) likewise keeps the readers' focus on the new understanding of God's purpose for Israel. The argument for why the apostles could not take care of the practical issues of the church centers on the interpretation of Scripture (Acts 6:2). Whatever else may be said in this connection about the discrepancy between this event and the earlier mentioning of the joyous sharing of material goods,[55] Luke's focus continues to dwell on how the early church divulged the *renewed* Israel in her dedication to the Law and the Prophets, the proclamation, and the practice of her faith.[56]

Stephen, his speech and the story of Israel. Keeping the focus on the church's reinterpretative role for Israel's understanding of her purpose, Luke uses the deacon selection event to transition to Stephen, whom he parallels with Jesus. When the reader "listens" to Stephen's speech in Acts 7, radical as it is in its reinterpretative force, it comes with the authority and following approval of Jesus Christ. Not only did Stephen evidence God's unquestionable presence through wonders and miracles,[57] but he was irrefutable in his wisdom and argumentation,[58] fulfilling the promises Jesus gave the Twelve when he predicted the persecution of his followers (Lk 21:15). Moreover, as Johnson notes, the apprehension of Stephen conjures up images of the events surrounding Jesus' passion—"the suborning spies, the agitation of the populace, the arrest, and the delivery to the council (Acts 6:10-12)."[59] In the mind of his opponents, what Stephen said about Jesus and did in the power of the Spirit was blasphemy against Moses and God (Acts 6:11). Like Jesus, he was charged with speaking against Moses and the temple.[60]

The literary setup for the speech gives the same interpretative framework. When Stephen answers their charge, they all notice that "his face was like the face of an angel" (Acts 6:15), a clear parallel to the concluding charge of his speech, where he chastises the Jewish leadership for not obeying the law that was instituted or ordained (*diatagē*) by angels (Acts 7:53). If the angels had mediated the law, as tradition held,[61] Stephen spoke with the authority of one of them. Furthermore, during the subsequent stoning

---

[55]See Craig S. Keener's remark that this was an uncommon practice in the ancient world, where "those with political power generally repressed complaining minorities; here the apostles hand the whole system over to the offended minority. This may thus be the first recorded instance of what we might today call 'affirmative action'" (*The IVP Bible Background Commentary: New Testament* [Downers Grove, Ill.: InterVarsity Press, 1993], 338).

[56]Notice the framing of this whole episode by references to the continued growth (Acts 6:1, 7). See also Robert C. Tannehill's discussion of how Luke does not merely try to glamorize the church but seems keen to focus on the outer effects of its witness (*The Narrative Unity of Luke-Acts 2: A Literary Interpretation* [Minneapolis: Fortress, 1990], 2:80-81).

[57]Compare the recognition Nicodemus gives Jesus (Jn 3:2) to the description of Stephen in Acts 6:8.

[58]Compare the response given to Jesus in, for example, Luke 20:26, 39.

[59]Johnson, *Acts,* 112.

[60]Compare also to Jesus' encounter with Pilate, Luke 23:2, 5, 14 // Acts 6:11, 13, 14.

[61]*Jubilees* 1:29; Josephus, *Ant,* 15:136: "We have learned from God the most excellent of our doctrines, and the most holy part of our law, by angels or ambassadors" (cf. Gal 3:19; Heb 2:2).

of Stephen, the God-ordained nature of his claims is highlighted through his vision of the resurrected Jesus at the right hand of God. Stephen had been affirmed; his interpretation followed Jesus' claims. Indeed, his last words before he dies echo Jesus' words on the cross. He surrenders his spirit to the Lord (Lk 23:46 // Acts 7:59) and prays for his opponents that their sin may not be held against them (Lk 23:34 // Acts 7:60). Stephen was not the one who broke the law and missed God's will; his opponents were the guilty ones. Stephen's speech had rightly interpreted Israel's history.

The speech itself stands as the climactic center pole in Acts. It is hardly incidental that Luke includes this particular speech in such detail at this point in his narrative. The narrative efficacy of having a Greek-speaking Jew from the Diaspora[62] give such a detailed outline of Israel's history with the convincing force and parallels to Christ outlined above can easily be overlooked by modern readers.[63] Stephen evidences, beyond the words of his proclamation, that God's new covenant calls forth a new people consisting of Israel *and* the nations—all who will believe what God has done through Christ and is accomplishing through his Spirit. Indeed, Stephen's speech moves the focus of Acts from Israel to the nations.[64] Following this speech, Christians are scattered into the Gentile areas and God's good news now moves to Samaria (Acts 8:4ff.), to Ethiopia (Acts 8:26ff.) and throughout the world (Acts 9ff). As Stephen has so amply shown, one does not have to be a Hebraic Jew to be able to understand what God has done and to explicate what he is about to conclude. As his speech argues, the traditional Hebraic understanding of the land, the law and the temple needs a serious reconsideration.[65] Stephen's powerful challenge to each of these pillars of Jewish identity as the people of God may be Luke's most compelling reason to include this speech in its full length and detail.

---

[62]Although we have no indication that Stephen was a proselyte like his fellow Hellenist deacon Nicolaus, Hebrew-speaking Jews "from the land" most likely saw themselves as distinct from the "others." See, for example, Paul's remark in Galatians 2:15—"Jews by birth" *(physei Ioudaioi)*.

[63]Beyond the point of Stephen being a Hellenistic Jew from "outside the land" interpreting Jewish history to the Hebraic leadership in Jerusalem, it is interesting to note how the modern Christian reading completely permeates our initial understanding of Israel's history. For example, I have not yet had a student who, before our discussion, could pinpoint what was "wrong" with Stephen's reading of Israel's history and why he was stoned. To them it is a straightforward reading of the Old Testament data and the story as they know it.

[64]Cf. Acts 11:19-20. "The reasons for the development of this [missionary] interest [among the Hellenists] are related to their biography. Since they had grown up as part of a minority group among Gentiles, they did not consider Gentiles as abominable people who were to be avoided as much as possible. Rather, the environment in which they grew up furthered manifold relationships, even friendships, between pagans and Jews. This explains why their communities of such synagogues had open door for gentiles" (Heinz-Werner Neudorfer, "The Speech of Stephen," in *Witness to the Gospel: The Theology of Acts,* ed. David Peterson and I. Howard Marshall [Grand Rapids, Mich.: Eerdmans, 1998], 278, n.11).

[65]For a good overview of the tension between the Hebraic Jews and the Hellenists, who "called for the eschatological abolition of the Temple worship and the revision of the law of Moses," see Hengel, *Acts,* 71-80.

Stephen's speech comes as a reply to a direct question charging that he speaks against the temple and the law. His answer is neither a no, as Ben Witherington suggests,[66] nor a straight yes, as several commentators affirm. Nor should it probably be seen as a mere restatement of the views held by the Hellenistic synagogues, as Hengel seems to suggest.[67] Rather, it expresses a distinctive Christian reinterpretation in light of their experience of God's eschatological fulfillment of Israel's history as foretold by the prophets. This, of course, may have looked like the teaching of some of the radical Hellenistic synagogues to those opposing Stephen; but in terms of Luke's narration, the purpose of the speech is to show that the Jewish leadership in Jerusalem read their history wrong and as a result were blinded to God's eschatological work through Jesus (Acts 7:51-52).

According to Stephen, the Jewish understanding of "the land" as "God's place" rested on a misinterpretation of their own history. Launching his reinterpretation from a restatement of the Abrahamic covenant as Paul would later do (Gal 3), Stephen argues that Abraham's promise did not include the land. He was called out of Mesopotamia but was not given an inheritance in the land of Canaan—"not even a foot's length" (Acts 7:5). Rather, his offspring would not live in Canaan but would be moved to a place where they would be treated as strangers without a land (Acts 7:6). Stephen's argument is clearly that although God would later give them the land, God's promise is tied to his presence among his people and their obedience to him. The actual possession of the land is at best secondary—a mere physical expression of God's blessing. Contemporary Judaism had turned this around and connected the blessing to the land itself.[68]

To drive home his point, Stephen argues that the patriarch Jacob (Israel), the father of the twelve tribes who would later be given the land, was honored and received his blessing outside the land (Acts 7:9-16). This point elevates the obvious disconnect in Israel's own history between God's blessing and the land. The illustration could not be clearer. It proved necessary for Israel (Jacob) to leave the land in order to survive. It was therefore the new group of believers in Christ who were the true heirs of Abraham and Jacob (Israel). They trusted God, evidenced his power and understood that his presence was not limited to Israel's land. The promise to Abraham and the blessing of Jacob would be fulfilled through them.

Continuing the outline of Israel's history, Stephen now shifts his focus to the second

---

[66]Ben Witherington, *The Acts of the Apostles: A Socio-Rhetorical Commentary* (Grand Rapids, Mich.: Eerdmans, 1998), 262-64.

[67]Hengel, *Acts,* 72-73.

[68]Paul Billerbeck and H. L. Strack, *Kommentar zum Neuen Testament aus Talmud und Midrash,* vol. 2, *Das Evangelium nach Markus, Lukas und Johannes und die Apostelgeschichte erläutert aus Talmud und Midrasch* [München: C. H. Beck'sche Verlagsbuchhandlung, 1924], 668-71.

major pillar of the Sanhedrin's self-understanding—the law. He divides Moses' life into three forty-year periods—ruler of Egypt (Acts 7:17-22), preparation in the desert (Acts 7:23-29), deliverer of Israel (Acts 7:30-43). As Israel's great law-giver, Moses stood, in the mind of the Sanhedrin, as the prophet who defined and made explicit the covenantal relationship between God and his people. The law, mediated through Moses, was the very evidence that Israel was God's chosen people. Because they had the law, only they knew how to live in God's presence.

Stephen, however, wastes no time dwelling on Israel's preferential position. To the contrary, he points immediately to their rejection of Moses as God's appointed ruler and deliverer (Acts 7:35). Even after everyone recognized that he was indeed God's chosen one, they refused to obey him (Acts 7:39) and preferred to go back to slavery (Acts 7:40-41). No listener (or reader of Acts) could miss the parallel to the contemporary situation in which they found themselves. Their forefather's treatment of Moses was a typology of their treatment of the prophet like Moses, Jesus.[69]

' Stephen's words to describe Moses (ruler and deliverer) are almost identical to Peter's words about Jesus in his speech before the same group—ruler and savior (Acts 5:31). In the flow of Luke's presentation, Israel's history affirms that the Sanhedrin has turned God's purpose upside down. It is not "having the law" that makes God's people blessed. Rather, blessedness comes when the presence of God's Spirit, as foretold by Jeremiah and Ezekiel, indwells people who trust him and enables them to fulfill God's purpose for the law.[70] In other words, according to Stephen, a true interpretation of the Moses story will convincingly prove that Jesus is the Coming One pointed to by Moses. Those who miss that have misunderstood God's story with Israel and placed themselves with the hypocrites and apostates of old. Rather than being set free from captivity and living in the guidance of God's presence, they would remain in exile (Acts 7:43).

Stephen's speech concludes by emphasizing the misinterpretation of first-century Judaism's third major pillar of identity—the temple. Following the line of thought from the earlier parts of his speech, he underscores that the true meaning of the temple is found in God's intentions, not in its physical manifestation. Indeed, God instructed

---

[69]F. F. Bruce sees in Stephen's treatment here a typological allusion to the reappearance of Jesus mentioned in Peter's speech in Solomon's portico (Acts 3:20). Joseph appeared twice to his brothers (Acts 7:13) and Moses twice to his (Acts 7:23, 35). Cf. the prophetic promise in Zechariah 12:10; *The Acts of the Apostles: The Greek Text with Introduction and Commentary* (Grand Rapids, Mich.: Eerdmans, 1990), 195. See also C. K. Barrett, *A Critical and Exegetical Commentary on the Acts of the Apostles,* International Critical Commentary, no. 1 (Edinburgh: T & T Clark, 1994), 363.

[70]"But this is the covenant that I will make with the house of Israel after those days, says the Lord: I will put my law within them, and I will write it on their hearts; and I will be their God, and they shall be my people" (Jer 31:33). "I will put my spirit within you, and make you follow my statutes and be careful to observe my ordinances" (Ezek 36:27).

In spite of intense human effort and apologetic fervor from the pinnacle of Sanhedrin understanding of Jewish identity, God's purposes could not be thwarted. With a twist that reads like divine humor, Luke parades how God changed the misguided Saul, who led the stoning of Stephen (Acts 7:58; 8:1), into the most prominent defender of God's eschatological work through Christ (Acts 9:20-22) and the most defining apostle to the Gentiles. The description of Paul's conversion in Acts 9 is replete with references to direct divine intervention. This event could not be explained as mere successful human efforts to confuse religious traditions; it was caused by God's direct persuasive intervention, which at first even confused the believers themselves (Acts 9:13, 26).

Indeed, this was so radical that even Peter struggled to understand. Although he could understand the spread of the gospel beyond the borders of Jerusalem and Judea, it was only a direct and indisputable vision from God that convinced him that God was serious about the fulfillment of his purposes for all nations (Acts 10:9-23). It would be impossible to exaggerate the significance of Peter's speech in Cornelius's house and its consequences for the flow of the Acts narrative. Acts 10 outlines how the final serious interpretative obstacle had now been overcome. God's persuasive vision to Peter changed his thinking and brought him into a Gentile setting that was unthinkable for a Jew.

Luke details the description of God's unquestionable guidance in bringing Peter to Cornelius's house (Acts 10:28-32). Through a lengthy description of a conversation between Peter and Cornelius, it becomes evident that it was the prayer of Cornelius (a Gentile!) that caused Peter's vision (Acts 10:30). Moreover, when Peter began to speak, sketching how Jesus was the fulfillment of Israel's history (Acts 10:36), the Holy Spirit fell upon the Gentile assembly even before he had finished. Peter's conclusion from this experience comes with razor-sharp clarity: "Can anyone withhold the water for baptizing these people who have received the Holy Spirit just as we have?" (Acts 10:47). In other words, since God had evidenced his acceptance of these people (Spirit baptism), they should be allowed entrance into the assembly of the Lord (water baptism). Since God's evident presence now dwelt among these Gentiles, they were already members of God's eschatological people.

Luke has now made his point, and the rest of his narrative simply shows how God continues to include people of all groups from all places "without hindrance" (Acts 28:31) because "they will listen" (Acts 28:28). When a new church is formed, an *ekklēsia* of the Lord in Antioch Syria, the Jerusalem church sends Barnabas, "a good man full of the Holy Spirit and faith" (Acts 11:24), to check it out. When he sees "evidence of the grace of God" in the new setting, the stage is set for a Gentile headquarters from which to launch a deliberate Christian missionary effort to bring all Gentiles to faith and inclusion into God's *ekklēsia*. When it proves apparent that some Jewish people loosely connected to the church in Jerusalem continue to work from the old interpretative framework, the church forms a council in Jerusalem (described in Acts 15) who, on the basis of Peter's and Paul's testimonies, decide that these Judaizers are wrong because God himself had included Gentiles who did not know the law of Moses (Acts 15:19-21).

Luke leaves the reader with no doubt. The story told in Acts (and in Luke) is the story about how Israel's history had come to its fulfillment and conclusion. Israel's sin had left her in exile, blinded to God's fulfillment of his promises. Through the outpouring of his Spirit, God manifested his presence among the true believers who understood how Jesus Christ had come to bring about the fulfillment of God's creative purposes. A new Israel was called forth! It was a people who experienced God's relational and guiding presence similarly to God's people of old—a people who brought the promises and aspirations of God's covenant to their fulfillment among all of God's creation. God had clearly accomplished his purpose. He had sent his salvation through a small group of believing Israelites to the Gentiles and created his people of the new covenant.

As the narrative ends, the story continues to be told "without hindrance" and Gentiles continue to find salvation. The Jewish leadership and those who follow their misguided interpretation of Israel's story remain in exile. Those who accept the interpretation detailed by Stephen and explicated throughout the book of Acts are filled with God's Spirit and included in God's new *ekklēsia*. Most of these are Gentiles—for "they will listen!" (Acts 28:28).

Supplemental Readings *in* New Dictionary of Biblical Theology

D. G. Peterson, "Acts," 285-91

D. J. Tidball, "Church," 407-11

M. Turner, "Holy Spirit: In Acts," 553-55

M. Turner, "Languages," 627-29

J. G. Millar, "People of God," 684-87

Study Questions

1. In what way is Luke's narrative teaching programmatic?

2. How does Luke connect Peter and Paul to each other and both to Jesus?

3. What is the significance of Acts 1:8 for a reading of Acts?

4. What is the theological significance of the Pentecost event?

5. What is the purpose of the speeches in Acts?

6. In what way does Acts 2:42-46 affirm the Christian community as the true fulfill-ment of the Old Testament prophetic call to Israel?

7. What is the special feature of Paul's conversion, the conversion in Cornelius's house and the baptism of the Ethiopian eunuch that enables Luke to portray these events as *evidence* or *proof* that the church fulfills God's purpose for Israel?

10

PAUL

The Reverse of the Curse

As the last chapters demonstrated, already in the Gospels and in Acts the retelling of the story of Israel is set in motion. There the crucified Jesus is portrayed as embracing the Deuteronomic curses while dispensing the blessings of the covenant upon all those who believe in him through his resurrection. In this chapter we will see that Paul furthers that reinterpretation. In fact, the apostle to the Gentiles par excellence, in light of the Christ event, reverses the covenantal curses and blessings: those who attempt to obey the law are necessarily under divine judgment, while those who believe in Jesus as Messiah, apart from the Torah, possess the long-awaited restoration of Israel. We will develop this thesis in four steps: the prelude to Paul's retelling of the story of Israel; the basis of that reinterpretation; its components; and the opposition such a subversion evoked.

Prelude to Paul's Retelling of the Story of Israel

Paul's pre-Christian career as a Pharisee inexorably placed him on a collision course with the message of early Christianity. Such a message centered on Jesus and his followers' relationship to the Mosaic law. Martin Hengel summarizes the conflicting viewpoints that erupted over that issue:

> As the result of the agitation of the new messianic Jesus movement, or more precisely the Jewish Christian "Hellenists," in the Greek-speaking synagogues of Jerusalem, considerable unrest developed there and there was an energetic reaction. The proclamation of the Greek-speaking followers of the messiah Jesus of Nazareth, crucified a short time earlier, which was critical of the ritual parts of the Torah and the cult, was a provocation to the majority who were loyal to the law. The most active spokesman of the new group, Stephen, was stoned to death after a tumultuous gathering in one of these synagogues. On this occasion Sha'ul/Paul, the scribal student and young teacher, played only a subsidiary role. But when the representatives of this enthusiastic group which was hostile to the law did not lie low, but continued to agitate, he took the initiative and brought about a "pogrom" within the limited sphere of the "Hellenistic" synagogues of Jerusalem against these

sectarians. Here he followed the example of Phinehas in his "zeal for the law" and did not shrink from the use of brute force. Presumably "Hellenists" were arrested as they discussed in the synagogues, and condemned to the usual punishment of thirty-nine lashes; some may even have suffered more serious physical hurt and even have been killed. In this way the relatively small community of the "Hellenists" was largely destroyed and fled from Jerusalem to neighbouring territories and cities. Sha'ul/Paul accepted a mission from these synagogues in Jerusalem to Damascus, to take proceedings against the agitators who had fled there and their local supporters.[1]

The pre-Christian Paul is best identified as espousing the theocratic interpretation of the law that characterized Sirach, Baruch and *Psalms of Solomon*.[2] That is to say, if Israel will strictly follow the Torah, God will restore her freedom by casting off the yoke of foreign oppression. This resolute commitment to the entirety of the Torah imprints two of Paul's key testimony statements, Galatians 1:13-14 and Philippians 3:4-6 (cf. Acts 22:3). As we will see, two characteristics unite those passages: nomism and particularism.

Galatians 1:13-14. The vivid terminology of Galatians 1:13-14 portrays the pre-Christian Paul's commitment to the Torah: *zēlōtēs* (zealous, Gal 1:14), *en tō Ioudaismō* (in Judaism, twice in Gal 1:13-14), *ediōkon* (persecute) and *eporthoun* (destroy, Gal 1:13). We have noted elsewhere that the term "zealot" occurs, among other places, in Sirach 51:17-18, with reference to ben Sira's defense of Torah vis-à-vis Hellenism's inroads. Paul's usage of this word seems to locate him in the same conceptual milieu.[3] "Judaism" (Gal 1:13, 14) confirms that observation, for as Richard Longenecker remarks, this *hapax* (one-time occurrence) in the New Testament occurs in 2 Maccabees 2:21; 8:1; 14:38; 4 Maccabees 4:26 with reference to the Jewish religion and way of life as contrasted to Seleucid Hellenism.[4] The other terms, "persecuted" and "destroyed" (v. 13), bespeak the vehemence of Saul's attack on the church of God. The language recalls the drastic and violent measures employed by righteous Jews in an effort to punish apostates whose behavior, in effect, aligned them with Gentiles (e.g., Num 25:1-5; 25:6-15; 1 Macc 2:23-28, 42-48; 2 Macc 6:13; IQS 9:22; IQM 7:5; 10:2-5;

---

[1]Martin Hengel, *The Pre-Christian Paul*, trans. John Bowden (Philadelphia/London: Trinity Press International/SCM Press, 1991), 85-86. Hengel reaches this conclusion after a careful analysis of Paul's testimony statements and the relevant Acts material. Hengel's recent work continues his investigation into the pre-Christian Paul's life as well as his early Christian ministry; see Martin Hengel and Anna Maria Schwemer, *Paul Between Damascus and Antioch: The Unknown Years,* trans. John Bowden (Louisville, Ky.: John Knox Press, 1997).

[2]See C. Marvin Pate, *The Reverse of the Curse: Paul, Wisdom, and the Law,* Wissenschaftliche Untersuchungen zum Neuen Testament II/114 (Tübingen, Germany: J.C.B. Mohr/Paul Siebeck, 2000), chap. 1.

[3]Ibid.

[4]Richard N. Longenecker, *Galatians,* Word Biblical Commentary 41 (Dallas: Word, 1990), 27.

IQH 14:13-15; *Pss Sol* 17:21-46; Bar 4:25). These four terms, then, attest to Saul's no-mism (commitment to the Torah), based probably on a theocratic interpretation. Per-haps, with Longenecker, we should also view Paul's persecution of the apostate Jews (the church of God) as related to the Pharisaic belief that the observance of the Mosaic law was a vital prerequisite for the coming of the messianic age (cf. *b Sanh* 97b-98a; *b Bat 10a; b Yoma* 86b), hence the need to purge Jewish communities of apostates who deterred other Jews from following the law.[5]

We began this section with a statement by Martin Hengel that equates the church Paul persecuted with Greek-speaking Jewish Christians in Jerusalem. On the basis that the "Hellenists" of Acts 6:1 and Acts 9:29 represented a Christian community of Greek-speaking Jews whose critique of the Torah and temple linked them with the his-torical Jesus, Hengel and others have put forth the view that this was the main group Paul persecuted.[6] This interpretation obviously accentuates the particularistic attitude of the pre-Christian Paul: his attack on that sector of the church was born out of zeal for the Torah and a deep-seated concern that that group was seriously undermining the Jewish faith. Moreover, such a Torah/temple critical movement would have added insult to injury if it indeed was made up of the type of people once attracted to the Greek-speaking synagogues in Jerusalem, the very sphere of Saul's teaching activity.[7]

Philippians 3:4-6 (cf. Acts 22:3). Our particular interest in the list of credentials in Philippians 3:4-6 lies in Paul's scrupulous adherence to the law: "as to the law, a Phar-isee" (Phil 3:5); "as to righteousness under the law, blameless" (Phil 3:6); "as to zeal, a persecutor of the church" (Phil 3:6). To these statements we should add Paul's remark in Acts 22:3, "I am a Jew, born at Tarsus in Cilicia, but brought up in this city [Jerus-alem] at the feet of Gamaliel, educated strictly according to our ancestral law, being zealous for God." These two texts demonstrate, as did Galatians 1:13-14, Paul's no-mism and particularism before becoming a Christian.

So we see that the pre-Christian Paul agreed with the traditional telling of the story of Israel: if Jews will embrace the Torah wholeheartedly, then God will restore her to the covenantal blessings. That perspective would drastically change, however, on Paul's way to Damascus to persecute Christians.

The Basis of Paul's Retelling of the Story of Israel

A key passage focusing on Paul's about-face understanding of the message of early Christianity is Galatians 3:13-14. There, in the aftermath of his Damascus road en-

---

[5]Longenecker, *Galatians*, 28-29.
[6]Martin Hengel, *Between Jesus and Paul: Studies in the Earliest History of Christianity*, trans. John Bowden (Philadelphia: Fortress, 1983), 1-19; cf. Pate, *Reverse of the Curse*, 157-67, 429-34.
[7]For defense of this view, see Pate, *Reverse of the Curse*, 157-67.

counter with the crucified and risen Christ, Paul portrays Jesus as the righteous one who, having obeyed the law fully, suffered the Deuteronomic curses (Gal 3:13, death) in order that those who believe in him (sinners though they are) might have the Deuteronomic blessings (life, Gal 3:14). Four comments are in order here.

The Deuteronomic context of Galatians 3:10-14. First, recent investigations of Galatians 3:10-14 call attention to the Deuteronomic context of the Old Testament verses that the apostle quotes or alludes to in this text, which we summarize here.[8] In Galatians 3:10 Paul quotes Deuteronomy 27:26 to make the point that the Deuteronomic curses (death) fall on those who do not obey the entirety of the Torah. That thought is echoed in Galatians 3:12 where, quoting Leviticus 18:5, Paul asserts that if one is to find life in the law, one must follow it completely (cf. Gal 5:3). Thus far in the apostle's argument, most Jews in the Second Temple period would have agreed with his contention, for they would have also shared Paul's sentiments that Israel was under bondage to the nations precisely because she disobeyed the divine law.

There, however, the similarity ends, for in Galatians 3:11-12 Paul contrasts the works of the law with the way of faith in his quotation of Habakkuk 2:4, a passage that anticipated the future revival of Israel.[9] Undoubtedly this did not set well with those Jews who espoused the conviction that only a new-found obedience to the law could effect Israel's restoration. Paul and his opponents (see below) will have therefore appealed to Habakkuk 2:4 for opposite reasons—the former as a basis for faith apart from works; the latter as support of their commitment to the Torah. What emerges from Galatians 3:10-12, then, is Paul's reversal of the Deuteronomic curses and blessings. Those who attempt to keep the law are under its curses; those who live by faith in Christ apart from the Torah experience the eschatological restoration of the Deuteronomic blessings.

Christ and the law. Second, Christ was the righteous one who perfectly kept the law. Three pieces of data confirm this observation: (1) Paul says as much elsewhere (e.g., Rom 5:6-11; 8:3; 2 Cor 5:21); (2) Paul omits "by God" after "cursed" in his quotation of Deuteronomy 21:23 in Galatians 3:13, most probably to avoid the inference that Christ on the cross was actually cursed by God, the implication being that it was the Torah that indicted Christ;[10] and (3) the fact that God raised Jesus from the dead must have signaled to Paul that he was blameless before God, otherwise he would have remained in the grave (cf. Gal 3:13-14 with Gal 1:1-5; 2:19-20; cf., e.g., Rom 4:25; Phil 2:9-11).

---

[8]For discussion and bibliography see ibid., 170-32.
[9]Frank Thielman makes this point; see *Paul and the Law: A Contextual Approach* (Downers Grove, Ill.: InterVarsity Press, 1994), 128, 275.
[10]See Pate for defense of this position, *Reverse of the Curse,* 215-16.

Christ and the Deuteronomic curses. The third comment to be made about Galatians 3:13-14 is that at the crucifixion, Jesus vicariously bore the Deuteronomic curses for the sins of others. At least three ideas comprise this assertion: (1) As we argued elsewhere, Jesus' death by crucifixion convinced many Jews, the pre-Christian Paul included, that Jesus could not be the Messiah.[11] Hence, early Christianity's quandary at interpreting Deuteronomy 21:23. Yet Paul's christophany on the Damascus road revealed to him that Jesus was the Messiah, now exalted. (2) It seems that it was Paul who first fully explored the nature of the judgment that fell on Jesus on the cross—it was the Deuteronomic curses that accrued to Israel because she had disobeyed the law (and if they fell on Israel, God's chosen people, then they fell on the whole world as well). Thus, the rationale for the apostle's quotation of Deuteronomy 27:26 (Gal 3:10). F. F. Bruce pinpoints Paul's contribution to the topic:

> It may well be that the argument of Gal. 3.10-14 was worked out in Paul's mind quite early in his Christian career. As soon as he came to acknowledge the crucified Jesus as the Son of God, the problem why the Son of God should have died under a curse clamoured for a solution. Previously, the very manner of Jesus' death had been sufficient to prove to Paul that he could not be what his followers claimed him to be, and more, his being "hanged on a tree" could not be left unexplained. The collocation of Deut. 21.23 and Deut. 27.26 pointed the way to an explanation.[12]

The end of the law. Finally, we reach the climax of our overall point regarding the sacrificial nature of Jesus' death and resurrection relative to the Deuteronomic curses with the argument that at the cross, according to Paul, the role of the Law was terminated. Four elements make up this assertion: (1) According to Deuteronomy 21:23, Jesus' crucifixion contradicted his claim to be the Messiah; that is, the law itself disallowed Jesus' messianic assertion. (2) Jesus' resurrection, on the contrary, proved him to be the Messiah, vindicated by God. This truth was revealed to Paul on the Damascus road (Gal 1:11-12, 15-16). (3) The law, therefore, was wrong in its condemnation of Jesus. That the law (personified) could be guilty of miscalculation is clear from Galatians 3:10-12, where Paul opposes the works of the law with the way of faith (contrast Hab 2:4 with Deut 27:26; Lev 18:5). So its culpability with regard to Jesus' death would not have been an unfeasible thought for the apostle. (4) Consequently, the Torah was replaced by Christ as God's revelation. Seyoon Kim expresses this idea well:

> Paul realized that the crucified Jesus of Nazareth was not accursed by God as the law had pronounced (Dt 21.23), but, on the contrary, exalted by him as his own Son (cf. Rom 1.3f). This means that God reversed or annulled the verdict of the law upon Jesus. Paul

---

[11]For this entire third point, see ibid., chap. 5.
[12]F. F. Bruce, "The Curse of the Law," in *Paul and Paulinism: Essays in Honour of C. K. Barrett,* ed. M. D. Hooker and S. G. Wilson (London: SPCK, 1982), 27-36, 32.

was thus compelled to recognize that it is no longer the Torah but Christ who truly represents the will of God, that Christ has superseded the Torah as the revelation of God. This is implied when Paul says in Rom 10.4: "Christ is the end of the law" . . .

However, that was not the only line of thinking concerning the law and the crucifixion of Jesus which Paul derived from the Damascus Christophany. There is another line, a line which recognizes the reality of the power of the law to curse its trespassers. Insofar as Jesus is the Messiah, the Son of God, who is both by definition and in reality sinless (2 Cor 5.21; Rom 8.3), the law cursed him wrongly, thus demonstrating that it no longer represented God's will.[13]

These four points, then, form the basis of Paul's retelling of the story of Israel: Galatians 3:13-14 is informed by the Deuteronomic tradition; Christ kept the law fully; his death and resurrection embraced the covenantal curses and offered the covenantal blessings, respectively, to those who believe in him; Christ's death terminated the Torah.

The Components of Paul's Retelling of the Story of Israel

Our last point broached the subject of Paul's retelling of the story of Israel. In this section we focus on the apostle's reversal of the Deuteronomic blessings and curses by examining the following passages: 1 Thessalonians 2:15-16; Galatians 3:10-14; Romans 1:16ff.; 2 Corinthians 3:1—4:6; Ephesians as a whole (cf. Colossians).

1 Thessalonians 2:15-16. These verses provide insight into Paul's understanding of the story of Israel:

> The Jews, who killed both the Lord Jesus and the prophets, drove us out; they displease God and oppose everyone by hindering us from speaking to the Gentiles so that they may be saved. Thus they have constantly been filling up the measure of their sins; but God's wrath has overtaken them at last.

James M. Scott perceives the Deuteronomistic tradition to be operative in this passage.[14] Thus: (1) Israel's past sin continues in Paul's day with its rejection of Jesus, which is in keeping with (2) and (3) Jews' rejection of the prophets from times past until the present, including Jesus[15] and Paul;[16] consequently, (4) God's wrath remains over the nation of Israel, having now reached its full force. At this point, however, Paul seems to

---

[13]Seyoon Kim, *The Origin of Paul's Gospel,* Wissenschaftliche Untersuchungen zum Neuen Testament 24 (Tübingen, Germany: J.C.B. Mohr/Paul Siebeck, 1981), 274-75.

[14]James M. Scott, "Paul's Use of Deuteronomic Tradition(s)," *Journal of Biblical Literature* 112 (1993): 651-57.

[15]For a thorough defense that Jesus was a prophet like Jeremiah, see Michael Knowles, *Jeremiah in Matthew's Gospel: The Rejected Prophet Motif in Matthaen Redaction,* Journal for the Study of the New Testament Supplement Series 68 (Sheffield: Sheffield Academic Press, 1993).

[16]For a defense that Paul considered himself a prophet, see Karl Olav Sandes, *Paul—One of the Prophets? A Contribution to the Apostle's Self-Understanding,* Wissenschaftliche Untersuchungen zum Neuen Testament 1/43 (Tübingen, Germany: J.C.B. Mohr/Paul Siebeck, 1991).

break stride with the Deuteronomistic tradition in that he omits components (5) (Israel will repent) and (6) (God will fully forgive the nation[17]), that is, the restoration of Israel.

Frank Thielman provides a rationale for this omission, namely, that according to Paul Gentiles have replaced Jews as the people of God. Thus terminology used of Israel in the Old Testament is now applied in 1–2 Thessalonians to Christian Gentiles: "church" (*ekklēsia*; cf. 1 Thess 1:1; 2 Thess 1:1 with Deut 23:1, 4, 9 LXX); "beloved of God" (cf. 1 Thess 1:4, 2:12; 2 Thess 1:1, 2:13-14 with Deut 4:37, 7:8, 10:15, 23:5); "called" (cf. 1 Thess 2:12, 4:7, 5:24; 2 Thess 1:11, 2:14 with Is 41:9, 42:6, 48:12); "saints"/sanctified" (cf. 1 Thess 4:1-8, 5:23-24; 2 Thess 2:13-14 with Lev 20:24, 26 LXX); people of the "spirit" and thus members of the new covenant of obedience to God (cf. 1 Thess 1:5-6, 4:8 with Ezek 36:25-27 LXX; see also Ezek 11:19, 18:31, 37:14; Jer 31 [LXX 38]:31-34, 32:40, 50:5).[18]

What emerges from this reading of 1 and 2 Thessalonians, therefore, is the surprising reality that Gentiles are now elevated to a status unrivaled in the Old Testament, while on the other hand, non-Christian Jews find themselves outside the sphere of God's blessings. How the law fits into this discussion Paul does not specifically say in 1–2 Thessalonians. That would change, however, with his writing of Galatians.

Galatians 3:10-14. The logic of Galatians 3:10-14 unfolds verse by verse. Verse 10 quotes Deuteronomy 27:26, asserting that those who do not obey the Mosaic law will suffer the curses of God. But for the apostle, this is not a challenge designed to motivate people to obey the Torah; rather, it is a warning that no one is capable of keeping the law perfectly. This is why the apostle draws on the Septuagint of Deuteronomy 27:26, which adds the word "all" to the Masoretic text, thereby accentuating the criterion necessary to escape the divine curse—one must abide by *all* the things written in the law. Thomas Schreiner, therefore, expresses the essence of Galatians 3:10 in a syllogism: (1) Those who do not keep everything in the law are cursed; (2) no one keeps everything in the law (implicit premise); (3) therefore, those who rely on the works of the law for salvation are cursed.[19]

Galatians 3:11 confirms the inability and undesirability of attempting to keep the

---

[17]Although some commentators do not think a future restoration of Israel is within the purview of 1 Thessalonians 2:15-16, others do, including Scott, "Paul's Use of Deuteronomic Tradition(s)," 655-57. For further discussion of both sides of the argument, see Scott's bibliography, 651, n. 22.

[18]See Thielman, *Paul and the Law,* 72-77.

[19]Thomas R. Schreiner, *The Law and Its Fulfillment: A Pauline Theology of the Law* (Grand Rapids, Mich.: Baker, 1993), 44. The next three books—Galatians, Romans and Philippians—are clustered together in our treatment because they clearly contain Paul's polemics against the Judaizers, those first-century professing Jewish Christians who maintained that justification was the result of God's grace and human works. Moreover, the discussion of these three books are indebted to Pate, *Communities of the Last Days: The Dead Sea Scrolls, the New Testament and the Story of Israel* (Downers Grove: InterVarsity Press, 2000), 165-77.

Torah by invoking Habakkuk 2:4, which Paul interprets to mean that a person lives—that is, is justified—by faith (cf. Rom 1:16-17). This prophetic principle, according to Galatians 3:12, is at odds with Leviticus 18:5 and its teaching that one must obey the law in order to live. Galatians 3:13 seems to harmonize the two statements by in effect indicating that Christ alone has kept the law and has taken on himself humanity's curse for breaking the Torah.[20] Christ thereby both fulfilled and ended the law for all who trust in him, which according to Galatians 3:14 includes Gentiles.

The preceding comments indicate that Paul reversed the covenant blessings and curses. The blessings reside on those who believe in Jesus apart from the Torah (Gentiles, especially), while the curses are reserved for those who attempt to commend themselves to God by works of the law (Jews most notably). Thus Paul replaces nomism and particularism with faith and a universal message respectively. Such a perspective continues in Romans, to which we now turn.

Romans. Here we examine three key passages in Romans that demonstrate Paul's reversal of the Deuteronomic blessings and curses: Romans 1:16—3:31; 5—8; 9:30—10:8.

Romans 1:16—3:31. As Richard B. Hays and James M. Scott have observed, the wrath texts in Romans 1:16—3:31 are informed by the theme of the Deuteronomic curses, such that Paul announces therein that divine judgment rests on Israel because it continues to disobey the law of Moses (cf. Rom 2:9 with Deut 28:53, 55, 57; Rom 2:5 with Deut 31:27; Rom 2:8 with Deut 27:26).[21] Romans 1:18-32 belongs on this list as well, thus also including Gentiles in the purview of the Deuteronomic curses.[22] One group, the Jews, is under judgment for disobeying God's written Law, the Torah. Another group, the Gentiles, is also under God's wrath for disobeying his law expressed in natural revelation. One is reminded here of a work like Wisdom of Solomon, which employs natural law to condemn Gentiles because they do not in fact live up to its light (Wis 13:1—15:17). Thus Paul places both Jew and Gentile under the Deuteronomic curses in Romans 1:18-32 (cf. Rom 2:9; 3:9). The driving force behind their rebellion,

---

[20] That Paul was not unique in applying Deuteronomy 21:23 to crucifixion is now clear, for the DSS did the same. See 4QpNah 1:7-8 and 11QTemple 64:6-13; see also J. A. Fitzmyer, "Crucifixion in Ancient Palestine, Qumran Literature and the New Testament," *Catholic Biblical Quarterly* 40 (1978): 493-513. On a related issue, how Paul can assume that Israel's failure to fully comply with the Torah implicates all of humanity in the divine curse is developed in Pate, *Reverse of the Curse*, 210, which agrees that Gentiles are included in the purview of Galatians 3:13-14.

[21] Richard B. Hays, *Echoes of Scripture in the Letters of Paul* (New Haven, Conn.: Yale University Press, 1989), 43; James M. Scott, "Paul's Use of the Deuteronomic Tradition(s)," 660, n. 64.

[22] That the divine condemnation for disobedience described in Romans 1:18-32 is intended by Paul to apply to both Gentile and Jew because it is rooted in Adam's sin is demonstrated by C. E. B. Cranfield, *Romans I-VIII* (Edinburgh: T & T Clark, 1975), 106ff.; Morna Hooker, "Adam in Romans 1," *New Testament Studies* 6 (1960): 297-306; James D. G. Dunn, *Romans 1–8*, Word Biblical Commentary 38A (Waco, Tex.: Word, 1998), 60ff. The upshot of the passage is that Paul is indicating that Israel is still in Adam and therefore fares no better than Gentiles in terms of obedience to God.

according to the apostle Paul, is surprisingly the law itself, which stirs up disobedience within the individual (Rom 3:19-20, 4:15; 5:20; cf. Gal 2:15, 3:10-12). In effect, then, Paul here reverses the Deuteronomic curses: both Jew and Gentile are under divine wrath because the law within them has become the catalyst for sin.[23]

While the Deuteronomic curses abide on Jews and Gentiles because they do not obey the Torah, according to Romans 1:16—3:31 the Deuteronomic blessings abide on Christians because of their faith in Christ alone. Hays has pointed out that Romans 1:15-17 is informed by the Old Testament promise of the restoration of Israel, the Deuteronomic blessings (cf. Rom 1:15-17 with Ps 24:2; 43:10; 97:2-3 LXX; Is 28:16; 51:4-5, 10; Hab 2:4).[24] Furthermore, according to Paul in Romans 3:21-31, the divine means for actualizing this promise was the atoning death of Christ (Rom 3:24-25), which is to be received by faith (Rom 3:21-24, 27-31). Looking at the total picture of Romans 1:16–3:31, then, we can see Paul's logic. The righteousness of God, which includes the Deuteronomic blessings and the prophetic promise of restoration, is available to both Jew and Gentile exclusively through faith in Christ, whose death and resurrection brought an end to the Torah and its curses (cf. Rom 1:16-17 with Rom 3:21-31). The role of the law was therefore temporary; it served to convict both Jew and Gentile of sin (see Rom 1:18–3:20) in order to drive them to the gospel (Rom 3:21-31). Because the Torah is now terminated, both Jew and Gentile can be saved, but by faith alone (Rom 1:16–3:30).

Romans 5—8. This passage can also be situated in the context of the story of Israel. In that connection, N. T. Wright's study, "The Vindication of the Law: Romans 8:1-11," offers a helpful synopsis of Paul's logic in Romans 5—8:

> It should not come as a surprise, then, to find that the Torah and the covenant are still central categories in Romans 5–8. It could even be argued that Romans 5.20 is the climax of the whole Adam-Christ passage, explaining the position of the law within the entire scheme of divinely ordered history: . . . ("but the law entered that the transgression might abound"). Certainly it is to that verse that the discussion of Torah in 7.1–8.11 looks back quite obviously, via the things—which fit happily into the same scheme of thought—in 6.14-15. The position Paul is arguing, just as in Galatians 3, is that the Torah has not alleviated, but rather has exacerbated, the plight of Adamic humanity. This can only mean that the recipients of Torah, i.e., Israel, have found themselves to be under its judgment because of their participation in Adamic humanity. Since therefore Christians have left the realm of the . . . (old man) in baptism, they have also left the realm of Torah coming out from the place where it could exert a hold over them.[25]

---

[23]Neither Hays (*Echoes of Scripture*) nor Scott ("Paul's Use of the Deuteronomic Tradition[s]") mentions this reversal motif in treating Romans 1–3.
[24]Hays, *Echoes of Scripture,* 193-219.
[25]N. T. Wright, "The Vindication of the Law: Romans 8:1-11," in *The Climax of the Covenant: Christ and the Law in Pauline Theology* (Edinburgh: T & T Clark, 1991), 195.

For Wright, then, Paul's solution to the human inability to obey the Torah is Christ, who as Israel's representative has drawn sin to himself on the cross and thereby defeated it (Rom 5:12-21; 7:7-25; 8:3). Because Christians are in Christ via baptism (Rom 6:1—7:6), they now possess the life of the covenant, which was the purpose for which the law was given in the first place (Rom 8:1-11).

Similarly, Frank Thielman's article, "The Story of Israel and the Theology of Romans 5—8"[26] locates the background of Paul's comments in that unit in the Deuteronomistic tradition. Table 10.1 lists some summary statements of Thielman's exegesis of those sections making up Romans 5—8. Thus Romans 5—8 can be viewed from the perspective of the story of Israel.

Table 10.1. Romans 5—8 and the Story of Israel

5:1-11	The hope of Israel's restoration is being fulfilled in Christ.
5:12-21	Christ is God's answer to Adam's sin and Israel's violation of the covenant.
6:1—7:25	Through identification with Christ's death and resurrection, Christians are delivered (Deuteronomic blessings) from Adam's disobedience, which is continued in Israel's sin (Deuteronomic curses).
8:1-39	Paul restates the promise of Israel's restoration, which is now occurring through Christ.

Paul reverses the Deuteronomic curses and blessing therein. For our purposes, Romans 5—8 can be divided into four sections: Romans 5:1-11; 5:12-21; 6:1—7:6; 7:7—8:11.

> a. *Romans 5:1-11* should be understood as making the following statement: Christians now experience the Deuteronomic blessings because Christ has absorbed the Deuteronomic curses. That Paul intends to say as much is evident in the covenantal benefits that he believes accrue to Christians because they are justified by faith in Christ. "Peace" (Rom 5:1), as James D. G. Dunn has indicated, is a covenant concept. It refers to the prophetic hope of the return of God's favor to Israel now realized in Christ.[27] "Life" (Rom 5:10), the goal of the covenant, is now available to Christians because the wrath of God—the Deuteronomic curses—has

---

[26]Frank Thielman, "The Story of Israel and the Theology of Romans 5–8," in *Pauline Theology*, ed. David M. Hay and E. Elizabeth Johnson (Minneapolis: Fortress, 1995), 3:169-95.

[27]Cf. Num 6:22-27; Ps 55:18-19; Is 9:6, 7; 48:17-22; 54:10; Jer 14:19-22; Ezek 34:25-31; 37:26; Mic 5:4; Hag 2:9; Zech 8:12; Sir 47:13; 2 Macc 1:2-4; *1 En* 5:7-9; 10:17; 11:2. Refer also to Dunn, *Romans 1–8*, 264.

been removed (Rom 5:9). "Reconciliation" (Rom 5:10-11) bespeaks the renewal of God's covenant with Israel but now applied to the church. Whereas *justification* deals with the legal aspect of the covenant, *reconciliation* addresses its relational side.[28] All of this is made possible because Christ embraced the Deuteronomic curses at the cross (Rom 5:6-11).

> b. *Romans 5:12-21.* Probably the best background for interpreting the Adam-Christ antithesis presented in Romans 5:12-21 is that of the Deuteronomic blessings and curses. Adam's sin (of coveting) was tantamount to breaking the Torah before it was promulgated by Moses (cf. Rom 5:13-14; 7:7 with 4 Ezra 7:11; *Tg Neof* 2:15; *Gen Rab* 16:5-6; 24:4; *Deut Rab* 2:25; *b Sanh* 56b). Therefore, if Adam's sin was perceived as committed against the Torah, then most likely we are to understand the ensuing judgments pronounced on Adam, Eve and the serpent (Gen 3:14-19) as anticipating the Deuteronomic curses.[29] This idea would help explain Paul's association of Adam and Moses in Romans 5:12-14.

As Wright has insightfully argued, however, the goal of Romans 5:20 ("Law came in, to increase the trespass") is to assert that Israel, though commonly thought to be the divinely intended replacement of Adam, has by breaking the Torah demonstrated itself to still be in Adam. Wright says of this, "The place 'where sin abounded' (v. 20b) is undoubtedly Israel, the 'place' where 'the law came in that the trespass might abound.' Adam's trespass, active though unobserved until Sinai (vv. 13-14, cf. 7.9a), found fresh opportunity in the arrival of the Torah. Again it could display its true colours as trespass, the flouting of the commands of God."[30] Thus, if Adam's sin anticipated the Deuteronomic curses, Israel's disobedience became the focal point of that judgment.

All of this was according to the divine plan which, as Romans 5:15-21 makes clear, was that Christ—Israel's representative—by his obedient death would bring the covenantal curses to their climax (see especially Rom 5:20, "but where sin increased, grace abounded all the more"). Consequently, Christ's acceptance of the death that humanity deserved made it possible for God to offer to others the life of the covenant (Rom 5:21).

> c. *Romans 6:1—7:6.* The preceding background enlightens Paul's logic in Romans 6:1—7:6, which can be simply put: through baptism, Christians have been united with Christ's death, and by that death the curse of the law over them has been dismissed; through Christ's resurrection they now participate in the Deuteronomic blessing of life.[31]

---

[28]See also remarks on Rom 5:1-11 in Thielman, "Story of Israel," 177-79.
[29]Refer to a more extensive discussion of this point in C. Marvin Pate, *Reverse of the Curse,* chap. 7.
[30]Wright, *Climax of the Covenant,* 39; cf. 198.
[31]Ibid., 195.

d. *Romans 7:7—8:11.* Thielman and Wright have (correctly, we think) suggested that the phrases in Romans 8:2—"the law of the Spirit of life" and "the law of sin and death"—correspond to the Deuteronomic blessings and curses, respectively. Regarding the latter, those authors argue that "the law of sin and death" (see Rom 7:10-11; 8:2) alludes to the Deuteronomic promise of life based on the law but that, according to Paul, actually provoked the opposite effect, death (Lev 18:5; Deut 4:1; 30:15, 19-20; 32:47). This ironic turn of events took place because of the law's inability to check sin (see Rom 4:15; 7:5; 8:3; cf. Gal 2:14; 3:21). The culprit, however, is not the divine law but sin, which distorts it (see Rom 7:13).[32] Thus, Paul reverses the Deuteronomic curse in Romans 8:2: whoever attempts to find life by obeying the Torah will suffer death.

Thielman and Wright also call attention to the new covenant nuance that informs the phrase "the law of the Spirit of life." Thus, those whose faith is in the atoning death of Christ (cf. the context of the words "the law of faith" in Rom 3:27) now experience the new covenant, which has inaugurated the Deuteronomic blessings. Such a reality has occurred for Christians because they died to the law through Christ's death (Rom 7:1-6) and now share in his resurrection life (Rom 8:10-11; cf. Rom 6:1-14).[33] So we see from Romans 7:7—8:11 that Paul reverses the Deuteronomistic tradition; its curses abide on those who attempt to keep the Mosaic law, while its blessings rest on those whose faith is in Christ, who took upon himself the judgment of the law in order to bring it to its conclusion (cf. Rom 8:1-11; 10:14; Gal 3:10-14). This powerfully alternates, like the Jews antiphonally responding to each other from Gerizim and Ebal, between presenting life (the Deuteronomic blessings) and death (the Deuteronomic curses), based on the choice to either believe Christ or follow the law.

Romans 9:30—10:8. By way of introducing this section of Romans, we should take note of the rather recent studies that call attention to the Deuteronomistic underpinning of Romans 9—11 as a whole. The first is by Richard B. Hays, who emphasizes the importance of Deuteronomy 32 for Romans in two respects. Deuteronomy 32 contains the salvation-historical scheme appropriated in Romans: God's election and care for Israel (Deut 32:6-14), Israel's rebellion (Deut 32:15-18; cf. Deut 32:5), God's judgment on them (Deut 32:19-35) and ultimately God's final deliverance and vindication of his own people (Deut 32:36-43). Here are contained both the prophecy that God would stir Israel to jealousy through the Gentiles, cited in Romans 10:19 (cf. Deut 32:21) and the invitation to the Gentiles to join with God's people in praise, cited in Romans 15:10 (cf. Deut 32:43).[34]

---

[32]Thielman, *Paul and the Law,* 202; Wright, *Climax of the Covenant,* 210-11.
[33]Thielman, *Paul and the Law,* 201-2; Wright, *Climax of the Covenant,* 211.
[34]Hays, *Echoes of Scripture,* 163.

The second author investigating the Deuteronomistic influence on Romans 9—11 is James M. Scott, who applies Odil Steck's sixfold description of the Deuteronomistic tradition to that material:[35]

1. Israel has been disobedient to the law of God throughout its history (Rom 9:31; 10:21; cf. Rom 2:1-19).

2-3. God has sent his prophets (including Paul) to call Israel to repentance, but they have been repeatedly rejected (Rom 11:2-5; cf. Rom 10:16; 15:31).

4. The Deuteronomic curses now rest on Israel in the form of foreign suppression (Rom 9:1-3; 10:3; 11:1, 5, 10, 16-25; cf. Rom 2:6-8; 3:5).

5. It is still possible for Israel to repent (Rom 9:22: 10:16, 19; 11:11, 14; cf. Rom 2:4-5).

6. Israel will repent and be restored (Rom 11:26-27).

We concur with these conclusions, except that neither of these authors takes the next step to detect whether Paul's reversal of the Deuteronomic curses and blessings is operative in Romans 9—11. Three indications combine to show that in Romans 9:30—10:8 Paul does indeed reverse the Deuteronomic curses and blessings. First, as was noted previously, the Deuteronomistic tradition is embedded in the overall argument of Romans 9—11. Second, more specifically, we have also seen that Romans 8:1-11 (cf. Rom 7) is well understood as Paul's reversal of the Deuteronomic curses and blessings. Third, Romans 9:25-29 continues Paul's thought along these lines when, in quoting Hosea 2:23 (Rom 9:25), Hosea 1:10 (Rom 9:26) and Isaiah 10:22-23 (Rom 9:27), he draws on the themes of the exile (Deuteronomic curses on the unfaithful Jew) and the remnant (Deuteronomic blessings on the faithful).

In light of these considerations, therefore, it can be understood that Romans 9:30—10:8 reverses commonly held Jewish expectations. According to Paul, those who do not attempt to be justified by the works of the law but who rather place their faith in Christ alone (Gentile believers) experience the Deuteronomic blessings, whereas those who attempt to be saved through adherence to the Torah (non-Christian Jews) are under the Deuteronomic curses. This ironic contrast surfaces when one observes the parallels in Romans 9:30—10:8 (table 10.2).

With regard to the first proposed parallel, Romans 9:30 and Romans 10:1, both statements speak of acquiring the righteousness of God or salvation. Romans 9:30 attests to the ironic fact that Gentiles, who do not pursue God's righteousness via the

[35]Scott, "Paul's Use of Deuteronomic Tradition(s)," 659-65.

Table 10.2. Parallels Between 9 and 10

9:30	The acquisition of salvation/righteousness	10:1
9:31	Israel's failure to obey the law	10:2
9:32-33	Israel's misunderstanding of the law	10:3-4

Mosaic law, have actually received that righteousness by faith (implied—through faith in Christ). Romans 10:1 expresses Paul's deep desire that Israel also will receive God's salvation or righteousness (implied—like the Gentiles already have).

The second parallel, Romans 9:31 and Romans 10:2, addresses Israel's failure to obey the Torah. The first part of each verse speaks of Israel's commitment to keep the law ("pursued the righteousness which is based on law"; "have a zeal for God"). The second part of each verse laments Israel's nonachievement of that objective ("did not succeed in fulfilling that law"; "it is not enlightened").

The third parallel, Romans 9:32-33 and Romans 10:3-4, exposes Israel's misunderstanding of the law. Each text presents two aspects of that confusion—one general, the other specific. In general, Israel failed to perceive that the divine intent was that the law should be pursued by faith, not by one's meritorious works (cf. Rom 9:32 with Rom 10:3). More specifically, Israel perpetuates that mistake in its rejection of Jesus Christ, the fulfillment of the law and the only means of acquiring God's righteousness (cf. Rom 9:33 and Rom 10:4).

Paul concludes his argument in Romans 9:30—10:8 by explicitly contrasting obedience to the law (cf. Rom 10:5 with Lev 18:5) with the righteousness that comes by faith in Christ (cf. Rom 10:6-8 with Deut 30:12-14). In doing so, he essentially reverses the Deuteronomic curses and blessings by replacing the law with faith and particularism with universalism.[36]

2 Corinthians 3:1—4:6. This passage presents an antithetical Moses typology. Seyoon Kim's chart of contrasts between the Mosaic covenant and the new covenant in Christ is a helpful summary of 2 Corinthians 3:1—4:6 (table 10.3).

Although an increasing number of recent interpreters argue that Paul does not say in 2 Corinthians 3:1—4:6 that the law and the old covenant are annulled,[37] the following four points made by Ben F. Witherington III seem to suggest other-

---

[36]For further discussion see Pate, *Reverse of the Curse,* chapter 7.

[37]Two major studies on 2 Corinthians 3:1–4:6 defending this view are Scott J. Hafemann, *Paul, Moses, and the History of Israel: The Letter/Spirit Contrast and the Argument from Scripture in 2 Corinthians 3,* Wissenschaftliche Untersuchungen zum Neuen Testament 81 (Tübingen, Germany: J.C.B. Mohr/ Paul Siebeck, 1995); and, to a lesser degree, Carol Kern Stockhausen, *Moses' Veil and the Glory of the New Covenant: The Exegetical Substructure of II Cor. 3, 1-4, 6,* Analecta Biblica 116 (Rome: Pontifical Biblical Institute Press, 1989), 94 (see also their bibliographies).

wise,[38] as indeed a straightforward reading of the previous contrasts might have indicated: (1) Paul is not merely talking here about a legalistic approach or attitude to the Mosaic law. The contrast is between the actual effect of the Mosaic law on humans (death, 2 Cor 3:6; condemnation, 2 Cor 3:9) as opposed to the opposite result of the Spirit and Christ on people (life, 2 Cor 3:6; righteousness, 2 Cor 3:9; enlightenment and spiritual obtuseness removed, 2 Cor 3:15). This contrast in ef-

Table 10.3. Old and New Covenants in 2 Corinthians 3:1—4:6

The Ministry of the Old Covenant	The Ministry of the New Covenant
1. It is a written code (3:6f.):	1. It is of the Spirit (3:6, 8):
of death (3:6)	of life (3:6)
of condemnation (3:9)	of righteousness (3:9)
in the process of abolition (3:11)	permanent (3:11)
of less glory	of greater glory (3:7-11)
2. Moses, its minister, veiled himself in order to prevent the Israelites from seeing the end of the covenant which was being abolished (3:13).	2. Paul, its minister, acts with confidence, hope, freedom and frankness (3:4, 12; 4:1ff.).
In consequence the old covenant remains veiled (3:14).	The new covenant reveals the glory of the Lord.
Its adherents, the Israelites, are also veiled in their hearts, so that they cannot understand the revelation of God (3:14f.; 4:3f.).	Its adherents, the Christians, have their veil removed in Christ, and see the glory of the Lord and are transformed into the image of Christ who operated as the Spirit (3:16-18; 4:4-6).
Implied: The glory and image of God were restored to Israel on Sinai; but they lost them through sin. The observance of the law does not restore them.*	

*Kim, Origin of Paul's Gospel, 214.

---

[38]Ben F. Witherington III, Jesus, Paul, and the End of the World: A Comparative Study in New Testament Eschatology (Downers Grove, Ill.: InterVarsity Press, 1992), 110-11.

fect is similar to what Paul says in Romans 2—3; 7—8. To read a passage like *Exodus Rabbah* 41.1 (on Ex 31:18)—"While Israel stood below engraving idols to provoke their Creator to anger . . . God sat on high engraving tablets which would give them life"—is to appreciate the uniqueness of Paul's stance regarding the result of the Torah. (2) Paul's usage of the verb "abolished" *(katargeō)* in various forms in 2 Corinthians 3:1—4:6 (2 Cor 3:7, 11, 13-14) is critical to the discussion. Twenty-two of its twenty-seven occurrences in the New Testament are found in the undisputed Pauline letters and always refer to something replaced, invalidated or abolished, not merely to something faded.[39] Consistency would dictate that Paul uses the word here with the same intended meaning. (3) The third point has to do with the removal of the veil over the hearts of unbelievers, thanks to the working of Christ and the Spirit. This too indicates that the Mosaic law and covenant had reached their end. Witherington writes of this:

> Only Christ the Lord or the Spirit can take away the veil over the hearts of the Israelites. But when the veil is taken away, what does Paul think the Israelites will see? His arguments suggest that they will see that the Mosaic law has a temporary, not a permanent glory, unlike the new covenant (v. 11, *to menon en doxē*), and thus a temporal and temporary part to play in the divine economy of salvation. His argument suggests that they will see the Mosaic covenant, far from giving life, had just the opposite effect on fallen human beings. When the veil, or hardheartedness, is removed, though the law will be seen as a good and glorious thing in and of itself, it will also be seen to have had bad effects, and thus in the end needed to be superseded by a more effective covenant that gives life and righteousness.[40]

(4) In view of the fact that the neuter participle in 2 Corinthians 3:11, "fading" *(katargoumenon)*, in accordance with the neuter substantive in 2 Corinthians 3:10, "have glory" *(to dedoxasmenon)*, should be interpreted as applying to the entire old covenant, it is likely that Paul in 2 Corinthians 3:14 says that the old covenant, not just the veil, is passing away. This is confirmed by the fact that when Paul speaks of the removal of the veil (2 Cor 3:16), he uses the more fitting term "is removed" *(periaireitai)*.

In light of these four considerations, we are led to the conclusion that the correlations in 2 Corinthians 3:1—4:6 between the new covenant and life, and the Mosaic covenant and death are rooted in the Deuteronomic curses and blessings, except that Paul reverses conventional Jewish thinking by attributing death to the law but life to those who believe in Christ.[41]

---

[39] Ibid., 110; cf. Victor Furnish, *II Corinthians,* Anchor Bible 32A (Garden City, N.Y.: Doubleday, 1984), 203.

[40] Witherington, *Jesus, Paul, and the End of the World,* 110-11.

[41] See Thielman's discussion, *Paul and the Law,* 110-12.

[42] Although we accept the Pauline authorship of these letters, our argument is not absolutely dependent on that assumption. For thorough defenses of the Pauline authorship of Colossians and Ephesians,

Ephesians and Colossians. The theme of Paul's reversal of the Deuteronomic curses and blessings continues, we suggest, in Ephesians and Colossians.[42] Our method in this section will be to uncover the Deuteronomic framework of Ephesians and Colossians, along with identifying Paul's replacement of the stipulations of the Torah with faith in Christ alone. We begin with Ephesians.[43]

Ephesians. Though it has apparently gone unnoticed by the commentators, Ephesians nicely matches the covenantal framework of the book of Deuteronomy.[44] The Torah was the covenant charter of Israel, establishing her relationship with God. Nowhere is this perspective of the Law more evident than in the book of Deuteronomy (see above, chapter two). Patterned after the Hittite suzerainty-vassal treaty (ca. second millennium B.C.?), Deuteronomy highlights the centrality of the Torah to ancient Judaism: preamble (Deut 1:1-5), historical prologue (Deut 1:6—3:29), stipulations (Deut 4—26), blessings and curses (Deut 28), appeal to witnesses (Deut 31:26—32:47), public display (Deut 31:9, 24-26). These features accentuate the importance of the Torah for Israel's relationship to God. To obey the covenant was to invite divine blessings for both people and land; to disobey it was to invoke God's curses in the form of defeat and exile suffered at the hand of foreign powers.[45]

We suggest that the six components outlined above are operative in Ephesians.

1. The preamble section of Deuteronomy (Deut 1:1-5) identifies Yahweh as the God of Israel's covenant, thus giving the historical setting for the book. Building on the work of others, Roy E. Ciampa has argued that Paul's opening references to God as Father extending his grace and peace (through Jesus Christ) are rooted in the Jewish concept of the exodus and restoration (see Deut 32:5-20, 36-43; Ex 4:22; Is 1:2; 63:16; 64:4-7, 9-12; Jer 3:12-18; 30:1; 21:9; Hos 1:9—2:1; 2:14-15, 21-23; 11:1-11; *Pss Sol* 17:27; *Jub* 1:24-25; *T. Jud* 24:3; 3 Macc 6:3, 8; Tob 13:4-6; Sir 4:10; 23:1, 4; 1 QH 9:33-36; Wis 2:16-18; etc.).[46] Ephesians 1:1-3, we suggest, is very much in keeping with the preceding notion, constituting the preamble to Paul's exposition of the new covenant of restoration in Christ, including both Jew and Gentile (cf. Eph 1:1-3 with Eph 2:11-13).

---

see Donald Guthrie, *New Testament Introduction* (Downers Grove, Ill.: InterVarsity Press, 1978), 551-55 and 479-508, respectively, and the bibliography contained therein.

[43]We could just have easily begun with Colossians, because it and Ephesians are significantly similar.

[44]The following discussion of Ephesians and Colossians is indebted to C. Marvin Pate and Douglas Kennard, *Deliverance Now and Not Yet: The New Testament and the Great Tribulation* (Baltimore, Md.: Peter Lang, 2004), chap. 4.

[45]For studies on the relationship between the suzerain-vassal treaties and the Old Testament, see G. E. Mendenhall, "Covenant Forms in Israelite Tradition," *Biblical Archaeologist* 17, no. 3 (1954): 50-76; Meredith G. Kline, *Treaty of the Great King: The Covenant Structure of Deuteronomy* (Grand Rapids, Mich.: Eerdmans, 1963).

[46]Roy E. Ciampa, *The Presence and Function of Scripture in Galatians 1 and 2,* Wissenschaftliche Untersuchungen zum Neuen Testament 2/102 (Tübingen, Germany: J.C.B. Mohr/Paul Siebeck, 1998), 40-44.

2. The historical prologue section of Deuteronomy (Deut 1:6—3:29) rehearses God's past saving acts on behalf of Israel. Ephesians 1:3-14 nicely qualifies to be Paul's counterpart of such a historical prologue, summarizing God's salvific acts in Christ on behalf of the church. Four ideas in Ephesians 1:3-14 are rooted in the Old Testament story of God's saving relationship to Israel, now reapplied to the Christian community: (a) "chosen" as sons (cf. Eph 1:3, 11 with, e.g., Deut 4:37; 7:6-9; 10:15; Is 41:8-9; 44:2; 28:12); (b) "beloved" of God (e.g., cf. Eph 1:4 with Deut 4:37; 10:15; 23:5); (c) "redeemed" at the exodus (cf. Eph. 1:7, 14 with, e.g., Deut 9:26; 13:5; 24:18; 1 Chron 17:21); (d) a people of God's own "possession/inheritance" (cf. Eph 1:14 with, e.g., Ex 19:5; Deut 7:6; 9:26; 14:2; 15:4; 26:18; Mal 3:17).[47] In addition to these four ideas, we should also mention that "saints" is rooted in the Old Testament relative to ancient Israel's status now applied to the church (cf. Eph 1:1 with, e.g., Ex 19:5-6; Lev 19:2; Deut 7:6).

3. The stipulations section of Deuteronomy (Deut 4—26) specifies the Mosaic law to be the condition to be met in order for Israel to maintain its status as the people of God. Ephesians 2:4-10 (cf. Deut 11—22) seems to be Paul's stipulation for entering the new covenant, which, ironically, is no longer the Torah but faith in Christ alone.

4. Deuteronomy 28 (cf. Deut 27—30; cf. Deut 11:26-28; 30:15-20) predicts blessings and curses for Israel, depending on her obedience or lack thereof to the Mosaic law. As a number of commentators have noted, Paul's virtue/vice lists in Ephesians 4:17—5:2 and Colossians 3:5-11 are rooted in the two-ways tradition of Deuteronomy, that is, the covenantal curses and blessings.[48] If so, such a background invites one to interpret the wrath upon the disobedient (Eph 5:6; cf. Eph 2:3) as the enforcement of the Deuteronomic curses. Indeed, Paul's warning in Ephesians 5:5 about sinners not inheriting the kingdom of Christ and God (the spiritualization of the land of Israel now applied to heaven) confirms the Deuteronomic nuance of Ephesians 5:6.

5. In Deuteronomy 31:26—32:47 history and creation are appealed to as witnesses that God has been faithful to Israel, that God would keep his word. This backdrop casts helpful light on Ephesians 3:8-10 (cf. Eph 1:8-10), for there the church (now made up of reconciled Jews and Gentiles in Christ) is the witness to God's promise that one day he will bring unity to the cosmos (Eph 1:10; 3:10-11).

6. Finally, in Deuteronomy 31:9, 24-26, we are told that Moses wrote down the Book of the Law and placed it beside the ark of the covenant. Such a public display stood as a testimony to Israel. Ephesians 2:11-18 seems to draw on such a concept but in reverse fashion, for the law that condemned humanity and separated Jew and Gen-

---

[47]For the connection between the Pauline concept of "inheritance" and the possession of the land of Israel, now spiritually interpreted, see again Pate, *Reverse of the Curse*, chap. 6.

[48]See discussion and bibliography in Andrew T. Lincoln, *Ephesians,* Word Biblical Commentary 42 (Waco, Tex.: Word, 1990), 296.

tile was nailed to the cross of Christ. It was the public display of Christ's death by
which the barrier of the law was removed.[49]

Colossians. We suggest that the same Deuteronomic framework informs Colossians.
Because that letter parallels Ephesians, we need only to show in chart form the correspondences between Colossians and the book of Deuteronomy (table 10.4).

Table 10.4 Deuteronomic Framework in Colossians

Deuteronomy	Colossians
A Preamble	1:1-3 (God the Father)
B Historical Prologue	1:4-20 (Inheritance in Christ)
C Stipulations	2:6-23 (Faith, Not Law)
D Blessings/Curses	3:5-11 (Two Ways)
E Witnesses	1:26-27 (Gentile and Jew Now One)
F Public Display	2:13-15 (Law Nailed to the Cross)

Opposition to Paul's Retelling of the Story of Israel

Predictably, not all were pleased with Paul's proclamation that God in Christ had reversed the Deuteronomic curses and blessings. In particular the Judaizers, Jewish
Christians who taught that faith in Jesus plus adhering to the Mosaic code was the
means to be justified before God, dogged Paul's footsteps, decrying his message (see
Acts 15:1-5). In this section we will summarize the Judaizers' message through the
eyes of Galatians and then, using Philippians 3, one of Paul's most polemical statements against the Judaizers, highlight the apostle's response.

The Judaizers' message. Attempting to reconstruct the Judaizers' theology (one
that taught that salvation comes by grace and observing the law) through a mirror-
reading of Galatians has inherent dangers; nevertheless, it provides evidence that we
could not otherwise obtain.[50] The following picture emerges in Galatians about the Ju-

---

[49]For a detailed attempt to uncover Jewish mysticism's preoccupation with the Torah as the background of Paul's polemic in Colossians, see Pate, *Communities of the Last Days,* chap. 7.

[50]The following is taken from Pate, *Reverse of the Curse,* 338-41. Mirror-reading a text is like overhear-
ing one end of a telephone conversation, which of course runs the risk of jumping to conclusions
about the nature of the discussion. But used judiciously, such an approach can be very helpful, as
John M. G. Barclay has demonstrated in his article, "Mirror-Reading a Polemical Letter: Galatians as
a Test Case," *Journal for the Study of the New Testament* 31 (1987): 73-93. For the application of this
approach in general to Paul's letters with a view to recovering the Judaizing message that he opposed,
see Pate, *Reverse of the Curse,* part 2.

daizers: in Galatians 1:1, 11—2:10 they portrayed Paul as deriving his message, which consisted of faith in Christ plus the need to follow the law, especially circumcision, from the Jerusalem apostles. But according to Galatians 1:6-10, Paul abandoned the latter aspect because he did not want to offend the sensitivities of the Christian Gentiles. In other words, the apostle watered down the gospel in order to please Gentiles. In Galatians 2:11-16, furthermore, the Judaizers indicated that the covenantal curses could be removed because Jesus the Messiah's death and resurrection inaugurated the long-awaited age to come, and with it the beginnings of the eschatological restoration of Israel envisioned by the Old Testament prophets. Now, according to Galatians 2:19-20, because of his resurrection life, Christians—Jews and Gentiles alike—have a new-found power for obeying God's law, thereby fully actualizing the age to come. However, Paul's antinomian (against law) message places Gentiles back under the slavery of sin and even makes Christ an instrument of unrighteousness, according to Galatians 2:17-18.

In Galatians 3:1-5 one can detect the Judaizing message that the Spirit, the sign of the age to come, now resides within Christians and empowers them to perform genuine works of faith—in effect, the ethics of the new covenant. Furthermore, according to Galatians 3:6-9, even Gentiles can now become children of Abraham if they believe in Jesus Messiah and submit to circumcision. As such, they, together with Jewish Christians, can experience the Deuteronomic blessings by obeying the Torah, because Christ has taken its curses unto himself, according to Galatians 3:10-14. In other words, the eschatological restoration of Israel has dawned, and the nations can participate in Israel's salvation, provided they become like Jews. Gentiles no longer need be enslaved to the curses of the covenant (once pronounced on Israel's enemies) because they do not follow the Torah; now they can experience the new exodus with its spiritual freedom born out of a new-found obedience. All of this has happened in light of the fullness of time, the dawning of the messianic age (Gal 4:1-7).

To complete their salvation, however, Judaizers argue that Gentile believers must submit to circumcision, the dietary laws and Sabbath keeping (Gal 4:8-11). If they want to be the children of Abraham, then they must live like the children of Abraham, the descendants of Israel (Gal 4:21-31). (If Paul were more forthright, he would admit to the Galatians that he preaches the very same thing, Gal 5:1-12.) With Christ and the Spirit, Gentiles can overcome the works of the flesh by permitting the Torah to inspire within them obedience to God and hence can participate in Israel's inheritance. Not to pursue this path, however, is to invite judgment (Gal 5:13-6:7). But the Christian message brings hope—Gentiles can become citizens of the new creation, the Israel of God. For their part, they must exercise faith in Christ and accept the message of circumcision (Gal 6:11-18).

We have already seen from Galatians 3:10-14 how Paul responds to such a message: Attempting to be justified by the works of the law brings about an ironic result—the covenantal curses. On the other hand, faith in Christ alone is the sole means for receiving the covenantal blessings. Philippians 3 sustains Paul's argumentation against works righteousness. We turn now to that passage.

Philippians 3. Paul's comments in Philippians 3 rank as some of his most polemical statements regarding the nomistic message of the Judaizers (cf. Gal 1:6-10; 3:10-13; 4:21-31; 6:12-15).[51] In effect, Paul's remarks reverse the Deuteronomic curses and blessings: those who rely on the Torah are under the divine curse, while those whose faith is in Christ, apart from the works of the law, enjoy God's acceptance. Thus, the Judaizers are labeled "dogs," nomenclature normally applied to Gentiles (Phil 3:2). Peter T. O'Brien says of this remark, "In an amazing reversal Paul asserts that it is the Judaizers who are to be regarded as Gentiles, they are 'the dogs' who stand outside the covenantal blessings."[52]

The next description, "evil workers" (Phil 3:2), is even more forceful. The language echoes the Psalter's characterization of the enemies of God (e.g., Ps 5:5 [LXX]; 6:8; 14 [13]:14; 36 [35]:12). Paul undoubtedly used this epithet because of his conviction that the Judaizers' confidence in the works of the law was misplaced. Rather than stimulating a person to obedience before God, the Torah ironically was the catalyst for their becoming his enemies through disobedience (see again Rom 3:20; 5:20-21; 7:7-13; Gal 3:10). In this concept we meet Paul's reversal of the Deuteronomic curses.

According to Philippians 3:3, the Judaizing message of circumcision only mutilates the flesh; it does not change the heart.[53] Those whose faith is in Christ apart from the Torah are the true circumcision, the ones in whom the Spirit dwells and produces genuine godliness. All of this bespeaks the actualization of the new covenant. Here, then, the apostle reverses the Deuteronomic blessings: not the works of Moses, but faith in Christ is the means for ensuring divine acceptance. O'Brien catches the irony of the apostle's comments in Philippians 3:3: "Circumcision, their [the Judaizers'] greatest source of pride, is interpreted by the apostle as a sure sign that they have no part in God's people at all."[54]

If Paul in the past had placed utmost importance on the Torah (Phil 3:4-6), since encountering Christ on the Damascus road he can no longer do so, according to Philippians 3:7-11.[55] The righteousness of the law is eternally inferior to the right-

---

[51]Thielman (*Paul and the Law,* 148-49) persuasively identifies Paul's opponents at Philippi as Judaizing Christians.

[52]Peter T. O'Brien, *The Epistle to the Philippians: A Commentary on the Greek Text* (Grand Rapids, Mich.: Eerdmans, 1991), 355.

[53]Ibid., 357.

[54]Ibid., 356.

[55]For support that Paul alludes to his Damascus road conversion in Philippians 3:7-11, see Seyoon Kim, *Origin of Paul's Gospel,* 66.

eousness that comes through Christ (Phil 3:7). Through the knowledge of Christ, Paul has been justified, thereby participating in the divinely intended restoration of Israel—not the earthy renewal of Jerusalem, the temple and the Law, but the prospect of resurrection and heaven had become the focus of the apostle's hope. This was made possible because of Christ's death on the cross, which embraced the curses of the law (Phil 3:8-11). But according to Philippians 3:12-16, the complete realization of the heavenly promise had not yet occurred; it awaits the parousia (Phil 3:20-21).[56] Until then, Paul would have to press on in faith.

In the meantime, Paul warned the Philippian church of the activities of the Judaizers, whose nomistic platform contradicted the message of the crucified Christ. These people were enemies of the cross (Phil 3:18) for two reasons. First, they failed to perceive that their law-keeping message was self-refuting; it stirred up disobedience rather than obedience. That is, they did not comprehend Paul's proclamation of the reversal of the Deuteronomic curses. Second, the Judaizers did not understand that the law misjudged Jesus (who perfectly obeyed God) and thereby rendered itself obsolete in the divine plan.[57] Stated another way, Paul's opponents did not grasp the truth that the cross of Christ, in ending the role of the law, opened up the Deuteronomic blessings for all. Instead, the message of the cross scandalized the Judaizers (cf. 1 Cor 1:18—3:23). Consequently, they remained under the curse of the law ("their end is destruction," Phil 3:19). The Torah in which they boasted, with its dietary law ("their god is the belly"),[58] observance of circumcision ("they glory in their shame")[59] and commitment to the national restoration of Israel ("with minds set on earthly things"), paradoxically secured their judgment.

Whereas the Judaizers are portrayed in Philippians 3 as being under the Deuteronomic curses, Christian Gentiles are presented as enjoying the covenantal blessings. This last point is made clear in two passages conveying Paul's positive attitude toward Gentiles—Philippians 2:14-15 and Philippians 3:3. Both of these texts promote the idea that Gentiles are now incorporated into the people of God. In Philippians 2:14-15, Paul tells the Philippians, "Do all things without murmuring or arguing, so that you may be blameless and innocent, children of God without blemish in

---

[56]This last paragraph is more fully developed in Pate, *Reverse of the Curse,* chap. 7.

[57]This last paragraph is more fully developed in ibid., chap. 6.

[58]Andrew T. Lincoln plausibly defends the view that the phrase "whose god is their belly" refers not to libertine conduct but to the Judaizers' boast in their food laws (cf. a similar use of "belly" in Rom 16:18); see Lincoln, *Paradise Now and Not Yet: Studies in the Role of the Heavenly Dimension in Paul's Thought with Special Reference to His Eschatology,* Society for the Study of the New Testament Monograph Series 43 (Cambridge: Cambridge University Press, 1981), 96.

[59]Ibid. The phrase "whose glory is their shame," argues Lincoln, is sarcastic, predicting future judgment (not glory) on those who practice circumcision as a means of salvation. (The "shame" alluded to is the nakedness required for circumcision.)

the midst of a crooked and perverse generation, in which you shine like stars in the world." As Thielman observes, these words echo the biblical record of Israel's wilderness wanderings. Philippians 2:15 in particular recalls the Song of Moses (Deut 32:4-5 [LXX]). Thielman writes of this parallel:

> The theme of the song, then, is that despite God's faithfulness, Israel severed its filial ties with him through its disobedience and became a blemished, crooked and perverse generation. In contrast, Paul describes the Philippians as "children unblemished" *(tekna amōma)* who live "in the midst of a crooked and perverse generation *(meson geneas skolias kai diestrammenēs)*. Paul's language seems intentionally formulated to signal the Philippians' status as the newly constituted people of God who, unlike Israel of old, as "unblemished" and who, rather than constituting "a crooked and perverse generation," stand in contrast to it.
>
> Paul then says that as this newly constituted and unblemished people, the Philippians "shine as stars in the world," a phrase that echoes the descriptions of Israel's vocation in Isaiah 42:6-7 and 49:6 as a "light to the Gentiles." With this comment Paul implies that the Philippians not only have taken over biblical Israel's role as the unblemished people of God but have been assigned Israel's vocation as "light to the Gentiles" as well.[60]

Thus, Gentile Christians now enjoy the Deuteronomic/covenantal blessings against the backdrop of Israel's current state of disbelief and judgment.

Philippians 3:3 also conveys the thought that Gentiles are now incorporated into the people of God through faith in Christ, "for we are the true circumcision, who worship God in spirit, and glory in Christ Jesus, and put no confidence in the flesh." Paul here applies the language of the Old Testament to the Philippian believers (who of course were composed of Gentiles and Jews). As was shown earlier, the phrase "true circumcision" refers to the biblical hope that Israel's heart would one day be circumcised for the purpose of obedience (Deut 10:16; Jer 4:4). Similarly, the word *worship* or *serve* adopts the language the Septuagint employs for Israel's service to God as his chosen people (Ex 3:12; Deut 10:12). Moreover, the phrase "in spirit" recalls the prophetic description of the restored Israel as a place where God's Spirit will dwell (Ezek 11:19; 36:27; 37:1-14).[61]

In effect, then, what Paul does in Philippians 3:3 is to spiritualize language once applied to ancient Israel by now ascribing it to the Gentiles. The concluding words of Philippians 3:3, "glory in Christ Jesus and put no confidence in the flesh," point in that direction as well. The descriptions in Philippians 3:3, then, indicate that Gentile Christians are true Israel to whom belong the covenantal blessings, while the Judaizers remain under the curses of the Torah.

---

[60]Thielman, *Paul and the Law,* 157. Translations of Philippians 2:15; 3:3 are his.
[61]Ibid., 155.

Conclusion

This chapter has highlighted Paul's retelling of the story of Israel. We began by uncovering how very different the pre-Christian Paul's message was. He taught that obeying the Torah restores the Deuteronomic blessings, while disobeying the Old Testament law ensures the continuation of the covenantal curses on Israel. However, with his encounter of the crucified Jesus now glorified in heaven, Paul underwent a radical change of perspective. He now realized that faith in Christ had replaced the law as the means to salvation in the divine plan. Consequently, his former values were switched—obedience to the law brings a curse; only faith in the Crucified One recovers the Deuteronomic blessings—this despite the protests of Paul's Judaizing opponents.

Excursus: The Restoration of Israel and Paul's Wider Thought

This chapter has rather narrowly focused on how the story of Israel influences Paul's thought as expressed in some of his letters. But the case can be made that the retelling of the story of Israel also influenced Paul's wider thinking. Space only permits us to take soundings of this theme in the major categories often used to interpret Paul's theology as a whole—theology proper, Christology, soteriology, anthropology, pneumatology, ecclesiology, and eschatology—some of which we already covered along the way.

Theology. Surprisingly, only rather recently has the central place of God in Paul's thought come to light, in particular the triumph of God over his creation.[62] Here we mention one aspect of that theme, namely, that Paul is convinced that God has been faithful to Israel, the crown of creation. More specifically, Paul is concerned to show that God's action in Jesus Christ fulfills the divine covenant with Israel. It will be recalled from our chapter that Paul reverses Israel's nomism and particularism, replacing that with fideism (faith alone) and universalism (all can become a part of the people of God by faith in Christ), respectively. But these are not some new and foreign ideas to the Old Testament, according to Paul. That salvation resulted from faith is clear in Genesis 15:6 ("Abraham believed in God and it was counted to him as righteousness"), according to Romans 4 and Galatians 3:6-18. Even Moses recognized that the law could not justify, only faith could, Paul argues in Romans 10:5-8. That the Old Testament envisioned that Gentiles should be included in the people of God is a point the apostle makes forcefully in Galatians 3:6-29 (quoting Gen 12:1-3—all nations will be blessed) and Romans 10:18-21 (which draws on Deut 32:21); the former with reference to Abraham and the latter concerning Moses. Actually, from Paul's perspective, the nomism and particularism that later characterized Israel are at odds with God's plan for the ages (see Rom 15:7-13; Eph 2:13-

---

[62]See C. Marvin Pate, *The End of the Age Has Come: The Theology of Paul* (Grand Rapids, Mich.: Zondervan, 1995), chap. 2.

THE STORY OF ISRAEL

22)—one that envisions both Jew and Gentile as one in Christ. In all of this, the
apostle to the Gentiles reaffirms that the Christ event has proven God to be faithful
to his promises to Israel.

Christology. Because much of the subject of this chapter has to do with Jesus the
Messiah, here we need only mention that a significant aspect of Paul's portrayal of
Christ is that he embraced the covenantal curses on the cross so that by his resurrec-
tion he might dispense the divine blessings on those who believe in him.

Soteriology. We have treated this too, so we simply note here that salvation, according to Paul, is not to be found through following the Torah, but by exercising simple
faith in Christ alone.

Anthropology. Salvation is by faith alone because, to Paul's way of thinking, humankind is depraved, with no merit to commend itself to God (Rom 3:1-20); hence, faith
in Christ's death for our sins is the only means to justification. It may even be, as we
argued elsewhere, that Paul thereby rejects the prevalent Jewish notion that the law
empowers the good inclination within a person toward obedience. On the contrary,
says Paul, the Torah stirs up the bad inclination within a person—not because the law
is evil, but rather because humans are sinful.[63] A powerful irony pertains, therefore, to
the law: if one attempts to follow the law, sin and spiritual exile persist; only through
faith in Christ does true restoration come.

Pneumatology. For Paul and the early church, the Holy Spirit was the sign par excellence that the age to come had dawned (see Rom 8; Acts 2; etc.). Moreover, like the
Old Testament, Paul envisioned that the pouring out of the Spirit would be a time
when the new covenant would finally be actualized among God's people, thus bringing
about Israel's long-awaited restoration (cf. 2 Cor 3:1—4:6 with Ezek 36:22-38; cf. Joel
2:23-32). Thus it is that, for Paul, the indwelling Spirit of God in the Christian is proof
that that day had arrived; one was born not out of an exterior adherence to the Torah,
but rather an inward change of heart.

Ecclesiology. It is easy to see from our comments on Paul in this chapter that the restoration of Israel is reinterpreted by the apostle along spiritual, not national lines. Consequently, both Jew and Gentile compose the new people of God, which is the church
in Christ.

Eschatology. And yet, according to Romans 11:25-27, Paul believed that God had
not yet finished with ethnic Israel. A day is coming when that nation will accept Jesus
as Messiah, thereby experiencing her ultimate restoration. This comprises components
5 and 6 of the Deuteronomistic tradition: Israel will have the opportunity to repent of
its sin, and receiving Christ, will be restored to God.

---

[63]See Pate, *Reverse of the Curse,* 56.

Supplemental Readings in New Dictionary of Biblical Theology

D. J. Moo, "Romans," 291-97.

M. J. Harris, "2 Corinthians," 306-11.

R. E. Ciampa, "Galatians," 311-15.

T. Moritz, "Ephesians," 315-19.

I. H. Marshall, "Philippians," 319-22.

M. J. Harris, "Colossians," 322-26.

P. D. Woodbridge, "Circumcision," 411-14.

P. R. Williamson, "Covenant," 419-29.

K. E. Brower, "Eschatology," 459-64.

M. A. Seifrid, "Righteousness, justice, justification," 740-45.

Study Questions

1. What components of the Deuteronomistic tradition occur in 1 Thessalonians 2:15-16?

2. Summarize the Judaizing message Paul opposed in Galatians.

3. How does Galatians 3:10-14 respond to the Judaizing message?

4. What components of the Deuteronomistic tradition occur in Romans 9—11?

5. Summarize Paul's response in Philippians 3 to the Judaizing message.

6. Summarize the contrasts between the old and new covenants discussed in 2 Corinthians 3:1—4:6.

7. Summarize the components of the covenantal framework of Deuteronomy that are operative in Ephesians.

11

THE GENERAL EPISTLES
AND HEBREWS

In Exile but on the
Brink of Restoration

Much of the Bible divides well into subgroups like the Gospels, the letters of Paul and so forth. After dividing up the New Testament into fairly obvious subsets, we are left with 1–2 Peter, James, Jude and Hebrews. These are commonly called the "General Epistles," although even in this grouping Hebrews is often separated.

Connected Letters or "Hodgepodge of Leftovers"?

Since the Reformation, our Western love affair with Paul has caused us to see his letters as the key to Christian living. Furthermore, the Gospels with their stories of Jesus, the writings of John with their simplicity and depth, Acts' story of the early church, and Revelation's story of the last days all seem to have compelling and immediately obvious reasons to be studied. But alas, the General Epistles have almost the taint of being the scattered remnants of the New Testament, "the leftovers." James Dunn has noted that New Testament theologies usually devote the majority of space to Jesus, Paul and John, sparing "only a few pages for others."[1]

Often separated from the General Epistles, Hebrews still enjoys the same fate, not so much because it shares the perceived low status of the other General Epistles but because its complex theology with its use of extensive Old Testament imagery has often mystified modern Western readers. However, although they are often neglected, the General Epistles (Hebrews, 1–2 Peter, James and Jude) contain a rich biblical theology.

Traditionally, these letters have been considered a distinct unit on the argument that

---

[1]James Dunn, "Editor's Preface," in Andrew Chester and Ralph Martin, *The Theology of the Letters of James, Peter, and Jude,* New Testament Theology Series (Cambridge: Cambridge University Press, 1994), ix.

they were not addressing a specific church but rather were "catholic," in the technical sense of "universal"; that is, they address Christians in general. Most scholars today, though, believe the General Epistles were addressed to specific congregations and particular issues just like the other New Testament letters.[2]

The General Epistles as a Tripartite Corpus

Since we now reject grouping these letters as "catholic," the question remains: Are these letters still to be grouped together because they are similar, or are they merely the "left-over" books? Hebrews stands the most apart. Thus, it is not uncommon to see the description, "Hebrews and the General Epistles." We shall consider them a loose group since they all write out of a Jewish-Christian church context.

Although they form a group, the group may be divided into three parts. James and 1 Peter share much commonality since they both emphasize how to live wisely while "in exile." They write from a primitive Jewish-Christian context. To make their point, each will present a midrash[3] (sermon) on a passage from an Old Testament prophet. Wisdom—Jewish teachings on how to live wisely—figures prominently in their writings. Jude and 2 Peter form a very tight group. 2 Peter appears to be a revision of Jude, keeping at its heart Jude's warnings against false teachers. Hebrews stands by itself. The author of Hebrews writes from a Hellenistic Jewish rather than a Palestinian Jewish context. Hebrews emphasizes a different aspect of the story of Israel. We will discuss the General Epistles in this tripartite format.

The Story of Israel

Old Testament background. When God called his people, he established a conditional covenant with them, setting out blessings (for obedience) and curses (for disobedience). These Deuteronomic blessings and curses form a major theme in the story of Israel. Despite divine warnings, Israel continued to violate the covenant and thus invoked the curses. As described in Deuteronomy 28:15-68, a foreign nation would dispossess them (Deut 28:36, 49-53), leaving them with no home, no resting place (Deut 28:65), and even returning them to slavery under a foreign power, Egypt

---

[2]This is not to imply New Testament writings were strictly focused only on their particular community (see Col 4:16). Richard Bauckham has convincingly argued that each Gospel was written for "any and every Christian community in the late-first-century Roman Empire" ("Introduction," in *The Gospels for All Christians: Rethinking the Gospel Audiences,* ed. Richard Bauckham [Grand Rapids, Mich.: Eerdmans, 1998], 1).

[3]The Hebrew term *midrash* can be translated "commentary" (2 Chron 13:22; 24:27). In biblical scholarship, midrash refers to a Jewish method of expounding Scripture; see Ellis, *Prophecy and Hermeneutic in Early Christianity: New Testament Essays* (Grand Rapids, Mich.: Eerdmans, 1978), 151. The emphasis was on contemporizing Scripture to make it applicable or meaningful for the current situation, much like modern preaching.

(Deut 28:68). The Babylonian exile actualized these curses.

Jeremiah repeatedly warned Israel of the coming exile. His message was for Israel to accept the just punishment of God and to prepare for life in Babylon: "Build houses, plant gardens" (Jer 29:5). Once in exile, many repented of the sins of their past. The covenant unfaithfulness that led to the exile no longer characterized their lives. They were committed to the covenant and to Torah-obedience.

The situation of the Jews had now changed. The message for the exiles was no longer "we're under a just punishment." A new message was needed: a call to restoration because the exile was ending (Ezek 36:8, 25-28). When God spoke to Ezekiel *while in exile,* God was indicating several things:

• He no longer dwelt in the temple.
• His presence was no longer confined to Jerusalem or Palestine.
• He was going to pour out his Spirit on his people.
• He would restore the Deuteronomic blessings.

Yet Israel's vision was not of a mere return to Canaan with a simple restoration of the old order:

> The captives dreamed not simply of a return but of a renewal, a rebirth of Israel in greater conformity to God's original design. . . . drawing up plans for a better future, a future in which Israel's sins will no longer come back to haunt them. . . . A radically new future could be conceived in which obedience to the Lord would no longer be a dream but a reality.[4]

This restoration required a change of heart in God's people: the Deuteronomistic pattern would be broken; God would not just restore their homes (Ezek 36:8) but would also change their hearts (Ezek 36:26), in effect, establishing a new covenant (Jer 31:31-34; Ezek 36:24-27).

The return of some exiles to Palestine under Cyrus is commonly viewed today as the fulfillment of the promises of restoration; yet many ancient Jews believed that this return fell short of the great expectations raised by the visions of Jeremiah and Ezekiel.[5] Although a new temple to Yahweh was built, God did not indwell it as he had the old temple (see the discussion above in Chapter 3). Many Jews concluded that Cyrus's return was not the true, promised return from exile because the promises of Ezekiel were not all realized:

• Israel was governed, not by the kingdom of God, but by the kingdom of Persia, or later, Alexander or the Seleucids or Rome.
• When they saw the rebuilt temple and city, they did not see God's promise that they

---

[4] I. M. Duguid, "Exile," in *New Dictionary of Biblical Theology* (Downers Grove, Ill.: InterVarsity Press, 2000), 477.
[5] So, among others, Duguid, "Exile," 477.

would "prosper more than before" (Ezek 36:11).

- The land did not always produce plenty, nor was it a land where famine did not come among them (Ezek 36:29).
- A son of David did not sit on Jerusalem's throne (Ezek 37:24).

The promised restoration had not yet happened.[6] Furthermore, for many Jewish Christians the temple no longer symbolized the presence of God, but rather the idolatry of Israel.[7]

Second Temple Judaism. As we noted earlier in this book, N. T. Wright has ably demonstrated that many Jews in the centuries up to and including the time of Christ still considered themselves to be living in the exile.[8] The restoration promised by Jeremiah and Ezekiel had not yet come. Many Christians (including Jesus) held this viewpoint. The message of Jeremiah to those in exile was thus still a word for God's people in the first century, even though the situation had changed somewhat from Jeremiah's time. The church was now God's Chosen Israel, albeit an Israel still in exile. The promised restoration was coming soon but was going to be different than they had expected. It was not merely a restoration of the Davidic monarchy. The Son of David had indeed come and had established a kingdom that would last forever as Nathan had prophesied to David (2 Sam 7:12-16), but it would not be David's kingdom (2 Sam 7:16) but God's kingdom as revealed to the Chronicler (1 Chron 17:14). The General Epistles fit into this framework.

Unlike gospels or books of history or of the prophets, letters are addressed to specific recipients. While we have long known that letters are rich sources of theology, we must take particular care to locate each letter's message in its original context. A brief glimpse at the structure of each letter of the General Epistles as well as its intended readers is necessary to mine each letter's theology.

Living in Exile: The Story of Israel in James and 1 Peter

The structure and readers of James. Ever since Martin Luther accused James of "throwing things together . . . chaotically,"[9] the letter of James has often been viewed as a loose

---

[6]In A.D. 90, when the tattered remains of Judaism convened to formalize their canon of Scripture, they ended their canon with 2 Chronicles, which tells the tragic story of how Israel lost the land and moved into exile. This book concludes with the decree of Cyrus, a hint of promised restoration. Yet ending their canon with Chronicles instead of Ezra may be yet another indicator that first-century Jews saw themselves as still in exile (especially after A.D. 70).

[7]See Mark 11:12-21; Acts 7:44-48; 21:30.

[8]For a very helpful survey of the ongoing discussion of Wright's thesis, see the essays in *Jesus and the Restoration of Israel: A Critical Assessment of N. T. Wright's "Jesus and the Victory of God,"* ed. Carey Newman, (Downers Grove, Ill.: InterVarsity Press, 1999).

[9]See D. O. Via, "The Right Strawy Epistle Reconsidered: A Study in Biblical Ethics and Hermeneutics," *Journal of Religion* 49 (1969): 253-67.

collection of barely connected paraenetic[10] sayings.[11] But the last twenty years has seen
a shift. Peter Davids argues that James is carefully structured around three themes: testing, wisdom (pure speech) and poverty/wealth.[12] Douglas Moo, in his fine commentary
on James, critiques Davids's structure for James by arguing that "godly speech" is not
clearly connected to wisdom in James.[13] Yet "proper speech" was such an integral part of
Wisdom literature that there was no need to verbally connect them (e.g., Prov 10:19;
13:3; 18:2-7). About 20 percent of Proverbs 10–29 deals with proper speech, which indicated a reflective life and was considered evidence of wisdom.

Moo notes well, though, that Davids's structure has no room for three other important
topics in James: faith, humility and the law. Moo returns to the view that James is a series
of brief, relatively independent, exhortations.[14] However, Davids is correct to see more
structure in James. James talks about poverty/wealth sometimes in the context of "testing" and sometimes in the context of obedience.[15] A modification of Davids's outline
might be helpful, using "obedience" as the third theme, since it is perhaps the underlying
message connecting poverty/wealth as well as faith, law and humility.

Let us suggest this structure: James begins with a double opening.[16] The first opening introduces the three themes:

- Testing (Jas 1:2-4)
- Wisdom (in speech and prayer) (Jas 1:5-8)
- Poverty as better than wealth (Jas 1:9-11)

---

[10]Paraenesis (or paranesis) refers to a literary genre, often a collection, of various practical moral exhortations whose goal is to alter the audience's behavior; see S. Stowers, *Letter Writing in Greco-Roman
Antiquity,* Library of Early Christianity Series (Philadelphia: Westminster Press, 1986), 91. In the
Greco-Roman world, paraenesis was commonly aimed at encouraging conformity to the rules of society; see Abraham Malherbe, *Moral Exhortation: A Greco-Roman Source Book* (Philadelphia: Fortress,
1986), 124.
[11]Dibelius (1964) is usually credited as the modern founder of this view; see Martin Dibelius, *A Commentary on the Epistle of James,* rev. H. Greeven, trans. M. A. Williams, Hermeneia Series (Philadelphia:
Fortress, 1975), 5-6. It is well argued again by Todd Penner, *The Epistle of James and Eschatology: Re-
reading an Ancient Christian Letter,* Journal for the Study of the New Testament, Supp. Ser. 121 (Sheffield: Sheffield Academic Press, 1996), 214-15.
[12]Peter Davids, *Commentary on James,* New International Greek Testament Commentary (Grand Rapids, Mich.: Eerdmans, 1982).
[13]Douglas Moo, *The Letter of James,* Pillar New Testament Commentary Series (Grand Rapids, Mich.:
Eerdmans, 2000), 45.
[14]Ibid., 44.
[15]Moo (*James,* 24) believes the socioeconomic situation of James's readers (seen in his warnings about
poverty and wealth) should not be given a controlling role in understanding the letter. While obviously important, it does not seem to be the interpretive crux.
[16]Double openings are a well-documented element of some ancient letters (e.g., Josephus, *Ant.* 8.50-
54; Eusebius, *Praep. Ev.* 9.33-34; 10.25-45; Philem 4-7; 1–2 Thess). See the definitive work of F. O.
Francis, "The Form and Function of the Opening and Closing Paragraphs of James and 1 John,"
Zeitschrift für die neutestamentliche Wissenschaft und die Kunde der älteren Kirche 61 (1970): 110-26.

The second opening repeats these themes (with some chiastic[17] blending):
- Testing (related to wealth) (Jas 1:12-18)
- Wisdom (Speech) (Jas 1:19-21)
- Obedience (when tested) (Jas 1:22-25)

James then summarizes these three themes in James 1:26-27 by mentioning the tongue, obedience,[18] and purity (from having passed the test). These three themes—testing (often connected with wealth),[19] speech, and obedience (often in the context of "passing the test")—are then elaborated by James in the remainder of the letter (chiastically):
- Obedience (Jas 2:1-26)
- Proper Speech (Jas 3:1—4:12)
- Tested by wealth (Jas 4:13—5:6)

James concludes by a final summary (chiastic):
- Endure the test (Jas 5:7-11)
- Watch your speech (oaths) (Jas 5:12-13)
- Generosity (in prayer and forgiveness) (Jas 5:14-20)

We do not want to be too rigid, but James seems to follow a general structure while feeling free to modify or blend his elements when it suited him. His book is not just a jumble of exhortations. He presented his material in what to a first-century Jew was an orderly manner.

To whom was James writing? Usually to solve this problem, we look at the letter's address. Ancient letters began with a format: "Sender to Recipient, Greetings." We might think the issue is thus resolved by the letter's address "James . . . To the twelve tribes in the Dispersion: Greetings" (Jas 1:1). James was writing to Jews living in the "Diaspora," that is, places outside Israel's borders where Jews had been "scattered" (Jn 7:35; 2 Macc 1:27). Since Diaspora letters, letters from a prominent Jewish teacher to Jews living in the Diaspora, were not uncommon,[20] it is often assumed that James was writing a general letter addressed to Jewish Christians living abroad. He was thus

---

[17]A *chiasm* is an orderly arrangement of material in which an idea is introduced, followed by another and perhaps another, etc. Eventually the last idea will be repeated, and then the next to the last, etc., in reverse order. An example of a simple chiasm is found in Romans 10:9-10:

> "If you confess with your lips" A
> "and believe in your heart" B
> "for one believes with the heart" B'
> "and one confesses with the mouth" A'

[18]James is clearly referring to biblical injunctions to care for the widow/orphan (Ex 22:22; Deut 10:17-18).

[19]Most commentators see James addressing the problem of poor church members being taken to court by the wealthy. James is encouraging them to endure the test.

[20]Peter Davids, "Book Review of Douglas Moo, *The Letter of James*," *Bulletin for Biblical Research* 12 (2002): 141, strongly critiques Moo for failing to recognize this genre in James.

stressing two common themes: (1) "the twelve tribes," was used for Christians to stress they are the true people of God in the last days, a usage that can be seen elsewhere in the New Testament;[21] (2) "the Dispersion" was emphasizing that the world was not the true homeland for Christians. They were still in exile and awaiting the restoration.

However, Moo argues that James was targeting a more specific audience and that his address should be taken more literally.[22] James was writing to Jewish Christians[23] forced to live away from their homeland. Yet if so, why not a specific letter address? Why say "to the twelve tribes in the Dispersion" if James meant specific congregations? One might counter that James was writing to multiple locations and so used a generic address. However, Peter felt free to list multiple locations (1 Pet 1:1). We are led to conclude that James did not list specific places because he wanted to emphasize the theme of *all Christians living in the Dispersion*.

Like other first-century Jews, James saw Israel as still living in the exile, but for James the church was the true Israel, eagerly awaiting the call to restoration out of her exile. Using the format and theme of a Diaspora letter, James was writing to specific people and places,[24] perhaps former members of his church in Jerusalem who were "scattered" after the persecution following the stoning of Stephen (Acts 8:1) or more likely the famine in Palestine (Acts 11:19-28). These Jews had previously come to Jerusalem on pilgrimage, converted to Jewish Christianity under James, and remained in the church there perhaps because they were expecting an imminent return of Christ (Jas 5:7-8). With the subsequent persecution or hardships, these converts had returned to their homes abroad, and thus James was writing to encourage them and to advise them in dealing with specific problems—both common Jewish problems such as the poverty/oppression pervasive among Jews living in the Dispersion and specific Jewish-Christian problems such as the influx of Pauline Christianity into the region.

The message of James: Live wisely in the exile as we await our imminent restoration. James was writing to particular churches with full confidence that his message was appropriate for all Christians, and he addressed the question: How do we live wisely during our brief remaining time in this exile? He approaches this message of

---

[21]See Moo, *James*, 49-50.

[22]Ibid., 23-24.

[23]Clearly James's readers are Jewish (or at least predominantly Jewish), since they meet in a synagogue (Jas 2:2) and James presupposes distinctively Jewish beliefs, like belief in "one God" (Jas 2:19).

[24]*Pace* Peter Davids, *James*, 24-25, who sees it as a "literary epistle," reflecting the *Sitz im Leben* (life situation) of James rather than any supposed recipients. For support, he notes the lack of personal details. Yet private letters often lacked personal details; see E. R. Richards, *The Secretary in the Letters of Paul*, Wissenschaftliche Untersuchungen zum Neuen Testament 2/42 (Tübingen, Germany: J.C.B. Mohr/Paul Siebeck, 1991), 131, and idem, *Paul and First Century Letter Writing* (Downers Grove, Ill.: InterVarsity Press, 2004), chap. 8.

"living wisely" in two parts. James 1—3 takes a traditional Wisdom approach. James 4—5 is a midrash of Isaiah 58.

Wisdom, "living wisely" (often described as choosing the right path[25]) has long been a cornerstone of Old Testament education:

> The path of the righteous is like the light of dawn . . .
> The way of the wicked is like deep darkness. (Prov 4:18-19)

It is important to note, as in the example above, that the distinction is not between Israel (the righteous) and the nations (the wicked), but rather between the wise Israelite and the foolish Israelite. So also in James, he is not describing the "saved" and the "lost," but rather the wise Christian and the foolish Christian; the former asks of God in faith, while the latter doubts (Jas 1:5-7). James frequently sets before his readers the two paths in stark contrast.

James begins the letter with the theme of "wisdom" (Jas 1:5). In Proverbs, a wise person is one who controls his speech (a major theme in Proverbs 10—29; see Prov 10:19; 13:3); so also James emphasizes controlling the tongue (Jas 1:19, 26; 3:1-12; 4:1-3; 5:12). Who is wise among you? he asks (Jas 3:13). He frequently admonishes his readers to select the right choice of the two paths before them (Jas 3:13-18; 4:4, 6, 13-15; 5:8-9, 12). When James speaks of "one who wanders from the truth" (Jas 5:19), he is not addressing the issue of apostasy, but the common theme in Wisdom literature of the fool who wanders from the path and stumbles in darkness (Prov 19:27; 4:19; Ps 119:10, 21, 113-120). Saving a soul from sin and death is a common Wisdom theme (Job 8:13; Ps 1:6; 2:12; Prov 2:18; 12:28; 14:12; *Jub* 23; 2 Esd 7:48; Syr Bar 85:13).[26]

By exhorting them to be "wise," James wants his readers to avoid the traps that put Israel in exile. He then illustrates this by a midrash on two Old Testament prophetic injunctions:

1. When admonishing his readers, James calls them "adulterers" (4:4). He actually uses the feminine form, "adulteresses." James is calling to mind for his readers the common portrayal of Israel's covenant relationship with Yahweh as a marriage, where Israel was the unfaithful wife (e.g., Is 57; Ezek 16; 23:37; also Jer 3:8; Hos 3:1).[27] Gone is the appellation "brothers." Now James calls them spiritual adulteresses, seeking to be "friends with the

---

[25]The origin of the "Two Paths" motif is probably Deuteronomy 30:15-20 (see C. Marvin Pate, *The Reverse of the Curse,* Wissenschaftliche Untersuchungen zum Neuen Testament 2/114 [Tübingen, Germany: J.C.B. Mohr/Paul Siebeck, 2000], 385-86). James, though, probably received it from its rich usage in the Wisdom literature.

[26]Davids, *James,* 199-201.

[27]J. Schmitt argues that James is thinking of the adulterous woman "Foolishness" in Proverbs ("You Adulteresses: The Image of James 4:4," *Novum* Testamentum 28 [1986]: 327-37). In such a scenario, James would be continuing a contrast of the "two paths."

world," thus forsaking Yahweh and provoking him to "holy jealousy."[28] James is encouraging his people to avoid the things that would cause them to stay in exile.

2. James preaches Isaiah 58 to his readers (as a midrash). Through his prophet Isaiah, Yahweh denounces a false piety that speaks of devotion to God yet is empty and ignores social justice. The prophet announces Israel's rebellion (Is 58:1; Jas 4:4); and warns his people: to stop being double-minded (Is 58:2-3; Jas 4:8), to draw near to God (Is 58:2; Jas 4:8) and be humble (Is 58:3; Jas 4:10), not to oppress workers (Is 58:3; Jas 5:4), not to use the Lord's time for personal business (Is 58:3; Jas 4:13-15), not to quarrel and fight (Is 58:4; Jas 4:1), but to care for the poor—feed the hungry, house the homeless, clothe the naked (Is 58:7; Jas 5:1-6; 2:1-16)—and to look after kin (Is 58:7; Jas 5:13-19). If they do not point fingers and speak evil (Is 58:9; Jas 4:11), then the Lord will answer (Is 58:9; Jas 5:15) and "your healing shall spring up quickly" (Is 58:8; Jas 5:15-16). If his people would do these things, then restoration would come (Is 58:9-14; Jas 5:16-20).[29]

In his message on Isaiah 58, James is admonishing his readers to live wisely while in the exile and to prepare for restoration. Although 1 Peter will emphasize the "stranger in a foreign land" motif, James only touches on it by speaking of the Dispersion. As with other General Epistles, James is not addressing *which* sin caused them to be in exile. The question: How did we come to be in exile? is not considered by James (or the other General Epistles). James likewise does not speak of the nature of the restoration. The end is near (Jas 5:8), but in what way we will be restored is not discussed. Rather, James stresses avoiding the path of foolishness described in Wisdom literature (the undisciplined tongue, disobedience) and a false piety described in Isaiah 58. We are encouraged to live wisely because the time of restoration is near (Jas 5:8).

The structure and readers of 1 Peter. While James may be difficult to outline, 1 Peter is fairly straightforward. Most commentators agree that the letter naturally breaks after 1 Peter 2:10 and again at 1 Peter 4:11.[30] Commentators debate the pur-

---

[28]See Moo, *James*, 46, and his convincing exegesis of James 4:4-5 (186-91).

[29]Other intertextual themes between Isaiah 58 and James can be seen: light, mismatch of words and deeds, injustice, judgment, etc. We can also ask if Isaiah was picking his themes from Leviticus 19 since there is much in common, including themes emphasized by James:

Lev 19:12	Jas 5:12
Lev 19:13	Jas 5:4
Lev 19:15	Jas 2:1, 9; 4:11-12
Lev 19:16	Jas 4:11
Lev 19:18	Jas 2:8; 5:9

Yet any similarities between Leviticus 19 and James are likely via Isaiah 58.

[30]See, for example, Leonhard Goppelt, *A Commentary on 1 Peter*, ed. F. Hahn, trans. and aug. J. Alsup (Grand Rapids, Mich.: Eerdmans, 1993 [1978]), 20-21; and Ralph Martin, "The Theology of Jude, 1 Peter, and 2 Peter," in Andrew Chester and Ralph Martin, *The Theology of the Letters of James, Peter, and Jude*, New Testament Theology Series (Cambridge: Cambridge University Press, 1994), 102-3.

pose of these three sections. We suggest a slightly different model. That 1 Peter is writing a Diaspora letter is obvious because (1) he addresses his letter to "the exiles in the Dispersion"; (2) he makes at least two more explicit references to being in exile (1 Pet 1:17; 2:11); and (3) he uses the cryptogram "Babylon."

Yet 1 Peter is more than a typical Diaspora letter. 1 Peter is using the *original* Diaspora letter, the one by Jeremiah to those in exile in Babylon (Jeremiah 29), as his example. Not only are there numerous allusions to Jeremiah's letter, but Peter draws the same general points (see table 11.1).

Table 11.1 Jeremiah's and Peter's Letters to the Diaspora

Theme	*Jeremiah*	*1 Peter*
1. God has a word for his people in exile in Babylon.	29:1-3	1:1-2
2. In order to mold his people, God has allowed a foreign empire to conquer them.	29:4	1:3—2:10 (see 1:6-7)
3. God tells his people to submit to the empire and live in peace while in exile.	29:5-7	2:11—4:11 (see 2:13-17 and the domestic code)

4. God has a plan that includes:
  a. Suffering
  b. Warnings and judgment
  c. Promise of restoration
	29:10-14
	(29:15-23)
	(29:24-32)
	(30:1—31:20)
		4:12
		(4:12-16)
		(4:17—5:9)
		(5:10)

5. Although they live in Babylon, God reminds them that they are aliens in that land.	31:21-26	5:12-14

Commentators have long noticed 1 Peter's similarity to sermonic material, even arguing that the letter is a modified baptismal sermon. They are correct that 1 Peter is sermonic: it is a midrash on Jeremiah 29.

In the first section of his Diaspora letter, Jeremiah reminds his hearers that God has sent them into the exile (Jer 29:4). In the letter, Jeremiah does not stress how this is part of the plan of God—though he stresses this in multiple places elsewhere (e.g., the famous potter's wheel sermon). 1 Peter does, however, elaborate on the plans God has for his people in Christ (1 Pet 1:10-20). The vague descriptions in Jeremiah (Jer 29:11) of

---

Cf. J. Ramsey Michaels, who sees "responsibilities" as a theme for each section; *1 Peter,* Word Biblical Commentary Series 49 (Waco, Tex.: Word, 1988), xxxvii.

future blessings and a new covenant are described by 1 Peter as realized in Christ (1 Pet 1:10-12). Jeremiah encouraged the people to seek God with all their hearts (Jer 29:13), while 1 Peter reminds them that even angels longed to see what they were seeing (1 Pet 1:12), that is, the working out of God's plan for his people in exile (1 Pet 1:17-20).

In the second section of his Diaspora letter, Jeremiah encourages those in exile to submit to the empire and live at peace with those around them (Jer 29:5-7), becoming members of society (building houses, planting gardens, etc.). First Peter elaborates this considerably since it is a theme he wishes to emphasize. 1 Peter's readers are to submit to the (Roman) empire (1 Pet 2:12-17). They are to live at peace with those around them. To encourage this, 1 Peter stresses a common Greco-Roman domestic code. Greeks and Romans believed the family unit was the building block of society. Therefore, to insure stability, they outlined how members of the family unit were to act. Often done in triplet manner (slaves, children, wives), these codes described how members of the family should relate to the male (as master, father, husband). First Peter only discusses slaves and wives and (like Paul) outlines also the responsibility of the male (1 Pet 2:18—3:7). He then reminds them to obey the laws of society. They are not to repay evil for evil (1 Pet 3:9) because God is against those who do evil (1 Pet 3:12). Rather, they are to suffer only for "doing what is right" (1 Pet 3:14). First Peter's purpose was to help his readers live at peace with those around them with a clear conscience (1 Pet 3:16).

In the third section of Jeremiah's letter, he describes how the trouble they are experiencing is the plan of God (Jer 29:10-14). First Peter echoes this assurance (1 Pet 4:12-19). God's plan and will are made known through his chosen leaders. Jeremiah spends quite some time denouncing the false leaders who have arisen among God's people (Jer 29:15-32). 1 Peter speaks of no false prophets in his churches; instead he warns the leaders (elders) there to lead wisely, not for sordid gain or by compulsion (1 Pet 5:1-9).

The book of Jeremiah then continues with material that speaks at great length about the restoration as the culmination of the plan God has for them (Jer 30—31). First Peter makes only a passing reference to the restoration (1 Pet 5:10). Like James, 1 Peter is not interested in describing the nature of the restoration, whether it will be a Platonic dualism (a place that is currently "up there somewhere") or a future physical kingdom (a place that will "one day come"). Like James, 1 Peter's focus is on how they all should live *now* while they are in the exile ("in Babylon"), awaiting their restoration.

Although we question if any of the General Epistles are truly "universal," clearly 1 Peter is the least generic. The original recipients of the letter are clearly defined geographically.[31] Peter was writing to churches in the region of northern Anatolia (mod-

---

[31]Furthermore, the order of the listing is not random but indicates the route the letter carrier was to take when circulating the letter; see the convincing arguments of Colin J. Hemer, "The Address of 1 Peter," *Expository Times* 89 (1978): 239-43.

ern-day Turkey). Jews were already an established part of the Persian Empire. In the centuries that followed, Jews migrated (sometimes were forced) into Anatolia.[32] Jews were never models of integration into Greco-Roman culture, and it is even less likely they integrated well into the indigenous cultures of northern Anatolia.[33] We are not surprised then to find Jews (and hence Jewish Christians) as the object of discrimination and even persecution in northern Anatolia by the time of 1 Peter.

The Message of 1 Peter: Living as Aliens in Babylon. Ralph Martin notes that the readers of 1 Peter faced three issues:[34]

1. They were "at odds" with society and even faced unofficial persecution from local leaders in the community (1 Pet 1:6; 3:13-14; 4:4, 12-16; 5:9-10).

2. They were alienated from any established part of society because they had converted to Christianity (1 Pet 2:10; 4:4). Thus they were still not "Galatian" or any of the other indigenous ethnic groups, but they were also no longer "Jewish."

3. They wrestled with some age-old questions, like "Why do God's people suffer?" and "Why is God allowing these trials to come?" (1 Pet 1:6; 2:19; 4:12).

According to Martin, 1 Peter answers each of these issues:

a. The readers should have exemplary conduct that commends them to the community (1 Pet 2:12, 16-17; 3:16; 4:12-16). While they were still "outsiders," they should be respected, even admired for their behavior.

b. They now belong to the "people of God," stretching back to Abraham and Sarah (1 Pet 3:5-6).

c. God has a plan that will be fully known at the end of history (1 Pet 1:5-9; 4:7; 5:10).

These issues and answers in 1 Peter arise from the story of Israel. If we restate them in terms of Israel's story, the issues the readers faced were two-fold: "Why are we in exile?" (issues 1 and 2) and "Why has the restoration not come?" (issue 3). These were the same questions Jews elsewhere were asking. First Peter's answers also come from the story of Israel:

---

[32]We are told that Antiochus III relocated 2,000 Jeish families into Lydia and Phrygia; see F. F. Bruce, *New Testament History* (Garden City, N.Y.: Doubleday, 1969), 274.

[33]The ethnic history of northern Anatolia is complex. Celts who had been gradually migrating from northern Europe through France, Romania and Macedonia crossed into northern Anatolia in 280-70 B.C. The Greco-Roman world came to call them Galatians; see the excellent summary by J. Daniel Hays, *From Every People and Nation: A Biblical Theology of Race*, New Studies in Biblical Theology Series (Downers Grove, Ill.: InterVarsity Press, 2003), 155-56.

[34]These are modified from his brief but excellent discussion, "The Theology of Jude, 1 Peter, and 2 Peter," 89-90.

a. Live wisely while in exile (1 Pet 2:11-17).

b. Remember you are the true Israel (1 Pet 2:9-10). You are suffering in exile, as are the other children of Abraham (1 Pet 5:9). Once again we note that 1 Peter, like James, did not address *why* we are in exile or the sin that causes exile. Rather, they both consistently write from the viewpoint of how we should live in exile while awaiting our restoration.

c. The end of the exile is coming and God will restore you (1 Pet 4:7, 12-13; 5:10).

The question is rightly asked: Was 1 Peter thinking of the story of Israel? The answer is clearly yes. There are obvious places where 1 Peter names the readers "a chosen race, a royal priesthood, a holy nation, God's own people" (1 Pet 2:9), terms reserved for Israel, complete with references to the temple (1 Pet 2:4-5), to Isaiah's Servant Songs (1 Pet 2:22-25), and so forth. He traces his readers' history through Old Testament figures (1 Pet 3:6, 20), and finally, he explicitly describes them as "in exile" (1 Pet 1:17; 2:11).

The story of Israel, though, is not found merely in the explicit references. The entire letter is steeped in the story. As Ralph Martin notes, "no New Testament book (with the possible exception of Romans and Hebrews) is so permeated with Old Testament hints and ideas as well as actual citations as 1 Peter."[35] Furthermore, the long-debated cryptic use of "she who is in Babylon greets you" (1 Pet 5:13)[36] calls toward the story of Israel on an emotional as well as a historical level. While other options are possible, Peter is most likely referring to Rome. Yet there is a double entendre, just as being in Babylon came to mean more than living in the physical environs of the city. Peter is probably reaching beyond one congregation in the city and is painting vivid images of the church in the Roman Empire in his appeal to the churches of remote Anatolia as "chosen together" with other churches in the empire.

For 1 Peter, the church was still in exile, living in Babylon,[37] awaiting God's deliverance. This explains the apparent mixed message 1 Peter seems to give: "fit in," but also "don't conform."[38] How can, and why should, one be told to do both? First Peter

---

[35]Martin, "Theology of Jude, 1 Peter, and 2 Peter," 88. It is noteworthy that the other two examples, Romans and Hebrews, also make extensive use of the story of Israel.

[36]NRSV: "Your sister church in Babylon."

[37]For Jeremiah, "in Babylon" was synonymous with "in exile" (Jer 29:20).

[38]D. L. Balch builds on 1 Peter's use of a Greco-Roman domestic code (1 Pet 2:13—3:18) to argue that the letter was an apology to demonstrate that Christians were good citizens of Rome. The letter, he says, encourages his readers to "fit in" with society (Balch, *Let Wives Be Submissive: The Domestic Code of 1 Peter*, Society of Biblical Literature Monograph Series 26 [Chico, Calif.: Scholars Press, 1981]). Yet Balch has been critiqued for downplaying 1 Peter's strong injunctions not to conform to society. Martin, "Theology of Jude, 1 Peter, and 2 Peter," correctly notes that 1 Peter's context for "family" is not Greco-Roman but his understanding of the church as "the new people of God who are

saw Christians as still living in exile, and hence they needed to be wise and work to live peacefully with their neighbors. Yet the exile was *not* their home. They were all aliens in Babylon. They should not conform to Babylon's ways. And the time was drawing near when they would be restored (1 Pet 4:7, 17; 5:10).

The Perils of Living in the Last Days: The Story of Israel in Jude and 2 Peter

The structure and readers of Jude. Jude has long been noted as a polemical document.[39] It is also clearly a letter.[40] Jude begins with a richly worded letter address (Jude 1-2) and ends with an even richer doxology. Jude omits any Christian word of thanksgiving ("I give thanks that you are . . . ") that often follows the letter address. Rather, he moves directly into the body of the letter. Is he implying that he cannot be thankful "for the salvation we share" (Jude 3) because the "faith that was once for all entrusted to the saints" (Jude 3) has been threatened by "intruders" (Jude 4)? The beauty of Jude's presentation is enhanced by his clever use of triads, which give us the key to his outline.[41] The letter breaks into three sections, each introduced by the appellation, "Beloved" (Jude 3, 17, 20).

Assuming Jude is the author, the readers are easily identified as Palestinian Jewish Christians. The theology of Jude, though, is not highlighted by describing his readers, but rather by identifying the false teachers and the nature of their teaching. These opponents—itinerant, charismatic preachers—are recent intruders (Jude 4), who claim

- to be super-spiritual,
- to have direct access to God, implying they are under no one's authority and need no mediator including angelic ones (Jude 8),
- to have no need to fear an eschatological judgment, allowing "fleshly" behavior since the actions of the body were irrelevant (Jude 4, 10, 16, 18), and
- to be ecstatic prophets (Jude 16) and thus the church was expected to support them (Jude 12).

The message of Jude: Beware of false teachers in the last days. Throughout his appeal, Jude assumes his readers are familiar with the story of Israel. Moreover, Jude

---

called to be both a holy nation in an alien world and a missionary force like the servant figure in Deutero-Isaiah" (127).

[39] A *polemical* document is one that is written in a context in which conflict is evident and the document defends or accuses. Martin, "Theology of Jude, 1 Peter, and 2 Peter," p. 66, views Jude as polemical. He also notes that there is a wide range of opinion as to the structure of this polemic, ranging from "simply an outpouring of venom in a disorderly fashion" to a carefully crafted example of a classic form of Greco-Roman rhetoric (82).

[40] So also, Richard Bauckham, *Jude, 2 Peter,* Word Biblical Commentary 50 (Waco, Tex.: Word, 1983), 3.

[41] Hillyer, *1 and 2 Peter, Jude,* 19, and Richard Bauckham, *Jude, 2 Peter,* New International Biblical Commentary Series (Peabody, Mass.: Hendrickson, 1992), 5-6, note some of these triads. I believe the entire letter can be outlined in detail using triads.

assumes it is *their* story. His brief letter is replete with Old Testament references: the straying angels of Genesis 6,[42] Sodom and Gomorrah, Moses, Cain, Balaam, and Korah. In each case, Jude assumes his readers easily recognize these stories, know the entire story, and accept these stories from Israel's history as authoritative. His readers are the true Israel, and they are living in the last days. Jesus' apostles predicted that scoffers would arise in the last days, and Jude pronounces the false teachers to be a fulfillment of this word (Jude 17-18).[43] As such, they will be judged in the last days, as seen in his Old Testament examples[44] as well as in the metaphors from nature.[45]

It is tantalizing to see echoes of Jeremiah's letter to the exiles (Jer 29) in Jude. Jeremiah warns against the false prophets as dreamers (Jer 29:8), as burned in a fire (Jer 29:22), and as adulterers (Jer 29:23). Jude makes similar statements about the false teachers, calling them "dreamers" (Jude 8), licentious (Jude 7, 8, 18), and needing to be saved from the "fire" (Jude 23). Nevertheless, these themes are too common to maintain that Jude had Jeremiah 29 in mind. Furthermore, Jude does not use the story of Israel as the framework for his presentation. He uses stories from Israel but not the story of Israel. Jude had a clear target, the false teachers threatening his church, and he builds a carefully constructed argument against them. This focus is too narrow, though, for us to determine Jude's overarching theological framework.

The structure and readers of 2 Peter. Second Peter is a mixture of two genres. It is a true letter, but it also draws on a style of Jewish literature called a "Testament." These

---

[42]Jude shares the intertestamental interpretation of Genesis 6. Jude uses *1 Enoch* 1:9 (Jude 14-15) to argue that the ungodly behavior of the false teachers (Jude 12-13) guarantees they will share the judgment God reserves for such people. (Note Jude's pronounced repetition of "ungodly," a theme common to *1 Enoch* as well and likely the catchword that caused Jude to connect the two situations). E. Earle Ellis argues that Jude 14-15 is a midrash pesher. Ellis demonstrates that the entire letter of Jude is a midrash on judgment (*Prophecy and Hermeneutic*, 223-26); so also Bauckham, *Jude, 2 Peter*, 3-5.

Jude cites *1 Enoch* because his opponents hold it in high regard, rather than because Jude considers it canonical and/or authoritative, argues J. Daryl Charles, *Literary Strategy in the Epistle of Jude* (Scranton, Penn.: University of Scranton Press, 1993); see also Hillyer, *1 and 2 Peter, Jude*, 18. Jude is fighting the false teachers who want "authority" to be located in immediate experience (charismatic utterances) rather than in traditional sources (apostles and transmitted teaching). Jude counters their claim to immediate inspiration by reminding his readers of Old Testament authoritative texts that pronounce judgment on such behavior, citing the false teachers' preferred text (*1 Enoch*), which also pronounces the same judgment on "ungodliness."

[43]Jude's eschatology is not only evident in explicit statements like Jude 17-18, but his way of interpreting scripture (midrash pesher) indicates his view that they are in the "last days"; so Ellis, *Prophecy and Hermeneutic*, 226, and Bauckham, *Jude, 2 Peter*, 5.

[44]Jude actually considers them to be "types" and not just examples; see Bauckham, *Jude, 2 Peter*, 63.

[45]*First Enoch* 80:2-3 lists three of Jude's examples. The fourth ("wild waves") may have come from Isaiah 57:20. Bauckham draws an interesting analogy: "In this lawlessness of nature, such as apocalyptic writers expected to characterize the last days, Jude sees pictures of the lawlessness of the false teachers of the last days" (*Jude, 2 Peter*, 92).

writings were a sort of farewell speech from an Old Testament hero. The Jewish exam-ples were all pseudonymous.[46] Testaments usually had two types of contents: exhorta-tions to maintain the ethical heritage they had received, and predictions of the last days, often with paraenetic admonitions.[47] Second Peter presents us with the Testa-ment of Peter as a letter to his churches.

The church of 2 Peter, like Jude's, faced false teachers. These become the heart of his letter. His arguments are strikingly parallel to Jude's. The relationship between 2 Peter and Jude has long been noted and hotly debated. Obviously the two letters are related. Not only are there numerous parallels, but they are in the same order. Further-more, 2 Peter mentions most of the Old Testament events and characters mentioned by Jude.[48] It seems more reasonable to argue that 2 Peter modified Jude rather than the other way around.[49] 2 Peter's events are in chronological sequence.[50] He also reduces the number of examples but explains each more thoroughly. Apparently, 2 Peter was concerned that his readers were not as familiar with the Old Testament stories.

Second Peter 3:1 identifies the readers as the same as 1 Peter.[51] In 2 Peter, his focus has shifted to a group of false teachers in at least one of those churches. Since 2 Peter says more about his opponents than Jude, we can draw a clearer picture of them. Second Peter's op-ponents were similar to Jude's—at least in the area of licentiousness, which accounts for his use of Jude.[52] Clearly, 2 Peter felt Jude's message was easily adapted for his needs.

---

[46]That is, written under a false *(pseudo)* name. For example, the *Testament of Abraham* speaks from the point of view of the dying words of Abraham but was not written by Abraham.

[47]See Bauckham, *Jude, 2 Peter,* 131-35.

[48]We see that 2 Peter eliminated Old Testament events or characters mentioned by Jude that were not in the order of the Old Testament biblical narrative. In two places, 2 Peter adds characters not mentioned by Jude. In each case (Noah and Lot), the character was next in sequence in the biblical narrative.

[49]Whether 2 Peter borrowed from Jude or vice versa is debated. Perhaps both drew from a third (and missing) document and that is why they vary. The similarity does not extend to vocabulary. Jude's ver-sion of the parallel material has 256 words, while 2 Peter's has 297. What is more striking is that only 78 words are the same; see Hillyer, *1 and 2 Peter, Jude,* 18. 2 Peter obviously felt free to choose his own language. What he borrowed from Jude was the framework. 2 Peter elaborated and modified as he felt led. While positing a third document removes any concerns about an author "modifying" another ca-nonical letter, we have no evidence of such a document, and until we do, we should work with the two documents we have: Jude and 2 Peter. *Pace* Hillyer, who argues that the differences between 2 Peter and Jude are "palpable" and indicate independence, I believe the differences are because 2 Peter was writing to an audience less familiar with the Old Testament stories. But see Hillyer, *1 and 2 Peter, Jude,* 13-14.

[50]Hillyer, *1 and 2 Peter, Jude,* 14, also notes that 2 Peter's events are in "chronological order" while Jude is not. Hillyer's conclusions, however, are different.

[51]2 Peter could be referring to a different letter. 2 Peter 1:16 might imply he knew the readers person-ally, while 1 Peter has no such indications. It seems more likely, though, that the addressees of 2 Peter are at least one of the congregations addressed by 1 Peter.

[52]So Bauckham, *Jude, 2 Peter,* 156. Second Peter omits Jude's references to his false teachers having the Spirit and receiving prophetic revelations. Yet 2 Peter's omission does not necessarily mean these were not characteristics of the false teachers. The evidence is really too scant to paint clear pictures of either group of opponents.

The message of 2 Peter: Building on Jude's message. Any unique theological contribution of 2 Peter will be found in the opening (chap. 1) and closing (chap. 3), which are not paralleled by Jude, and in his additions to Jude.[53] This material offers us an all-too-brief glimpse of 2 Peter's theology. For example, he adds Noah and Lot to the story (2 Pet 2:5-8). He wants to remind his readers that in both of these Old Testament scenarios, the judgment of God was upon their society. Yet individuals could be saved from this judgment by living godly lives: "The Lord knows how to rescue the godly from trial, and to keep the unrighteous under punishment until the day of judgment" (2 Pet 2:9). Second Peter exhorts his readers to godly lives as a means of escape from the coming judgment (3:11-13).[54]

Second Peter uses stories from Israel, but does he use the story of Israel as a framework for his theology? Although his unique contribution (and hence his discernible theology) is very brief, the answer is a guarded yes. We see a tendency in the General Epistles to view Wisdom as the key to living in the exile while awaiting restoration, as in 1 Peter and James. Obviously, 2 Peter saw the false teachers as on the wrong path (2 Pet 2), but there are also small indications that he was visualizing the "Two Paths" of Wisdom literature.[55] Second Peter describes the false teachers using "Two Paths" language. In the material 2 Peter adds to Jude's argument, we find three references to picking the right path (*hodos*): "the way (*hodos*) of truth" (2 Pet 2:2), "the straight way (*hodos*)" (2 Pet 2:15), and "the way (*hodos*) of righteousness" (2 Pet 2:21). Second Peter warns his readers "many will follow their [the false teachers'] licentious ways" (2 Pet 2:2). These false teachers "have left the straight road (*hodos*) and have gone astray, following the way (*hodos*) of Balaam" (2 Pet 2:15). Indeed, "it would have been better for them never to have known the way (*hodos*) of righteousness than, after knowing it, to turn back" (2 Pet 2:21). It is not coincidental that 2 Peter immediately quotes for support Proverbs 26:11, a passage making a protracted description of the one who chooses the foolish way. Furthermore, 2 Peter 1:3-4 and 2 Peter 3:17-18 form an inclusio,[56] whereby he encourages his readers to pick the right path.

---

[53]Second Peter details what the "scoffers" are saying (2 Pet 3:4), leading him into a discussion of the delay of the parousia, including another passing allusion to Noah (2 Pet 3:6-7)—Peter seems to have a fondness for passing references to Noah (see also 1 Pet 3:20-21). Perhaps his readers were quite familiar with Noah. Jewish evangelists may have used the Noachian laws as a theology for the inclusion of Gentiles apart from the law. Jude's concluding exhortations for his readers to lead godly lives is expanded somewhat by 2 Peter (2 Pet 3:11-18a). Jude's beautiful doxology is abbreviated by 2 Peter (2 Pet 3:18).

[54]Bauckham adds, "Since the Flood and the judgment of Sodom and Gomorrah are prototypes of eschatological judgment, the situations of Noah and Lot are typical of the situation of Christians in the final evil days before the Parousia" (*Jude, 2 Peter,* 253).

[55]C. Marvin Pate and Douglas Kennard (*Deliverance Now and Not Yet: The New Testament and the Great Tribulation* [New York: Peter Lange, 2003]) point in this direction, although they see these as indicative of the Messianic Woes.

[56]An *inclusio* is a literary device where a key idea is mentioned at the beginning and then repeated at the end to bring the reader's thought back to the beginning. It is a well-known method for helping an audience to grasp the argument as a whole. The inclusio brackets the argument.

A Better Restoration: The Story of Israel in Hebrews

If Jude and 2 Peter seem to provide little theology, Hebrews seems awash in it. The modern reader is often overwhelmed with Old Testament quotations and allusions, arguments that ebb and flow like the tide, with digressions that seem to lead nowhere yet later resurface in the letter as a prominent theme. The modern Western reader is swept along by a flood of theological ideas, grasping at objects as they swirl past in the torrent of concepts we would not have thought to use, applied in ways we do not understand.

It is also not necessary to argue that Hebrews uses the story of Israel as a framework. Long before it was thought that the story of Israel might underlie all of Scripture, Hebrews was recognized as describing Jesus in terms of "better than" some aspect of Israel's story. Hebrews uses the sin–exile–restoration motif of the story of Israel but focuses upon "restoration": the community of God entering her promised "rest." In the restoration, the church, as the True Israel, receives the eschatological blessings (obedience, the new covenant, and true worship).[57] Christ provides these blessings, Hebrews argues, in better ways than does Judaism.

The structure and readers of Hebrews. We can see these three eschatological blessings—obedience, new covenant, and true worship—appearing in Hebrews in a chiastic pattern:

A. Jesus as Superior (1:1—2:4)

      B. Obedience (Adam and Israel) (2:5—4:13)

           C. True Worship (Priesthood) (4:14—7:28)

              D. New Covenant (8)

           C'. True Worship (Tabernacle and Sacrifice) (9—10)

      B'. Obedience (examples culminating in Jesus) (11:1—12:2)[58]

A'. Jesus as Superior (12:3—13:25)

This is not to say we have outlined Hebrews. This letter is far too complex rhetorically to be reduced to a simple, chiastic outline.[59] But in the midst of the complex argument being woven by the author, he discusses the three eschatological blessings in what for a first-century writer was an "orderly fashion"—a chiasm.

---

[57]Following Tom Wright's paradigm for Second Temple Judaism; see N. T. Wright, *The New Testament and the People of God* (Minneapolis: Fortress, 1992), 244-79. Marvin Pate demonstrates well that various groups in Israel were asserting themselves as the True Israel and hence recipients of the eschatological blessings. Christianity became a competing voice in this milieu; see C. Marvin Pate, *Communities of the Last Days: The Dead Sea Scrolls, the New Testament and the Story of Israel* (Downers Grove, Ill.: InterVarsity Press, 2000), 197-213.

[58]Note the inclusio of Jesus as "pioneer" in Hebrews 2:10 and Hebrews 12:2.

[59]For an excellent discussion of the rhetorical nature of Hebrews, see George Guthrie, *Hebrews,* NIV Application Commentary Series (Grand Rapids, Mich.: Zondervan, 1998), esp. 27-35.

The lofty rhetoric and complex argumentation can mislead us into forgetting that Hebrews is a letter, written as a practical response to an urgent need. The author is dis-
traught that his readers are on the verge of making a tragic mistake that would lead to
denying the Christian faith. Some members are discouraged about some seemingly un-
realized promises of the Christian faith and, in light of increased hostility from their society, are tempted to return to Judaism.[60] The author of Hebrews is bringing the weapons
in his impressive rhetorical arsenal to bear on the problem in order to persuade them.

From the letter we can learn several things about the author's readers. They were
steeped in the Old Testament. Hebrews has 35 quotations from the Old Testament, 34
allusions to it, 19 summaries of an Old Testament story and 13 mentions of an Old
Testament name or subject.[61] He focuses on the threat of his readers leaving the faith
and returning to Judaism. We also notice that Hebrews repeats theological ideas that
were more popular in Hellenistic Judaism than in Palestine. From these clues, it is
commonly agreed that Hebrews was written to a church (or perhaps a cluster of
churches) that were primarily Jewish, probably located in Rome (Heb 13:24).

The message of Hebrews: Enter the promised rest. Unlike the other General Epistles, Hebrews speaks from the context of Hellenistic Judaism with its mild Platonic fla-
vor. Hebrews 3—4 describes the Christian "rest" (restoration), not in terms of entering
Canaan, but in terms of "ceasing from work" (Heb 4:10).[62] Hebrews emphasizes "today" as the opportune time (Heb 4:7) to reach the heavenly homeland (Heb 11:16).[63]
He contrasts the earthly tent with the heavenly reality (Heb 8:5), and the law as "a
shadow of the good things to come" (Heb 10:1). Yet some in the community have *now*
fallen short of finding "rest." Nevertheless, because of the work of Christ, just men are
made perfect (Heb 12:23).

In spite of his emphasis on a "spiritual" understanding of restoration, Hebrews does
not forsake entirely the future orientation of the kingdom shared by the rest of the New
Testament.[64] We do await "the city to come" (Heb 13:14) when God will shake heaven
and earth, remove what is shaken and leave us an unshaken kingdom (Heb 12:27-28).
In this eschatological dimension at the end of his letter, Hebrews (like the other Gen-

---

[60]I am following Guthrie's reconstruction here; see ibid., 19-22.

[61]See ibid., 19.

[62]This is a much-debated topic, with some scholars seeing "rest" as eschatological only (e.g., Otto
Hofius), while others see it as a present reality not limited to time and space (Gerd Theissen); see the
helpful brief discussion in Guthrie, *Hebrews*, 151-53.

[63]In Hebrews 3–4, the author draws heavily upon Psalm 95, a call to obedience and worship. The
psalmist appeals to the wilderness wanderings. Hebrews exhorts his readers not to be disobedient
like their ancestors in the wilderness, but rather to enter the Promised Land. "Rest" here refers to an
earlier part of the story of Israel. Pate connects it to Moses' warnings in Deuteronomy 32:5 and hence
to the Deuteronomic blessings and thus to "restoration" (*Communities of the Last Days*, 206-7).

[64]This tension between the present reality and future hope of "rest" is well articulated by Harold Attridge, *The Epistle to the Hebrews*, Hermeneia (Philadelphia: Fortress, 1989), pp. 127-28.

eral Epistles) does not discuss how such a coming city would fit in with his general spiritualizing of the promised blessings earlier in the letter.

Hebrews does not present a full-blown Platonism.[65] He differs in at least two regards. First, while Hebrews allegorizes, he does not allegorize like the Platonist Philo, who places no significance on the historical event. Hebrews' use is more typological than purely allegorical.[66] The priesthood (Heb 7), covenant (Heb 8), temple (Heb 9), law (Heb 10) and sacrifice (Heb 10) are not just inferior "copies" as in a Platonic model, but "types" foreshadowing a fuller future fulfillment in Christ. They were not just concepts or metaphors pointing toward a fuller spiritual reality, but actual historical events, ways in which God had previously interacted with his people, foreshadowing the present way God was interacting with his people through Christ.[67] These "various ways," although from "long ago" (Heb 1:1), are all part of the story of Israel.

Second, in most Platonic systems the path to virtue is by educating the soul through higher teachings.[68] Hellenistic Judaism modified this approach.[69] The suffering endured by the community of God led them to maturity; that is, suffering matures the soul.[70] The author of Hebrews encourages readers to endure suffering because it leads to perfection (Heb 10:32-39), as it did for Christ (Heb 2:10). Yet unlike Plato, this perfection still has a future orientation, when those who endure will "receive what was promised. For yet, in a very little while, the one who is coming will come" (Heb 10:36-37).

In spite of these hints of an eschatological fulfillment, Hebrews speaks mainly from the perspective that the church has *already* entered the "promised rest" in at least some ways. Thus, he must show how these eschatological blessings (obedience, new covenant, true worship) were currently being realized in the community.

Obedience. In Second Temple Judaism, membership in the community of God, and hence the eschatological rest, relied on observing the law of Moses. In Hebrews, the revelation of God was found formerly in the prophets (Heb 1:1-2) and in the law of Moses as mediated by angels (Heb 1:4), but now it is found in Christ. Some still fail to enter (Heb 4:1, 6) because of "disobedience" (Heb 4:6, 11), which is also described as

[65]See the argument by Barnabas Lindars, *The Epistle to the Hebrews,* Hermeneia (Philadelphia: Fortress, 1989), 23-24.

[66]See, e.g., Randall Gleason, "The Old Testament Background of Rest in Hebrews 3:7–4:11," *Bibliotheca Sacra* 157 (2000): 280-302.

[67]See Ellis, *Prophecy and Hermeneutic,* 165-69. The classic work on typology remains Leonhard Goppelt, *Typos: The Typological Interpretation of the Old Testament in the New,* trans. D. Madvig (1939; reprint, Grand Rapids, Mich.: Eerdmans, 1982).

[68]Pheme Perkins, *Reading the New Testament: An Introduction* (New York: Paulist Press, 1988), 273, sees Hebrews 5:11–6:12 as teaching this Platonic view by urging readers to move beyond "milk" to mature teaching.

[69]Wisdom, 2 and 4 Maccabees; see Pate and Kennard, *Deliverance Now and Not Yet,* 373.

[70]See Charles Talbert, *Learning Through Suffering: The Educational Value of Suffering in the New Testament and Its Milieu,* Zacchaeus Studies, New Testament Series (Collegeville, Minn.: Liturgical Press, 1991).

unbelief (Heb 3:19; 4:2). Entering the promised rest comes from faith in Christ, described as obedience to God's new revelation, his new covenant.

New covenant. Because of Israel's unfaithfulness to the old covenant, she lost the Deuteronomic blessings for faithfulness (Deut 28:1-14) and received the curses (Deut 28:49-68). As warned by the prophets, Israel's faithlessness voided the Deuteronomic covenant. God was now offering his people a new covenant. Although better than the old covenant, it was still part of the continuing story of Israel. This new covenant (Jer 31:31-34) will return them from Babylon—a name synonymous with exile (Jer 29:20)—and provide Israel with "rest" (Jer 31:2) in a manner that surpasses all God's mercies of old. Hebrews considers the Christian community to be inheritors of the old covenant, beginning with Abraham (Heb 7). Yet they were also divinely chosen by God to participate in the new covenant of Jeremiah (Jer 31:31-34), which they were now in (Heb 3:1, 14; 6:4; 9:15).

True worship. During the Babylonian exile, Jews came to believe they had lost the temple (and hence the ability to worship God) because of their disobedience to the law. Hence, when they returned to Torah-observance, they would have another temple (with a priesthood) where they could experience true worship again because God would again inhabit the temple. The Qumran community considered itself the true observers of Torah and the true inheritors of the Aaronic priesthood. Yet the sacrifices offered were spiritualized as the holy lives of the community's members, particularly when they suffered persecution.[71] The community atoned for the sins of Israel. Hebrews builds on both ideas. He shares many concepts with Qumran,[72] but with several significant differences. Like Qumran, he saw his community (the church) as the true inheritor of the priesthood, but of a purer priesthood, that of Melchizedek. Like Qumran, sacrifice was spiritualized beyond animals in the temple to the holy lives of believers. Yet in Hebrews it is the ultimate holy life of Christ that is the final sacrifice, ending the sacrificial system. Hebrews sees atonement now solely in the completed work of Christ on the cross (Heb 10:11-12).[73]

Conclusion: The Story of Israel in the General Epistles
The sin–exile–restoration motif in the story of Israel forms a framework for most of the General Epistles. However, none of the General Epistles use the entire framework to present their theologies. Most of them, though, use one aspect of the story of Israel.

---

[71]Rule of the Community 8:1-10; see Pate, *Communities of the Last Days,* 209-10.
[72]Susanne Lehne shows the Qumran Community viewed themselves in strikingly parallel ways; see Lehne, *The New Covenant in Hebrews,* Journal for the Study of the New Testament Series 44 (Sheffield: Sheffield Academic Press, 1990).
[73]They differed in other ways as well. Hebrews breaks with the Aaronic priesthood (Heb 4:13–7:28). Furthermore, true worship is already occurring when the Christian community worships (Heb 9).

Sin. We must be careful in saying that the writers of the General Epistles saw the church as "Israel still in exile," for this remains true only in a specific sense. The major Old Testament imagery of the exile was God's judgment and the subsequent separation from his presence. Many first-century Jews saw that as the *cause* of the exile. Now, although still in exile, they saw themselves as living according to Torah. They were keeping the covenant, so why were they still suffering in the Diaspora? Many contended that restoration would only come when the Messiah reestablished David's kingdom in Jerusalem, when God reentered Zion.[74]

For the prophets, Israel could not be restored until she repented. The General Epistles do not have a call to repentance. (Hebrews is a warning against falling into sin, not an appeal for them to repent.) Christians saw themselves as having fulfilled God's call to faithful living and thus were eligible to be restored. They were the true Israel ready to be called home from the exile.

Exile. The General Epistles (except Hebrews) write of the exile only in the sense of already being in exile. They do not address how they came to be in exile or why. They address how to live in exile, which is soon to be over. While Jeremiah told the people to settle down in Babylon because they were to be there for awhile, Ezekiel tells them later that the end of the exile is coming. This is the message of the General Epistles (except Hebrews). Christians are not to settle down and make their homes in exile any longer. God has poured out his Spirit on them (Ezek 39:29), *but they have not yet been moved to the home prepared for them* (Ezek 39:26-27). They are now sojourners in a land no longer their home. Because they are not yet in their home, they are still susceptible to suffering. For Peter, James and Jude, the restoration is not yet here.

Restoration. For the General Epistles (except Hebrews), the "restoration" is not presented in the "already accomplished in Christ" view that we might see in the Gospels. It is also not presented in the "already/not fully" view we see in Paul. Instead, they speak from the view of an earlier Palestinian Jewish Christianity. The restoration is temporal (future but imminent) and probably expected in Palestine.

Hebrews, however, speaks from a different perspective. The restoration of Israel in Hebrews is seen more as spatial ("heavenly") and as atemporal ("rest," Jer 29). He argues that the church is already experiencing in Christ at least some of the eschatological blessings of the restoration, although he does not forsake an eschatological consummation which is still imminent (Heb 9:28; 10:13, 25, 36-37; 13:14). In the limited confines of the letter, however, Hebrews does not explain how he sees these events fitting together.

---

[74]It can be argued the New Testament describes the triumphal entry as God's presence reentering the temple. Before the exile, sin drove God from the temple, which was subsequently destroyed. The New Testament presents the same image in Mark 11:12-21 and Acts 21:30.

In summary, the tripartite corpus of the General Epistles uses the story of Israel in some ways as a framework for theology. James and 1 Peter speak of how Christians should live wisely in these final days of the exile because the time of our restoration is near. Jude and 2 Peter warn the church of perils in exile, all the more present because our restoration is near. Hebrews, taking a little different tack, encourages us by reminding us that we can already taste some of the blessings of the restoration, and therefore we should not lose heart.

Supplemental Readings in New Dictionary of Biblical Theology

See the individual articles for each of the General Epistles:

P. H. Davids, "James," 342-46.

G. L. Green, "1 Peter," 346-49.

P. H. Davids, "Jude," 355.

P. H. Davids, "2 Peter," 350-51.

P. Ellingworth, "Hebrews," 337-42.

For additional reading on particular themes in Hebrews, see also

R. C. Ortlund Jr., "Apostasy," 383-86.

D. G. Peterson, "Sanctification according to Hebrews" in "Holiness," 547-48.

D. G. Peterson, "Melchizedek," 658-60.

D. G. Peterson, "Drawing near to God through Jesus as high priest" in "Worship," 861-63.

Study Questions

1. Do you think these books (James, Hebrews, 1-2 Peter, and Jude) should be considered a corpus (a connected subgroup) of the New Testament? Why or why not?

2. N. T. Wright argues that many Jews at the time of Christ still considered themselves to be living in the exile. What does this mean? What evidence can you cite from a General Epistle that suggests the writer saw himself as still living in the exile?

3. Concerning "living in exile," Hebrews seems to present a different viewpoint than the other General Epistles. Describe how Hebrews seems to stand apart from the others in its use of the story of Israel.

4. How do you see these letters fitting together (complementing, contradicting, etc.)? Why?

5. Define the following terms: chiasm, midrash, the exile, the "Two Paths" in Wisdom literature, Diaspora letter, and pseudonymity.

12

REVELATION
The Transforming Vision

I n the final chapter of the Bible, the "grand finale" of the drama of salvation, God pulls back the curtain to allow his people to see his plans for human history, plans that center around Jesus Christ. Revelation draws together in spectacular fashion the central elements of the story of Israel—sin, exile and restoration. The story began in Genesis 1—2 with God's creation of the world. What God made was good, and he gave it his blessing. In Act II of the cosmic drama (Genesis 3—11), God's good world is spoiled when the man and the woman give in to the serpent's temptation and experience exile from the presence of God as a consequence. While there are hints in Genesis 4—11 that God is not finished with his creation, restoration proper begins in Genesis 12, where God establishes his covenant with Abraham and his descendants.

The entire story pivots on the life, death and resurrection of Jesus Christ, but the full implications and consequences of this climactic event are not immediately visible. The book of Revelation presents in colorful language and powerful imagery the final chapter in God's story, where he reverses the curse of sin, restores his creation and lives among his people forever. As we shall see in what follows, Revelation constitutes a transforming vision, empowering those who embrace its heavenly perspective to live faithfully in this fallen world until their Lord returns.

The Context of the Vision
The historical situation of the book is one in which false religion has formed a partnership with pagan political power. As a result, those who claim to follow Christ are facing tremendous pressure to conform to the system at the expense of faithfulness to Christ. As is often the case in war (and how much more so in the ultimate cosmic battle portrayed in Revelation), people must choose sides and live (or die) with the consequences of their choices. War divides people into two groups, and like the prophets of old, Revelation has a strong message for both groups. For those who are remaining faithful to Christ and suffering for it, Revelation brings comfort and hope. For those who are compromising with the pagan powers to avoid persecution, Rev-

elation conveys a formidable warning.

In terms of literary context, Revelation combines three different genres: letter, prophecy and apocalyptic. As a *letter* the whole book of Revelation (and not just Rev 2—3) is a single letter addressed to seven churches in Asia Minor: Ephesus, Smyrna, Pergamum, Thyatira, Sardis, Philadelphia and Laodicea.[1] Because the number seven symbolizes wholeness or completeness in Revelation, a letter to seven churches is in reality a letter to the whole church. When we read Revelation as a letter originally written for seven particular churches, we can have confidence that God is also speaking to all Christians everywhere. As Jesus says to the churches, "Let anyone who has an ear listen to what the Spirit is saying to the churches."[2]

Revelation is also a *prophetic* letter. Both in the letter's opening (Rev 1:3) and its closing (Rev 22:7, 10, 18-19), the contents of the book are described by the term "prophecy." Biblical prophecy includes both *prediction* of the future and *proclamation* of God's truth for the present, with the emphasis falling on the latter. Often in the very places where Revelation is described as a prophecy, the readers are commanded to *obey* the prophecy (Rev 1:3; 22:7, 18-19). We know that the emphasis falls on proclamation rather than prediction because it is difficult to imagine someone being commanded to *obey* a prediction. Revelation is certainly about the future, but it is also about what God wants to see happen in the here and now. John writes at the climax of prophetic revelation with the intent of showing how the story of Israel was being fulfilled for Christians living in "the last days" (i.e., the time between Christ's death/resurrection and his glorious return).[3] John is disclosing the final chapter of the biblical story, a story that highlights a slaughtered lamb as the hero in God's grand plan to conquer his enemies, restore creation and live forever in intimate fellowship with his people.

Finally, Revelation is a prophetic-*apocalyptic* letter. As an apocalypse, Revelation uses vivid images to create a symbolic world for the readers to inhabit during the time they are reading (or hearing) the book. When they enter this symbolic world, their whole way of thinking is cleansed and purified so that their perspective on the world in which they live is changed. They are able to see things from a heavenly perspective as they are transformed by the visions of Revelation. Transported to the final future, they can see the present from the perspective of God's ultimate victory over his ene-

---

[1] Richard Bauckham, *The Theology of the Book of Revelation* (Cambridge: Cambridge University Press, 1993), 2.

[2] For more on the historical and literary context of Revelation along with guidelines for interpreting the book, see J. Scott Duvall and J. Daniel Hays, *Grasping God's Word: A Hands-On Approach to Reading, Interpreting, and Applying the Bible* (Grand Rapids, Mich.: Zondervan, 2001), 271-89.

[3] Hence the meaning behind the title of Richard Bauckham's extremely significant work, *The Climax of Prophecy: Studies in the Book of Revelation* (Edinburgh: T & T Clark, 1993).

mies. In this way Revelation provides Christians with a set of "prophetic counter-images" to purge their imagination of the pagan view of the world and replace it with a view of what things will be like after God's ultimate restoration.[4] When Christians who are facing hostile circumstances hear again and again the message of Revelation, they are reminded that "what they believe is not strange and odd, but truly normal from God's perspective."[5]

By using images in this way, Revelation answers the question, Who is Lord? During times of oppression and persecution, the righteous suffer and the wicked seem to prosper. God's people want to know: Is God still on his throne? Revelation says that in spite of how things appear, Caesar is not Lord, and Satan is not Lord, but Jesus is Lord. And he is coming soon to restore his creation and establish his eternal kingdom. Satan, sin and death will not have the final word. The main message of this grand finale of the biblical story is "God wins!" Those who are being persecuted have their hearts and minds immersed in hope and their eyes opened to see God's future. Those who are selling their souls to the pagan powers are shown God's future to shock them into repentance. One way or the other, Revelation is indeed a transforming vision.

The Transforming Vision

Revelation transforms its hearers by immersing them in God's story in a masterful way.[6] John has skillfully woven together the story using seven main threads or themes (see table 12.1).

These seven themes amplify the traditional story of Israel by highlighting the main characters (Creator, enemies, Restorer, followers) and the central storyline (sin–exile–restoration). The final theme brings to bear on the readers the determinative choices they face ("keeping the words of the prophecy" vs. "practicing falsehood") with the hope that they will endure.

The God of the Story (Sovereign Creator). Revelation's highly theocentric (God-centered) theology is "its greatest contribution to New Testament theology."[7] A closer look reveals a sovereign God who is firmly in control. Thus the Creator God of Genesis 1 brings the story of Israel to its final conclusion. Because he acts to redeem his people, judge his enemies and restore his creation, he alone is worthy of worship.

---

[4]We are indebted here to Richard Bauckham's insights into the role of apocalyptic. See his *Theology of Revelation*, 5-12, 17-22.

[5]G. K. Beale, *The Book of Revelation*, New International Greek Testament Commentary (Grand Rapids, Mich.: Eerdmans, 1999), 175.

[6]Although we don't know everything that John saw and experienced, we do have access to an elaborate and complex "literary work which communicates their message to others" (Bauckham, *Theology of Revelation*, 117).

[7]Bauckham, *Theology of Revelation*, 23.

Table 12.1 Seven Main Themes of Revelation

	Themes	Main Characters	Reader's Decision	Central Storyline
1	God of the Story	Creator		
2	The Enemies of God	Enemies		Sin
3	The Lamb of God	Restorers		
4	The People of God	Followers		
5	The Judgment of God			Exile
6	The Paradise of God			Restoration
7	The Battle of God		Choices	

On his throne. The salutation (Rev 1:4-8) anchors the letter in God's sovereign control of all history through a vivid, threefold description of God: the "Alpha and the Omega," "the one who is and who was and who is to come," and "the Lord God, the Almighty." Alpha and Omega, the first and last letters of the Greek alphabet, portray God as the beginning and the end of all things (cf. Is 41:4; 44:6; 48:12). He is not only the Creator of all things, but also the end (purpose or goal) of all things. He is the Supreme God, victorious over every contender. This title also tells us that God is the final judge of his creation—an encouraging thought for Christians being threatened by worldly powers that seem invincible from a human perspective.

God is also described as "the one who is and who was and who is to come." John alludes here to Exodus 3:14, where God identifies himself to Moses as "I AM WHO I AM" (Rev 1:4, 8; 4:8; 11:17; 16:5). Throughout the story of Israel, God is not just the beginning and the end; he is also the One who is always with us. He is Lord of the past and the future and everything in between. All of time and eternity is in his hands. As God spoke to Moses, he now speaks to his people (one of just two places in Revelation where God officially speaks; cf. also Rev 21:6)—"I am the God who is always there for you." The addition of "and who is to come" reminds us that the God who originally delivered Israel from slavery in Egypt will in the future also deliver his people from all enslaving powers. He will come in great power to judge his enemies and make things right.

The third expression, "Lord God, the Almighty," is used throughout the Old Testament to speak of God's universal supremacy. The title "Almighty" (*pantokratōr*, cf. Rev 1:8; 4:8; 11:17; 15:3; 16:7, 14; 19:6, 15; 21:22) carries special significance for John's original audience. Caesar, the *autokratōr* or emperor, may rule Rome, but the Lord God Almighty, the *pantokratōr,* rules over the entire universe. He is in control.

The powerful description of God in the first part of the letter sets the stage for the most magnificent depiction of God's sovereignty in all of Revelation. In Revelation 4—5 we read of John being summoned to heaven, where he sees a throne with One seated on it. The centrality of the throne signifies God's sovereign rule as the centerpiece of ultimate reality around which everything else revolves. All subsequent visions in the book emerge from these introductory visions of God's sovereignty. The faithful witness and suffering of believers, the rebellion and punishment of unbelievers and the fulfillment of God's promise to redeem his people and live among them are all under God's control. And because only God is supreme over his creation, he alone is worthy of worship.

Worthy of worship. At times John's visionary experience overwhelms him to the point that he falls down and begins to worship the angel bearing the message (Rev 19:10; 22:8-9). As a faithful messenger, however, the angel quickly corrects John and tells him, "Worship God!" In this and other ways, Revelation sends a clear message that God alone is worthy of worship.

God is worshiped as the Sovereign Creator. The heavenly beings that surround the throne worship God because he has created all things: "You are worthy, our Lord and God, to receive glory and honor and power, for you created all things, and by your will they existed and were created" (Rev 4:11). Later in the book another angel proclaims the eternal gospel that calls people to "worship him who made the heaven and earth, the sea and the springs of water" (Rev 14:7; notice also the clear connection to Genesis 1). God is worthy of worship because he reigns supremely as Creator of heaven and earth (Rev 4:8, 11; 19:6).

God is also worshiped for his role in redemption. Due to the destructive invasion of sin, all is not well with God's world. Hostile powers of evil jeopardize his grand plan. But God (not Caesar or the dragon or any beast) will have the final word. The One who sits on the throne grips the scroll of his divine plan firmly in his right hand (Rev 5:1), and the only one worthy to open the scroll (i.e., to carry out God's plan) is the Lamb who was slaughtered. We see, therefore, that the cross was God's means of reversing the curse. John's vision of the great multitude in Revelation 7 pictures the ultimate fulfillment of God's covenant promises to Abraham in Genesis 12 that he would be the ancestor of a multitude of blessed nations:

> Now the LORD said to Abram, "Go from your country and your kindred and your father's house to the land that I will show you. I will make of you a great nation, and I will bless you, and make your name great, so that you will be a blessing. I will bless those who bless you, and the one who curses you I will curse; and in you all the families of the earth shall be blessed." (Gen 12:1-3)
>
> After this I looked, and there was a great multitude that no one could count, from every

nation, from all tribes and peoples and languages, standing before the throne and before
the Lamb, robed in white, with palm branches in their hands. They cried out in a loud
voice, saying, "Salvation belongs to our God who is seated on the throne, and to the
Lamb!" And all the angels stood around the throne and around the elders and the four
living creatures, and they fell on their faces before the throne and worshiped God, singing,
"Amen! Blessing and glory and wisdom and thanksgiving and honor and power and
might be to our God forever and ever! Amen." (Rev 7:9-12)

Every creature in heaven and on earth worships God and the Lamb for creating a people and overcoming evil (Rev 5:11-14; 7:9-12). God's story has a happy ending.

Perhaps most surprising to those of us not immediately threatened by persecution
is that God is worshiped in Revelation chiefly for his holy character, which leads him
to judge evil and vindicate his people. In language reminiscent of Isaiah 6, the heavenly beings surrounding the throne cry out "Holy! Holy! Holy!" in worship of the sovereign Lord (Rev 4:8). In Revelation 15 we read of a group that has conquered the beast
(most certainly through martyrdom) and now stand beside the sea of glass singing
praises to God:

And they sing the song of Moses, the servant of God, and the song of the Lamb: "Great
and amazing are your deeds, Lord God the Almighty! Just and true are your ways, King
of the nations! Lord, who will not fear and glorify your name? For you alone are holy. All
nations will come and worship before you, for your judgments have been revealed."

The expression "song of Moses" recalls Exodus 15 (and perhaps also Deut 31—32)
where the people praise God by the sea for his deliverance and his destruction of their
enemies. In Revelation the people sing an additional song, the Lamb's song that celebrates God's full and final deliverance of his people from sin and evil (Rev 15:3-4).

The language of righteous vindication as the occasion for worship is even stronger
elsewhere in Revelation, where again the people sing praises to God (cf. Rev 16:5-7;
19:1-2). The wrath of God for his enemies stands in contrast to God's compassion for
his people.

An ever-present help. While Revelation portrays God as holy and awesome, it also
reveals him as an ever-present help for his people. We read of God protecting his people from the judgment by sealing them with his name as a sign of his ownership (Rev
7:2-3; 14:1). In contrast to those who are labeled with the sign of the beast, the divine
marking protects God's people from wrath and judgment, though it does not exempt
them from suffering or even martyrdom.

Revelation paints a stunning picture of God as the compassionate father who comforts his children who have endured terrible trials. We are told that "the one seated on
the throne will shelter" his people (Rev 7:15), "wipe every tear from their eyes" (Rev
7:17; 21:4), abolish death, mourning, crying and pain (Rev 21:4), and "give water as

a gift from the spring of the water of life" (Rev 21:6). He has not forgotten his children; rather, he is making all things new for them to enjoy in his presence.

When God speaks in Revelation for the second and final time, he announces the fulfillment of a longstanding, three-part promise that he would live *(skenoō)* among his people (see table 12.2).

Table 12.2. God's Promise to Dwell with His People

Exodus 29:45-46	I will dwell among the Israelites, and I will be their God. And they shall know that I am the LORD their God, who brought them out of the land of Egypt.
Leviticus 26:11-12	I will place my dwelling in your midst, and I shall not abhor you. And I will walk among you, and will be your God, and you shall be my people.
Ezekiel 37:27	My dwelling place shall be with them; and I will be their God, and they shall be my people.
Zechariah 2:10-11	Sing and rejoice, O daughter Zion! For lo, I will come and dwell in your midst, says the LORD. Many nations shall join themselves to the LORD on that day, and shall be my people; and I will dwell in your midst.
Revelation 21:3	And I heard a loud voice from the throne saying, "See, the home of God is among mortals. He will dwell with them as their God; they will be his peoples, and God himself will be with them."
Revelation 21:7	Those who conquer will inherit these things, and I will be their God and they will be my children.

The Jewish hope for restoration was that God would live among his people in a future temple. Revelation transfers this hope to an entire city (a temple city or a New Jerusalem) that is shaped like the most holy place (Rev 21:10, 16). More precisely, John says, "I saw no temple in the city, for its temple is the Lord God the Almighty and the Lamb" (Rev 21:22). As Craig Keener observes, "This will be the most explicit "tabernacling" of God with humanity since the Incarnation."[8] An ever-present help indeed.

God's desire for eternal intimacy with his people comes into full view in Revelation 22:1-5:

---

[8]Craig S. Keener, *Revelation*, NIV Application Commentary (Grand Rapids, Mich.: Eerdmans, 2000), 487. Keener notes in support John 1:14, "which declares that Jesus, the Word, 'made his dwelling' [lit., 'tabernacled'] among us, the only New Testament use of *skenoo* outside Revelation."

Then the angel showed me the river of the water of life, bright as crystal, flowing from the throne of God and of the Lamb through the middle of the street of the city. On either side of the river is the tree of life with its twelve kinds of fruit, producing its fruit each month; and the leaves of the tree are for the healing of the nations. Nothing accursed will be found there any more. But the throne of God and of the Lamb will be in it, and his servants will worship him; they will see his face, and his name will be on their foreheads. And there will be no more night; they need no light of lamp or sun, for the Lord God will be their light, and they will reign forever and ever.

Especially striking is the statement in Revelation 22:4 that "they will see his face." This takes them even beyond the level of freedom granted to Moses, God's servant (Ex 33:20). God's children are given unhindered access to, and fellowship with, their Father for an eternity. The story does indeed have a happy ending. And yet there are those out to thwart God's plan.

The enemies of God (advocates of sin). Although God is seated on the throne as the high king and is worshiped by all who submit to his rule, he does have enemies who oppose him and his people. From the time the serpent chose to sabotage God's plan (see Gen 3), the grand story took on an element of danger. God is engaged in a war of cosmic proportions.[9] The dragon, God's chief enemy, amasses and empowers worldly empires and systems in an attempt to thwart the purposes of God. Revelation portrays this evil alliance as the advocates of sin and exile, but it is they who are ultimately doomed to divine banishment.

The Dragon. At war with the One seated on the throne stands the dragon (also known as Satan, the devil, the serpent, the accuser). We see glimpses of this archenemy of God in the messages to the seven churches, where he sponsors false religion that opposes Christians (Rev 2:9-10, 13, 24; 3:9), but not until Revelation 12 do we get the full picture. There a sign appears in heaven of a woman who is about to give birth to a male child (Jesus). Waiting to devour the child is a great red dragon. To the dragon's surprise, after the child is born he is snatched up and taken away to God (likely a reference to the resurrection and ascension of Jesus). The woman (from our perspective a symbol for the community of faith) flees from the dragon to the wilderness, where she is nourished and protected by God for 1,260 days. Beginning in Revelation 12:7, John retells the same story from the vantage point of a war in heaven, where Michael and his angels fight against the devil and his angels. The great dragon is defeated and is thrown out of heaven to the earth, where he turns his wrath against the woman and the rest of her children (lit. *sperma* or "seed"; cf. Gen 3:15). As Revelation 12 closes, we see the dragon taking his stand on the shore of the sea.

---

[9]See the insightful and well-argued contribution by Gregory A. Boyd, *God at War* (Downers Grove, Ill.: InterVarsity Press, 1997).

The two beasts. The first beast (traditionally known as the "antichrist") rises out of that same sea (Rev 13:1) and is empowered by Satan (Rev 13:2, 4; 16:13-14) to carry out his purposes of blaspheming God (Rev 13:1, 5-6) and destroying God's people (Rev 13:7).[10] The parody of Christ's death and resurrection becomes clear when we read that this beast had a fatal wound that had been healed (Rev 13:3, 12). John's readers would certainly have identified this sea beast as Rome, the dominant pagan empire at the time. John also describes Rome or "Babylon" (cf. 1 Pet 5:13) in Revelation 17 as the "great whore" who sits on the scarlet monster that we first encounter in Revelation 12:3. The prostitute is full of materialistic indulgence, abominable immorality and blasphemous idolatry, and she is said to be "drunk with the blood of the saints" (Rev 17:6; 18:24). She partners with the "kings of the earth," a phrase John uses regularly to describe political powers aligned against God (Rev 17:2, 18; 18:3, 9; 19:19). But the reference surely extends beyond the first century. We understand Rome to represent world powers of all ages that are opposed to God. Any politico-economic power that demands absolute allegiance (or "worship") in place of loyalty to God would fit the description.

The second beast (called the "false prophet" in Rev 19:20 and Rev 20:10) rises out of the earth. Also deriving its power from Satan, this second beast represents religious power and propaganda organized in support of the evil politico-economic system. The false prophet's main task is to deceive people into worshiping the first beast through the use of great and miraculous signs (Rev 13:11-15).

The "Inhabitants of the Earth." The dragon, the beast from the sea (antichrist), and the beast from the earth (false prophet) constitute the satanic trinity. Just as God has a people for himself, so this diabolical trio also claims a following. When John refers to the "inhabitants of the earth," he is usually describing human beings who have chosen to align themselves with the dragon and the beasts. Because they have been deceived (Rev 13:14), they give themselves over to sin (Rev 17:2) and worship of the beast (Rev 13:8, 12). These earth-dwellers gladly participate in persecuting Christians (Rev 6:10; 11:10), but their celebration is short-lived. They do not have their names written in the Lamb's book of life and will suffer God's judgment (Rev 6:10; 8:13).

The two signs of allegiance. God and Satan are truly at war, and there is no middle ground. Every human being is marked or sealed with one of two signs of loyalty: the seal of God (Rev 7:2-3; 9:4) or the mark of the beast (Rev 13:16-17; 14:9, 11; 16:2; 19:20; 20:4). The sealing is a spiritual mark that reveals the very essence of a person's allegiance. The two marks not only represent two opposing kingdoms, but they also forecast two contrasting destinies. Restoration is complete only when there is no more threat from the powers of evil. The negative side of restoration is God's judgment of

---

[10]The sea is often associated with evil in the Old Testament. Revelation 13 draws heavily on Daniel 7, where the sea is viewed as the origin of the beasts (e.g., Dan 7:2-3).

his enemies. We read of the final demise of the satanic trinity in Revelation 20:10: "And the devil who had deceived them was thrown into the lake of fire and sulfur, where the beast and false prophet were, and they will be tormented day and night forever and ever." Likewise, those who bear the mark of the beast share a fate of death and ultimate exile from the presence of God.

On the other hand, those marked as God's people overcome Satan "by the blood of the Lamb and by the word of their testimony," even though it very well might cost them their lives (Rev 12:11). They rely on Christ's decisive victory and cling to him even in the face of physical danger. They endure and experience ultimate restoration, a restoration promised to Abraham and made possible by the Lamb.

The Lamb of God (the Restorer). The book is a "revelation of Jesus Christ" (Rev 1:1), but John prefers the designation "Lamb" for Jesus since it communicates vividly his central role in the story of salvation. In the grand biblical story that moves from sin to restoration, the Lamb of God who takes away the sin of the world becomes the focal point. More specifically, Revelation speaks of the Lamb as God, the Lamb as the victorious sacrifice, and the Lamb as the returning warrior-judge.

The Lamb as God. John consistently emphasizes the Lamb's oneness with God. In the opening greeting with its reference to the triune God (Rev 1:4b-5), John's high Christology begins to shine through: "Grace to you and peace from him who is and who was and who is to come [the Father], and from the seven spirits who are before this throne [the Holy Spirit], and from Jesus Christ, the faithful witness, the firstborn of the dead, and the ruler of the kings of the earth."

Further into the first chapter, as John explains his vision of "one like the Son of Man," he uses terms that are often found in the Old Testament when referring to God himself (e.g., the description of God as the "Ancient of Days" in Dan 7:9-10). Throughout Revelation expressions that refer to God are also used of Jesus, thereby affirming Jesus' deity. For example, in Revelation 1:8 we read, "'I am the Alpha and the Omega,' says the Lord God" only later to hear Jesus state: "I am the Alpha and the Omega" (Rev 22:13). In addition, the word "Lord" is used to refer both to God (Rev 1:8; 4:8; 11:4, 15, 17; 15:3-4; 16:7; 18:8; 19:6; 21:22; 22:5-6) and to Jesus (Rev 1:10; 11:8; 14:13; 17:14; 19:16; 22:20-21).

The primary sign of the divine identity of the Lamb in Revelation is that he is explicitly worshiped as God. In the great throne-room vision of Revelation 4—5, after the slaughtered Lamb takes the scroll from the One seated on the throne, the heavenly choir responds with a new song of worship—"Worthy is the Lamb that was slaughtered to receive power and wealth and wisdom and might and honor and glory and blessing!" (Rev 5:9-14). Later the great multitude of Revelation 7 cries out in praise, "Salvation belongs to our God who is seated on the throne, and to the Lamb!" (Rev 7:10). In fact, all through Revelation we see the Lamb sharing in God's authority (Rev

5:6; 7:17; 12:10; 22:1, 3) and glory (Rev 5:13; 21:22-23). Whereas God is found worthy of worship because he has created all things, the Lamb is found worthy because of his role as Redeemer (Rev 5:9). He has conquered evil and created a people, and he has done so in a most unexpected and paradoxical manner.

The Lamb as conquering sacrifice. John breaks down in tears when no one is found worthy to open the scroll (Rev 5:4). An elder comforts him by telling him not to weep because "the Lion of the tribe of Judah, the Root of David, has conquered, so that he can open the scroll and its seven seals" (Rev 5:5). What a shock for John when he looks up expecting to see a fierce and powerful lion only to see instead a slaughtered lamb (Rev 5:6)! The image of a lamb reminds us of the Passover lamb associated with the exodus—the greatest saving act of God in the Old Testament. The book of Revelation draws on exodus imagery to portray Jesus as the Passover lamb who sacrifices himself in order to bring about the ultimate or "eschatological" deliverance of his people.

The divine paradox is that the Lamb's victory comes through suffering and sacrifice. He "freed us from our sins by his blood" (Rev 1:5). He was slaughtered, and by his blood he "ransomed for God saints from every tribe and language and people and nation" (Rev 5:9). The Lamb is faithful in his witness unto death (Rev 1:5, 18) and this sacrificial death becomes the crucial event in God's ultimate victory over evil. The Lamb's death is of course followed by his resurrection, "Do not be afraid; I am the first and the last, and the living one. I was dead, and see, I am alive forever and ever; and I have the keys of Death and of Hades" (Rev 1:17-18). As the slaughtered yet resurrected Lamb, he is able to empathize with his people who now endure tribulation as part of their identification with him (Rev 1:9; 12:17; 20:4). And he has promised to return as the warrior Lamb to bring ultimate deliverance and restoration.

The Lamb as the returning warrior-judge. Jesus came to earth the first time as the sacrificial Lamb, but he promises to return a second time as the warrior-judge. His return is mentioned as early as the letter's salutation, where John quotes Daniel 7:13, "Look! He is coming with the clouds" (Rev 1:7). Jesus promises the church at Philadelphia that he is coming soon (Rev 3:11), and when the sixth angel pours out his bowl of judgment, Jesus announces, "See, I am coming like a thief!" (Rev 16:15). In the final chapter of the book we see a special emphasis on Jesus' return as the church's prayer/cry of hope (Rev 22:7, 12, 17, 20), but Revelation 19:11-21 presents the most detailed and captivating account of the return of the warrior-judge. Jesus is identified in Revelation 19, not as the Lamb, but as the one who "judges and makes war" (Rev 19:11). He is mounted on a white stallion. His eyes are a flame of fire. He is crowned with many crowns and wears a robe dipped in blood. Out of his mouth comes a sharp sword, and he will rule the nations with a rod of iron. He "treads the wine press of the fury of the wrath of God the Almighty" (Rev 19:15). He is called "Faithful and True," "the Word of God," and "King of kings and Lord of lords" (Rev 19:11, 13, 16; cf. also

Rev 17:14). This last title is applied consistently in the Old Testament to the supreme ruler, God (Deut 10:17; Ps 136:3; Dan 2:47; Zech 14:9), but is now applied to Jesus.[11]

The beast and his armies who have tormented the people of God on earth now gather to make war against the rider on the white horse and his army (Rev 19:19). But somewhat surprisingly, the great battle itself is described in only a few words at the beginning of verse 20: "And the beast was captured." Some battle! The antichrist and the false prophet are then condemned to the lake of fire (Rev 19:20), and their followers become the banquet meal for the birds of prey (contrast the wedding supper of the Lamb in Rev 19:9). The two beasts who seemed to have the upper hand up to this time are now defeated and judged by the Lamb.

Jesus conquers sin and Satan through his sacrificial death and resurrection (Rev 3:21; 5:5), but he also will conquer when he returns as the warrior-judge (Rev 17:14). He brings both salvation and judgment since both are needed to reverse the curse and restore God's people.

The people of God (following the Lamb in a foreign land). Throughout this book we have traced the story of Israel. We have seen that the story is actually about the people of God. At the climax of the story, Scripture has much to say about who the people of God are and how they should live.

A redeemed people. The traditional term "church" is used at the beginning and end of Revelation to refer to seven local congregations of Christians in Asia Minor (Rev 1—3; 22:16). But as we mentioned earlier, these seven particular churches represent the universal church, and John uses a variety of expressions and images in the body of his letter to portray God's people. They are called "saints" (e.g., Rev 5:8; 13:10; 14:12; 17:6), the "144,000" (Rev 7:4, 14:1, 3), the "great multitude" (Rev 7:9; 19:1, 6), the "bride" of the Lamb (Rev 18:23; 21:2, 9; 22:17), and the "new Jerusalem" (Rev 21:2, 10), just to name a few. Above all, what sets these people apart is that they have been redeemed by the blood of the slaughtered Lamb (Rev 1:5; 5:9; 14:3-4). In spite of fierce opposition, they have continued to rely on the Lamb's sacrificial death on their behalf to free them from their sins and make them to be a kingdom of priests (Rev 1:6; 5:10; 20:6; cf. also Ex 19:5-6). The seven occurrences of the fourfold formula—every "tribe, language, people, and nation"—indicate that the Lamb's redemptive sacrifice creates a genuinely multicultural people (Rev 5:9; 7:9; 10:11; 11:9; 13:7; 14:6; 17:15).[12] What binds them together in eternal unity is their service to, and worship of, the One seated on the throne and the Lamb (Rev 5:13; 7:10, 15; 14:2-3; 15:3-4; 19:1-5; 6—7; 22:3).

---

[11]Keener, *Revelation*, 454.

[12]See Bauckham, *Climax of Prophecy*, 326-337 for a discussion of this fourfold formula. For a broader discussion of the multicultural people of God, see J. Daniel Hays, *From Every People and Nation: A Biblical Theology of Race*, New Studies in Biblical Theology (Downers Grove, Ill.: InterVarsity Press, 2003).

A persecuted people. Contrary to much popular teaching on Revelation in our day, the book actually bears out very clearly what Jesus said to his disciples: "In the world you face persecution" (Jn 16:33; "tribulation" in the NIV). John wastes no time in turning our attention to the root cause of this trouble—their corporate identity with their suffering Savior, Jesus Christ: "I, John, your brother who *share with you in Jesus the persecution* and the kingdom and the patient endurance" (Rev 1:9; italics added). The word translated "persecution" by the NRSV is the Greek word *thlipsis,* which is also translated "put to death" (Mt 24:9), "suffering" (Mt 24:29) or "ordeal" (Rev 7:14; "tribulation" in NIV) in New Testament apocalyptic contexts. Jesus cautions the church at Smyrna (and by extension the universal church) about the real possibility of persecution:

> I know your affliction and your poverty, even though you are rich. I know the slander on the part of those who say that they are Jews and are not, but are a synagogue of Satan. Do not fear what you are about to suffer. Beware, the devil is about to throw some of you into prison so that you may be tested, and for ten days you will have affliction. Be faithful until death, and I will give you the crown of life. (Rev 2:9-10)

This is no mock military exercise where the enemy fires blanks. This is real spiritual warfare where God's people are mocked and mistreated (Rev 11:9-10), deprived economically (Rev 13:16-17), falsely accused (Rev 12:10) and sometimes even put to death (Rev 6:9-11; 16:6; 17:6; 18:24; 19:2) for following the Lamb and refusing to worship the evil powers (Rev 13:15; 20:4). They are at war with Satan (Rev 12:17; 13:7), and while their defeat may at times appear certain (Rev 11:7; 13:7), the God of life will himself give them life and victory.[13] No wonder that the saints' prayers in Revelation are focused on asking God to vindicate his people and judge the ungodly (Rev 5:8; 6:9-11; 8:3-4). The book even closes with the repeated prayer, "Come, Lord Jesus" (Rev 22:17, 20). In the meantime, the reality of persecution demands endurance and faith on the part of the saints (Rev 13:10).

A faithful people. After being thrown out of heaven, the dragon makes war on those who "keep the commandments of God and hold the testimony of Jesus" (Rev 12:17). The importance of faithfulness is emphasized in two main ways. First, God's people are characterized throughout the book as those who are obedient to the word or commandments of God (Rev 1:2, 9; 6:9; 12:17; 14:12; 20:4; 22:9). They have not defiled themselves (Rev 14:4-5) but have put on righteous deeds consistent with their relationship to the Lamb (Rev 19:8; 22:11, 14). Second, they are faithful in their witness to the testimony of/for Jesus (Rev 1:2, 9; 6:9; 19:10; 20:4). Put simply, they "follow the Lamb wherever he goes" (Rev 14:4).

---

[13]See Bauckham, *Theology of Revelation,* 84-88, 113-15; Keener, *Revelation,* 289-93, for discussions of the view taken here that the two witnesses of Revelation 11 represent the prophetic witness of the church.

A tempted people. Their faithfulness is not beyond temptation, however, and the book has its share of pointed warnings calling the saints to endure in faith (Rev 13:10; 14:12). One of the most vivid occurs in Revelation 18 when the heavenly voice urges believers to separate from Babylon and her idolatry—"Come out of her, my people, so that you do not take part in her sins, and so that you do not share in her plagues" (Rev 18:4). The historical context of Revelation suggests that those who face persecution also face the temptation to compromise. Although their faithfulness is emphasized, God's people are nevertheless reminded to stay alert for Christ's return (Rev 16:15) and to conquer evil by holding fast to their confession, even to the point of death (Rev 12:11). With this in mind, the last words of Revelation could not be more appropriate, "The grace of the Lord Jesus be with all the saints" (Rev 22:21).

The judgment of God (ultimate exile). Throughout the story of Israel we have come to understand the term *exile* to refer to God's discipline of his own people for their disobedience (and we see remnants of this meaning in Jesus' words of warning to the seven churches). The word *exile* is never used in Revelation, but the reality of exile is present in full force. The meaning of the concept takes an ironic twist in that the enemies of God (rather than the people of God) are now the ones who face exile. God created a good world, but Satan and sin have invaded it like a cancer. God's wrath constitutes his righteous response to wickedness. His judgment of evil is an expression of his holy and perfect character. Revelation speaks of the ultimate exile of God's enemies, or to put it another way, the curse of the curse.

In the central section of Revelation we see God's judgment of evil played out in three series of seven judgments—the seals (Rev 6:1—8:1), the trumpets (Rev 8:2—11:19) and the bowls (Rev 16:1-21).[14] While the judgments grow more intense and severe as we move from the first to the third series, all three series bring us the final end, though not in strict chronological order (cf. Rev 6:12-17; 11:15-19; 16:17-21). To a large extent many of these judgments are modeled on the plagues of Egypt in the book of Exodus. We read of hail, darkness, sores, locusts and frogs and bodies of water turning to blood. In Revelation as in Egypt, God sends the plagues on his enemies to show his power and vindicate his people. These powerful images, drawn from the most familiar of Old Testament stories, overwhelm the reader and force a decision. Unbelievers are warned to repent or face the ultimate exile, while believers are reminded that God will be victorious over evil. As Paul Spilsbury puts it, "After the plagues, the exodus!"[15] We see the same movement toward a decision in Revelation 14.

Although the interlude of Revelation 14 comes between the trumpet and the bowl

---

[14]See the summary charts in Beale, *Revelation*, 128; and Paul Spilsbury, *The Throne, the Lamb & the Dragon: A Reader's Guide to the Book of Revelation* (Downers Grove, Ill.: InterVarsity Press, 2002), 117.
[15]Spilsbury, *Throne, Lamb & Dragon*, 118.

judgments in the book, its subject matter relates to the very end of time when the beast and his followers are judged. The war between God and the beast presents a clear choice for "those who live on the earth—to every nation and tribe and language and people" (Rev 14:6). They are told to "fear God and give him glory" (Rev 14:7) or else face God's tormenting judgment reserved for "Babylon the great" (Rev 14:8) and "those who worship the beast and its image" (Rev 14:9). God's judgment will be inescapable and eternal (cf. Rev 14:11, where "the smoke of their torment goes up forever and ever"). Two images dramatize the impending judgment: the grain harvest (Rev 14:14-16) and the winepress (Rev 14:17-20). The gruesome image of the beast-followers being crushed in the "winepress of the wrath of God" (cf. Rev 19:15) so that their blood flows as high as a horse's bridle for two hundred miles drives home the point that God's judgment of evil will be absolute.

Revelation 17:1—19:6 reports in greater detail God's final judgment on "Babylon the great, the mother of whores." In contrast to the New Jerusalem as the bride of Christ, Babylon constitutes the worldly system that blasphemes God and puts Christians to death. (John and his readers would certainly have seen Rome and her emperors as the evil political-economic-religious system in their day.) At the end of Revelation 17 we are told that part of God's judgment on these enemies is that they will make war with the Lamb, but "the Lamb will conquer them" (Rev 17:14). We also see, somewhat surprisingly, that God's judgment includes using evil powers to destroy other evil powers (Rev 17:16-17). When Babylon falls, God's people rejoice because his judgment demonstrates not only his justice but also the value of their faith: "Rejoice over her, O heaven, you saints and apostles and prophets! For God has given judgment for you against her" (Rev 18:20). And in Revelation 19:

> After this I heard what seemed to be the loud voice of a great multitude in heaven, saying, "Hallelujah! Salvation and glory and power to our God, for his judgments are true and just; he has judged the great whore who corrupted the earth with her fornication, and he has avenged on her the blood of his servants." Once more they said, "Hallelujah! The smoke goes up from her forever and ever." And the twenty-four elders and the four living creatures fell down and worshiped God who is seated on the throne, saying, "Amen. Hallelujah!" And from the throne came a voice saying, "Praise our God, all you his servants, and all who fear him, small and great." Then I heard what seemed to be the voice of a great multitude, like the sound of many waters and like the sound of mighty thunderpeals, crying out, "Hallelujah! For the Lord our God the Almighty reigns." (Rev 19:1-6)

As Keener says, God's judgment of Babylon not only stops her oppression but also "avenges her incomprehensible injustices" and becomes the occasion when God begins to reign as King of the universe (cf. Rev 19:6-10).[16]

The final battle is recorded in more detail in Revelation 19:11-21. Throughout his-

---

[16]Keener, *Revelation*, 449-50.

tory, the forces of evil make war against the people of God and appear to conquer them. In this final battle, however, they pick on the wrong opponent when they make war against the Lamb. Here Jesus is described as the rider on the white horse that "judges and makes war" (Rev 19:11). The Lamb has returned as the mighty warrior-judge. He captures the beast and the false prophet and throws them "alive into the lake of fire that burns with sulfur" (Rev 19:20). Eventually Satan himself is doomed to the very same fate: "And the devil who had deceived them was thrown into the lake of fire and sulfur, where the beast and the false prophet were" (Rev 20:10). The satanic trinity suffers God's eternal wrath as a result of their rebellion as they are "tormented day and night forever and ever" (Rev 20:10).

At the beginning of Revelation 20 we read of righteous people who are raised to life in order to reign with Christ (Rev 20:4). Those who experience this "first resurrection" (Rev 20:5-6) will not be affected by the "second death" (Rev 20:6). In contrast to this resurrection of the righteous, we read later of Death and Hades and the sea giving up their dead to stand before God's great white throne (Rev 20:11-15). With the devil and both beasts condemned, these people now stand before God with no place to hide and no evil power to delay their judgment. God judges them all "according to their works, as recorded in the books" (Rev 20:12). Any person whose name is not found in the book of life is thrown into the lake of fire to experience the second death (Rev 20:14-15).[17] By also casting Death and Hades into the lake of fire God's ultimate exile of evil is complete and the story turns to God's ultimate restoration of his people and his creation.

The paradise of God (ultimate restoration). The story of God's ultimate restoration of his people and his creation is recounted in detail in Revelation 21—22. Perhaps the best way to see the depth and richness of the victorious conclusion to the story of Scripture is to set the beginning elements in Genesis side by side with the concluding elements in Revelation (see table 12.3). The panorama of the creation–sin–exile–restoration story becomes apparent.

As Revelation 22 opens, the sea that produced the beast is no more, and we now see a river of life flowing from the throne of God and of the Lamb. This recalls the inaugural visions of Revelation 4—5 and the focus on God's throne, a symbol of his sovereign rule over all of reality. The centrality of the throne vision has proven true: God kept his promise to conquer his enemies, vindicate his people and restore his creation.

The river that flowed out of Eden (Gen 2:10) is replaced with a river of life that flows through the middle of the city. In contrast to toiling with a cursed ground to get their food (Gen 3:17-19), God's people may now eat freely of the tree of life that grows

---

[17]Throughout Revelation the "book of life" refers to a heavenly register of those overcomers who do not worship the beast, but instead follow the Lamb and live accordingly (see Rev 3:5; 13:8; 17:8; 20:12, 15; 21:27).

Table 12.3 **Genesis and Revelation Compared**

Genesis	Restoration in Revelation	
Sinful people scattered	God's people unite to sing his praises	19:6-7
"Marriage" of Adam and Eve	Marriage of Last Adam and his bride, the church	19:7; 21:2, 9
God abandoned by sinful people	God's people (New Jerusalem, bride of Christ) made ready for God; marriage of Lamb	19:7-8; 21:2, 9-21
Exclusion from bounty of Eden	Invitation to marriage supper of Lamb	19:9
Satan introduces sin into world	Satan and sin are judged	19:11-21; 20:7-10
Serpent deceives humanity	The ancient serpent is bound "to keep him from deceiving the nations"	20:2-3
God gives humans dominion over the earth	God's people will reign with him forever	20:4, 6; 22:5
People rebel against the true God, resulting in physical and spiritual death	God's people risk death to worship the true God and thus experience life	20:4-6
Sinful people sent away from life	God's people have their names written in the book of life	20:4-6, 15; 21:6, 27
Death enters the world	Death is put to death	20:14; 21:4
God creates first heaven and earth, eventually cursed by sin	God creates a new heaven and earth where sin is nowhere to be found	21:1
Water symbolizes unordered chaos	There is no longer any sea	21:1
Sin brings pain and tears	God comforts his people and removes crying and pain	21:4
Sinful humanity cursed with wandering (exile)	God's people given a permanent home	21:3
Community forfeited	Genuine community experienced	21:3, 7

Genesis	Restoration in Revelation	
Sinful people are banished from presence of God	God lives among his people	21:3, 7, 22; 22:4
Creation begins to grow old and die	All things are made new	21:5
Water used to destroy wicked humanity	God quenches thirst with water from spring of life	21:6; 22:1
"In the beginning, God . . ."	"I am the Alpha and the Omega, the beginning and the end."	21:6
Sinful humanity suffers a wandering exile in the land	God gives his children an inheritance	21:7
Sin enters the world	Sin banished from God's city	21:8, 27; 22:15
Sinful humanity separated from presence of holy God	God's people experience God's holiness (cubed city = holy of holies)	21:15-21
God creates light and separates it from darkness	No more night or natural light; God himself is the source of light	21:23; 22:5
Languages of sinful humanity confused	God's people is a multicultural people	21:24, 26; 22:2
Sinful people sent away from garden	New heaven/earth includes a garden	22:2
Sinful people forbidden to eat from tree of life	God's people may eat freely from the tree of life	22:2, 14
Sin results in spiritual sickness	God heals the nations	22:2
Sinful people cursed	The curse removed from redeemed humanity and they become a blessing	22:3
Sinful people refuse to serve/ obey God	God's people serve him	22:3
Sinful people ashamed in God's presence	God's people will "see his face"	22:4

beside the river and bears fruit throughout the year. This scene has much in common with Ezekiel, who also envisions a restored garden where water flows from the sanctuary and nurtures fruit-bearing trees. In Ezekiel 47:12 we read that "their fruit will be for food, and their leaves for healing." Revelation adds the phrase "of the nations" to the word "healing" to show that redeemed peoples from the various nations will be permitted to reside in the heavenly city. We now see the fulfillment of the very heart of the Abrahamic blessing in Genesis 12 that God would bless "all the families of the earth" in him. What God initiated with Abraham and expanded at Pentecost, he now consummates with the restored multicultural community living in the new heaven and new earth. The curse has been totally and completely abolished. In its place we find only blessing. This is the grand fulfillment of the story of the people of God.

This celestial city is identified primarily as the place where God lives with his people. They will "see his face" and bear "his name on their foreheads." These are profound expressions of intimate and personal fellowship with God. The communion that God desired with Adam and Eve is finally realized with those who have been redeemed by Jesus Christ, the last Adam. We are also told again that the Lord God in all his glory will be their light and that there "will be no more night." No darkness, no night; only God's light! Keener encourages us to see the light as directly related to seeing God's glorious face, just as Moses reflected God's glory after he saw God's face (Ex 34:30).[18] As a community of priests to God (Rev 1:6; 5:10; 20:6), they will worship him (NIV "serve"). As a community of kings, they will "reign forever and ever" with him.

God is a God of restoration and has planned a restored paradise for his people. There will be no more Satan, no more sin, and no more pain or death. God's glory will completely banish all darkness. He will live among his people, and they will know him face to face. They will join the multitude of heavenly beings in worshiping God forever for all the good he has done. They have a bright future in God's grand plan. But what about their present? What about the pressure to confess Caesar as Lord? What about the temptation to deny Christ in order to avoid economic distress? What about the constant pull to switch to an acceptable and "safe" religion approved by Rome? Why not compromise with the dragon and the beast to steer clear of trouble? What does Revelation say about living God's story here and now?

The battle of God (living by God's story). As the final chapter of the story of Israel, Revelation clearly shows that God and his people are at war with the forces of evil. The Creator has enemies who advocate sin and attempt to thwart his plan and destroy his people. Jesus Christ, the Restorer, has dealt a death blow to sin and Satan through his death and resurrection. Those who follow him are promised eternal life and all that it entails, yet the Lamb's followers continue to live in enemy territory and face choices

---

[18]Keener, *Revelation*, 501.

that test their true identity. The promises are genuine, but overcoming is prerequisite to inheriting the promises.

The word translated "overcome" or "conquer" (*nikaō*) is a battle term that Jesus uses to challenge all seven churches at the beginning of the book. The promises he makes to those who overcome are all associated with ultimate restoration: eternal life, provision, justice, participation in Christ's victory and the very presence of God. Then, at the end of the book, in the vision of the new heaven and new earth, the term reappears to describe those who will inherit God's eternal kingdom, "Those who conquer will inherit these things, and I will be their God and they will be my children" (Rev 21:7). While Jesus challenges people to overcome in the book's introduction and rewards those who have overcome in the conclusion, what it means to overcome (or conquer) becomes clear only as the entire book unfolds.

From what we know of the historical situation of Revelation, the threat of evil is real for Christians. False religion has joined with pagan political power to pressure believers to compromise their faith in Christ. In the heat of the battle we read that the beast comes up from the Abyss, attacks the two witnesses who represent the witnessing church, overpowers (*nikaō*) and kills them (Rev 11:7). Later we hear that the beast is "given power to make war against the saints and to conquer (*nikaō*) them" (Rev 13:7). Throughout history the forces of evil have "conquered" God's people by inflicting on them physical persecution and death. But that is not the end of the story.

Revelation leaves no doubt that Jesus has conquered or triumphed. In the heavenly throne vision of Revelation 4—5 John is told not to weep because the "Lion of the tribe of Judah, the Root of David, has conquered, so that he can open the scroll and its seven seals" (Rev 5:5). Since John turns to see a "Lamb standing as if it had been slaughtered" (Rev 5:6), we may conclude that Jesus conquered by means of his death on the cross (cf. Rev 3:21). The victory over evil that Revelation describes is "no more than the working-out of the decisive victory of the Lamb on the cross."[19] The means of Jesus' victory has significant implications for how God's people will conquer evil.

To live by God's story means to conquer as the Lamb conquered—by being faithful to the end, despite suffering and even death. Revelation 12:11 summarizes the story better than any other single verse: "They [Christians] have conquered him [Satan] by the blood of the Lamb and by the word of their testimony, for they did not cling to life even in the face of death." While Christians may suffer earthly defeat at the hands of Satan through persecution and even death, they actually conquer him by holding fast to their testimony of Christ crucified and resurrected. Satan's victory over them is at the same time their victory over Satan.

The powerful paradox of how God's people conquer (eternal victory through physical

---

[19]Bauckham, *Theology of Revelation*, 75.

suffering and death) rests ultimately on their devotion to truth rather than their surrender to deceit. Bauckham is surely right when he says, "Perhaps the most important contrast between the forces of evil and the army of the Lamb is the contrast between deceit and truth."[20] Satan deceives the whole world (Rev 12:9; 20:3, 8, 10), the false prophet deceives the inhabitants of the earth (Rev 13:14; 19:20), and Babylon deceives all nations (Rev 18:23); but God's people are completely without deceit (Rev 14:5; cf. Rev 21:27; 22:15).[21] By choosing the right God, the God of life, they outlast their enemies, who are all subject to the second death. In the end, God's people are left standing in his presence. They have overcome because they have followed the one true God.

But what exactly does overcoming entail for the people of God? The seven beatitudes (or "blessings") of Revelation offer insight into the specific nature of overcoming (table 12.4).

Table 12.4 The Seven Beatitudes of Revelation

1:3	**Blessed** is the one who reads aloud the words of the prophecy, and **blessed** are those who hear and who keep what is written in it; for the time is near.
14:13	**Blessed** are the dead who from now on die in the Lord. "Yes," says the Spirit, "they will rest from their labors, for their deeds follow them."
16:15	See, I am coming like a thief! **Blessed** is the one who stays awake and is clothed, not going about naked and exposed to shame.
19:9	**Blessed** are those who are invited to the marriage supper of the Lamb.
20:6	**Blessed** and holy are those who share in the first resurrection. Over these the second death has no power.
22:7	See, I am coming soon! **Blessed** is the one who keeps the words of the prophecy of this book.
22:14-15	**Blessed** are those who wash their robes, so that they will have the right to the tree of life and may enter the city by the gates. Outside are the dogs and sorcerers and fornicators and murderers and idolaters, and everyone who loves and practices falsehood.

The blessing of God is given to those who (1) hear and obey his Word, (2) turn away from sin, and (3) persevere in following the Lamb to the end. Here Revelation correlates the blessings and curses throughout the story of Israel (e.g., in Deut 28) with

---

[20]Ibid., 91.
[21]Ibid.

the blessings and curses associated with following Christ and the beast respectively. In the story of Israel these options have always been there.

Jesus gets even more specific about the nature of blessing in his messages to the seven churches in Revelation 2—3. Overcoming necessitates following Jesus by rejecting false teaching, abstaining from sexual immorality, resisting idolatry and refusing to compromise. Positively, it demands both faith and the good works that demonstrate its authenticity, along with patient endurance that will almost certainly involve suffering and perhaps even death. Overcoming involves making ethical decisions in everyday life that please God. The two summary statements at the end of Revelation (Rev 21:7-8; 22:14-15) illustrate clearly the contrast between a conquering life and a compromising life, as has been the consistent pattern throughout the history of God's people (table 12.5). To overcome, therefore, means to follow the Lamb with one's whole life until the very end of one's life.

Table 12.5 Blessings and Curses in Revelation 21—22

Revelation 21:7-8	Revelation 22:14-15
Those who conquer will inherit these things, and I will be their God and they will be my children.	Blessed are those who wash their robes, so that they will have the right to the tree of life and may enter the city by the gates.
Vs.	Vs.
But as for the cowardly, the faithless, the polluted, the murderers, the fornicators, the sorcerers, the idolaters, and all liars, their place will be in the lake that burns with fire and sulfur, which is the second death.	Outside are the dogs and sorcerers and fornicators and murderers and idolaters, and everyone who loves and practices falsehood.

Conclusion

As Genesis 1—11 presented the problem (sin–exile) and Genesis 12 began the journey toward restoration, so Revelation climaxes the story by presenting the final restoration and the ultimate solution to the sin problem of Genesis. Since the time the book was written, those who have entered the symbolic world created by the visions of Revelation have been transformed as they see what God has planned. The transforming vision we call Revelation may be compared to a tapestry that has been woven by the seven theological threads: God, his enemies, the Lamb, his followers, God's judgment,

God's restored paradise, and the battle of God. This seventh and final theme connects the story back to the hearers by locating them in the battle and reminding them that their temporal choices have eternal consequences. Such has been the case throughout the story of Israel. As Noah "did all that God commanded him" (Gen 6:22) and Abraham "believed" and "obeyed" God (Gen 15:6; 26:5) and Jesus submitted to the Father's plan that would take him to the cross (Mk 14:36), so God's people are challenged to obey what is written in the prophecy (cf. Rev 1:3; 22:17-18). In the end, living by God's story means "hearing what the Spirit says to the churches."

Supplemental Reading in New Dictionary of Biblical Theology

G. K. Beale, "Revelation (book)," 356-63.
H. A. G. Blocher, "Evil," 465-67.
K. E. Brower, "Eschatology," 459-64.
T. Longman III, "Warfare," 835-39.
J. A. Motyer, "Judgment," 612-15.
P. D. Woodbridge, "Lamb," 620-22.

Study Questions

1. Describe the historical situation and literary context of the book of Revelation.

2. How does Revelation as a prophetic-apocalyptic work attempt to transform its readers?

3. What are the seven main themes of the book of Revelation? Briefly describe how each theme contributes to the overall theology of the book.

13

CONCLUSION

Does the Bible have a grand theme? Is there a single idea that is pervasive enough to establish unity within the Bible while at the same time encompassing diverse motifs such as people of God, new covenant, promise/fulfillment, wisdom, kingdom of God, and new creation? *The Story of Israel* provides our yes answer to the question. We believe that the story of Israel—the story of God's creation, humanity's sin and resulting exile, and God's mission to restore his people—represents a prominent theological theme of Scripture.

The story begins with God's design for his creation and its attendant blessings (Gen 1—2). The story of blessing gives way to the story of sin and the cursing of the creation (Gen 3—11). The good, blessed creation unravels as Adam and Eve's sin leads into exile away from the paradise of God's intimate presence. What was once blessing has now become a curse. The key question now is, How will humanity be restored to right relationship with God? How will the curses be removed so that the blessings of God may be restored? The rest of the Bible explains God's answer to that crucial question.

The most obvious beginning point for restoration is God's covenant with Abraham. God narrows the focus from all of humanity to one man and his family. God will bless Abraham so that in time he may offer hope and restoration to all the families of the world. In the book of Exodus the story of Israel expands from one family to an entire nation (Israel). Out of slavery God calls Israel, his son, and this redemption from bondage becomes the anchor of salvation history. God takes the initiative to choose Israel for restoration and blessing, but Israel must respond in faithful obedience. The assumption is that those who have been rescued by God will respond with obedience appropriate to the blessings. Disobedience will result in curses. At the heart of the covenant between Israel and God is the threefold formula: I will be your God; you will be my people; I will dwell in your midst. More than anything, God wants a restored relationship.

The Pentateuch closes with a new generation of Israelites preparing to enter the Promised Land in fulfillment of the promises made to Abraham in Genesis. Before they enter, however, God calls them to covenant renewal, exhorting them to be faithful to the Mosaic covenant as presented in Deuteronomy. The central focus in Deuteronomy is obedience to God's word. Those who obey God's instructions can enter the Promised Land, where they will experience abundance, peace, victory over enemies, fulfillment of the covenant and God's presence. Those who disobey will be cursed with unproductive land, opposition from God himself, destruction from enemies and exile. At the end of Deuteronomy, the people accept the Mosaic covenant with these terms clearly understood. In Deuteronomy the decisive moment is "today," and this decision will determine whether the people will experience blessings or curses. The ultimate blessing, the Promised Land, is reminiscent of a return to the garden of Eden and a reminder of God's program of restoration.

In the historical books that follow the Pentateuch (Joshua, Judges, Ruth, 1–2 Samuel, 1–2 Kings) the central question is, Will Israel be faithful in following God into the Promised Land, as spelled out in the book of Deuteronomy? The tragic but simple answer to this question is no. We read in these books of Israel's failure to live by the Mosaic covenant. One simple truth is repeated over and over—humanity is sinful and is unable to sustain a life of obedience to God. Instead of enjoying the blessings of God, they choose instead a life of stubborn rebellion that leads to judgment.

The historical books also teach us much about God's patience with his people. Their inability to keep the Mosaic law is counterbalanced by his loving promises made first to Abraham and then to David. At the peak of David's reign, and climaxing the restoration of Israel after the disaster of Judges, Yahweh makes an everlasting covenant with David (2 Sam 7). He promises that a future heir of David will reign forever. This Davidic covenant combines with the Abrahamic covenant (promise of blessings on all the nations) to create a hopeful expectation of restoration. It also suggests the need for a king greater than David and a new covenant in which God's covenant promises can find final fulfillment. This hope of ultimate restoration and blessing drives the story of salvation through the Prophets and into the New Testament, where Christ appears as the resolution.

In the Prophets we find the message of sin, exile and restoration more clearly and powerfully presented than in any other portion of the Old Testament. They declare that Israel has violated the Mosaic covenant. They call on the people to turn from their idolatry, social injustice and religious ritualism and return to a faithful walk with God—but the people refuse. As a result, the prophets announce that God will bring judgment on his people. This judgment will result in exile away from the land and away from the blessings described in Deuteronomy.

The prophets, however, look beyond judgment and exile to the glorious time of restoration. They preach a much-needed message of hope beyond sin, judgment and exile. The hope championed by the prophets goes beyond the national aspirations of Israel to return to the land. It extends far beyond the ethnic borders of Israel to include all peoples. The prophets promise a whole new way of relating to God in a brand new covenant inaugurated by the Davidic Messiah. In this way the prophets look back be-yond the Mosaic covenant to God's covenant with Abraham. They expand the message beyond the local story of Israel (from Genesis 12 to 2 Kings 25) to the universal story of God's dealings with all people (Gen 1—11). This ultimate restoration will bring Is-rael and the nations together as one people of God who experience God's healing for-giveness, participate in glorious worship and experience God's intimate presence through the indwelling of his very Spirit.

From the Prophets we move to the Wisdom literature. Much of what we read there reflects an attempt to apply to life the theology of the blessings and curses found in Deuteronomy. The historical psalms, for instance, rehearse the events in the life of Is-rael that best represent the movement from sin to exile and finally to restoration. The psalmist makes it clear that the people's rebellion will be met with the destructive con-sequences of exile.

We also find in the Wisdom literature a caution against simplistic answers to com-plex issues. Job and Ecclesiastes suggest that we don't always have enough information to understand why God blesses and why he curses. These two works of wisdom insert an element of mystery into the story of Israel and remind us that our human perspec-tive is indeed limited.

With the literature of Second Temple Judaism, we discovered that a basic unity un-dergirds its telling of the story of Israel: If Israel is to experience true and lasting res-toration she must take the Torah seriously. Only then will she realize her destiny as God's chosen people among the nations. Such nomism and particularism, however, do not find approval in the Christian canon.

The New Testament opens with the Synoptic Gospels—Matthew, Mark and Luke. What God has been about all the time in his relationship with Israel and the nations is now made evident in the Gospel story. The Synoptics recount the events in Jesus' ministry as a way of reinterpreting God's relationship to Israel. They offer evidence of how God is remembering his covenant with Abraham and is now bringing the history of Israel to fulfillment in Jesus. Without a doubt, the Gospel writers view Jesus as *the* central figure for God's new covenant relationship with Israel and the nations.

The eschatological purpose of God's history with Israel is not to restore the Mosaic covenant. The Prophets were correct, a new covenant was needed. God's Spirit would be poured out upon all true believers, and the Son of Man would show his glory and power. Faithless Israel would remain in spiritual exile, while faithful followers of Jesus, the true believers in God's eschatological purpose, would be restored and saved.

The reign of God among his people, which had been promised by the prophets, be-came a reality in Jesus. The whole point of Jesus' ministry and message was to say and show that the time of waiting was over. What Judaism understood to be the age *to come* has now broken into their present reality. With Jesus, the kingdom of God has arrived, and the distance between God and his people caused by sin and experienced as exile has been narrowed significantly. God is again near. God's presence now dwells dynamically among people, though not fully until the return of Christ. Nevertheless, true believers are now the living evidence of God's eschatological purposes and of his restoring power that calls his creation together from all nations of the earth under his kingship.

For John, the story of Israel is the interpretive grid for his understanding of Jesus. What the Creator had done and was now doing in the world (*kosmos*) became focused on what Jesus was doing in Israel. The activities of Jesus in Palestine have *cosmic* repercussions. They are the culmination of God's saving activity, stretching back through Israel's history, through Abraham, to creation itself. John's one overarching purpose in writing his Gospel is to share that God himself was finally redeeming Israel from her exile.

John accomplishes his purpose by demonstrating that in Jesus, God was again living among his people in the person of Jesus. When John makes his case for Jesus as "God in our midst," he does not use Greco-Roman or gnostic imagery. He uses the story of Israel and Old Testament Wisdom language. As God was present with his people in the tabernacle as evidenced by signs and wonders, so also now God in Jesus is present with his people. As the presence of God was an abiding glory in the tabernacle, so also John emphasizes this theme. But in place of the elements familiar to the Israelites in the Old Testament (shekinah, Torah, Jerusalem temple and covenant code), we see the *logos* becoming a human being—Jesus of Nazareth. In Jesus, God tabernacles among his people and reveals his divine glory.

The book of Acts makes it clear that the story of Israel does not stop at the ascension of Jesus. The ministry of Jesus in the Gospels continues programmatically in the ministry of the Spirit of Jesus through the early church. As Jesus preached, they preached; as Jesus healed, they healed; as Jesus engaged in exorcism, they engaged in exorcism; filled with his Spirit they continued his ministry.

Luke advances the story in Acts chiefly through narrative and speeches. The narrative of Acts, rather than merely serving as "filler" material between teaching points, sustains the story at a theological level. The events of the ongoing story become teaching moments in their own right. Acts makes it clear that God's purpose for Israel as shown in the Gospels is being fulfilled in the Christian church. As the Gospel of Luke offers the story of Israel and her misunderstanding of God's eternal purpose, so Acts supplies the story of God's fulfillment of this eternal purpose in spite of Israel's misunderstanding. Just as the historical Jesus reveals God's original plan and enables its fruition, the Spirit of Jesus reveals and enables God's plan to be fulfilled throughout his creation. God's purpose for Israel to be a light to the nations through the power of his presence is now accomplished through the new Israel, Jesus' disciples, who are empowered by the presence of God's Spirit.

The speeches in Acts function as summary statements of sorts, but in terms of theology, they are the pillars to which the narrative sections connect. They reinforce Luke's message that Israel's story is now coming to its climactic fulfillment and conclusion. In Acts 2, we read of the fulfillment of Joel's prophecy. From this grand display of God's presence, Peter's first public speech moves the readers to an awareness of Israel's wickedness and need for repentance (Acts 2:22-40). Sounding the prophetic message once again, Peter's second speech, beginning in Acts 3:12, focuses on the need for Israel to repent and turn from her sins. This moves to an all-out charge of being stiff-necked in Stephen's speech to the Jewish leadership in Acts 7 (Acts 7:51). As Stephen retells Israel's story, it becomes evident that Israel has misinterpreted God's actions in their midst and missed the purpose of her calling. Indeed, it is the Gentiles, not Israel, who are calling upon God and being visited by his Spirit (Acts 10).

Peter is invited to speak in the home of a devout and God-fearing Gentile and is convinced by God himself to accept the invitation (Acts 10:9-23). This leads to an outpouring of God's Spirit upon Gentiles, who are now marked by the very evidence of God's presence, the Holy Spirit (Acts 10). Peter can conclude nothing other than that "God shows no partiality, but in every nation anyone who fears him and does what is right is acceptable to him" (Acts 10:34).

Paul's speech in Acts 13 takes this even further. Beginning with a recounting of God's history with Israel (Acts 13:16), the emphasis now falls on restoration and forgiveness of sin (Acts 13:38). The forgiveness that comes through God's final work in Jesus frees people from "all those sins from which you could not be freed by the law of Moses" (Acts 13:39). As a crescendo to the Acts narrative, Luke ends with Paul's speech to the Roman guard (Acts 28:17ff.) where a quote from Isaiah (Is 6:9, 10) makes it evident that although Israel's story had been intricately tied to God's plan for the nations, they are now being fulfilled in spite of Israel's obstinacy. Israel would not listen, but the Gentiles will (Acts 28:28). Israel missed her appointment and forfeited the purpose of her calling—yet God's plan for his creation moves unhindered toward its completion (Acts 28:31).

The Gospels and Acts are founded on the belief that the crucified Jesus has embraced the Deuteronomic curses and (by virtue of his resurrection) dispensed the blessings of the new covenant on all those who believe in him. The apostle Paul advances that reinterpretation by arguing that the curse has actually been reversed. It is now those who attempt to obey the works of the law who are under divine judgment, while those who believe in Jesus as Messiah experience the long-awaited restoration of Israel.

Prior to his conversion, Paul's message was that obedience to the Old Testament law brought Deuteronomic blessings, whereas disobedience to the law made certain the continuation of the covenantal curses on Israel. Paul's dramatic Damascus road experience with the risen Christ changed his perspective and caused him to reinterpret the story of Israel. In Galatians 3:13-14, for example, he now portrays Jesus as the righteous one who (having obeyed the law fully), suffered the Deuteronomic curses (Gal 3:13, death) in order that those who believe in him (sinners though they are) might experience the Deuteronomic blessings (life, Gal 3:14). Christians now enjoy the Deuteronomic blessings as they put their faith in Christ, who has absorbed the Deuteronomic curses (cf. Rom 5:1-11).

As the story of Israel continues through the New Testament, each of the General Epistles uses some aspect of the story to encourage and instruct its readers. James and 1 Peter both emphasize how Christians should live wisely while "in exile." As sojourners in a land no longer their home, they are susceptible to poverty and persecution. Although they are suffering, they are the true Israel and should live wisely because the time of their restoration is near.

Jude and 2 Peter are also addressed to the true Israel living in the last days. Both warn of the perils in exile. 2 Peter appears to be a revision of Jude, keeping at its heart Jude's warnings against false teachers. These false teachers are on the wrong path, and these two letters encourage their readers to stay true to the story by selecting the correct path.

Hebrews uses the sin–exile–restoration motif of the story of Israel but focuses on restoration—the community of God entering her promised "rest." The church as the true Israel is already experiencing at least some of the eschatological blessings of the restoration. Christ provides these blessings, Hebrews argues, in better ways than Judaism. In spite of these hints of an eschatological fulfillment, Hebrews speaks mainly from the perspective that the church has *already* entered the promised rest, in at least some ways.

As Genesis 1—11 presented the problem (sin–exile), and Genesis 12 began the journey toward restoration, so Revelation concludes the story by presenting the final restoration and the ultimate solution to the sin problem of Genesis. The entire story pivots on the life, death and resurrection of Jesus Christ, but the full implications and consequences of this climactic event are not immediately visible. The book of Revelation presents in colorful language and powerful imagery the final chapter in God's story, where he judges his enemies, reverses the curse of sin, restores his creation and lives among his people forever. The transforming vision we call Revelation may be compared to a tapestry that has been woven by the seven theological threads: God, his enemies, the Lamb, his followers, God's judgment, God's restored paradise and the battle of God. This seventh and final theme connects the story back to the hearers by locating them in the battle and reminding them that their temporal choices have eternal consequences.

Throughout the story of Israel we have seen God's people responding to him in faith. Abraham "believed" and "obeyed" God (Gen 15:6; 26:5). Jesus submitted to the Father's plan that would take him to the cross (Mk 14:36). For the story of Israel to become our story, we must cling to the cross and resurrection of Jesus and stay faithful to our confession even in the face of death.

BIBLIOGRAPHY

Allen, Leslie. *Psalms 101—150*. Word Biblical Commentary 21. Waco, Tex.: Word, 1983.

Attridge, Harold. *The Epistle to the Hebrews*. Hermeneia Series. Philadelphia: Fortress, 1989.

Aune, David E. *Revelation*. 3 vols. Word Biblical Commentary 52. Dallas: Word, 1997-98.

Baer, D. A., and R. P. Gordon, "חסד," in *New International Dictionary of Old Testament Theology and Exegesis*, 2:210-18. Edited by Willem A. VanGemeren. Grand Rapids, Mich.: Zondervan, 1997.

Balch, David L. *Let Wives Be Submissive: The Domestic Code of 1 Peter*. Society of Biblical Literature Monograph Series 26. Chico, Calif.: Scholars Press, 1981.

Barclay, John M. G. "Mirror-Reading a Polemical Letter: Galatians as a Test Case." *Journal for the Study of the New Testament* 31 (1987): 73-93.

Barr, James. *The Semantics of Biblical Language*. Oxford: Oxford University Press, 1961.

Barrett, C. K. *A Critical and Exegetical Commentary on the Acts of the Apostles*. International Critical Commentary, no. 1. Edited by J. A. Emerton, C. E. B. Cranfield and G. N. Stanton. Edinburgh: T & T Clark, 1994.

Bauckham, Richard J. *The Climax of Prophecy: Studies in the Book of Revelation*. Edinburgh: T & T Clark, 1993.

———. "Introduction," in *The Gospels for All Christians: Rethinking the Gospel Audiences*, ed. Richard Bauckham, 1-7. Grand Rapids, Mich.: Eerdmans, 1998.

———. *Jude, 2 Peter*. Word Biblical Commentary 50. Waco, Tex.: Word, 1983.

———. *The Theology of the Book of Revelation*. Cambridge: Cambridge University Press, 1993.

Bauer, Bruno. *Die Apostelgeschichte: Eine Ausgleichung des Paulinismus und des Judenthums innerhalb der christlichen Kirche*. Berlin: Verlag von Gustav Hempel, 1850.

Baylis, Albert H. *From Creation to the Cross: Understanding the First Half of the Bible*. Grand Rapids, Mich.: Zondervan, 1996.

Beale, G. K. *The Book of Revelation*. New International Greek Testament Commentary. Grand Rapids, Mich.: Eerdmans, 1999.

Beasley-Murray, George R. *Jesus and the Kingdom of God*. Grand Rapids, Mich.: Eerdmans, 1987.

———. *Jesus and the Last Days: The Interpretation of the Olivet Discourse*. Peabody, Mass.: Hendrickson, 1993.

———. *The Book of Revelation*, rev. ed. New Century Bible. Grand Rapids, Mich.: Eerdmans, 1981.

Bergen, Robert D. *1, 2 Samuel*. New American Commentary. Nashville, Tenn.: Broadman & Holman, 1996.

Billerbeck, Paul, and H. L. Strack. *Kommentarzum Neuen Testament aus Talmud und Midrash*, 2 vols. München: C. H. Beck'sche Verlagsbuchhandlung, 1922, 1924.

Blenkinsopp, Joseph. *Wisdom and Law in the Old Testament*. Oxford: Oxford University Press, 1995.

Block, Daniel I. *The Book of Ezekiel: Chapters 1-24*. New International Commentary on the Old Testament. Grand Rapids, Mich.: Eerdmans, 1997.

———. *Judges, Ruth*. New American Commentary. Nashville, Tenn.: Broadman & Holman, 1999.

———. "Recovering the Voice of Moses: The Genesis of Deuteronomy." *Journal of the Evangelical Theological Society* 44 (2001): 385-408.

———. "Will the Real Gideon Please Stand Up? Narrative Style and Intention in Judges 6—9." *Journal of the Evangelical Theological Society* 40 (1997): 353-66.

Blomberg, Craig. "The Wright Stuff: A Critical Overview of *Jesus and the Victory of God*." In *Jesus and the Restoration of Israel: A Critical Assessment of N. T. Wright's "Jesus and the Victory of God,"* ed. Carey C. Newman, 19-39. Downers Grove, Ill.: InterVarsity Press, 1999.

Brown, Colin. *Miracles and the Critical Mind*. Grand Rapids, Mich.: Eerdmans, 1984.

Brown, Raymond E., Joseph A. Fitzmyer and Roland E. Murphy. *The New Jerome Biblical Commentary*. Englewood Cliffs, N.J.: Prentice Hall, 1990.

Bruce, F. F. *New Testament History*. Garden City, N.Y.: Doubleday, 1969.

———. *The Acts of the Apostles: The Greek Text with Introduction and Commentary*. Grand Rapids, Mich.: Eerdmans, 1990.

———. "The Curse of the Law." In *Paul and Paulinism: Essays in Honour of C. K. Barret*, ed. M. D. Hooker and S. G. Wilson, 27-36. London: SPCK, 1982.

Brueggemann, Walter. "Exodus." In *The New Interpreter's Bible*, vol. 1. Nashville, Tenn.: Abingdon, 1994.

———. *1 & 2 Kings*. Smith & Helwys Commentary. Macon, Ga.: Smyth & Helwys, 2000.

———. *First and Second Samuel*. Interpretation. Louisville, Ky.: John Knox Press, 1990.

———. *Genesis*. Interpretation. Louisville, Ky.: Westminster John Knox, 1982.

Bruner, Frederick Dale. *A Theology of the Holy Spirit*. Grand Rapids, Mich.: Eerdmans, 1970.

Bullock, C. Hassell. *An Introduction to the Old Testament Prophetic Books*. Chicago: Moody, 1986.

Bultmann, Rudolf. *The History of the Synoptic Tradition*. New York: Harper & Row, 1963.

Cadbury, Henry J. *The Book of Acts in History*. New York: Harper & Bros., 1955.

———. *The Making of Luke-Acts*. 2nd ed. Peabody, Mass: Hendrickson, 1958.

Caird, G. B. *The Revelation of St. John the Divine*. Black's New Testament Commentary. Peabody, Mass.: Hendrickson, 1966.

Cairns, Ian. *Deuteronomy: Word and Presence*. International Theological Commentary. Grand Rapids, Mich.: Eerdmans, 1992.

Caragounis, C. C. "Kingdom of God/Heaven." In *Dictionary of Jesus and the Gospels*, ed. J. B. Green, Scot McKnight and I. H. Marshall, 417-30. Downers Grove, Ill.: InterVarsity Press, 1992.

Casey, Maurice. "Where Wright is Wrong: A Critical Review of N. T. Wright's *Jesus and the Victory of God*." *Journal for the Study of the New Testament* 69 (1998): 77-94, 95-103.

Charles, J. Daryl. *Literary Strategy in the Epistle of Jude*. Scranton, Penn.: University of Scranton Press, 1993.

Charlesworth, James H. *The Old Testament Pseudepigrapha*, vol. 1. Garden City, N.Y.: Doubleday, 1983.

———. *The Old Testament Pseudepigrapha*, vol. 2. Garden City, N.Y.: Doubleday, 1985.

Childs, Brevard S. *Biblical Theology in Crisis*. Philadelphia: Fortress, 1970.

Christensen, Duane. *Deuteronomy 21:10—34:12.* Word Biblical Commentary 6B. Nashville: Thomas Nelson, 2002.

Ciampa, Roy E. *The Presence and Function of Scripture in Galatians 1 and 2.* Wissenschaftliche Untersuchungen zum Neuen Testament 2/102. Tübingen, Germany: J.C.B. Mohr/ Paul Siebeck, 1998.

Clements, Ronald E. *Old Testament Prophecy: From Oracle to Canon.* Louisville, Ky.: Westminster John Knox, 1996.

Coggins, Richard. *Sirach.* Guides to Apocrypha and Pseudepigrapha Series. Sheffield: Academic Press, 1998.

Collins, John J. *Between Athens and Jerusalem: Jewish Identity in the Hellenistic Diaspora.* New York: Crossroad, 1986.

———. *Daniel with an Introduction to Apocalyptic Literature.* The Forms of the Prophetic Literature 20, edited by Rolf P. Knierim and Gene M. Tucker. Grand Rapids, Mich.: Eerdmans, 1984.

———. *Jewish Wisdom in the Hellenistic Age.* Louisville, Ky.: Westminster John Knox, 1997.

———. *The Apocalyptic Imagination: An Introduction to the Jewish Matrix of Christianity.* New York: Crossroad, 1989.

Colson, F. H. *Philo.* LCL 341. London/Cambridge: Heinmann/Harvard University Press, 1939.

Cootes, Robert. "Joshua." In *New Interpreter's Bible,* vol. 2. Nashville: Abingdon, 1998.

Craig, C. T. "Biblical Theology and the Rise of Historicism." *Journal of Biblical Literature* 62 (1942): 281-94.

Craig, William Lane. "The Problem of Miracles: A Historical and Philosophical Perspective." In *Miracles of Jesus,* ed. David Wenham and Craig Blomberg, 9-48. Sheffield: JSOT Press, 1986.

Craigie, Peter C. *The Book of Deuteronomy.* New International Commentary on the Old Testament. Grand Rapids, Mich.: Eerdmans, 1979.

Cranfield, C. E. B. *Romans I—VIII.* Edinburgh: T & T Clark, 1995.

Cullmann, Oscar. *Christ and Time: The Primitive Christian Conception of Time and History.* Philadelphia: Westminster Press, 1950.

Dahl, Nils. "The Johannine Church and History." In *The Interpretation of John,* ed. J. Ashton, 122-40. Philadelphia: Fortress, 1986.

Dalbert, P. *Die Theologie der hellenistisch-jüdischen Missionsliteratur unter Ausschluss von Philo und Josephus.* Hamburg: Reich, 1954.

Davids, Peter. "Book Review of Douglas Moo *The Letter of James.*" *Bulletin for Biblical Research* 12 (2002): 141-42.

———. *Commentary on James.* New International Greek Testament Commentary Series. Grand Rapids, Mich.: Eerdmans, 1982.

Davies, W. D., and D. C. Allison. *The Gospel According to Matthew 8-18.* International Critical Commentary, no. 2. Edinburgh: T & T Clark, 1991.

Day, John. "Pre-Deuteronomic Allusions to the Covenant in Hosea and Psalm LXXVIII," *Vetus Testamentum* 36 (1986): 1-12.

Dentan, Robert C. *Preface to Old Testament Theology,* 2nd ed. New York: Seabury, 1968.

Dibelius, Martin. *A Commentary on the Epistle of James,* revised by H. Greeven; translated by M. A. Williams. Hermeneia Series. Philadelphia: Fortress, 1975.

Drury, John. *Tradition and Design in Luke's Gospel: A Study in Early Christian Historiography.* London: Darton, Longman & Todd, 1976.

Duguid, I. M. "Exile." In *New Dictionary of Biblical Theology,* edited by T. Desmond Alexander, Brian S. Rosner, D. A. Carson and Graeme Goldsworthy, 475-78. Downers Grove, Ill.: Inter-Varsity Press, 2000.

———. "Zechariah." In *New Dictionary of Biblical Theology,* edited by T. Desmond Alexander, Brian S. Rosner, D. A. Carson and Graeme Goldsworthy, 257-60. Downers Grove, Ill.: Inter-

Varsity Press, 2000.

Dunn, James D. G. "Let John Be John: A Gospel for Its Time." In *Das Evangelium und die Evangelium, Wissenschaftliche Untersuchungen zum Neuen Testament* 28, ed. Peter Stuhlmacher, 309-39. Tübingen, Germany: Mohr, 1983.

———. "Matthew 12:28/Luke 11:20 - A Word of Jesus?" In *Eschatology and the New Testament: Essays in Honor of George Raymond Beasley-Murray*, ed. W. H. Gloer, 29-49. Peabody, Mass.: Hendrickson, 1988.

———. *Romans 1—8*. Word Biblical Commentary 38a. Waco, Tex.: Word, 1988.

———. "Editor's Preface." In Andrew Chester and Ralph Martin, *The Theology of the Letters of James, Peter, and Jude*, ix-x. New Testament Theology Series. Cambridge: Cambridge University Press, 1994.

Duvall, J. Scott, and J. Daniel Hays. *Grasping God's Word: A Hands-On Approach to Reading, Interpreting, and Applying the Bible*. Grand Rapids, Mich.: Zondervan, 2001.

Eichrodt, Walther. *Theology of the Old Testament*. 3 vols. Philadelphia: Fortress, 1961, 1967.

Ellis, E. Earle. *The Making of the New Testament Documents*. Boston: Brill Academic, 1999.

———. *Prophecy and Hermeneutic in Early Christianity: New Testament Essays*. Grand Rapids, Mich.: Eerdmans, 1978.

Elwell, Walter A., ed. *Evangelical Dictionary of Biblical Theology*. Grand Rapids, Mich.: Baker, 1996.

Eschel, Esther, and Frank Moore Cross. "Ostraca from Khirbet Qumran." *Israel Exploration Journal* 47/1-2 (1997): 17-28.

Evans, Craig A. "Aspects of Exile and Restoration in the Proclamation of Jesus and the Gospels," in *Exile: Old Testament, Jewish, and Christian Conceptions*, ed. James M. Scott, 299-328. Leiden/New York: E. J. Brill, 1997.

———. "Jesus and the Continuing Exile of Israel." In *Jesus and the Restoration of Israel: A Critical Assessment of N. T. Wright's "Jesus and the Victory of God,"* ed. Carey C. Newman, 77-100. Carlisle, U.K.: Paternoster Press/Downers Grove, Ill.: InterVarsity Press, 1999.

———. *Word and Glory: On the Exegetical and Theological Background of John's Prologue*. Journal for the Study of the New Testament, Supplement Series 89. Sheffield: JSOT, 1993.

Fee, Gordon D., and Douglas Stuart. *How to Read the Bible for all its Worth*. 2nd ed. Grand Rapids, Mich.: Zondervan, 1993.

Fensham, Charles. "Nehemiah 9 and Pss 105, 106, 135 and 136. Post-exilic Historical Traditions in Poetic Form." *Journal of Northwest Semitic Languages* IX (1981): 35-51.

Ferguson, Everett. *Backgrounds of Early Christianity*. Grand Rapids, Mich.: Eerdmans, 1987.

Fishbane, Michael. "Torah and Tradition." In *Tradition and Theology in the Old Testament*, ed. D. Knight, 275-300. Philadelphia: Fortress, 1977.

Fitzmyer, J. A. "Crucifixion in Ancient Palestine, Qumran Literature and the New Testament." *Catholic Biblical Quarterly* 40 (1978): 493-513.

———. *The Gospel According to Luke (I-IX)*. Anchor Bible 28a. New York: Doubleday, 1970.

Foakes-Jackson, F. J., and Kirsopp Lake, eds. *The Beginnings of Christianity: Part 1, The Acts of the Apostles*. London: Macmillan, 1922.

Fox, Michael. *Proverbs 1—9*. Anchor Bible 18a. New York: Doubleday, 2000.

Francis, F. O. "The Form and Function of the Opening and Closing Paragraphs of James and 1 John." *Zeitschrift für die neutestamentliche Wissenschaft und die Kunde der älteren Kirche* 61 (1970): 110-126.

Fretheim, Terence E. *First and Second Kings*. Westminster Bible Companion. Louisville, Ky.: Westminster John Knox, 1999.

Friedländer, M. *Geschichte der jüdischen Apologetik*. Zürich: Schmidt, 1903.

Furnish, Victor. *II Corinthians*. Anchor Bible 32a. Garden City, N.Y.; Doubleday, 1984.

Gabler, J. P. "About the Current Distinction of Biblical and Dogmatic Theology and the Right Definition of their Goals." Inaugural address in Altdorf, March 30, 1787. In *Opuscula Adademica* 1 (1831): 179-94.

Georgi, D. *Die Gegner des Paulus im 2 Korintherbrief.* Wissenschaftliche Monographien zum Alten und Neuen Testament 11. Neukirchen-Vluyn: Neukirchener Verlag, 1964.

Gerstenberger, Erhard. *Leviticus: A Commentary.* Old Testament Library. Louisville, Ky.: Westminster John Knox, 1996.

Gleason, Randall C. "The Old Testament Background of Rest in Hebrews 3:7—4:11," *Bibliotheca Sacra* 157 (2000): 280-302.

Goldingay, John E. *Daniel.* Word Biblical Commentary 30. Dallas: Word, 1989.

Goppelt, Leonhard. *A Commentary on 1 Peter.* Edited by F. Hahn. Translated and augmented by J. Alsup. Grand Rapids, Mich.: Eerdmans, 1993 [1978].

———. *Typos: the Typological Interpretation of the Old Testament in the New.* Translated by D. Madvig. Grand Rapids, Mich.: Eerdmans, 1982 [1939].

Gowan, Donald E. *Theology of the Prophetic Books: The Death and Resurrection of Israel.* Louisville, Ky.: Westminster John Knox, 1998.

Guelich, Robert A. *Mark 1—8:26.* Word Biblical Commentary 34a. Edited by David A. Hubbard and Glenn W. Barker. Dallas: Word, 1989.

Gundry, Robert H. *Mark: A Commentary on His Apology for the Cross.* Grand Rapids, Mich.: Eerdmans, 1993.

Gunkel, Hermann. *An Introduction to the Psalms.* Translated by James Nogalski. Macon, Ga.: Mercer University Press, 1998.

Guthrie, Donald. *New Testament Introduction.* Downers Grove, Ill.: InterVarsity Press, 1978.

Guthrie, George. *Hebrews.* NIV Application Commentary Series. Grand Rapids, Mich.: Zondervan, 1998.

Hafemann, Scott J. *Paul, Moses, and the History of Israel: The Letter/Spirit Contrast and the Argument from Scripture in 2 Corinthians 3.* Wissenschaftliche Untersuchungen zum Neuen Testament 81. Tübingen, Germany: J.C.B. Mohr/Paul Siebeck, 1995.

Haglund, Erik. *Historical Motifs in the Psalms.* Stockholm: CWK Gleerup, 1984.

Hagner, Donald A. *Matthew 14—28.* Word Biblical Commentary 33b. Dallas: Word, 1995.

Hamilton, Victor P. *Handbook on the Historical Books.* Grand Rapids, Mich.: Baker, 2001.

———. *The Book of Genesis: Chapters 1—17.* New International Commentary of the Old Testament. Grand Rapids, Mich.: Eerdmans, 1990.

Hardon, John A. "The Miracle Narratives in the Acts of the Apostles." *Catholic Biblical Quarterly* 16 (July 1954): 303-18.

Hasel, Gerhard. *Old Testament Theology: Basic Issues in the Current Debate,* rev. ed. Grand Rapids, Mich.: Eerdmans, 1977.

Hays, J. Daniel. *From Every People and Nation: A Biblical Theology of Race.* New Studies in Biblical Theology, ed. D. A. Carson. Leicester, U.K.: Inter-Varsity Press/Downers Grove, Ill.: InterVarsity Press, 2003.

———. "Has the Narrator Come to Praise Solomon or to Bury Him? Narrative Subtlety in 1 Kings 1—11." *Journal for the Study of the Old Testament* 28 (2003): 163-88.

Hays, Richard B. *Echoes of Scripture in the Letters of Paul.* New Haven, Conn.: Yale University Press, 1989.

Helyer, L. "The Separation of Abram and Lot: Its Significance in the Patriarchal Narratives." *Journal for the Study of the Old Testament* 26 (1983): 77-88.

Hemer, Colin J. "The Address of 1 Peter." *Expository Times* 89 (1978): 239-43.

———. *The Letters to the Seven Churches of Asia in Their Local Setting.* Biblical Resources Series. Grand Rapids, Mich.: Eerdmans, 1989.

Hengel, Martin. *Acts and the History of Earliest Christianity.* Translated by John Bowden. Philadelphia: Fortress, 1979.

————. *Between Jesus and Paul: Studies in the Earliest History of Christianity.* Translated by John Bowden. Philadelphia: Fortress, 1983.

————. *Judaism and Hellenism: Studies in Their Encounter in Palestine During the Early Hellenistic Period.* Minneapolis: Fortress, 1974.

————. *The Pre-Christian Paul.* Translated by John Bowden. Philadelphia/London: Trinity Press International/SCM Press 1991.

Hengel, Martin, and Anna Maria Schwemer. *Paul Between Damascus and Antioch: The Unknown Years.* Translated by John Bowden. Louisville, Ky.: John Knox Press, 1997.

Hess, Richard S. *Joshua.* Tyndale Old Testament Commentaries. Leicester, U.K.: Inter-Varsity Press/Downers Grove, Ill.: InterVarsity Press, 1996.

Hillyer, Norman. *1 and 2 Peter, Jude.* New International Biblical Commentary Series. Peabody, Mass.: Hendricksen, 1992.

Hooker, Morna D. "Mark's Parables of the Kingdom." In *The Challenge of Jesus' Parables,* ed. Richard N. Longenecker, 79-101. Grand Rapids, Mich.: Eerdmans, 2000.

————. *The Gospel According to Mark.* Peabody, Mass.: Hendrickson, 1991.

————. "Adam in Romans 1." *New Testament Studies* 6 (1960): 297-306.

House, Paul R. *Old Testament Theology.* Downers Grove, Ill.: InterVarsity Press, 1998.

Hurtado, Larry W. *Mark.* New International Biblical Commentary. Peabody, Mass.: Hendrickson, 1983.

Jaubert, Annie. *La notion d'alliance dans le judaïsme aux abords de l'ère chrétienne.* Patristica Sorbonesia 6. Paris: Éditions du Seuil, 1963.

Jeremias, Joachim. *New Testament Theology: The Proclamation of Jesus.* New York: Scribner, 1971.

————. *The Parables of Jesus.* London: SCM Press, 1978.

Johnson, Luke Timothy. *The Acts of the Apostles.* Sacra Pagina, no. 5. Edited by D. J. Harrington. Collegeville, Minn.: Liturgical Press, 1992.

————. *The Gospel of Luke.* Sacra Pagina, no. 3. Edited by D. J. Harrington. Collegeville, Minn.: Liturgical Press, 1991.

Kaiser, Walter. "Leviticus." In *The New Interpreter's Bible,* Vol. 1. Nashville, Tenn.: Abingdon Press, 1994.

Keener, Craig S. *Revelation.* NIV Application Commentary. Grand Rapids, Mich.: Zondervan, 2000.

————. *The IVP Bible Background Commentary: New Testament.* Downers Grove, Ill.: InterVarsity Press, 1993.

Kim, Seyoon. *The Origin of Paul's Gospel.* Wissenschaftliche Untersuchungen zum Neuen Testament 24. Tübingen, Germany: J.C.B. Mohr/ Paul Siebeck, 1981.

Klausner, Joseph. *The Messianic Idea in Israel from Its Beginning to the Completion of the Mishnah.* London: Allen & Unwin, 1956.

Kline, Meredith G. *Treaty of the Great King: The Covenant Structure of Deuteronomy.* Grand Rapids, Mich.: Eerdmans, 1963.

Knibb, M. A. "The Exile in the Literature of the Intertestamental Period." *Heythrop Journal* 17 (1976): 253-72.

Knowles, Michael. *Jeremiah in Matthew's Gospel: The Rejected Prophet Motif in Matthean Redaction.* Journal for the Study of the New Testament Supplement Series. 68. Sheffield: Sheffield Academic Press, 1993.

Köstenberger, Andreas. *The Missions of Jesus and the Disciples According to the Fourth Gospel.* Grand Rapids, Mich.: Eerdmans, 1998.

Kraabel, A. T. "Unity and Diversity among Diaspora Synagogues." In *The Synagogue in Late Antiquity,* ed. Lee I. Levine, 49-60. Philadelphia: American Schools of Oriental Research, 1987.

Kraus, Hans-Joachim. *Psalms 1—59: A Commentary. Continental Commentary.* Translated by H. C. Oswald. Minneapolis: Augsburg, 1988.

————. *Psalms 60—150.* Minneapolis: Augsburg, 1993.

Kümmel, Werner G. *Promise and Fulfilment: The Eschatological Message of Jesus,* 2nd. ed. Studies in Biblical Theology 23. Translated by Dorothea M. Barton. London: SCM Press, 1961.

Ladd, George E. *A Commentary on the Revelation of John.* Grand Rapids, Mich.: Eerdmans, 1972.

Lane, William L. *The Gospel of Mark. International Commentary on the New Testament.* Grand Rapids, Mich.: Eerdmans, 1974.

Lehne, Susanne. *The New Covenant in Hebrews.* Journal for the Study of the New Testament Series 44. Sheffield: Sheffield Academic Press, 1990.

Levine, Baruch. *Leviticus.* Philadelphia: Jewish Publication Society, 1989.

Liebreich, Leon J. "The Impact of Nehemiah 9:5-37 on the Liturgy of the Synagogue." *Hebrew Union College Annual* 32 (1961): 227-37.

Lincoln, Andrew T. *Paradise Now and Not Yet. Studies in the Role of the Heavenly Dimension in Paul's Thought with Special Reference to his Eschatology.* Society for the Study of the New Testament Monograph Series 43. Cambridge: Cambridge University Press, 1981.

————. *Ephesians.* Word Biblical Commentary 42. Waco, Tex.: Word, 1990.

Lindars, Barnabas. *The Theology of the Letter to the Hebrews.* New Testament Theology Series. Cambridge: Cambridge University Press, 1991.

Longenecker, Richard N. *Biblical Exegesis in the Apostolic Period.* Grand Rapids, Mich.: Eerdmans, 1975.

————. *Galatians.* Word Biblical Commentary 41. Dallas: Word, 1990.

Malherbe, Abraham. *Moral Exhortation: A Greco-Roman Source Book.* Philadelphia: Fortress, 1986.

Mann, Thomas. *The Book of the Torah: The Narrative Integrity of the Pentateuch.* Louisville, Ky.: Westminster John Knox, 1988.

Marshall, I. Howard. *Luke: Historian and Theologian.* Grand Rapids, Mich.: Zondervan, 1970.

Martin, Ralph. "The Theology of Jude, 1 Peter, and 2 Peter." In Andrew Chester and Ralph Martin, *The Theology of the Letters of James, Peter, and Jude,* 63-163. New Testament Theology Series. Cambridge: Cambridge University Press, 1994.

Martínez, Florentino García. *The Dead Sea Scrolls Translated: The Qumran Texts in English.* Leiden: E. J. Brill, 1994.

Mattill, A. J. "The Purpose of Acts: Schneckenburger Reconsidered." In *Apostolic History and the Gospel: Biblical and Historical Essays Presented to F. F. Bruce on his 60th Birthday,* edited by W. Ward Gasque and Ralph P. Martin, 108-22. Grand Rapids, Mich.: Eerdmans, 1970.

Mays, James L. *Psalms.* Interpretation. Louisville, Ky.: Westminster John Knox, 1994.

McConville, J. Gordon. *Grace in the End: A Study in Deuteronomic Theology.* Studies in Old Testament Biblical Theology. Grand Rapids, Mich.: Zondervan, 1993.

McKnight, Scot. "John the Baptist." In *New Dictionary of Biblical Theology,* ed. T. Desmond Alexander, Brian S. Rosner, D. A. Carson and Graeme Goldsworthy, 602-4. Downers Grove, Ill.: InterVarsity Press, 2000.

Mendenhall, G. E. "Covenant Forms in Israelite Tradition." *Biblical Archaeologist* 17, no. 3 (1954): 50-76.

Metzger, Bruce M. *Breaking the Code: Understanding the Book of Revelation.* Nashville, Tenn.: Abingdon, 1993.

Metzger, Bruce, ed. *The Apocrypha of the Old Testament. Revised Standard Version.* Oxford/New York: Oxford University Press, 1977.

Michaels, J. Ramsey. *1 Peter.* Word Biblical Commentary 49. Waco, Tex.: Word, 1988.

————. *Interpreting the Book of Revelation.* Grand Rapids, Mich.: Baker, 1992.

————. *Revelation.* The IVP New Testament Commentary Series. Downers Grove, Ill.: InterVarsity Press, 1997.

Milgrom, Jacob. *Leviticus 23—27.* Anchor Bible Commentary 3B. New York: Doubleday, 2001.

Moo, Douglas. *The Letter of James.* Pillar New Testament Commentary Series. Grand Rapids,

Mich.: Eerdmans, 2000.

Moore, Carey A. "Toward the Dating of the Book of Baruch." *Catholic Biblical Quarterly* 36 (1974): 312-20.

Morris, Leon. *The Book of Revelation,* rev. ed. Tyndale New Testament Commentaries. Grand Rapids, Mich.: Eerdmans, 1987.

Mounce, Robert H. *The Book of Revelation,* rev. ed. New International Commentary on the New Testament. Grand Rapids, Mich.: Eerdmans, 1997.

Neirynck, F. "The Miracle Stories in the Acts of the Apostles." In *Les Actes des Apôtres: Traditions, Rédaction, Théologie, Bibliotheca Ephemeridum Theologicarum Lovaniensium* 48, edited by J. Kremer. Leuven: University Press, 1979.

Nelson, Richard D. *First and Second Kings.* Interpretation. Louisville, Ky.: John Knox Press, 1987.

———. *Joshua: A Commentary.* Old Testament Library. Louisville, Ky.: Westminster John Knox, 1997.

Neudorfer, Heinz-Werner. "The Speech of Stephen." In *Witness to the Gospel: The Theology of Acts,* edited by David Peterson and I. Howard Marshall, 275-94. Grand Rapids, Mich.: Eerdmans, 1998.

Neusner, Jacob. *Self-Fulfilling Prophecy: Exile and Return in the History of Judaism.* Boston: Beacon, 1987.

Neusner, J., W. S. Green, and E. Frerichs. *Judaisms and Their Messiahs at the Turn of the Christian Era.* Cambridge: Cambridge University Press, 1987.

Newman, Carey C., ed. *Jesus and the Restoration of Israel: A Critical Assessment of N. T. Wright's "Jesus and the Victory of God."* Downers Grove, Ill.: InterVarsity Press, 1999.

Newsome, Carol. "Job." In *The New Interpreter's Bible,* vol. 4. Nashville, Tenn.: Abingdon, 1994.

Nickelsburg, George W. E. *Jewish Literature Between the Bible and the Mishnah: A Historical and Literary Introduction.* Philadelphia: Fortress, 1981.

Nineham, Dennis E. "Some Reflections on the Present Position with Regard to the Jesus of History." *Church Quarterly Review* 166 (January 1965): 5-21.

North, C. R., "OT Theology and the History of Hebrew Religion." *Scottish Journal of Theology* 2 (1949): 113-26.

Noth, Martin. *Überlieferungsgeshichtliche Studien I.* Halle: Niemeyer, 1943.

O'Brien, Peter T. *The Epistle to the Philippians: A Commentary on the Greek Text.* New International Greek Testament Commentary. Grand Rapids, Mich.: Eerdmans, 1991.

Osborne, Grant. *Revelation.* Baker Exegetical Commentary. Grand Rapids, Mich.: Baker, 2002.

Osborne, Grant R., and Clark H. Pinnock. "A Truce Proposal for the Tongues Controversy." *Christianity Today,* October 1971, 6-9.

Oswalt, John. "Isaiah: Theology of." In *New International Dictionary of Old Testament Theology & Exegesis,* ed. Willem A. VanGemeren, 4:725-32. Grand Rapids, Mich.: Zondervan, 1997.

Overland, Paul. "Did the Sage Draw from the Shema? A Study of Proverbs 3:1-12," *Catholic Biblical Quarterly* 62 (2000): 424-41.

Pannenberg, Wolfhart. "Redemptive Event and History." In *Basic Questions in Theology: Collected Essays,* vol. 1. Translated by George H. Kehm. Philadelphia: Westminster Press, 1970.

Parsons, Mikeal C., and Richard I. Pervo. *Rethinking the Unity of Luke and Acts.* Minneapolis: Fortress, 1993.

Pate, C. Marvin, ed. *Four Views on the Book of Revelation.* Grand Rapids, Mich.: Zondervan, 1998.

———. *Communities of the Last Days: The Dead Sea Scrolls, the New Testament and the Story of Israel.* Downers Grove, Ill.: InterVarsity Press, 2000.

———. *The End of the Age Has Come: The Theology of Paul.* Grand Rapids, Mich.: Zondervan, 1995.

———. *The Reverse of the Curse: Paul, Wisdom, and the Law.* Wissenschaftliche Untersuchungen zum Neuen Testament II, 114. Tübingen, Germany: J.C.B. Mohr/Paul Siebeck, 2000.

Pate, C. Marvin, and Douglas Kennard. *Deliverance Now and Not Yet: The New Testament and the Great Tribulation.* New York: Peter Lang, 2003.

Penner, Todd. *The Epistle of James and Eschatology: Re-reading an Ancient Christian Letter.* Journal for the Study of the New Testament, Supplement Series 121. Sheffield: Sheffield Academic Press, 1996.

Perdue, Leo. *Wisdom and Creation: The Theology of the Wisdom Literature.* Nashville, Tenn.: Abingdon, 1994.

Perkins, Pheme. *Reading the New Testament: An Introduction.* New York: Paulist Press, 1988.

Peterson, Eugene H. *First and Second Samuel.* Westminster Bible Companion. Louisville, Ky.: Westminster John Knox, 1999.

Priest, J. "Testament of Moses." In *The Old Testament Pseudepigrapha,* ed. James Charlesworth, 1:919-26. Garden City, N.Y.: Doubleday, 1983.

Rad, Gerhard von. "Gerichtdoxologie." In *Gesammelte Studien zum Alten Testament Band II,* ed. Rudolf Smend, 246-47. TBS. AT 48. Munich: Kaiser, 1973.

―――. *Old Testament Theology.* 2 vols. London: Harper & Row, 1962, 1965.

―――. *Wisdom in Israel.* Nashville, Tenn.: Abingdon, 1972.

Rengstorf, Karl Heinrich. "Hepta," In *Theological Dictionary of the New Testament,* edited by Gerhard Kittel and G. Friedrich, 627-35. Grand Rapids, Mich.: Eerdmans, 1964.

Richards, E. Randolph. *Paul and First Century Letter Writing.* Downers Grove, Ill.: InterVarsity Press, 2004.

―――. *The Secretary in the Letters of Paul.* Wissenschaftliche Untersuchungen zum Neuen Testament 2/42. Tübingen, Germany: J.C.B. Mohr/Paul Siebeck, 1991.

Ross, Allen P. *Creation and Blessing: A Guide to the Study and Exposition of Genesis.* Grand Rapids, Mich.: Baker, 1988.

Sanders, E. P. *Jesus and Judaism.* Philadelphia: Fortress, 1985.

―――. *Paul and Palestinian Judaism: A Comparison of Patterns of Religion.* Philadelphia: Fortress, 1977.

Sandes, Karl Olav. *Paul—One of the Prophets? A Contribution to the Apostle's Self-Understanding.* Wissenschaftliche Untersuchungen zum Neuen Testament 1/43. Tübingen, Germany: J.C.B. Mohr/ Paul Siebeck, 1991.

Sandy, D. Brent. *Plowshares & Pruning Hooks: Rethinking the Language of Biblical Prophecy and Apocalyptic.* Downers Grove, Ill.: InterVarsity Press, 2002.

Schiffman, Lawrence H. *The Halakhah at Qumran.* Studies in Judaism in Late Antiquity 16. Leiden: E. J. Brill, 1975.

―――. *Reclaiming the Dead Sea Scrolls: Their Meaning for Judaism and Christianity.* Anchor Bible Reference Library. New York: Doubleday, 1995.

Schmitt, J. "You Adulteresses: The Image of James 4:4," *Novum Testamentum* 28 (1986): 327-37.

Schnabel, Eckhard. *Law and Wisdom from Ben Sira to Paul.* Wissenschaftliche Untersuchungen zum Neuen Testament 2/16. Tübingen, Germany: J.C.B. Mohr/Paul Siebeck, 1985.

Schreiner, Thomas R. *The Law and Its Fulfillment: A Pauline Theology of the Law.* Grand Rapids, Mich.: Baker Books, 1993.

Schweizer, Eduard. *The Good News According to Mark.* Translated by Donald H. Madvig. Richmond, Va.: John Knox Press, 1970.

Scobie, C. H. H. "History of Biblical Theology." In *New Dictionary of Biblical Theology: Exploring the Unity and Diversity of Scripture,* ed. T. Desmond Alexander, Brian J. Rosner, D.A. Carson Graeme Goldsworthy, 11-20. Leicester, U.K.: Inter-Varsity Press/Downers Grove, Ill.: Inter-Varsity Press, 2000.

Scott, James M. *Adoption as Sons of God: An Exegetical Investigation into the Background of ΥΙΟ-ΘΕΣΙΑ in the Pauline Corpus.* Wissenschiftliche Untersuchungen zum Neuen Testament 2/24. Tübingen: J.C.B. Mohr/Paul Siebeck, 1992.

————. *Paul and the Nations: The Old Testament and Jewish Background of Paul's Mission to the Nations with Special Reference to the Destination of Galatians*. Wissenschaftliche Untersuchungen zum Neuen Testament 84. Tübingen, Germany: J.C.B. Mohr/ Paul Siebeck, 1995.

————. "Paul's Use of Deuteronomic Tradition(s)." *Journal of Biblical Literature* 112 (1993): 645-65.

————. ed. *Exile: Old Testament, Jewish, and Christian Conceptions*. Leiden/New York: E. J. Brill, 1997.

Scott, Martin. *Sophia and the Johannine Jesus*. Journal for the Study of the New Testament, Supplement Series 71. Sheffield: JSOT, 1992.

Soards, Marion L. *The Speeches in Acts: Their Content, Context, and Concerns*. Louisville, Ky.: Westminster John Knox Press, 1994.

Spilsbury, Paul. *The Throne, The Lamb & The Dragon: A Reader's Guide to the Book of Revelation*. Downers Grove, Ill.: InterVarsity Press, 2002.

Steck, Odil H. *Israel und das gewaltsame Geschick der Propheten: Untersuchungen zur Überlieferung des deuteronomistischen Geshichtsbildes im Alten Testament, Spätjudentum und Urchristentum*. Wissenschaftliche Monographien zum Alten und Neun Testament 23. Neukirchen-Vluyn, Germany: Neukirchener, 1967.

Stockhausen, Carol Kern. *Moses' Veil and the Glory of the New Covenant: The Exegetical Substructure of II Cor. 3,1-4,6*. Analecta Biblica 116. Rome: Pontifical Biblical Institute Press, 1989.

Stott, John R. W. *The Baptism and Fullness of the Holy Spirit*. Downers Grove, Ill.: InterVarsity Press, 1964.

Stowers, Stanley. *Letter Writing in Greco-Roman Antiquity*. Library of Early Christianity Series. Philadelphia: Westminster Press, 1986.

Stronstad, Roger. *The Charismatic Theology of St. Luke*. Peabody, Mass.: Hendrickson, 1984.

Sweeney, Marvin A. *Isaiah 1—39*. Forms of the Old Testament Literature XVI. Grand Rapids, Mich.: Eerdmans, 1996.

Talbert, Charles H. *Learning Through Suffering: The Educational Value of Suffering in the New Testament and Its Milieu*. In the Zacchaeus Studies, New Testament Series. Collegeville, Minn.: Liturgical Press, 1991.

————. *Literary Patterns, Theological Themes, and the Genre of Luke-Acts*. SBL Monograph Series 20. Missoula, Mont.: Scholars Press, 1975.

Tannehill, Robert C. *The Narrative Unity of Luke-Acts: A Literary Interpretation*, Vol. 2. Minneapolis: Fortress, 1990.

Tcherikover, Victor. "Jewish Apologetic Literature Reconsidered." *EOS commentarii societatis philologae polonorum* 48 (1956): 169-93.

Thielman, Frank. *Paul and the Law: A Contextual Approach*. Downers Grove, Ill.: InterVarsity Press, 1994.

————. "The Story of Israel and the Theology of Romans 5—8." In *Pauline Theology*, ed. David M. Hay and E. Elizabeth Johnson, 3:169-95. Minneapolis: Fortress, 1995.

Thompson, J. A. *The Book of Jeremiah*. New International Commentary on the Old Testament. Grand Rapids, Mich.: Eerdmans, 1980.

Tinsley, E. J. *The Imitation of God in Christ: An Essay on the Biblical Basis of Christian Spirituality*. London: SCM, 1960.

Troeltsch, Ernst. "Über historische und dogmatische Methode in der Theologie." In *Gesammelte Schriften, zweiter band, "Zur religiösen Lage, Religionsphilosophie und Ethik,"* edited by Ernst Troeltsch. Berlin: Scientia Verlag Aalen, 1962.

Vanderkam, James C. "Exile in Jewish Apocalyptic Literature." In *Exile: Old Testament, Jewish, and Christian Conceptions,* ed. James M. Scott, 89-109. Leiden/New York: E. J. Brill, 1997.

————. *The Dead Sea Scrolls Today*. Grand Rapids, Mich.: Eerdmans, 1994.

Via, Dan O. "The Right Strawy Epistle Reconsidered: A Study in Biblical Ethics and Hermeneutics," *Journal of Religion* 49 (1969): 253-67.

Vischer, W. *The Witness of the Old Testament to the Christ.* London: Lutterworth, 1949.

Walton, John H. *Genesis.* NIV Application Commentary. Grand Rapids, Mich.: Zondervan, 2001.

Weinfeld, Moshe. *Deuteronomy and the Deuteronomic School.* Oxford: Clarenden, 1972.

Wenham, Gordon J. *Story as Torah: Reading the Old Testament Ethically.* Old Testament Studies. Edinburgh: T & T Clark, 2000.

————. *The Book of Leviticus.* The New International Commentary on the Old Testament. Grand Rapids, Mich.: Eerdmans, 1979.

Williamson, H. G. M. *Ezra, Nehemiah.* Word Biblical Commentary 16. Waco, Tex.: Word, 1985.

Wise, Michael, Martin Abegg, and Edward Cook. *The Dead Sea Scrolls: A New Translation.* San Francisco: HarperCollins, 1996.

Witherington, Ben, III. *The Acts of the Apostles: A Socio-Rhetorical Commentary.* Grand Rapids, Mich.: Eerdmans, 1998.

————. *The Gospel of Mark: A Socio-Rhetorical Commentary.* Grand Rapids, Mich.: Eerdmans, 2001.

————. *Jesus, Paul, and the End of the World. A Comparative Study in New Testament Eschatology.* Downers Grove, Ill.: InterVarsity Press, 1992.

————. *Revelation.* New Cambridge Bible Commentary. Cambridge: Cambridge University Press, 2003.

Wright, Christopher. *Deuteronomy.* New International Biblical Commentary. Peabody, Mass.: Hendrickson, 1996.

Wright, N. T. *The Climax of the Covenant: Christ and the Law in Pauline Theology.* Edinburgh: T & T Clark, 1991.

————. *Jesus and the Victory of God.* Minneapolis: Fortress, 1997.

————. *The New Testament and the People of God.* Minneapolis: Fortress, 1992.

————. *The Resurrection of the Son of God.* Minneapolis: Fortress, 2003.

————. "Theology, History, and Jesus: A Response to Maurice Casey and Clive Marsh." *Journal for the Study of the New Testament* 69 (1998): 105-12.

AUTHORS

Contributions to this volume are listed in bold type at the end of each author's information.

J. Scott Duvall, Ph.D., is Dean of the Pruet School of Christian Studies at Ouachita Baptist University and Professor of Biblical Studies. His publications include *Grasping God's Word: A Hands-On Approach to Reading, Interpreting, and Applying the Bible,* coauthored with J. Daniel Hays (Zondervan, 2001), and *Biblical Greek Exegesis,* coauthored with George Guthrie (Zondervan, 1998). **Revelation, Conclusion**

J. Daniel Hays, Ph. D., is Elma Cobb Professor of Biblical Studies at Ouachita Baptist University. His publications include *From Every People and Nation: A Biblical Theology of Race* (InterVarsity Press, 2003), and *Grasping God's Word: A Hands-On Approach to Reading, Interpreting, and Applying the Bible,* coauthored with J. Scott Duvall (Zondervan, 2001). **Old Testament Historical Books, Old Testament Prophets**

C .Marvin Pate, Ph. D., is Professor of Biblical Studies at Ouachita Baptist University. His publications include *The Reverse of the Curse: Paul, Wisdom, and the Law* (Mohr/Siebeck, 2000) and *Communities of the Last Days: The Dead Sea Scrolls, the New Testament, and the Story of Israel* (InterVarsity Press, 2000). **Introduction, Second Temple Judaism, Paul, volume editor**

E. Randolph Richards, Ph.D., is Professor of Biblical Studies and Christian Missions at Ouachita Baptist University. His publications include *Paul and First Century Letter Writing* (InterVarsity Press, 2004) and *The Secretary in the Letters of Paul* (Mohr/Siebeck, 1991). **John, General Epistles, Hebrews**

W. Dennis Tucker Jr., Ph.D., is Assistant Professor of Christian Scriptures at George W.

Truett Theological Seminary, Baylor University. He is coeditor of *An Introduction to Wisdom Literature and the Psalms* (Mercer Press, 2000). **Pentateuch, Psalms and Wisdom Literature**

Preben Vang, Ph.D., is J. C. and Mae Fuller Professor of Theology at Ouachita Baptist University. His publications include *Telling God's Story* (forthcoming from Broadman & Holman, 2005), coauthored with Terry Carter. **Synoptics, Acts**

Author Index

Subject Index

Apocrypha Index

Scripture Index

10, 62
11—12, 62, 63
13, 63
15, 63
16, 63
20, 63
21, 63
22, 61

1 Kings
1—11, 64, 289
7:10-11, 68
8, 68
8:46-51, 18
10:23-29, 65
11, 65
11:12-13, 65
11:29-39, 65
11:34-39, 65
12, 65, 66
12:25-33, 65
12:28, 66
17, 52, 66
18, 66
19, 66
19:8, 129
19:11-12, 190

2 Kings
2:11, 190
2:11-12, 188
4:42-44, 142
9, 52
13:23, 66
17, 52, 65, 66
17:23, 18
17:25, 52
25, 18, 50, 52, 67, 88,
   91, 97, 103, 280
25:5, 51
25:21, 51
25:26, 51
25:27, 18

25:27-30, 52

1 Chronicles
17:14, 235
17:21, 223

2 Chronicles
13:22, 233
24:27, 233

Ezra
6:13-18, 68
9, 20
9:8-9, 21
9:15, 21

Nehemiah
1, 102
9, 20, 68, 72, 288
9:5-37, 22, 291
9:26, 19
9:32, 18
9:36-37, 68

Job
4—27, 80
4:7-8, 81
5:17, 81
7:11, 81
8:13, 239
9, 81
24:9-12, 81
42:7, 82
42:8, 82

Psalms
1—59, 196, 290
1:6, 239
2:12, 239
5:5, 226
16, 192
16:8-11, 192
24:2, 214

43:3, 135
43:10, 214
44, 71
55:18-19, 215
60—150, 73, 74, 291
66, 71
68, 71
69:25, 189
77, 71
78, 71, 72
78:10-11, 72
78:40, 73
78:58-59, 73
78:63, 73
78:64, 73, 74
80, 71
81, 71
83, 71
89, 72
89:9, 168
91, 71
95, 71
97:2-3, 214
99, 71
101—150, 74, 285
105, 71, 72
106, 71, 72, 75
106:14, 73
106:34, 73
106:39, 73
106:41, 74
106:43, 75
106:45, 75
107, 71, 72
109:8, 189
110, 192
114, 71
118, 195
118:22, 122
119:10, 239
119:21, 239
119:105, 135
119:113-120, 239

132, 72
135, 71, 72
136, 72
136:3, 266
136:23-24, 75
137, 72
144, 72

Proverbs
1—9, 77, 288
1:8, 76, 83
2:1, 76
2:18, 239
3:1, 76
3:1-12, 78, 292
3:3, 78, 79
3:5, 78
3:17, 166
3:18, 166
3:19, 165
3:21, 76
4:18-19, 239
4:19, 239
6, 80
6:20, 79
6:20-35, 78, 79
6:21, 79
6:22, 79
6:23, 135
6:25, 80
6:29, 80
6:30-31, 79
6:32, 79
8, 25, 163
8:1-5, 163
8:22-23, 165
8:22-30, 163
8:27-30, 163
8:30, 165
8:34, 166
8:35, 166
9:1-6, 77
9:5, 166